Essentials of Child Psychopathology

Essentials of Behavioral Science Series

Founding Editors, Alan S. Kaufman and Nadeen L. Kaufman

Essentials

of Child

Psychopathology

Linda Wilmshurst

 John Wiley & Sons, Inc.

Published by John Wiley & Sons, Inc., Hoboken, New Jersey.
Published simultaneously in Canada.

This publication is designed to provide accurate and authoritative information in regard to the subject matter covered. It is sold with the understanding that the publisher is not engaged in rendering professional services. If legal, accounting, medical, psychological or any other expert assistance is required, the services of a competent professional person should be sought.

Designations used by companies to distinguish their products are often claimed as trademarks. In all instances where John Wiley & Sons, Inc. is aware of a claim, the product names appear in initial capital or all capital letters. Readers, however, should contact the appropriate companies for more complete information regarding trademarks and registration.

For general information on our other products and services please contact our Customer Care Department within the United States at (800) 762-2974, outside the United States at (317) 572-3993 or fax (317) 572-4002.

Wiley also publishes its books in a variety of electronic formats. Some content that appears in print may not be available in electronic books. For more information about Wiley products, visit our website at www.wiley.com

Library of Congress Cataloging-in-Publication Data:

Wilmshurst, Linda.
     Essentials of child psychopathology / Linda Wilmshurst.
          p. ; cm. — (Essentials of behavioral science series)
     Includes bibliographical references and index.
     ISBN 0-471-65624-0 (pbk.)
          1. Child psychopathology. I. Title. II. Series.
     [DNLM: 1. Mental Disorders—Child. 2. Psychopathology—methods—Child.
     WS 350 W744e 2005]
     RJ499.W463 2005
     618.92'89—dc22

                                                                              2004042294

Printed in the United States of America.

10   9   8   7   6   5   4   3   2   1

CONTENTS

SERIES PREFACE

In the *Essentials of Behavioral Science* series, our goal is to provide readers with books that will deliver key practical information in an efficient, accessible style. The series features books on a variety of topics, such as statistics, psychological testing, and research design and methodology, to name just a few. For the experienced professional, books in the series offer a concise yet thorough review of a specific area of expertise, including numerous tips for best practices. Students can turn to series books for a clear and concise overview of the important topics with which they must become proficient to practice skillfully, efficiently, and ethically in their chosen fields.

Wherever feasible, visual cues highlighting key points are utilized alongside systematic, step-by-step guidelines. Chapters are focused and succinct. Topics are organized for an easy understanding of the essential material related to a particular topic. Theory and research are continually woven into the fabric of each book, but always to enhance the practical application of the material, rather than to sidetrack or overwhelm readers. With this series, we aim to challenge and assist readers in the behavioral sciences to aspire to the highest level of competency by arming them with the tools they need for knowledgeable, informed practice.

Essentials of Child Psychopathology provides an overview of child and adolescent disorders that begins with a historical look at the evolution of the field of child psychopathology. The introductory chapters focus on child and environmental characteristics (family, school, economics, culture) that shape developmental pathways toward normal or deviant behaviors, and the role of theoretical perspectives in guiding our understanding of the underlying processes. Current trends and issues in the areas of professional ethics, research, assessment, diagnosis, and treatment are also addressed. Following a discussion of conceptual issues and trends in child psychopathology, the remaining ten chapters of the book focus on the etiology, theory, assessment, and treatment of the major disorders and psychosocial problems of childhood and adolescence.

Alan S. Kaufman, PhD, and Nadeen L. Kaufman, EdD, Founding Editors
Yale University School of Medicine

Essentials of Child Psychopathology

One

INTRODUCTION TO CHILD PSYCHOPATHOLOGY: DEVELOPMENT, THEORIES, AND INFLUENCES

Recognition of clinical child psychology as a unique discipline has only emerged in the past 30 years, despite auspicious beginnings. The end of the 19th century ushered in an era of social reform that addressed the need to protect children's rights concerning health and education, to provide protection within the judicial system, and to free children from working within the adult workforce (Culbertson, 1991). In the wake of this movement, child labor laws and mandatory education became a reality. At the turn of the century, Lightner Witmer established the first psychology clinic to treat children with learning disabilities, and by 1909 more than 450 cases had been seen at the clinic. However, Witmer fell out of favor with colleagues, due to his refusal to adopt Terman's revision of the Stanford-Binet tests of intelligence and his reluctance to accept Freud's theories on behavior disorders.

William Healey, an English-born psychiatrist who shared America's enthusiasm for Freud's theories, opened the first child guidance clinic in Chicago in 1909. By 1933, 42 child guidance clinics were in operation in a wide variety of locations, including juvenile institutions, courts, hospitals, schools, and universities. As the popularity of the child guidance clinics grew, the emphasis shifted from delinquency to problems evident at home and at school, with a primary interest in parent-child difficulties.

The underlying philosophy of the time was that the source of children's problems could be found in parenting and the family (Horn, 1989, p. 27). In 1948, 54 child guidance clinics came together to form the American Association of Psychiatric Clinics for Children (AAPCC). According to Horn this marked a shift from identification to training and treatment, a movement riddled with debate over standards, roles, and status among psychiatrists, psychologists, and social workers. For a summary of the time lines in historical perspective, refer to Rapid Reference 1.1.

Despite the popular rise of the child guidance clinics, the field of clinical child

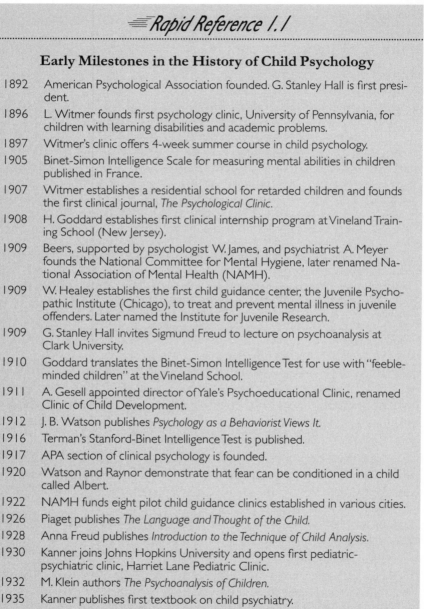

≡≡Rapid Reference 1.1

Early Milestones in the History of Child Psychology

1892	American Psychological Association founded. G. Stanley Hall is first president.
1896	L. Witmer founds first psychology clinic, University of Pennsylvania, for children with learning disabilities and academic problems.
1897	Witmer's clinic offers 4-week summer course in child psychology.
1905	Binet-Simon Intelligence Scale for measuring mental abilities in children published in France.
1907	Witmer establishes a residential school for retarded children and founds the first clinical journal, *The Psychological Clinic*.
1908	H. Goddard establishes first clinical internship program at Vineland Training School (New Jersey).
1909	Beers, supported by psychologist W. James, and psychiatrist A. Meyer founds the National Committee for Mental Hygiene, later renamed National Association of Mental Health (NAMH).
1909	W. Healey establishes the first child guidance center, the Juvenile Psychopathic Institute (Chicago), to treat and prevent mental illness in juvenile offenders. Later named the Institute for Juvenile Research.
1909	G. Stanley Hall invites Sigmund Freud to lecture on psychoanalysis at Clark University.
1910	Goddard translates the Binet-Simon Intelligence Test for use with "feeble-minded children" at the Vineland School.
1911	A. Gesell appointed director of Yale's Psychoeducational Clinic, renamed Clinic of Child Development.
1912	J. B. Watson publishes *Psychology as a Behaviorist Views It*.
1916	Terman's Stanford-Binet Intelligence Test is published.
1917	APA section of clinical psychology is founded.
1920	Watson and Raynor demonstrate that fear can be conditioned in a child called Albert.
1922	NAMH funds eight pilot child guidance clinics established in various cities.
1926	Piaget publishes *The Language and Thought of the Child*.
1928	Anna Freud publishes *Introduction to the Technique of Child Analysis*.
1930	Kanner joins Johns Hopkins University and opens first pediatric-psychiatric clinic, Harriet Lane Pediatric Clinic.
1932	M. Klein authors *The Psychoanalysis of Children*.
1935	Kanner publishes first textbook on child psychiatry.
1937	Adolescent psychiatric ward opens at Bellevue Hospital.
1944	Kanner describes autistic behaviors and attributes illness to "refrigerator mother."

1945	Studies by R. Spitz raise concerns about negative impact of institutional life on children.
1948	American Association of Psychiatric Clinics for Children (AAPCC) is formed as 54 child guidance clinics come together.
1950's	Behavior therapy emerges as a treatment alternative for child and family problems.
1951	Bowlby publishes on attachment.
1952	American Psychiatric Association (APA) publishes the *Diagnostic and Statistical Manual of Mental Disorders* (*DSM-I*). The DSM contains two disorders of childhood: Adjustment Reaction and Childhood Schizophrenia.
1953	The American Academy of Child Psychiatry is established.
1968	*DSM-II* published and adds "hyperkinetic reaction of childhood."
1977	Thomas and Chess publish work on the nine categories of temperament.
1980	*DSM-III* is first version of DSM to make specific developmental recommendations regarding childhood disorders.
1984	Sroufe and Rutter introduce domain of child psychopathology as offshoot of developmental psychology; *Developmental Psychopathology Journal* is introduced.
1999	Clinical Child Psychology established as the 53rd division of American Psychological Association, renamed Society of Clinical Child and Adolescent Psychology (2001).

Note: See Nietzel, Bernstein, and Milich, 1994, and Slaff, 1989, for details.

psychology encountered many roadblocks that delayed the establishment of child psychopathology as a unique discipline until 30 years ago. One reason for the delay was the fact that theories of child development were firmly entrenched in the nature/nurture controversy.

Toward the end of the 19th century there was a growing belief that mental illness had a biological basis, and Emil Kraepelin's (1856–1926) textbook published in 1883 argued that physical ailments could cause mental dysfunction. The disease model was a mixed blessing, with some intent on finding a cure while

CAUTION

The nature (heredity) and nurture (environment) debate has waged for centuries. John Locke, the 17th-century English philosopher, proposed that children came into the world as a blank slate (tabula rasa) and it was the parents' responsibility to fill the slate with the proper environmental controls and discipline. By contrast, the 18th-century French philosopher Jean-Jacques Rousseau envisioned the child as a flower that would grow and flourish, naturally, in a laissez-faire approach. Caring, nurturing, and opportunity were the parents' gifts to the growing child. Most psychologists today appreciate the interaction of heredity and environment.

DON'T FORGET

Henry Goddard is credited with establishing one of the largest training schools for the mentally retarded. However, the belief system upon which it was constructed did much to harm attitudes about the mentally retarded. Goddard's beliefs were summarized in his fictional book that chronicled two sets of offspring of Martin Kallikak: descendants from his union with a barmaid, who were plagued by feeblemindedness, delinquency, and alcoholism, and descendents of his union with a "nice girl," who all became respectable citizens.

others feared that diseases could be transmitted to others or passed on genetically to offspring. Fear and misunderstanding resulted in the placement of adults and children with mental retardation and mental illness in institutions for the next half century.

Another roadblock to the establishment of clinical child psychology as a unique discipline was the shift in emphasis from treatment to identification. Psychologists became increasingly involved in intellectual assessments of children and adults for placement in education and the military. By 1918, psychologists had screened over two million potential candidates for the army.

Abnormal behavior in children continued to be interpreted from the vantage point of adults, and thus childhood maladjustment was described in adult terms and treated with adult treatment methods (Peterson & Roberts, 1991). By the mid-1930s, child guidance clinics were firmly entrenched in linking child problems to adult problems. After years of viewing children's problems from the vantage point of adult psychopathology, the current trends are to refine our understanding of how many characteristic features of these child and adolescent disorders differ from adult disorders. Since the 1970s, several journals have emerged that are exclusively devoted to research about child and adolescent clinical concerns (*Journal of Clinical Child Psychology, Journal of Abnormal Child Psychology, Journal of the American Academy of Child and Adolescent Psychiatry, Journal of Child Psychology and Psychiatry and Allied Disciplines,* etc.).

In the mid-1980s, the field of clinical child psychology witnessed the evolution of yet another stage of development. At this time, the domain of developmental psychopathology (Sroufe & Rutter, 1984) emerged as an offshoot of developmental psychology, complete with its own journal, *Development and Psychopathology.* Within this framework, atypical behavior is conceptualized as deviating from the normal developmental pathway.

Organizational principles of developmental psychopathology define a system that considers human development as *holistic* (the interactive and dynamic concept of the total child) and *hierarchical* (movement toward increasing complexity;

Cicchetti & Toth, 1998). Increased emphasis has been placed on determining processes that can inhibit (protective factors) or escalate (risks) the development of maladaptive behaviors.

DON'T FORGET

Conceptually, since normal and abnormal behaviors stem from the same developmental principles and are part of the same continuum, increased emphasis is placed on having knowledge of normal behavior (its stages and underlying processes) as a precursor to abnormal behaviors.

PRACTICAL APPLICATIONS: CASE STUDY ILLUSTRATIONS OF CHILD PSYCHOPATHOLOGY

The following cases will serve as an introduction to some of the practical issues faced by child clinicians and provide a framework for better understanding the importance of considering developmental contexts and environmental influences in understanding child psychopathology.

The Cases of Jason, Winnie, and Brian

The psychologist is asked to observe three children in Mrs. Skill's grade 4 classroom: Jason, Winnie, and Brian. All three children have been rated as demonstrating the following behaviors: has problems sustaining attention, loses things necessary for tasks, is easily distracted, is forgetful, is restless, doesn't seem to listen, is disorganized, doesn't complete assignments, and demonstrates poor follow-through. The psychologist's observations of the children verify information obtained from the teacher rating scales. A review of the children's cumulative folders reveals that all three children scored within the average range on the Otis-Lennon group intellectual screening test given during the previous grade 3 school year.

Question: Is a diagnosis of Attention-Deficit/Hyperactivity Disorder (ADHD) an appropriate classification for Jason, Winnie, or Brian? Why?
According to the *Diagnostic and Statistical Manual of Mental Disorders*–fourth edition, text revision (*DSM-IV-TR;* APA, 2000), all three children demonstrate many symptoms associated with ADHD. The psychologist has verified the teacher's ratings of these behaviors through classroom observation, has reviewed the school records, and is fairly comfortable ruling out any contributing intellectual difficulties. Furthermore, these problems have been documented on an ongoing basis.

What's missing from this picture?

In order for the psychologist to diagnose whether the three children have ADHD, or rule out the possibility of ADHD in favor of a different diagnosis (a process called *differential diagnosis*), information is required from several key sources, including the home and school environments. What is missing, therefore, is information from the child's home environment. The psychologist schedules interviews with all three parents to obtain additional information.

The Case of Brian

According to Brian's mother, Brian has "always been this way." His mother describes Brian as a "space cadet" who constantly misplaces things and often gets distracted when trying to do his homework. Brian eats standing up and is always on the go. His mother adds that Brian is just like his father, who is also restless, active, and distracted. Brian seems very capable (his mother and teacher both feel he is a bright boy) but has problems completing assignments because of his distractibility. Everything seems to take his attention away from the task at hand.

After talking to the mother, the psychologist develops a *case formulation* (a hypothesis about why the problem behavior exists and how it is being maintained). The case formulation is based on information obtained from the family history, consistency in Brian's behaviors across situational contexts (home and school), and the longevity of the problem (he has always been that way). The psychologist is now more confident in suggesting that Brian does have ADHD, probably the predominantly Inattentive Type, and discusses possible interventions with Brian's parents.

Based on all the information, the psychologist makes a provisional diagnosis for Brian of ADHD, Predominantly Inattentive Type.

The Case of Winnie

Winnie's mother arrives at the interview out of breath and very anxious to hear about her daughter. Her mother describes Winnie as a "real worrier" and admits that she is that way herself. Winnie has always been very timid, and as an infant she was cautious, fearful, sensitive to noises and touch, and "slow to warm up to others." Socially, Winnie has a few close friends. Homework is a painful process, as perfectionistic tendencies get in the way of completing assignments because Winnie keeps erasing her work. Because of the extent of her fears and anxieties, Winnie is often overwhelmed by tasks and appears inattentive, distracted, and forgetful.

Winnie's provisional diagnosis is General Anxiety Disorder. Rule out possible Obsessive-Compulsive Disorder.

The Case of Jason

Jason's foster mother arrives at the interview with her social worker. This is Jason's fourth foster placement in the past 2 years. Jason has been in his current foster placement for the past 6 months. According to the social worker, Jason was a witness to family violence from an early age. Jason's family was well known to Social Services, and Jason has been in care several times in the past for reported neglect and possible abuse. Shortly after Jason and his brother rejoined their parents 2 years ago, Jason's father shot his mother and then himself, while Jason and his younger brother slept in an adjoining bedroom. Jason has been receiving play therapy for the past 2 years. Jason continues to have trouble sleeping and is often agitated and restless. In relationships, his behavior vacillates between being overly inhibited (shy and withdrawn) or disinhibited (socially precocious). His ability to sustain his attention and concentration is impaired, and he is often forgetful and appears disorganized.

Jason's provisional diagnosis is Posttraumatic Stress Disorder (chronic). Rule out possible Reactive Attachment Disorder and Attention Deficit Disorder.

Summary of the Three Child Study Cases

Although the three children demonstrated similar symptoms in the classroom and in the home environment (pervasive across situations), only one of the three children was likely demonstrating ADHD.

Given high rates of *comorbidity* (disorders occurring together) in childhood disorders and the fact that many disorders present with similar symptom clusters, the need for developing a case formulation based on information from multiple sources cannot be overemphasized.

The Case of Matthew

The next day, the psychologist is asked to observe another child in the fourth grade: Matthew, an 11-year-old who is repeating the grade 4 program. Matthew has a behavior problem, and his emotions often escalate out of control. This day is no exception. When the psychologist observes Matthew in the classroom, he demonstrates a full-blown temper tantrum, throwing himself on the floor, kicking, and crying.

The psychologist makes an appointment to meet with Matthew's father. She leaves the elementary school and stops on her way home to pick up her 3-year-old daughter, Rachel, at the day care center. To the psychologist's dismay, Rachel is lying on the floor, kicking and screaming because another child took her favorite toy from her.

When the psychologist meets with Matthew's father, he states that Matthew's behavior problems have been ongoing from an early age. Matthew can be aggressive, moody, and irritable. Tantrums are frequent and often unpredictable. Matthew is oppositional and defiant at home and at school, and he often refuses to comply with even the smallest request. Often Matthew seems to deliberately annoy others.

Question: Are the temper tantrums produced by Matthew and Rachel indicative of a disruptive behavior disorder?

Disruptive behavior disorders, classified as Conduct Disorder (CD) and Oppositional Defiant Disorder (ODD) by the *DSM-IV-TR* (APA, 2000), are highly prevalent in children and adolescents. Of these disorders, ODD is represented by a constellation of symptoms of aggression, anger, and disobedience. Children with ODD have recurrent displays of negative behaviors toward authority that are defiant, disobedient, and hostile (APA, 2000). Matthew's provisional diagnosis is Oppositional Defiant Disorder or depression.

The Case of Rachel

The psychologist's 3-year-old daughter throws tantrums at the day care center when she is frustrated. These tantrums have been increasing in frequency for the past 6 months. Talking to the day care staff, the psychologist finds out that there is one particular child, Arty, who seems to trigger these tantrums. Arty joined the day care center about 6 months ago. Rachel does not throw tantrums at home and is a relatively easy-to-manage child. The psychologist is aware that, developmentally, tantrum behavior in toddlers normally peaks at around 3 years of age. The day care center staff members are not concerned and see Rachel's behavior as reactive to increasing frustration. The provisional diagnosis is a developmentally appropriate response to frustration.

DON'T FORGET

Although Matthew and Rachel displayed the same behavioral response to frustration (temper tantrums), when viewed within a developmental context, tantrums are a normal expression of frustration at 3 years of age but more deviant behavior at 11 years.

DISTINGUISHING NORMAL FROM ABNORMAL BEHAVIOR

Although many of the professional skills and competencies required to distinguish normal from abnormal behavior are shared by clinicians who serve adult and child populations, there are also several unique skills and competencies that distinguish these two populations as separate clinical fields.

Determining whether a behavior pattern is normal or abnormal requires, at a minimum, a fundamental understanding of normal expectations and the range of behaviors that constitute the broad limits of the average or normal range. In order to determine whether a behavior falls outside the normal range, clinical judgement is often based on a series of decision-making strategies. One way of measuring how the behavior compares to normal expectations is the use of "the four Ds" as a guideline to evaluating the behavior: *deviance, dysfunction, distress,* and *danger* (Comer, 2001).

Rachel, the psychologist's 3-year-old daughter, was previously observed throwing a temper tantrum at the day care center. Consider the severity of Rachel's tantrum behavior in relation to the tantrum behavior of another 3-year-old child, Arty.

The psychologist observes Rachel throwing a temper tantrum because Arty has taken her favorite toy. Rachel is lying on the floor, crying and kicking her legs into the floor mat. This behavior occurs whenever Arty takes this toy away (about twice a week) and lasts until the teacher intervenes. Rachel's mother has not seen this behavior at home. Arty also causes a similar reaction from Sara, another child in the program. Arty is constantly fighting with other children. Arty takes what he wants, when he wants it. If stopped, Arty throws temper tantrums that escalate in proportion and can last up to half an hour. On two occasions, Arty has injured a teacher by throwing an object wildly into the air. When frustrated, Arty will strike out, and he has bitten others to get his way. Arty's mother has asked for help with managing Arty's behavior. She is afraid Arty will injure his new baby brother.

In evaluating Rachel's and Arty's behaviors, we know that tantrum behavior peaks at 3 years of age and that biting is not uncommon among preschoolers. However, although Rachel's tantrum behavior would likely be considered to fall within the range of normal expectations, Arty's behaviors are more concerning, be-

DON'T FORGET

Clinical decisions are often based on measures of the *intensity, duration,* and *frequency* of a behavior relative to the norm. In addition, evaluating whether a behavior is pervasive across situations can also provide information regarding the nature and severity of the behavior in terms of eliciting *mild, moderate,* or *severe* levels of concern.

cause the behaviors demonstrate deviance from the norm on all measures: intensity (he has injured others); frequency (he has done so repeatedly), and duration (his tantrums last at least a half hour). In contrast, Rachel's behaviors are isolated to the school situation and to Arty's advances in particular. Rachel's tantrums would likely elicit a mild level of concern and possibly result in the development of a behavioral intervention plan to assist Rachel in coping with Arty's advances. However, in addition to all the aforementioned concerns, Arty's behaviors would also be considered more severe due to the pervasive nature of the behavior, which is evident at home as well as at school. Furthermore, the behaviors pose a danger to those around him (he has injured a teacher), and Arty has not developed appropriate skills in areas of self-control or social relationships (dysfunction). Arty's ease of frustration, low frustration tolerance, and habitual tantrum behavior all signal high levels of distress. In addition, Arty's behaviors are disturbing and distressing to others. Based on the nature of Arty's problem behaviors, a more intensive treatment program would be required to modify his behavior.

The use of the four Ds can provide helpful guidelines in determining normal from abnormal behavior in the following ways.

Deviance. Determining the degree that behaviors are deviant from the norm can be assisted through the use of informal assessment (interviews, observations, symptom rating scales) or more formal psychometric test batteries (personality assessment). Classification systems can also provide clinicians with guidelines for evaluating the degree of deviance.

Clinicians working with children and adults must also be aware that several disorders can share common features, and often additional data gathering is required to rule out or confirm the existence of a specific disorder (*differential diagnosis*). In addition to disorders sharing similar features, some disorders also occur together more frequently, a condition known as comorbidity.

CAUTION

There has been an increasing awareness of the need to integrate cultural variations into our understanding of deviant behaviors and psychopathology (Fabrega, 1990; Rogler, 1999). The *DSM-IV-TR* (APA, 2000) includes sections acknowledging cultural factors and cultural reference groups in describing disorders.

DON'T FORGET

Symptoms of inattentiveness, lack of concentration, restlessness, fidgeting, forgetfulness, and disorganization may signal a case of ADHD. However, differential diagnosis may be required to rule out anxiety, depression, Posttraumatic Stress Disorder, child abuse, learning problems, and a host of other potential problems that share similar features.

Dysfunction. Once a disorder is identified, the relative impact of the disorder on the individual's functioning must be determined. Child clinicians may be interested in the degree of dysfunction in such areas as school performance (academic functioning) or social skills.

Distress. An area closely related to dysfunction is the degree of distress the disorder causes. Children often have difficulty articulating feelings and may provide little information to assist the clinician in determining distress. Interviews with parents and teachers can provide additional sources of information. Some disorders may present little distress for the individual concerned but prove very distressing to others.

Danger. In order to determine whether a given behavior places an individual at risk, two broad areas are evaluated: risk for self-harm and risk of harm to others. Historically the focus has been on victimization and maltreatment of children (abuse or neglect) or the assessment of risk for self-harm (suicide intent). However, more recent events, such as the 1999 Columbine shootings and increased awareness of bullying, have increased concerns regarding children as perpetrators of harm. Accordingly, increased emphasis has been placed on methods of identifying potentially dangerous children and conducting effective threat assessments.

Normal and Abnormal Behaviors: Developmental Considerations

Evaluation of psychopathology from a developmental perspective requires the integration of information about child characteristics (biological and genetic) and environmental characteristics (family, peers, school, neighborhood). Therefore, understanding child psychopathology from a developmental perspective requires an understanding of the nature of cognitive, social, emotional and physical competencies, limitations, and task expectations for each stage of development. This understanding is crucial to an awareness of how developmental issues impact psychopathology and treatment. Examples of developmental tasks, competencies, and limitations are presented in Rapid Reference 1.2.

The Impact of Theoretical Perspectives

The ability to distinguish normal from abnormal behavior and select developmentally appropriate child interventions can be guided by information obtained from various theoretical frameworks. Different theoretical perspectives can provide the clinician with guidelines concerning expectations for social, emotional, cognitive, physical, and behavioral outcomes. In addition, a therapist's theoretical

≡ Rapid Reference 1.2

Examples of Developmental Tasks, Competencies, and Limitations

Age or Stage of Development	Task or Limitations
Birth to 1 year	Trust vs. mistrust (Erikson)
	Secure vs. insecure attachment (Bowlby)
	Differentiation between self and others
	Reciprocal socialization
	Development of object permanence (Piaget: objects exist when out of sight)
	First steps; first word
Toddler: 1–2.5	Autonomy vs. shame and doubt (Erikson)
	Increased independence, self-assertion, and pride
	Beginnings of self-awareness
	Social imitation and beginnings of empathy
	Beginnings of self-control
	Delayed imitation and symbolic thought
	Language increases to 100 words
	Increase in motor skills and exploration
Preschool: 2.5–6	Initiative vs. guilt (Erikson)
	Inability to decenter (Piaget: logic bound to perception; problems with appearance/reality)
	Egocentric (emotional and physical perspective; one emotion at a time)
	Increased emotion regulation (under-regulation vs. over-regulation)
	Increased need for rules and structure
	Can identify feelings: Guilt and conscience are evident
	Emergent anxieties, phobias, fears
School age: 6–11	Industry vs. inferiority (Erikson)
	Sense of competence, mastery, and efficacy
	Concrete operations (Piaget: no longer limited by appearance, but limited by inability to think in the abstract)
	Can experience blends of emotions (love-hate)
	Self-concept and moral conscience
	Realistic fears (injury, failure) and irrational fears (mice, nightmares)

Teen years	Identity vs. role diffusion (Erikson)
	Abstract reasoning (Piaget)
	Emotional blends in self and others (ambiguity)
	Return of egocentricity (Piaget/Elkind: imaginary audience and personal fable)
	Self-concept relative to peer acceptance and competence

assumptions will also influence how the disorder is conceptualized and guide the course of the treatment focus.

Biomedical Theories

Biological and physiological theories are concerned with the impact of biological and genetic factors on individual differences. There has been increasing recognition of the interactive contribution of environmental (health, nutrition, stress) and genetic influences. Emphasis has been placed on several factors in this area, including temperament, genetic transmission, and brain structure and function.

In defining abnormal behavior, a biomedical model would seek to determine which parts of the body or brain were malfunctioning, whether genetics, brain chemistry, or brain anatomy. Twin studies have been instrumental in providing information concerning the role of genetics, while refined neurological approaches, such as magnetic resonance imaging (MRI), have also contributed to our knowledge of underlying brain-based differences in some disorders.

Psychodynamic Theories

Freud initially envisioned abnormal behavior resulting from fixations or regressions based on earlier unresolved stages of conflict. His psychosexual stages provide potential insight into unconscious drives and conflicts that may influence the underlying dynamics of certain pathologies. The role of unconscious defense mechanisms that serve to protect the vulnerable ego stem from battles between the id (more primitive pleasure principle) and the superego (moral con-

DON'T FORGET

Historically, psychoanalytic applications have been very difficult to support empirically. Influenced by Bowlby's theories of self-development and attachment, recent research by Fonagy and Target (1996) has provided empirical support for psychodynamic developmental therapy for children (PDTC). Working through the medium of play, therapists assist children to develop skills in the self-regulation of impulses and enhanced awareness of others.

science). These defense mechanisms add depth to our understanding of more primitive child defenses, such as denial, or more socially constructive defenses, such as humor.

Erik Erikson (1902–1994) also supported the notion of stages; however, his psychosocial stages outline socioemotional tasks that must be mastered to allow for positive growth across the lifespan. As can be seen in Rapid Reference 1.2, theorists have adapted the concept of developmental tasks and stages of development to explain and predict a wide variety of behaviors based on competencies and limitations (social, emotional, cognitive, and physical) evident at each of the stages.

According to Erikson, in the first year of life, the major task is to develop a sense of basic trust versus mistrust. From the foundation of a secure attachment, the preschooler is free to explore the environment. Either a growing sense of autonomy develops or the insecure child may shrink from these experiences, producing feelings of shame and self-doubt. The school-age child masters school-related subjects and peer socialization, which increase a sense of industry versus inferiority. In adolescence, the task becomes one of identity versus role confusion.

Behavioral Theories

Behavioral theory is based on the fundamental credo that behavior is shaped by associations (contingencies) resulting from positive (reinforcement) and negative (punishment) consequences. Consequences are *positive* if

- They add a benefit (positive reinforcement; e.g., finish your work in class and you will be given ten minutes of free activity time), or
- They remove or avoid (escape) a negative consequence (negative reinforcement; e.g., if you finish your work in class, you will not have to stay after school).

Consequences are *negative* if

- They add an adverse or negative consequence (punishment), or
- They remove or avoid a positive consequence (penalty).

Some punishments can be so severe that behavior is eliminated altogether, a condition known as *extinc-*

DON'T FORGET

The concept of negative reinforcement is more difficult to understand than positive reinforcement because negative reinforcement is often confused with punishment. Remember that punishments deliver negative consequences and serve to reduce rather than increase behaviors.

tion. If behavior is no longer reinforced and continually punished, extinction is often the result. Determining whether the behavior is an excess or deficit also requires knowledge of what to expect based on developmental level. Optimally, a behavioral plan will target increasing a deficit behavior rather than reducing an excessive behavior. For example, it is preferable and often more successful to attempt to increase on-task behavior than to attempt to reduce off-task behavior, since increasing the positive behavior will ultimately reduce negative consequences.

Although the majority of learned behavior occurs through operant conditioning or observational learning, behaviorists use the paradigm of classical conditioning to explain the development of irrational fears or phobias. For example, a child may develop a fear of sleeping alone if awakened by a very loud thunderstorm. Furthermore, the fear might generalize to fear of the dark, fear of loud noises, or fear of his or her own bed or bedroom. Pairing the loud noise with sleeping alone can result in the child's developing a conditioned response of fear of his or her own bed.

> ## DON'T FORGET
>
> Behaviors can also be categorized as a *behavioral excess* (externalizing, acting-out behaviors) or a *behavioral deficit* (internalizing, withdrawn behaviors).

> ## CAUTION
>
> Parents or teachers can be very frustrated when a child continues to engage in repeated negative behaviors despite warnings, punishments, and various other acts of negative consequences. However, what they fail to understand is that all the nagging and cajoling serves as a positive reinforcement to the child because the outcome is increased adult attention. Therefore, the more nagging continues, the more the behavior is reinforced and will be sustained.

Cognitive Theories

Cognitive theorists are primarily interested in the relationship between thoughts and behaviors and how faulty assumptions can impact on social relationships as well as influencing self-attributions in a negative way. Jean Piaget's stages of cognitive development are outlined in Rapid Reference 1.2. Piaget was highly influential in his attempts to chart the course of cognitive development. According to Piaget, children in the preoperational stage (ages 2 to 7) can be easily mislead by dominant visual features due to their inability to consider two aspects simultaneously, what Piaget calls an inability to decenter. A very young child will say that there is more liquid in a tall thin glass than a short fat one, even though the child witnessed the same amount of liquid being poured into the two glasses. Visual dominance also contributes to difficulties separating appearance and reality (a dog wearing a cat mask is now a cat). Taking another's perspective or point of view is also very limited due to the child's egocentrism or self-focus. The school-aged child (the concrete operations stage) is capable of reasoning beyond that of the preschool child; however, this stage is limited by concrete observations. According to Piaget, abstract thinking is not achieved until adolescence, when hypothetical and deductive reasoning emerges. Although Piaget believed that all children progress through a series of fixed stages, recent research has recognized that children of differing abilities may progress at different rates and that Piaget's stage theories may not be universal.

Social cognitive theories.   Albert Bandura's (1977, 1986) contributions to the field of social cognition stem from his early work on social learning processes, observational learning, and aggression. Bandura's (1977) understanding of the social aspects of learning has been instrumental in increasing our awareness of observational learning. Children's observation and subsequent modeling of adult behavior can have positive (nurturing and empathic caring behaviors) or negative consequences (aggressive responses; e.g., witness to domestic violence).

Research concerning children's understanding of social relationships has also been applied to the development of social skills and problem solving in social situations. Studies in this area have revealed that children rejected by peers are often aggressive, argumentative, and retaliatory towards others (Dodge, Bates, & Pettit, 1990). Furthermore, negative behaviors often resulted from tendencies to misinterpret ambivalent social situations as hostile, or what has come to be known as the *hostile attribution bias.*

> ## DON'T FORGET
>
> The concept of *triadic reciprocity* was developed by Bandura to explain the complex nature of people, behaviors, and the environment. According to Bandura behavior not only is the outcome of the person in a given environment or situation but also itself serves to influence the person and the environment.
>
> Person   Environment
>   ↑↓
>   Behavior

> ## DON'T FORGET
>
> Aggression from the social cognitive perspective might be explained by observational learning (the child is potentially a witness to violence at home; Bandura) or as resulting from an interpretation of a situation based on faulty attributions, *hostile attribution bias* (Dodge et al., 1990).

Cognitive behavioral theories.   The cognitive behavioral approach seeks to understand associations between thoughts and behaviors. Therefore, emphasis is placed on understanding how the child's faulty belief system contributes to maladaptive behaviors, such as aggression, depression, and anxiety. Cognitive theorists, such as Aaron Beck (1976), posit that depression develops and is sustained by self-attributions arising from a *cognitive triad* producing thoughts of helplessness, hopelessness, and worthlessness. Seligman and Peterson (1986) suggest that learned helplessness can develop from repeated negative self-attributions, which produce feelings of powerlessness and lack of control that ultimately become a self-fulfilling prophecy.

Theories of Attachment and Parenting

John Bowlby's (1908–1990) *adaptation theory* was influenced by Darwin's theory of evolution and Freud's emphasis on internal working models. Bowlby believed that early attachment relationships carry a profound influence throughout the lifespan. Later, Mary Ainsworth explored attachment issues using the strange situation experiments and revealed that securely attached infants were more independent and better problem solvers than insecurely attached infants. Infants who demonstrated avoidant attachment rarely showed distress when separated from caregivers, while infants who demonstrated resistant attachment often demonstrated clingy behaviors and greater upset at separations from caregivers who responded with unpredictable behavioral extremes (love and anger). In the late 1970s, working with a population of maltreated infants, Main and Weston (1981) ultimately added a fourth category of disorganized behavior to describe distressful and frightened responses to caregivers.

Baumrind (1991) also investigated parenting styles and found three approaches to parenting that impacted on child behaviors for better or worse. Children raised by authoritarian parents (high on structure, low on warmth) tend to react with behaviors that are aggressive and uncooperative, tend to be fearful of punishment, and are generally weak on initiative, self-esteem, and peer competence. Children who are raised in permissive households (high on warmth, low on structure) often fail to develop a sense of responsibility and self-control. Authoritative par-

CAUTION

Although attachment theory was developed to explain how children develop an organized schema of relationships (internal working models), Main and Hesse (1990) reasoned that disorganized responses were the result of an inability to construct a schema, since attachment in these maltreated infants activated two competing and irreconcilable response systems: attachment (approach) and fear (avoidance).

ents (high on warmth and high on structure) provide the optimum conditions for growth, and as a result children often demonstrate high degrees of self-reliance, self-esteem, and self-controlled behaviors.

Family Systems Theory

Family systems theory is represented by a variety of approaches that emphasize the family unit as the focus of assessment and intervention. This theoretical framework acknowledges the family system itself, as a unit made up of many sub-systems: parent and child, marriage partners, siblings, extended family, and so on. Within families, behaviors are often directed toward maintaining or changing boundaries, alignment, and power. Boundaries are the imaginary lines that serve to define the various subsystems. Often a family's degree of dysfunction can be defined by boundaries that are poorly or inconsistently defined or those that are too extreme (too loose or too rigid). Salvador Minuchin (1985), a proponent of structural family therapy, has suggested that enmeshed families (lacking in boundaries) may interpret a child's need to individuate as a threat to the family unit.

> **DON'T FORGET**
>
> A theorist from a family systems perspective might view the aggressive behaviors of a child in the context of behaviors motivated to undermine the importance of the primary marital relationship. Triangular relationships that serve to shift the balance of power include the parent-child coalition (parent and child versus parent), triangulation (child caught between two parents), and detouring (maintaining the child as focus of the problem to avoid acknowledging marital problems).

> **DON'T FORGET**
>
> An understanding of developmental pathways includes an awareness that there are several possible pathways that may produce the same outcome, an occurrence known as *equifinality* (e.g., many factors may cause a single outcome, such as childhood depression), and that similar risks may produce different outcomes, which is known as *multifinality* (e.g., childhood neglect may result in aggressive behavior in one child and withdrawal in another; Cicchetti & Rogosch, 1996).

Influences and Developmental Change

Most clinicians today recognize that in addition to understanding child characteristics (temperament, developmental stage) it is equally important to consider environmental influences (family, peers, school, community, economics and culture) when evaluating child and adolescent disorders. Ultimately, the importance of including the developmental context in understanding child and adolescent disorders is crucial to comprehending not only the child's present level of distress or dysfunction but also how the difficulties came to be (developmental pathway).

The child clinician must also consider the impact of environmental influences as predisposing, precipitating, and maintaining (reinforcing) factors regarding the behavior in question. While theoretical assumptions can guide our understanding of the nature of developmental change, our knowledge of individual differences (stage of development, personality or temperament) can refine our understanding of a child's unique nature. Ultimately, our awareness and understanding of how these forces are embedded in the child's environmental context provide the key to fully comprehending child psychopathology.

According to Bronfenbrenner (1979, 1989), developmental contexts consist of a series of concentric circles emanating from the child, who occupies the innermost circle. At the core are the child's individual characteristics (biological context, such as genetic makeup, temperament, intelligence). Moving outward, the child's immediate environment (family, school, peers, community, neighborhood), the surrounding social and economic context (poverty, divorce, family stress), and the cultural context provide additional ripples and sources of influence. Within this framework, understanding a child's mental disorder requires an understanding of the influences of all contextual variables.

Understanding multiple levels of influence also requires emphasizing the dual nature of influence, since child and parent mutually influence each other. Therefore, the bidirectional nature of these influences, or *reciprocal determinism* (Bandura, 1985), becomes a crucial aspect of interpreting how interactive effects of these influences may be instrumental in constructing different developmental pathways.

Sameroff's *transactional model* (Sameroff & Chandler, 1975) captures the ongoing and interactive nature of developmental change between the child and the environment. A transactional model is also crucial to understanding the dynamics of various disorders in order to trace the developmental pathway and construct meaningful case formulations and relevant treatment alternatives. For example, in their discussion of depressive disorders in children and adolescents, Cicchetti and Toth (1998) stress the need to use an ecological transactional model in order to comprehend the complex

CAUTION

One major influence that has often been overlooked is the compatibility between the environmental systems. According to Bronfenbrenner, the *mesosystem*, which represents the interaction between two microsystems (e.g., home and school environment), predicts the degree to which a system remains healthy, functional, and in balance.

DON'T FORGET

Several theories have been developed to assist our understanding of the complex dynamics that exist between individual and environmental influences. Bandura developed the concepts of triadic reciprocity (1977) and reciprocal determinism (1985) to emphasize the bidirectional nature of the influence. Bronfenbrenner (1979, 1989) envisioned ecological influences from the inner child to the outer world (family, community, culture). Sameroff's transactional model (Sameroff & Chandler, 1975) focuses on how interactive forces can shape the course of developmental change, while Cicchetti and Toth (1998) have applied the model to explain potential pathways for the development of depressive disorders in children and adolescence.

nature of depressive disorders in children and youth and understand the diverse and multiple influences that contribute to the emergence of the disorder.

Theories in Context

Viewing the child within the contexts of developmental influences provides an enhanced level of insight into the underlying dynamics of potentially disordered behaviors and can guide and improve our ability to make case formulations that have ecological validity.

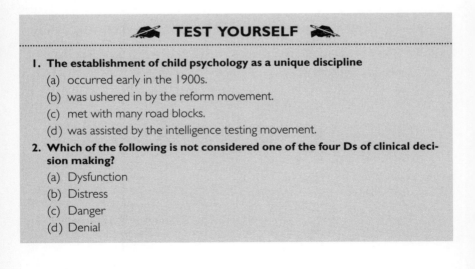

🦅 TEST YOURSELF 🦅

1. **The establishment of child psychology as a unique discipline**
   (a) occurred early in the 1900s.
   (b) was ushered in by the reform movement.
   (c) met with many road blocks.
   (d) was assisted by the intelligence testing movement.

2. **Which of the following is not considered one of the four Ds of clinical decision making?**
   (a) Dysfunction
   (b) Distress
   (c) Danger
   (d) Denial

3. **According to Erikson, the first psychosocial task sets the stage for development of**
   (a) autonomy versus shame.
   (b) trust versus mistrust.
   (c) industry versus inferiority.
   (d) identity versus role confusion.

4. **The existence of several possible pathways that may produce the same outcome (e.g., many factors may be responsible for depression) is an example of**
   (a) multifinality.
   (b) equifinality.
   (c) triadic finality.
   (d) triadic reciprocity.

5. **According to Bronfenbrenner, the outermost circle of influence is represented by**
   (a) culture.
   (b) school and family.
   (c) the child.
   (d) economics.

6. **Negative reinforcement is the same as**
   (a) punishment.
   (b) a negative consequence.
   (c) a penalty.
   (d) escape.

7. **According to Piaget, preschool children's reasoning is faulty because**
   (a) they have limited memories.
   (b) they can only consider one visual feature at a time.
   (c) vision acuity is not clearly established.
   (d) they have limited attention spans.

Answers: 1. c; 2. d; 3. b; 4. b; 5. a; 6. d; 7. b

ISSUES IN CHILD PSYCHOPATHOLOGY: ETHICAL ISSUES IN RESEARCH AND PRACTICE AND RESEARCH METHODOLOGY

Mental health professionals working with children and families are guided by ethical principles and professional standards developed and monitored by their professional organizations. Psychologist's scientific, educational and professional activities are guided by an ethics code (Ethical Principles of Psychologists and Code of Conduct) developed by the American Psychological Association. The most recent revision of the ethics code (American Psychological Association, 2002) includes a set of general guiding principles as well as specific standards to be enforced across a wide variety of psychological roles (clinical, counseling, school psychology) and applied practices (research, education, test construction and design, or administrative or supervising capacities).

Other professional bodies, such as the American Counseling Association (ACA; 1995), the American School Counselors Association (ASCA; 1998), and the National Association of School Psychologists (NASP; 2000), have also developed ethical guidelines and principles for professional practice in schools and mental health settings. The ethical codes mentioned are all available in their entirety on the internet and can be accessed using the contact information provided in Appendix A. Common general principles among these different practicing bodies include principles of beneficence and nonmaleficence, fidelity, justice, and autonomy.

The American Psychological Association's ethical standards cover issues in twelve areas of practice, including resolving ethical issues, competence, human relations, pri-

---

> ## DON'T FORGET
> ....
> The five general principles are considered to be aspirational goals, and although these general principles are not considered to be enforceable rules, they provide the foundation from which psychologists can seek direction in making ethically based decisions. The five general principles are
>
> - Beneficence and nonmaleficence
> - Fidelity and responsibility
> - Integrity
> - Justice
> - Respect for rights and dignity of others

> ## DON'T FORGET
>
> Common principles across ethical codes of the American Psychological Association, ACA, and NASP, include
> - Beneficence and nonmaleficence (do not harm)
> - Fidelity (maintain relationships of trust and ethical compliance)
> - Justice or competence (fairness, equality, minimization of bias, and recognition of boundaries of professional competence)
> - Autonomy (self-direction) and respect for the rights of others

vacy and confidentiality, advertising and public statements, record keeping and fees, education and training, research and publications, assessment, and therapy.

RELATIONSHIP BETWEEN ETHICAL GUIDELINES AND LAWS

The majority of mental health laws and statues that apply to mental health practitioners fall within the realm of civil rather than criminal law. Ethical guidelines are not laws and as such are not legally binding. However, the professional bodies do monitor and sanction violations of their members. Although a professional body such as the American Psychological Association may sanction its members for violation of the ethics code, it can also inform other professional groups or state and federal associations of nonmembers who violate the ethics code.

ETHICAL DILEMMAS

Ethical principles become very important when practitioners are faced with ethical challenges, such as ethical dilemmas. Practitioners face ethical dilemmas

> ## Putting It Into Practice
>
> Balancing a client's right to fidelity (maintaining relationships of trust) with the principle of beneficence (benefit) and nonmaleficence (doing no harm) might occur if a therapist is faced with the following dilemma. A teenager (15 years of age) is receiving counseling at a private clinic, and her parents are paying for the sessions. The girl has disclosed to the counselor that she is having unprotected sex with a 17-year-old male. The teen has asked that the counselor not tell her parents. The parents suspect that their daughter might be sexually active, but they have no proof. They demand that the counselor provide the information to confirm their suspicions. In this case, the therapist must face a number of ethically challenging questions, including "Who is the client?"

when two or more ethical principles are in conflict with one another. These principles can result in challenging decision-making choices that can become even more complex when one of the clients is a child.

ETHICAL ISSUES IN ASSESSING, TREATING, AND CONDUCTING RESEARCH WITH CHILDREN

One of the key clinical considerations in obtaining children's consent for involvement in assessment, treatment, or research is determining their level of competence in understanding the nuances and nature of what they are agreeing to. However, although the concepts of competency and informed consent overlap to a degree, one argument could be that competency is actually a necessary precursor to obtaining informed consent (Koocher & Keith-Spiegel, 1990). From this perspective, informed consent requires that the child demonstrate sufficient comprehension of the decision, which includes weighing potential outcomes and anticipating possible future consequences. Therefore, understanding how cognitive limitations might compromise decision making developmentally is a necessary precursor to obtaining informed consent.

Ethical Considerations in Research

- Research programs involving children as subjects must adhere to standards set by professional organizations such as the American Psychological Association (1992), NASP (2000), and the Society for Research in Child Development (1996).
- Another safeguard is a requirement that the research program be subject to an ethical review board to insure compliance with the American Psychological Association's guidelines for research with human subjects and to evaluate the benefits and any potential risks. If there is no ethical review committee, NASP (2000) suggests the use of peer review ("preferably a school psychologist") of the research proposal and methodology.
- Children with physical vulnerabilities due to their diminutive size and cognitive limitations may also have a limited ability to comprehend significant issues such as the full nature of their participation or inherent appearance/reality distinctions.
- Due to cognitive limitations, informed consent for participation is obtained from the parents of children who are minors. However, even under these circumstances, the child's assent, or consent and willingness

to participate, should be obtained by providing explanations of the process to the child in language suited to the child's developmental level.

Ethical Considerations in Practice

Since children rarely self-refer, therapists are most often asked to see a child at the request of an adult (parent, teacher, guardian). Although parents or guardians are assumed to be

> ### DON'T FORGET
>
> Although the age of majority is typically 18 (34 states), it can range up to 21 (Mississippi, D.C., New York) in the United States and between 18 (50% or six provinces) and 19 in Canada. The Canadian Code of Ethics for Psychologists recommends that children 12 years of age or older be involved in providing informed consent for their participation in research or assessment.

acting in the best interests of the child, there are many situations that can place professionals in a position of a conflict of interest. The Putting It into Practice case study illustrates how a parent's wishes may not be in the best interest of the child and may actually infringe on the psychologist's ethical standards to do no harm and to demonstrate fidelity and integrity.

Issues of Confidentiality

In the vast majority of cases, parents or legal guardians of children under 18 years of age (or the given age of majority in the practicing state or province) are responsible for signing releases of information and/or obtaining or releasing reports pertaining to a child's medical or educational records. However, ethical issues can often result, especially when working with parents and adolescents regarding the

Putting It Into Practice

Nancy and George have recently separated. Nancy is afraid that her son Joel is not responding well to the separation, and furthermore she does not approve of his visiting his father on the weekends. Nancy feels that Joel is more upset when he comes back on Sunday evenings and complains that it takes him all week to get over the visit, and then it is time to leave again.

Nancy is hoping that the psychologist can interview Joel to determine that the visits with his father are not in Joel's best interests. Nancy also does not want the psychologist to give any feedback to Joel's father about the assessment, because she intends to use this information in court to stop the visitation.

In this case, the therapist is faced with a case of parent interests that are not necessarily in line with the best interests of the child. Furthermore, the parent is also asking the psychologist to compromise ethical standards.

limits of confidentiality. Clinicians working with adolescents or older children should always define the limits of confidentiality at the onset of the therapeutic relationship. Limits of confidentiality include ethical duties to report any indications of harm to self or others or reports of abuse. However, the limits of confidentiality with respect to parent access to other information discussed during therapy sessions may be far more difficult to address.

CAUTION

When working with adolescents and older children, a therapeutic rule of thumb is to discuss and negotiate rules of confidentiality and issues of privacy (between parent and child) prior to beginning therapeutic sessions.

CAUTION

In obtaining parental consent for children whose parents are divorced or in custody litigation, the therapist must exercise special care in determining who is the custodial parent.

CAUTION

Be aware of state laws for reporting abuse. For example, failure to report abuse in the state of Florida is a misdemeanor of the first degree, subject to 1 year's imprisonment or a $1,000 fine.

DON'T FORGET

Researchers are primarily concerned with seeking answers to *nomothetic* truths, regarding the causes, nature, course, and treatment of childhood disorders.

Parents who seek therapeutic resources for older children and adolescents often can be persuaded that the clinician's ability to establish a trusting relationship with the child may initially require the therapist not to disclose information to the parents. By building a sense of rapport and trust, the psychologist will likely be able to develop the child's gradual understanding that sharing these private thoughts and feelings with parents will ultimately improve the parent-child relationship.

Confidentiality does not outweigh the therapist's mandated duty to report. The majority of mental health practitioners are legislated by state law to report issues of child abuse, neglect, or abandonment. Lack of reporting a suspected case of abuse can often result in legal ramifications.

RESEARCH METHODS IN CHILD PSYCHOPATHOLOGY

Clinical child researchers seek scientific truths guided by the four objectives of the scientific method: description, prediction, control (prevention), and understanding. Hypothesis testing can take two broad forms:

1. An investigation of the relationship among a set of variables (e.g., age, gender, aggression, leisure habits), known as *correlational research*.

2. Attempts to demonstrate a cause-and-effect relationship between two or more variables (e.g., how leisure activities might influence aggressive tendencies).

The Experimental Method

In conducting a true experiment, the researcher puts his hypothesis (hunch) about a behavior to the test. The researcher manipulates the experimental situation by randomly assigning subjects to one of two grouping conditions: a control group (which is not exposed to the variable in question) and an experimental group (which is exposed to the variable).

> **CAUTION**
>
> *Correlation does not imply causation.* While correlational research need only establish a relationship (either positive or negative) between the variables, experimental research has the more daunting task of delineating a cause-and-effect relationship.

> **DON'T FORGET**
>
> In an experiment, the researcher manipulates a variable and observes the effect of that variable on another variable. In the following experiment, the independent variable (violent versus nonviolent TV program) is manipulated by the experimenter, while the dependent variable (level of aggression) is the variable (behavior) that is monitored for expected change resulting from manipulation of the independent variable.

In the example provided in the Putting It into Practice box, a researcher wants to examine the relationship between TV viewing and aggressive behavior. The research hypothesis is that watching TV violence increases aggressive behavior. In order to test this hypothesis, the researcher would set out to disprove (or reject) the null hypothesis. The null hypothesis would reflect a condition of no difference in level of aggressive behavior in children who watch violent versus nonviolent TV programs. One possible way to examine this research question would be to randomly assign subjects to the two conditions presented in the Putting It into Practice box.

Several research questions can be generated about the study.

1. Does the study have *internal validity?* How well has the researcher linked increased aggression to the TV program that children watched (cause-and-effect relationship)?

2. Does the study have *external validity?* To what extent can the results of this study be generalized beyond the clinical laboratory?

Putting It Into Practice

One hundred 4-year-old low socioeconomic status (SES) boys are randomly assigned to one of two groups: violent cartoon group (VCG) and nonviolent cartoon group (NCG). Each group is observed in the playroom (25 children at a time) while raters obtain a 15-minute baseline record for aggressive versus nonaggressive play for each child. Children are then exposed to a 15-minute cartoon: In the VCG group the cartoon's main character is involved in several fight scenes involving swords, guns, and body contact, whereas the NCG group watches a Winnie the Pooh cartoon story. Observations of play behaviors after cartoon watching are recorded for aggressive versus nonaggressive play. Results reveal that aggressive acts increased significantly for children who were in the VCG during the second play period and continued to be evident when the children returned for a third observation period 2 weeks later.

Internal Validity

The researcher has made a good attempt to match his samples for age, SES, and gender, as well as limiting the extraneous confounds. Objective measures were taken of play behaviors before and after TV viewing. The researcher has also included a repeat observation 2 weeks later to evaluate longer-term effects. In evaluating internal validity, it would be informative to know how observations were conducted to rule out any potential observer/experimenter bias effects (e.g., were observers aware of the group affiliation, or was the rater unaware of group affiliation? How was interrater reliability established?).

External Validity

Can findings be generalized to different populations? While this experimental design produces high internal validity (experimental control), the artificial or contrived nature of the experimental situation may detract from ecological validity (validity of context). Generalizability of results would improve as the study was replicated, if findings were similar for males at different age levels, females at any age, and populations other than low-SES populations.

CAUTION

It could be strongly argued that the hypothetical study violates the ethical principle of beneficence and nonmaleficence, or the clinician's duty to do no harm. Ethically, the researcher's exposure of children in the experimental group to the violent cartoon condition resulted in increased and prolonged negative behaviors (aggression), which might produce long-term maladaptive consequences.

Quasi-Experimental Design

In clinical studies, randomized placement is often difficult to achieve and in some cases may not be advised. One way to circumvent this problem is the use of a matched control group.

Putting It Into Practice

A researcher wants to investigate the role of maternal depression on child abuse. Children who have been abused are matched to a group of children with the same demographics and characteristics (age, gender, SES, birth order, etc.) who have not been abused. Comparing prevalence rates of maternal depression for the two groups would provide an index of whether mothers of abused children were more depressed.

Empirically Based Treatments

There has been growing emphasis on empirically based treatments, specifically what works best for children who present with specific problems. In 1995, the Task Force on Promotion and Dissemination of Psychological Procedures established by the American Psychological Association produced a report on empirically validated psychological treatments. *Well-established treatments* documented treatment effectiveness in comparison to another form of treatment, or placebo, in at least two between-group experimental studies. Further criteria included the need for inclusion of a treatment manual and clear delineation of subject characteristics. *Probably efficacious treatments* were those that demonstrated that the treatment was superior to a wait list control group.

Single-Subject Experiment

Clinical studies that focus on intervention may also use the subject as their own control, in what is called a single-subject design. In this case, the variable to be manipulated (indepen-

DON'T FORGET

The report of the Task Force (1995) suggested classification of treatment efficacy based on a number of research criteria. Treatments were identified as *well-established treatments, probably efficacious treatments,* and *experimental treatments.*

DON'T FORGET

An *experimental treatment* is an empirically supported treatment approach that has been validated by comparisons of a treatment group with a no-treatment or alternative treatment control group.

DON'T FORGET

The wait list control group is used in quasi-experimental studies where treatment facilities keep a wait list for services. Treatment effects for children benefiting from treatment (experimental group) are compared to a no-treatment condition (wait list control group). Ethically, this is satisfactory because children in need of service are not deprived of treatment, since wait list children will benefit from treatment once their wait list status is removed.

dent variable) would be a clinical intervention and the subject would be observed prior to intervention (for baseline data) and again after the intervention was introduced. A comparison of behavior before and after intervention would provide an index of the degree to which the intervention was responsible for the behavior change.

Correlational Research

Researchers interested in how characteristics covary set out to compare how characteristics of one sample (participants) relate to characteristics in the same sample or another comparison sample. Correlations vary from −1 to +1, with +1 indicating a perfect positive correlation and −1 indicating a perfect negative correlation. Characteristics at zero are unrelated. In the hypothetical research study in the Putting It into Practice box, the researcher investigates the relationship between studying and grades.

External and Internal Validity.   Correlational studies have high external validity, meaning that a wide variety of variables can be generalized across large samples

Putting It Into Practice

A researcher wants to study the relationship between time spent studying and grades on a multiple-choice psychology exam. Students are randomly assigned to one of three groups: group 1 (60 minutes), group 2 (90 minutes), and group 3 (120 minutes). Groups are given an introductory psychology chapter to study, and after the allotted study times they are given a multiple-choice test. The researcher plots the results to find an upward-sloping line, as study time increases test scores increase. Results of study 1 confirm a strong positive correlation (.80) between study time and test scores. In study 2, students' study times are reduced by 30 minutes across the board. Results reveal a modest negative correlation (−.40) between decreased study time and test scores, producing a downward-sloping line.

Based on the researcher's study, can the researcher say that studying causes better grades? The answer is no.

of subjects and replicated to include greater sample variance. However, due to the descriptive nature of the correlational research and the inability to draw inferences of causation between variables, internal validity is low.

Epidemiological studies represent one form of correlational research that is important to clinical studies. These studies inform clinicians of the incidence and prevalence of disorders in the population.

Naturalistic observation. When a laboratory study is neither possible nor desired, the researcher may choose to observe children in their natural environment, such as in their homes, or on the playground in order to document naturally occurring behaviors. This method can be used in research or clinical practice. As a research design, emphasis is not on controlling the environment but rather on systematically controlling how behaviors are defined (operationalized) and the methods used to record the observations.

DEVELOPMENTAL CONSIDERATIONS IN CLINICAL CHILD RESEARCH

The Study of Behavior over Time

Research studies in the area of child psychopathology are often concerned with the study of how mal-

---

CAUTION

It is important to remember that *correlation is not causation* because two characteristics might be caused by a third factor. In the research program about studying and grades, other factors, such as anxiety, might impact on the outcome as well. Students with less study time might have had greater test anxiety, which served to lower scores.

DON'T FORGET

- *Incidence rate* refers to the number of new cases of a disorder within a given time period (e.g., the number of new cases in a year).
- *Prevalence rate* refers to the total number of cases of a disorder in the population within a given time frame.
- *Lifetime prevalence rate* refers to the number of cases of a disorder that might be expected to occur in one's lifespan.

Prevalence rates may differ significantly depending on the populations described (clinical versus nonclinical), how the disorder is classified (categorical versus dimensional), and how the disorder is measured.

DON'T FORGET

Some problems that may interfere with reliability of observed data include observer bias, observer drift, poor categories for coding, and central tendency (tendency to pick the middle category more frequently when rating behaviors).

adaptive behavior unfolds over the course of time, or the developmental pathways that serve as detours to normal development. These studies often seek to chart the course of maladaptive behavior by attempting to uncover factors that may serve to protect (buffer) the individual from harm or that place the child at greater risk of harm. Other studies may concentrate on the various forms (symptoms and behaviors) that maladaptive behavior may take at various ages as they are evident in the behavioral transformations that might be demonstrated at various stages of development (Sroufe, 1989). For example, depression may be expressed as acting-out behaviors at 2 years of age and as social withdrawal at 11 years. The study of developmental pathways has also emphasized the need to consider the role of *equifinality* (the possibility that different pathways can lead to the same outcome) and *multifinality* (the possibility that similar paths can produce different outcomes) in determining outcomes.

Longitudinal, Cross-Sectional, and Accelerated Longitudinal Designs

A clinical researcher is interested in studying the impact of insecure attachment across the life span. In particular, he is interested in how insecure attachment might impact academic achievement and social popularity with peers in preschool, in elementary school, and at the completion of the first year of high school. One method available to study long-term development is the *longitudinal study*. In this particular case, the researcher would be committed to a research program that would require approximately 15 years of data input. Using this method, the researcher would probably select two groups of infants (infants who were securely attached and infants who were insecurely attached) that were matched for demographic characteristics (SES, family constellation, etc.) and follow the children over the next 20 years of development, collecting data at specified periods. Although the value of this approach is self-evident, there are also significant drawbacks to the longitudinal approach, namely in the potential for subject shrinkage over the longevity of the research (subject attrition) and the cost of the research program.

A combination of the longitudinal and cross-sectional approaches, the *accelerated longitudinal design,* reduces the time involved while protecting against potential cohort effects. Using this approach, the researcher would study several age groups of children at the same time and then follow these groups for the next several years. In our hypothetical example, the researcher might select

> **DON'T FORGET**
>
> The cross-sectional approach allows researchers to study different groups of children (matched for similar demographics) simultaneously at different developmental times. In the study described, the researcher could follow two groups of children at the end of each of the following age levels: 5, 8, 11, and 14 years. Disadvantages of this approach are loss of information regarding developmental pathways and the potential for cohort effects (generational effects).

groups at three time periods—5, 8, and 11 years—and follow these groups at three-year intervals. In this manner, depending on the researcher's intent, the study could be completed within 3 to 6 years instead of 15 years.

Prevention: Risk Factors and Protective Factors

Improved research methodology and advances in technology (such as brain imaging and molecular biology) have all increased our understanding of the role of multiple influences (behavioral, psychological, and biological factors) in the etiology and course of child psychopathology. In addition, increased recognition that multiple influences can affect the trajectory of development for better or for worse has led to a greater emphasis on understanding how certain risk factors can contribute to vulnerability while other protective factors can buffer a child from harm.

In his review of over 1,200 prevention outcome studies, Durlak (1998) identified several common risk and protective factors that were shared across six areas of concern: social or behavior problems, academic problems, child maltreatment, physical injuries, drug use, and physi-

> **DON'T FORGET**
>
> Bronfenbrenner's (1979, 1989) emphasis on the contextual nature of development has expanded our awareness of the role of external forces in shaping developmental pathways. This knowledge has led to a greater understanding that the child's individual (biological) characteristics are continually influenced by the child's immediate environment (family, school, peers, community, neighborhood), social and economic environment, and cultural environment, in a reciprocal and mutual way.

≡ *Rapid Reference 2.1*

Common Risk and Protective Factors for Behavior Problems and School Failure

Environmental Context	Risk Factors	Protective Factors
Community	Poverty-stricken neighborhood	Adequate social norms
	Ineffective school policies	Effective school policies
School	Poor quality schools	Quality schools
Peers	Negative peer influence or role models	Positive peer influence or role models
Family	Low SES	Positive parent-child relationship
	History of parent psychopathology	
	Marital conflict	
	Harsh or punitive rearing	
Individual	Early onset of problem	Good social skills
	Additional problems	Self-efficacy
Other	Direct or indirect stressful conditions (any or all levels)	Direct or indirect social support (any or all levels)

Note: Data are from Durlak's (1998) meta-analysis of 1,200 prevention outcome studies.

cal health problems (sexuality, teen pregnancy, etc.). One major contribution of Durlak's review is the presentation of findings sorted by level of influence: individual, family, peer, school, community, and other. This analysis is particularly well suited to the models of environmental influence discussed in Chapter 1. Durlak's meta-analysis reveals 10 common risk factors and eight shared protective factors that influence behavior problems and school failure. A very brief summary of these findings is presented in Rapid Reference 2.1.

The following discussion provides a description of how risk and protective factors can impact on the trajectory of development at different levels of influence.

Inner Circle

The inner circle represents the child's individual makeup and includes the biological beginnings, including the DNA code that makes the individual unique. Newborns present with varying levels of activity and wariness, and some researchers believe that these are genetically determined and enduring traits. Newborns also present with varying levels of curiosity and attentiveness, which have also been attributed to varying degrees of later intellectual development. Other risk factors at this level can include male gender, difficult temperament, low birth weight and/or birth trauma, intellectual level, and genetic links to psychopathology. Protective influences have been associated with normal ability and good health.

Immediate Environment (Microsystem)

The family system becomes the child's world and can either buffer the child from harm or be unable to provide the protection and support the child needs. Violence in the home or inconsistent parenting can lead to poorly developed mechanisms of self-control, impulsive responding, and tendencies to act aggressively, which will also impact on social contacts. Children who are aggressive are often rejected by peers. As the child develops, the influences of the school (teachers and peers) and community (extracurricular contacts) begin to assert greater influence on development. Research has demonstrated that peer relationship problems are predictive of long-term outcomes of maladjustment in areas of school dropout, criminal behaviors, and delinquency (Blum et al., 2000; Parker & Asher, 1987).

Risk factors at this level might include maternal depression, insecure attachment, poor parenting style, domestic violence, poor peer relations, and academic lags. Protective factors might include successful peer relations, involvement in extracurricular activities, and having a supportive parent.

Social and Financial Context (Exosystem)

Families feeling the strain of financial or emotional hardship, or teenage mothers faced with their own personal distress, may be unable to provide solace or comfort to a distressed and challenging child. Living in poverty or unsafe neighborhoods can add to an already stressful environment. In addition, disadvantaged children often lack opportunities or experience barriers to participation in organized recreation (Jones & Offord, 1989) and may experience limited access to nutrition and health care (H. R. Rogers, 1986). Low parent education can also be associated with greater risk for reduced academic expectations in children (Stevenson, Chen, & Uttal, 1990).

Cultural Context (Macrosystem)

Since low income is often associated with single-parent families and ethnic minorities, many studies have confounded the influence of these factors. However, when children are both impoverished and members of an ethnic minority, the long-term implications of living in poverty increase dramatically (Wilson & Aponte, 1985). Culturally, there may be a need to integrate potentially conflicting

CAUTION

Ethnicity can influence a number of mental health issues for children and adolescents: parental beliefs about what constitutes mental illness, how symptoms are likely to be expressed or repressed (internalizing, somatization, externalizing), and whether seeking assistance for mental health issues outside of the family is an acceptable alternative (Gibbs & Huang, 2001).

belief systems involving family, school, and peer norms or expectations. Children may be stressed by environmental pressures and forced to develop conflicting sets of behaviors in an attempt to accommodate diverse systems, behaving in different ways with family members, teachers, and peers.

Some risk factors related to cultural context include high risk for suicide in native populations and dropout rates for ethnic minorities.

A review of research concerning risk factors across the areas of influence reveals that additional risks can have a multiplier effect, such as the combined effect of poor school performance and social maladjustment on later maladjustment (Sameroff, 1993). Knowledge of potential protective factors can also guide our observation and understanding to assist in enhancing positive mental health and in the design of preventative interventions.

🖋 TEST YOURSELF 🖋

1. **Which of the following is *not* one of the five general principles of the American Psychological Association code of ethics?**

    (a) Beneficence and maleficence

    (b) Fidelity and responsibility

    (c) Justice

    (d) Integrity

2. **Which of the following is *not* true regarding informed consent in working with minors?**

    (a) Due to cognitive limitations, informed consent is required from parents of children who are minors.

    (b) A child's assent or willingness to participate should also be obtained.

    (c) In situations of divorce with two custodial parents, obtaining permission from one parent is adequate.

    (d) The clinician should encourage parents of adolescents in a therapeutic relationship to waive their access to privacy information in the initial stages of rapport building.

3. **In a correlational study of eating habits and obesity, a researcher concludes that eating bananas causes obesity in males. This statement is faulty because**

(a) bananas are a low-calorie food.

(b) the researcher did not include information about the age of the subjects.

(c) the researcher's finding are limited only to males.

(d) correlation does not imply causation.

4. **Which of the following is true regarding experimental studies?**

(a) Studies have good ecological validity.

(b) Studies have strong internal validity.

(c) Studies have strong external validity.

(d) All of the above.

5. **The term *incident rates* refers to**

(a) the number of new cases in a lifetime.

(b) the number of existing cases in a decade.

(c) the most recent number of cases cited.

(d) the number of new cases within a given time period.

6. **Which of the following family characteristics was *not* considered a risk factor for behavior problems in Durlak's (1998) meta-analysis?**

(a) Low SES

(b) History of parent psychopathology

(c) Number of siblings

(d) Harsh parenting practices

Answers: 1. a; 2. c; 3. d; 4. b; 5. d; 6. c

Three

ISSUES IN CLINICAL DECISION MAKING: DIAGNOSIS, ASSESSMENT, AND TREATMENT OF CHILDHOOD DISORDERS

The assessment process involves several key steps, including determining individual differences and diagnosing signs and symptom presentations that are suggestive of specific mental disorders (U.S. Department of Health and Human Services [USDHHS], 1999). The purpose of diagnosis is to classify the problem within the context of other known behavioral clusters or disorders for the purposes of being able to draw on clinical knowledge regarding potential etiology, course, and treatment alternatives. The primary purpose of an assessment is to diagnose the nature of the problem in order that the most appropriate treatment can be selected.

> ## DON'T FORGET
>
> Assessment, diagnosis, and treatment are the fundamental steps in treatment planning. Monitoring and evaluation are often keys to how successful a treatment will be.

GOALS OF ASSESSMENT AND DIAGNOSIS

Assessment is a process. The initial stages of the process focus on clinical decision making regarding differential diagnosis (determine the specific nature of the disorder while ruling out the possibility that symptoms are not better explained by another disorder). The following sections will summarize current issues and trends in areas of assessment (what should be assessed and how assessment should be conducted), diagnosis (how to categorize or classify childhood disorders), and treatment (clinical interventions).

Kronenberger and Meyer (2001) present a framework for diagnosis, assessment, and treatment that evolves around three pivotal questions that must be answered by the child clinician, regardless of the presenting problem.

1. What are the characteristics of the child's problem?
2. How should the clinician conduct an in-depth evaluation of the problem?
3. What are the appropriate intervention strategies?

THE NATURE OF THE CHILD'S PROBLEM: ISSUES IN DIAGNOSIS

Kronenberger and Meyer (2001) suggest that each of the questions addresses a specific issue or aspect of child psychopathology. Clinicians respond to the first question when they choose to characterize a child's problem through the use of a diagnostic category or provide a provisional diagnosis or case formulation based

> **DON'T FORGET**
>
> **Three Questions that Guide Assessment:**
>
> - What is the nature of the child's problem?
> - How should I evaluate the problem?
> - How should I intervene to correct the problem?

> **CAUTION**
>
> Contrary to our concept of the clinician as expert, research has demonstrated that clinicians' judgments can actually reflect underlying personal biases toward such areas as gender, SES, race, and age (Rosenthal & Berven, 1999).

upon presenting information of symptoms and features. As will become increasingly apparent, the diagnostic method used can predict what types of measures might be selected.

Furthermore, clinicians can and do disagree regarding a patient's diagnosis. Because psychology is not an exact science and is subject to personal opinion and interpretation, there have been concerns about the negative impact that certain labels might have. In addition, fears that labels can become a self-fulfilling prophecy have been supported by research. The classic study by Rosenthal and Jacobson (1968) is a case in point (see Putting It into Practice).

Diagnosis as Classification: The Nature of Defining Outcomes

Although most clinicians would agree that a major goal of child assessment is to determine where the child's presenting behavior fits within the realm of adaptive or maladaptive behaviors, how the behavior is classified may vary depending on the classification system used.

There are two main systems currently used for classifying child and adolescent disorders or problem behaviors: the categorical classification system and the em-

Putting It Into Practice

In order to demonstrate the impact of teacher expectations on student achievement, Rosenthal and Jacobson (1968) administered IQ tests to students at the beginning and end of the school year. The researchers then labeled 20% of the students as having exceptional potential for intellectual growth in the upcoming school year. In fact, selection of these students was on a random basis and was not related to IQ scores. However, at the end of the school year, students identified as intelligent actually demonstrated significantly greater gains in IQ on retest than the students who were not so identified. The researchers reasoned that inflated teacher expectations had become responsible for this "Pygmalion effect" in the classroom, so called after the teacher in George Bernard Shaw's play *Pygmalion*.

pirical or dimensional classification system. The main comparative features of each of these classification systems are presented in Rapid Reference 3.1.

Categorical Classification: The DSM

Historical Background and Theoretical Orientation

While the most widely used classification system in the United States is the American Psychiatric Association's *Diagnostic and Statistical Manual of Mental Disorders* (*DSM*), in Europe the *International Classification of Diseases* (*ICD-10*), published by the World Health Organization, is the most commonly used system. Both systems rely on a categorical approach to defining disorders based on a medical model that views a disorders as present or absent (discrete categories with mutually exclusive boundaries). The *DSM* was originally published in 1952. The most recent revision, the *DSM-IV-TR* (2000) was undertaken to update information from empirical investigations and bridge the span between the *DSM-IV* (1994) and the future *DSM-V.* Clinicians use the *DSM* to evaluate whether symptoms meet established criteria for specific diagnoses.

Historically, the original version of the *DSM* (*DSM-I*) contained only two childhood disorders: Adjustment Reaction and Childhood Schizophrenia (APA, 1952). The *DSM-IV-TR* contains over 20 disorders that may *first* appear in childhood (Disorders Usually First Diagnosed in Infancy, Childhood, or Adolescence).

DON'T FORGET

The approach to classification adopted by the *DSM* is a clinical or categorical approach that determines whether an individual meets the criteria for a specific disorder. The disorder is present or absent based on whether a specified number of symptoms match the defining criteria.

Rapid Reference 3.1

Systems of Classification

System	Bases of Classification	Conceptualization of Disorders	Strengths and Weaknesses
Categorical Classification (DSM)	• Observation • Matching symptom criteria • Medical model: diagnostic categories • Structured and semistructured interviews (NIMH DISC-IV, K-SADS, CSI-4)	• Present or absent (all or nothing) • Qualitative and distinct entities of homogeneous features • Mutually exclusive: distinct boundaries	Strengths • Widespread usage among professionals in clinical practice (often an insurance requirement) and clinical trials (research) • Multiaxial presentation • Comprehensive documentation of disorder features Weaknesses • Subjectivity • Dichotomous (yes/no) • Mutually exclusive and comorbid disorders • Reliability and validity issues
Dimensional Classification (ASEBA, BASC, Conners)	• Multirater scales • Research-based statistical model (factor analysis) • Dimensions: levels or degree • Multirater rating scales (e.g., ASEBA, CRS, BASC)	• Continuum or degree of disorder • Adaptive to maladaptive range • Uses empirically based normative benchmarks (age, gender) • Multirater format • Focus on syndromes of co-occurring problems • Quantitative and continuous • Two broad-band behavioral dimensions • Externalizing and internalizing	Strengths • Can compare present status to normative peers (whether deviation is clinically significant) • Can compare degree of change pre- and posttreatment (whether change is statistically significant) • Use of multiple raters • Quantitative rating system Weaknesses • Not as well accepted by some clinical entities (e.g., insurance companies) • Problems integrating reports from multiple raters • Reliability and validity issues

DON'T FORGET

Many other disorders throughout the *DSM* can also have early onset (e.g., Mood Disorders, Anxiety Disorders, Panic Disorder, Posttraumatic Stress Disorder, Eating Disorders, Sleep Disorders, etc.). In these cases, when applicable, the manual outlines symptom presentations that may vary due to age or gender effects in sections devoted to specific culture, age, and gender features.

Application of the DSM Categorical Classification System for Child and Adolescent Disorders

Structured and semistructured interviews have been developed to assist child clinicians in identifying *DSM* criteria in children and adolescents. Some of the instruments that have been developed to assist with *DSM* classification are outlined in Rapid Reference 3.2 and include the following:

- Anxiety Disorders Interview Schedule for *DSM-IV:* Child and Parent Versions (ADIS for *DSM-IV;* Silverman & Albano, 1996). Semistructured interview: 7–17.
- Schedule for Affective Disorders and Schizophrenia for School Age Children (K-SADS; Ambrosini, 2000). Semistructured interview: 6–18.
- National Institute of Mental Health (NIMH) Diagnostic Interview

≡Rapid Reference 3.2

Common Structured and Semistructured Interviews

Interview	Ages	Child Version	Adult Version
Anxiety Disorders Interview Schedule for *DSM-IV* (ADIS for DSM-IV: C/P; Silverman & Albano, 1996; Silverman et al., 2001)	7–16 years	Yes	Yes
NIMH Diagnostic Interview Schedule for Children Version IV (NIMH DISC-IV; Shafter et al., 2000)	9–17 years	Yes	Yes
Schedule for Affective Disorders and Schizophrenia for School-Age Children (K-SADS; Ambrosini, 2000)	6–18 years	Yes	Yes

Note: References for all instruments can be found in Appendix B.

Schedule for Children (DISC), Version IV (NIMH DISC-IV; Shaffer et al., 2000). Structured interview: 6–17.

Strengths of the DSM Classification System

Benefits of using the *DSM* system include widespread usage, multiaxial presentation, and comprehensive documentation of the disorder, including diagnostic features; specific culture, age, and gender features; prevalence; course; familial patterns; and aids to differential diagnosis. Increased emphasis on empirically based treatments has increased the need for a common classification system across studies (Holmbeck, Greenley & Franks, 2004; Ollendick & King, 2004). Furthermore, *DSM* diagnostic categories are most often mandated by third-party payers in clinical practice.

Limitations of the DSM for Child Populations

The *DSM-IV-TR* cites several self-limiting features of the categorical approach. Although the categorical system works well for medical diagnosis (discrete and mutually exclusive), this is rarely the case with mental disorders. Conceptually, the system is especially problematic when considering high levels of comorbidity of disorders in child and adolescent populations. Limitations in applying the categorical system to child and adolescent disorders were summarized Rapid Reference 3.1.

Developmentally, the *DSM* approach has several shortcomings, including the fact that defining features do not take into account symptom presentations that change with age (Wenar & Kerig, 2000). The *DSM-PC Child and Adolescent Version* (American Academy of Pediatrics, 1996) improves upon existing *DSM* criteria by

CAUTION

More recent revisions of the *DSM* have recognized the need to incorporate *heterogeneity* or individual differences in symptom presentation by including several symptoms for each disorder, from which only a subset of items is required for the diagnosis. However, many clinicians find that the system continues to be flawed due to its all-or-nothing approach to diagnosis and its disregard for the degree to which a child matches the criteria.

Putting It Into Practice

Are parents or youth more reliable informants in predicting DSM disorders?

Bird, Gould, and Staghezza (1992) compared parent and child responses to the DISC and found that, while parents are better predictors than youth of externalizing behaviors (attention deficit disorder, oppositional disorder), parents and youth were equally effective informants of internalizing disorders (separation anxiety, overanxious disorder, dysthymia).

adding possible symptom presentations at various developmental stages and levels of severity.

Dimensional (Empirical) Classification

Historical Background and Theoretical Orientation

An alternative method of classification and diagnosis looks at behavior in terms of a continuum rather than in discrete all-or-nothing categories. Proponents of the dimensional approach conceptualize maladaptive behaviors as symptom clusters, patterns, or syndromes. Statistically, when two populations are compared (normative and referred children), behaviors that go together and are pronounced in the referred population become identified as clinical patterns or clusters of symptoms. While the *DSM* categorical system relies upon structured and semistructured interview schedules to obtain information regarding potential diagnoses, the dimensional system assesses behaviors through the use of behavior rating scales or problem checklists. Three widely used behavioral ratings scales that use the dimensional approach are the Achenbach System of Empirically Based Assessment (ASEBA; Achenbach & Rescorla, 2001), the Behavior Assessment System for Children (BASC; Reynolds & Kamphaus, 1992), and the Conners' Rating Scales—Revised (CRS-R; Conners, 1997). These multi-informant rating scales produce several sets of subscales, which were derived through empirical methods (factor analysis).

DON'T FORGET

Two broadband dimensions of behavior which have been revealed from factor and cluster analysis are the dimensions of internalizing behaviors and externalizing behaviors. Internalizing behaviors, which have also been referred to as overcontrolled behaviors, include such behaviors as anxiety, depression, social withdrawal, somatization, and shyness. Externalizing behaviors, also referred to as undercontrolled behaviors refer acting-out behaviors, such as aggression, rule breaking, and delinquency.

The Achenbach System of Empirically Based Assessment (ASEBA)

The ASEBA is one of the most popular rating scales used clinically and in research to identify problem behaviors in children and youth. The system includes a series of parallel rating scales for parents (Child Behavior Checklist [CBCL/6–18]), teachers (Teacher Rating Form [TRF]) and youth between 11 and 18 years of age (Youth Self Report [YSR]). The CBCL 2001 is a revision of an earlier version (Achenbach,

1991). The behavioral categories, clinical cutoff scores, and T scores were derived from two samples of children: normative children (children across 40 U.S. states, the District of Columbia, one Australian state, and England who participated in the 1999 national survey and who had not been referred for behavioral or emotional help in the past 12 months) and children receiving mental health services from 20 outpatient and inpatient facilities. Almost 5,000 children contributed to the norms

> **DON'T FORGET**
> ....
> T scores have a mean of 50 and a standard deviation of 10. Children who score above a T score of 70 on the ASEBA syndrome scales are said to be within the *clinical range* (2 standard deviations above the mean and at the 98th percentile) relative to peers of similar ages and gender. A score between 65 and 69 (1.5 standard deviations beyond the mean, or the 93rd to 97th percentiles) is considered to be in the borderline clinical range.

for this scale. The syndrome scales, as well as the Internalizing, Externalizing, Total Problem, and *DSM*-oriented scales, were obtained from normative (nonreferred) data available from the national survey sample. Children whose T scores are within a range of 40 to 60 are considered to score within normal limits.

In addition to the narrow band scales or syndromes, the ASEBA also includes three broadband scales, and composite scores can be obtained for Internalizing Problems, Externalizing Problems, and Total Problems. Two additional scales, Adaptive Functioning and Social Competence, can provide information concerning a child's overall success academically and in the social arena.

Empirical Support for the Dimensional Classification System

Multivariate studies of child and adolescent behavioral and emotional problems provide support for the identification of two broad groupings of problems: externalizing behaviors (disruptive behaviors such as aggression, delinquent or rule-breaking behaviors, and hyperactivity) and internalizing behaviors (anxiety, depression, somatic complaints, and withdrawal).

Children with externalizing problems are referred more often than children with internalizing problems and have been found to score significantly lower than internalizers on measures of intelligence, academics, and social acceptance.

Although the behaviors listed can be grouped into two different types of problems, recent research has also noted that children can and do demonstrate co-occurring externalizing and internalizing behaviors (Angold, Costello, & Erkanli, 1999; McConaughy & Skiba, 1993; Wilmshurst, 2002).

Putting It Into Practice

In her evaluation of 86 Canadian youth with severe emotional disabilities (SED) referred for treatment at a mental health facility in Ontario, Wilmshurst (2001) found that 90% of the population showed clinical elevations for externalizing disorders (T score 70+) with 74% having co-occurring internalizing disorders. Almost half the population (47%) had a cluster of four co-occurring disorders, with the most commonly occurring cluster involving Oppositional Defiant Disorder (ODD), ADHD, Conduct Disorder (CD), and, not surprisingly, depression. In this study, those children with elevated levels for the Anxiety Disorders actually got worse when assigned to the residential rather than the home-based treatment alternative.

Application of the CBCL Dimensional/Empirical Classification System for Child and Adolescent Disorders: A Cautionary Note on the Use of Rating Scales
Several concerns arise regarding the use of rating scales in general. The first concern is that the reliability of the behavioral observation is dependent upon the rater's perception, which in turn can be influenced by numerous extraneous variables (e.g., mood, recent history, stress). In their review of over 119 studies using the CBCL, Achenbach, McConaughy, and Howell (1987) found that agreement among informants from similar settings (interparent agreement) were much higher (.66) than correlations of observations (.28) collected from informants in different settings (parent and teacher). These results suggest the importance of collecting information across contexts in order to enhance understanding of how environmental contexts might influence the behavior in various settings (Frick & Kamphaus, 2001).

In addition, ratings have also been noted to vary across age levels, gender, and type of problem rated. Research has also noted that parents are more likely to identify more troublesome or external behaviors than less observable internalizing disorders, and that parent and child agreements are better for observable behaviors and for older (rather than younger) children (Offord, Boyle, & Racine, 1989).

CAUTION

Gender Effects and Rating Scales

Parents and teachers tend to report more problem behaviors in males compared to females at all age levels, although adolescent girls tend to self-report more problems than adolescent males (Stanger & Lewis, 1993). Within deviant populations, research has consistently shown that emotionally disturbed adolescents (typically male) tend to rate themselves as socially adequate (Matson & Ollendick, 1988; Versi, 1995).

Recent Trends in Combining Information from Categorical and Dimensional Systems

While proponents of the dimensional system have gained increased appreciation of this system's usefulness in classifying childhood disorders, increased pressure has been placed on the rigorous use of *DSM* categories to establish empirically based treatments (Ollendick & King, 2004). Within the wake of these movements, the debate regarding which system best serves the needs of children and adolescents has given way to more recent concerns regarding how to combine the merits of both systems. Rubio-Stipec, Walker, and Murphy (2002) investigated the probability of being classified with a psychiatric disorder (dichotomous classification) using empirically derived (dimensional) symptom scales. The authors ultimately suggest that a full description of a child's mental health status should contain not only the dichotomous measure of whether or not a child meets the diagnostic criteria (nosology) but also valuable information regarding dimensional status, such as the probability of meeting the diagnostic criteria.

The current revision of the ASEBA, like the more recent revision of the Conner's Scales (1997), has included information concerning both syndrome scales as well as *DSM* categories. A comparison of syndrome and *DSM* categories can be found in Rapid Reference 3.3.

ISSUES IN ASSESSMENT: HOW THE CLINICIAN SHOULD EVALUATE THE PROBLEM

Assessment is the process of conducting an in-depth evaluation to determine the nature of the child's problem. Assessment requires knowledge of appropriate interview and observational techniques, as well as general assessment instruments (e.g., measures of cognitive, behavioral, and emotional functioning) and specific assessment inventories (e.g., measures of anxiety, depression, etc.). Information obtained using these assessment techniques will assist the clinician in confirming certain hypotheses while providing sufficient evidence to rule out other potential diagnoses (differential diagnosis).

Individual Clinical Assessment

While the underlying theoretical assumptions discussed in Chapter 2 provide a framework for understanding child psychopathology at a general or nomothetic level, clinicians must apply this understanding in their assessment of the unique aspects of psychopathology evident in the individual child (the ideographic level).

Rapid Reference 3.3

A Comparison of Dimensional Syndromes and *DSM*-Oriented Scales of the CBCL/6–18 with Actual *DSM-IV* Diagnostic Categories

Syndrome Scales	DSM-IV–Oriented Scales	DSM-IV Disorders
Internalizing		
Anxious/depressed	Affective problems	Generalized Anxiety Disorder
Withdrawn/ depressed	Anxiety problems	Mood Disorders (Major Depressive Disorder, Dysthymic Disorder, Bipolar Disorder)
Somatic complaints	Somatic problems	Somatization Disorder
Externalizing		
Rule-breaking behavior	Oppositional defiant problems	ODD
Aggressive behavior	Conduct problems	CD
Other		
Social problems	N.A.	N.A.
Thought problems		Obsessive-Compulsive Disorder; Asperger's Disorder or Autistic Disorder Schizophrenia
Attention problems	Attention-deficit/hyper-activity problem	ADHD

Note: N.A. = not applicable.

DON'T FORGET

A primary goal of the assessment process in child psychopathology is to develop a *case formulation,* or hypothesis, concerning the underlying influences that cause and maintain the maladaptive behavior, including the impact of environmental influences such as family, school, and community.

For the child clinician, this investigation requires not only assessing the individual child but also obtaining information regarding important environmental influences, such as the child's family, peers, and school community. In addition, the clinician must also weigh the role of developmental considerations, such as the impact of the child's age level and gender, in evaluating the relative normalcy of the child's behaviors, thoughts, and feelings.

> **DON'T FORGET**
> ....
> Assessment is a multimodal or multimethod process of obtaining information from a variety of informants (parents or caregivers, teachers, child, peers) using a multitude of procedures (interviews, questionnaires, rating scales, standardized tests, self-report inventories) across a variety of settings (e.g., home and school).

Methods of Clinical Assessment

The process of clinical assessment can be conducted in several ways, and various clinicians will favor different approaches and instruments based on the nature of the problem and their own theoretical bias and training.

Why Use a Multimodal Assessment Model?

There are several reasons for using a multimethod assessment model, especially in the assessment of child and adolescent problems, including the nature of the problem (observable versus more covert), developmental limitations (parent report versus child self-report), and the need to verify the impact of situational influence. The multimodal assessment model provides a checks-and-balances approach to determining the nature of the problem. Multiple informants provide different perspectives on how the problem may appear or not appear in different settings. Ultimately, the clinician faces the ultimate challenge of defining the nature of the problem by integrating information from a variety of sources, settings, and instruments.

The Clinical Interview

The clinical interview is a goal-directed interaction between the clinician and the client (or the client's parent or teacher) and provides the opportunity of obtaining information that will assist in the clinical decision-making process. Interviews can vary considerably regarding the degree of structure: They can be unstruc-

DON'T FORGET

The *mental status evaluation* uses a series of questions as probes to determine a child's general orientation (name, place, date, and time), long- and short-term memory (general information and personal history), insight (abstract reasoning), and concentration or attention. This type of interview is often used to determine the potential of brain injury or thought disorders.

DON'T FORGET

While the structured interview attempts to increase reliability and validity through the use of formatted questions, most of the structured interviews (such as the DICA-IV) are modeled on the categorical classification system (*DSM*). Since this system considers disorders as discrete units that are either present or absent, information concerning the degree of symptom presentation along an adaptive to maladaptive continuum may be lost.

tured, semistructured, or structured (Edelbrock & Costello, 1988). Clinical interviews can be very helpful in obtaining background information and in providing contextual information to assist in evaluating the severity (duration and intensity) and pervasiveness (existence across situations) of the child's problems.

Advantages and Disadvantages

While the interview can be a rich source of information, there are several concerns regarding the reliability and validity of this technique, especially in the unstructured format. The interviewer's theoretical background may bias the direction of the questions or interpretation of the responses. Informants may also misinterpret questions or provide faulty information based on poor recall.

Behavioral Observation

Once the goals of the assessment are established, the clinician may have a number of potential hypotheses to consider regarding the nature and severity of the child's problem. One method of obtaining an overall impression of the child's behavioral responses is to conduct a behavioral observation. Although the first step in observation might be to perform a general observation of overall behavior (e.g., classroom behaviors), inevitably systematic observation will require selecting specific behaviors (target behaviors) for later in-depth observation and specifying the type of observational technique used (e.g., time sampling, event recording, etc.). For example, Sattler (2002) presents several coding systems that have been developed for observing children's behavior ranging from a two-category system (e.g., on-task versus off-task behavior) to a comprehensive 10-category list of inappropriate classroom behaviors (see Sattler for a complete review).

The Use of Clinical Tests: A Retrospective View

The tendency to equate assessment with testing produced a ripple effect—an equally strong tendency to equate testing with aptitude or achievement testing. Beginning with Goddard's translation of the Binet Simon Intelligence Test in 1910 for use with "feeble-minded children" and culminating in the famous *Larry P. versus Riles* case, issues in child assessment have resulted in strong opposition toward psychometric tests at many levels.

Professionally, dissatisfaction with testing was based on the disproportionate amount of time school psychologists were spending in conducting aptitude or achievement tests or in conducting *administrative assessments* (assessments designed to determine eligibility, placement, and diagnosis) instead of *functional assessments* (assessments designed to develop and evaluate interventions; Batsche & Knoff, 1995).

Issues Regarding What Should Be Assessed and How Assessments Should Be Conducted

The questions of what should be assessed and how the assessment should be conducted are inextricably tied together. Similar to the way research questions often determine the research design, different procedures will be required to obtain different types of information. Similarly, the way in which we conduct our assessment will be instrumental in determining the types of information we obtain.

DON'T FORGET

The *Larry P. versus Riles* case (1972) in California found the use of standardized IQ tests on Black children unconstitutional for the purposes of placement in programs for the educable mentally retarded (EMR), unless the court provided approval prior to testing.

DON'T FORGET

Other issues contributing to the negativism surrounding psychometric assessment concerned potential stigmatization of labeling, categorizing, and placing of children in diagnostic categories.

CAUTION

It is important to note that the goals in conducting a functional assessment will be different from those of a norm-based assessment. While a clinician conducting norm-based assessments will be concerned with the degree to which a behavior is deviant relative to the norm (nomothetic formulation), the clinician who conducts a functional assessment will be more concerned with the reason the specific behavior is occurring and the situational determinants of the behavior (ideographic or case formulation).

DON'T FORGET

Contemporary efforts toward the most recent (2004) reauthorization of the IDEA have continued to lobby for increased reliance upon applied behavioral analysis and the replacement of standardized assessments with curriculum-based measures (CBM). This trend continues earlier efforts to shift the emphasis from assessment (testing) to consultation (problem solving) and from standardized tests to the use of data from CBM to measure intervention efforts and treatment effects (Rechsley, 2003).

Functional versus Norm-Based Assessment

With the 1999 reauthorization of the Individuals with Disabilities Education Act (IDEA) Amendments of 1997, functional behavioral assessment (FBA) and behavioral intervention plans (BIP) became mandatory for students with emotional difficulties. Although aptitude or achievement tests are still required to determine eligibility for special education services, the inclusion of a functional analysis of a child's problems within the context in which they were occurring was seen as a major victory for many child advocates.

Proponents of functional assessments stress the need to develop intervention plans that have ecological validity relative to what is causing and sustaining the problem behavior. The referral question, they say, should firmly address why behaviors were occurring. Within this paradigm, the need for normative testing or linking behaviors to systems of classification or diagnostic categories has little merit or value.

Question of How Much or Degree

Norm-referenced assessment measures (psychometric tests) intend to answer questions relative to How much, or the degree to which a given behavior deviates from the norm. The focus is on determining the severity of the problem. Psychometric instruments are available to evaluate a given child's functioning, relative to peers of similar age, in several areas: intellectual functioning, neurological functioning, behavior, emotional status (anxiety, depression, etc.), personality, and social functioning. Psychometric tests may be administered in the form of rating scales or paper-and-pencil tests, and they may be administered to a group or as an individual test battery.

Proponents of psychometric assessment value the availability of measures that can provide a reliable and valid index of the severity of the child's problem relative to similar-aged peers. The wide range of available instruments enhances a multimodal approach. In addition, parallel forms of rating scales exist for many instruments that allow for a comparison of evaluations across a number of different informants (parents, teachers, child self-report).

Critics of psychometric assessment have been most vocal regarding the overemphasis on aptitude or achievement testing in the schools. There are also many criticisms levied at inherent weaknesses in psychometric measures, such as cultural bias and the role of environmental stimulation on performance outcomes. Concerns might address the snapshot quality of a test result that portrays merely a point in time or, at best, a point within a definable range, rather than a dynamic ongoing process. At a conceptual level, critics may suggest that knowledge of the severity of a problem does not address issues as to why a problem is occurring or how to intervene.

Why Assess Intelligence?

Historically, intelligence scales have been used as well-standardized, valid, and reliable predictors of academic achievement. The two most popular intelligence scales, the Wechsler Scales and the Stanford-Binet, have both seen recent major revisions. The Wechsler Intelligence Scale for Children—Fourth Edition (WISC-IV), provides a measure of overall intellectual functioning, based on scores obtained for four general indices: Verbal Comprehension, Perceptual Reasoning, Processing Speed, and Working Memory. The Stanford-Binet, now in its fifth revision, provides an index of overall intellectual functioning as well as separate indices of functioning in the visual and verbal areas. Results of an intellectual assessment can also provide information regarding strengths and weaknesses in information processing as well as providing information concerning brain dysfunction or thought disorders.

A Question of Why

Functional behavioral assessments (FBAs) purport to answer questions relative to why a given behavior exists.

Proponents of FBA emphasize the ecological validity of an assessment approach that is linked to the situational determinants of behavior. Framed within a problem-solving approach, there are several steps that might be involved in conducting FBAs, including gathering information from multiple sources regarding problem behaviors, determining probable functions, formulating hypotheses

> **DON'T FORGET**
> ....
> An FBA can be defined as the identification of important, controllable, causal functional relationships applicable to a specific set of target behaviors or an individual client (Haynes & O'Brien, 1990, p. 654).

regarding causes, and ultimately generating and monitoring interventions. An example of an FBA is presented in Rapid Reference 3.4.

Once the FBA information is completed, the BIP is developed, which outlines specific goals and proposed interventions and designates the persons responsible for implementing the plan. An example of a BIP is also available in Rapid Reference 3.4.

≡Rapid Reference 3.4

Functional Behavioral Assessment (FBA) and Behavior Intervention Plan (BIP)

Josh is referred to the psychologist because he is aggressive toward peers. After observing Josh and interviewing the teachers, the psychologist assists in the completion of the FBA work sheet, adding the following information:

Specific problem behaviors	• Verbal aggression: name calling • Physical aggression: pushing, shoving
Precipitation conditions	• Teacher is working with another student (independent work time) • Teacher is correcting homework (student has not done homework)
Consequences	• Teacher sends Josh to the office (removal from class)
Function of the behavior	• Removal from class (escape/avoidance) • Office is at hub of activity (attention)

Once the FBA is completed, then a BIP can be developed for Josh.

Specific goals	1. Josh will increase positive comments. 2. Josh will complete daily homework assignments with 80% accuracy. 3. Josh will complete independent seatwork with 80% accuracy.
Interventions	1. Contract for positive comments +1 bonus star. 2. Parent will sign completed homework assignments. 3. 15 minutes of independent work completed (80% accuracy) earns 3 minutes of free computer time at the end of day.
Person responsible for monitoring	Intervention #1: teacher Intervention #2: parent Intervention #3: teacher

Critics of the FBA approach emphasize the lack of norm-referenced information and subjectivity involved in this assessment procedure. Although behavior is assessed from multiple vantage points, linking behaviors to situational determinants may result in incorrect assumptions. For example, a child may be frustrated at home and act out in school or vice versa. A high level of expertise is needed to assimilate and integrate assessment information from multidisciplinary sources and to select appropriate intervention strategies that are developmentally appropriate.

It is important to note, however, that despite current emphasis on behavioral assessment in the schools, behavioral analysis is a multisituational analysis requiring the gathering of information concerning the child's behavior, cognitions, and affects as they present across various situations and as seen by various informants. Despite the undisputed importance of attention to situational variables in conducting behavioral assessments, giving situational factors their due importance has often been neglected in child assessment (Mash & Terdel, 1997).

CHILD TREATMENT INTERVENTIONS

Issues in Treatment: Intervention and Prevention

Many of the adult therapies are also available for children. The most common therapeutic techniques used for children are psychodynamic (play therapy), ego-supportive, behavioral and cognitive behavioral, interpersonal (social skills), and family systems. Over 400 different forms of psychosocial therapies currently exist (Comer, 2001). Given the complexities inherent in child treatment issues, it is not surprising to find that current trends have revealed an increased emphasis on the use of combined and multimodal treatment methods (Kazdin, 1996). The issue of treatment effectiveness can be addressed by posing questions at three levels:

1. Is therapy generally effective?
2. Are particular therapies generally effective?
3. Are particular therapies effective for particular problems? (Comer, p. 111)

Treatment Effectiveness

Are Particular Therapies Generally Effective?
Meta-analyses of treatment effectiveness have produced the following summation: Therapy effects are strongest for outcome measures that target specific

DON'T FORGET

Treatment Effectiveness and the Dodo Verdict

In *Alice's Adventures in Wonderland,* Lewis Carroll's Dodo bird announces that "everyone has won, and all must have prizes" (Carroll, 1865/1988). This phrase has become a popular summation in psychological writings, called the *Dodo verdict*. In essence, the quotation has been used often as an analogy to demonstrate the lack of research support for specificity of treatment effects. Child and adolescent outcomes studies (Weisz et al., 1995) have demonstrated that treatment is more effective than no treatment or placebos.

problems; effects for behavioral interventions are stronger than nonbehavioral approaches; and effects are strongest for adolescent girls (Weisz et al., 1995). However, since the majority of studies analyzed were laboratory-based (analogue) interventions, the authors caution that results might not reflect child and adolescent practice as it existed in clinical settings.

Are Particular Therapies Effective for Particular Problems?

Family preservation using multisystemic therapy (MST) has been demonstrated to be an effective treatment approach for substance-abusing adolescents (Henggeler, Melton, & Smith, 1992) and as an alternative to hospitalization for seriously emotionally disturbed youth (Schoenwald, Ward, Henggeler, & Rowland, 2000). Multimodal programs that combine parent education, psychosocial treatment (behavior and contingency management), and pharmacology have proven effective for children with ADHD (Barkley, 1997). Promising approaches to anxiety reduction have been demonstrated by the use of cognitive behavioral training techniques (Kendall et al., 1992), while parent training in behavioral methods has been determined as the most effective treatment method for dealing with disruptive disorders (Spaccarelli, Cotler, & Penman, 1992).

The American Psychological Association Task Force and Evidence-Based Treatments

In order to address the need for greater accountability regarding evidence-based treatment, the American Psychological Association convened two special task forces. After conducting an extensive research review, the Task Force on Psychological Intervention Guidelines (1995) developed two sets of criteria to assist in the classification of treatment programs. The first set of criteria, which is the most rigorous, classifies treatment programs that are deemed *well-established psy-*

chosocial interventions. The second set of less demanding criteria defines programs that are *probably efficacious psychosocial interventions* (Lonigan, Shannon, Saylor, Finch, & Sallee, 1998). Within these guidelines, emphasis has been placed on evaluating treatments with respect to treatment efficacy (internal validity) and treatment effectiveness or clinical utility (external validity).

> # DON'T FORGET
>
> The goal of the American Psychological Association Task Force was to focus on identifying psychosocial interventions for high-frequency problems encountered in children's mental health: depression, Anxiety Disorders, CD, ADHD, and autism.

Addressing issues of internal validity, the Task Force recommended the use of clinical trials or randomization, comparisons of alternative treatment approaches, and replication by different research teams. Clinical utility issues addressed questions about a program's feasibility, generalizability, and cost-benefit analysis. Results of the Task Force review can be found in a special issue on empirically supported psychosocial interventions for children appearing in the June 1998 *Journal of Clinical Child Psychology.*

Overall, the Task Force found more research initiatives directed toward the treatment of externalizing disorders (conduct problems, ADHD) than internalizing disorders (anxiety, depression) and significantly more studies that matched the probably efficacious treatment category than the category for well-established psychosocial treatments.

Does Specific Therapy Work for Specific Groups of Children?

According to Ollendick and King (2004), significant progress in recent years has effectively abolished the Dodo verdict and moved toward investigating "efficacy of specific treatments for children who present with specific behavioral, emotional and social problems" (p. 4). The authors go on to emphasize the need to incorporate more rigorous scientific methods, such as randomized clinical trials (RTC), in research programs designed to verify empirically supported treatments. In their review of well-established and probably efficacious psychosocial treatments for children and adolescents, Ollendick and King (2004) point out several continuing areas of concern. The authors suggest that there is a lack of identified empirical support of treatments for some of the most common disorders, such as Anxiety and Depression. In addition, verification of efficacious treatments have largely relied on cognitive behavioral or behavioral treatments, while other theoretically based treatments, such as psychodynamic or family systems, have had less opportunity for scrutiny. Ultimately, the authors summarize three areas of controversy between clinicians and researchers that have been problematic and have presented obstacles in the past:

- Some treatments are more effective than others.
- There is a need for treatment manuals to ensure treatment fidelity.
- The portability of laboratory findings to real-life clinical settings is important.

Developmental Issues in Treatment

While significant emphasis has recently been placed on the need to develop a wider body of research concerning empirically based treatments for child and adolescent concerns, Holmbeck, Greenley, and Franks (2004) suggest that it is equally important that treatment alternatives also consider methods that are sensitive to developmental issues. The authors point out several developmental trends that can influence and direct the course of therapeutic involvement.

In addition to level of cognitive appraisal, the authors also stress the need to consider the impact of the disorder in three other developmental areas:

CAUTION

Holbeck, Greenley, and Franks (2004) raise a number of red flags concerning the portability of treatment plans across developmental levels, especially cognitive behavioral programs, which emphasize higher-level thinking (such as self-reflective thinking, recursive thought and metacognition, or thinking about thinking).

- The role of the disorder in inhibiting normal development in other areas.
- The use of a developmental perspective to prioritize targets for intervention.
- Predicting the potential for children and adolescents to revisit earlier problems from a new cognitive vantage point.

🐟 TEST YOURSELF 🐟

1. **In Europe, the most common system used for diagnosis is**
   - (a) the *Diagnostic and Statistical Manual of Mental Disorders.*
   - (b) the Abridged Mental Health Index.
   - (c) the International Classification of Diseases.
   - (d) the *Mental Health Primer for International Codes.*

2. **One of the major criticisms regarding the use of the *DSM* for childhood disorders is that**
   - (a) the *DSM* considers mental disorders as present or absent.
   - (b) the *DSM* does not take different developmental presentations of disorders into consideration.
   - (c) the *DSM* was primarily designed to diagnose adult disorders.
   - (d) All of the above

3. **The Achenbach System of Empirically Based Assessment (ASEBA) provides behavioral ratings according to the**
   - (a) dimensional system.
   - (b) categorical system.
   - (c) medical model.
   - (d) dimensional and categorical systems.

4. **When a child is brought in for emergency treatment, the psychiatrist asks a series of questions as probes to determine the child's general orientation, long- and short-term memory, insight, and concentration or attention. The psychiatrist is conducting a**
   - (a) projective evaluation.
   - (b) mental status evaluation.
   - (c) functional assessment.
   - (d) behavioral plan.

5. **The outcome of the *Larry P. versus Riles* case was that**
   - (a) projective assessments were banned in California.
   - (b) clinical child interviews were deemed unconstitutional.
   - (c) special education programs were closed to minorities.
   - (d) the use of IQ tests on Black children for educational placement was deemed unconstitutional.

(continued)

6. In their study of the Pygmalion effect in the classroom, Rosenthal and Jacobson (1968) found that at the end of the school year random students identified as intelligent

(a) were given preferential treatment by teachers, resulting in increased IQ scores.

(b) were ignored by teachers, who then concentrated on less advantaged students.

(c) actually lowered their IQ scores due to lack of teacher input during the year.

(d) were less popular with peers than students not so identified.

7. Which of the following is a criticism of the Functional Behavior Assessment (FBA) approach?

(a) Lack of norm-referenced information

(b) Lack of multiple vantage points

(c) Linking behaviors to situational determinants

(d) Lack of research support

8. The Dodo verdict refers to

(a) inadequate research to support treatment effects.

(b) lack of specificity of treatment effects.

(c) improper use of multimethod effects.

(d) inadequate assessment techniques.

Answers: 1. c; 2. d; 3. d; 4. b; 5. d; 6. a; 7. a; 8. b

Four

ATTENTION-DEFICIT/HYPERACTIVITY DISORDER (ADHD)

H istorically, in the 1930s and 1940s, "restless and inattentive" behaviors currently associated with ADHD were attributed to minimal brain dysfunction (MBD) resulting from brain trauma to the frontal lobe. However, the MBD theory lost momentum when research evidence failed to support the claims. Several years later, the *DSM-II* (APA, 1968) categorized the symptoms of "overactivity, restlessness and inattention" as the Hyperkinetic Reaction of Childhood. Controversy and debate continued about the heterogeneity of seemingly incompatible symptoms of this disorder, which affected some children with passive inattentive symptoms while unleashing hyperactive and impulsive behaviors in others.

In the third revision of the *DSM,* the *DSM-III* (APA, 1980), an attempt was made to address both versions of the disorder by replacing the unified Hyperkinetic Reaction of Childhood with a new category, called Attention-Deficit Disorder (ADD). The disorder of ADD would recognize two distinct subtypes: ADD with Hyperactivity and ADD without Hyperactivity. However, by the time the *DSM* was revised (*DSM-IIIR;* APA, 1987), the disorder was once again the topic of significant debate. Lack of research support for subtyping from *DSM* field trials reversed thinking, and once again a single categorical domain prevailed: Attention-Deficit Hyperactivity Disorder.

CLINICAL DESCRIPTION AND ASSOCIATED FEATURES

The most recent revision of the *DSM* (APA, 2000) has once again reverted to subtyping the disorder. Currently classified as Attention-Deficit/Hyperactivity Disorder, the disorder recognizes three subtypes. The subtypes are identified on the basis of the degree to which the child demonstrates three core features of the disorder: inattention, hyperactivity, and impulsivity. The three subtypes are

1. Primarily Inattentive Type
2. Primarily Hyperactive-Impulsive Type
3. Combined Type

As with many *DSM* disorders, there is an additional category, Not Otherwise Specified (NOS), for atypical cases that match most, but not all, of the symptoms. The *DSM-IV-TR* suggests that ADHD NOS be used for cases where onset is after 7 years of age or when inattentive symptoms are accompanied by *hypoactive* behavior patterns (e.g., sluggishness and daydreaming). In our case scenario in the

Putting It Into Practice

For the third time in the past 5 minutes, Jeremy's fourth-grade teacher has had to tell him to sit in his seat and keep his hands to himself. It is as if Jeremy's feet are attached to springs. He doesn't walk; he bounces. He doesn't sit; he squirms. It's not just the motor activity that sets him apart from the rest of the class: Jeremy also has a motor mouth. He talks incessantly. He can't resist sharing his ideas with the class, whether they are welcomed or not, as soon as he thinks about them, regardless of whether the time is right, Jeremy blurts out answers, disrupts the classroom, and adds considerable stress to his teacher's already stressful job.

Jeremy is almost the polar opposite of his classmate Leonard. For Leonard, Jeremy's antics just fade into the background of other classroom stuff. Unlike Jeremy, Leonard is very quiet and rarely participates in classroom discussions, unless the discussions are about something that really interests him. Leonard spends most of his time staring out the window or off into space. The word *daydreamer* seems to fit Leonard perfectly.

Leonard always seems to be at least one step behind everyone else. Leonard is rarely on task; he drifts off in the middle of assignments and often has to be reminded to return to earth. Leonard is doing poorly academically. He just doesn't seem to tune in to whatever channel the rest of the class is on. Initially, the teacher thought that Leonard was a slow learner, until the class began to discuss different computer programs. The teacher was shocked at Leonard's sophisticated knowledge base and expertise in the area. That was when his teacher began to think that there was something else getting in the way of Leonard's academic success.

In this case study, Jeremy and Leonard share more than the same classroom and same teacher. As incredible as it might seem, they both probably share variations of the same disorder: Attention-Deficit/Hyperactivity Disorder (ADHD). How can two children who seem so different fall into the same diagnostic category? This is a question that has plagued theorists for the past 100 years. Although ADHD is among one of the most prevalent disorders in childhood, it continues to challenge professionals. It has been a topic for considerable discussion and controversy, especially regarding the overprescription of stimulant medications (Diller, 1996).

Putting It into Practice box, Leonard's inattentive behaviors certainly have a quality of the "sluggishness and daydreaming" characteristics; however, he more than meets the other criteria required for the Inattentive Type of ADHD.

Inattentive Type

The *DSM-IV-TR* lists nine possible symptoms as diagnostic criteria for ADHD Inattentive Type. According to the *DSM-IV-TR* a diagnosis of ADHD Inattentive Type requires a match with six of a possible nine symptoms:

- Careless attention to details
- Problems sustaining attention over time
- Does not appear to listen
- Poor follow-through (schoolwork, homework, chores)
- Poorly organized
- Poor ability to sustain mental attention (e.g., homework, independent seatwork at school)
- Loses necessary materials (e.g., pencils, notebooks, assignment sheets, homework)
- Easily distracted
- Forgetful

In addition to having six of the nine symptoms listed here, the *DSM-IV-TR* also stipulates that the child must meet four other conditions to be diagnosed with ADHD: (a) symptoms must have persisted for at least 6 months' duration, (b) symptoms must cause significant impairment (in relationships, performance, etc.), (c) the symptoms must be pervasive across situations, and (d) symptoms must be evident prior to 7 years of age.

DON'T FORGET

The *DSM-IV-TR* requires only six of nine possible symptoms in order to allow for some latitude in symptom presentation. This is a relatively new approach of the *DSM* and evolved in response to criticisms that the *DSM* criteria were too rigid and did not allow for individual variations or heterogeneity of symptom presentation (not all ADHD children are identical).

DON'T FORGET

There are several reasons why the *DSM-IV-TR* would include additional qualifiers concerning onset, duration, and pervasive nature of symptoms. As was discussed in the introductory chapter, several disorders share the same features as ADHD. These additional criteria assist in making differential diagnoses. Symptoms occurring later in childhood (after age 7) may be indicative of an emotional response to maltreatment, an anxiety disorder, or recent changes in the family constellation. Symptoms that are evident only at school may signal a more specific learning disability.

CAUTION

Undiagnosed, the Inattentive Type of ADHD is to education what high cholesterol is to those with heart problems: It can be a silently destructive force.

Unlike their highly active and highly visible counterpart, children with the Inattentive Type of ADHD are often misunderstood and undiagnosed; they often suffer painful consequences of internalizing disorders and have academic problems (Weiss, Worling, & Wasdell, 2003).

Reviewing the symptoms associated with ADHD Inattentive Type, it is not difficult to understand why these children would encounter problems academically. One of the major developmental tasks of the school-aged child is to develop a sense of competence, mastery, and efficacy. However, children with ADHD face significant challenges in meeting increased academic and social demands.

According to Barkley (1998), the Inattentive Type of ADHD is characterized by a "sluggish" information-processing style (slow to process information) and problems with focused or selective attention. Therefore, against the backdrop of "academic noise," these children are unable to filter essential from nonessential details. Lack of attention to details often results from information overload and an inability to selectively limit the focus of attention. This processing deficit also reduces grade scores due to careless errors. Other academic concerns are evident in difficulties completing homework assignments (sustaining attention for boring tasks) and apparent lack of motivation. If homework assignments are completed, often under intense parent scrutiny, the disorganized student may forget to bring them to school or lose them somewhere in the mess of papers at the bottom of his or her backpack. Academic endeavors are a frustration for these children, their parents, and their teachers.

DON'T FORGET

The symptoms of ADHD must have persisted for at least six months, must cause significant impairment, must be in excess of developmental expectations, and must occur in more than one setting (e.g., home and school). Symptoms must be evident prior to 7 years of age.

Hyperactive-Impulsive Type

The *DSM-IV-TR* requires six of a possible nine symptoms for a diagnosis of ADHD Hyperactive-Impulsive Type. The nine symptoms include six hyperactive and three impulsive symptoms. The following are the symptoms of hyperactivity:

- Fidgety or squirmy behavior
- Problems remaining seated
- Excessive motion
- Problems engaging in quiet play
- Constantly being on the go
- Incessant talking

The following are the symptoms of impulsivity:

- Blurts out answers, comments
- Is impatient, has problems with turn taking
- Is intrusive to others

In the Putting It into Practice case study, Jeremy demonstrates many of the symptoms of ADHD Hyperactive-Impulsive Type: problems remaining seated, squirminess, always being in motion, incessant talking, blurting out answers, and problems with turn taking. If during the parent interview the clinician determines that Jeremy has always been that way, that Jeremy is the same way at home and school, and that this behavior is causing problems across situations (home, school, church), then it becomes increasingly likely that Jeremy has ADHD Hyperactive-Impulsive Type.

In addition to their social problems, children with ADHD Hyperactive-Impulsive Type also experience academic problems because of their impulsive nature. These children tend to rush through their assignments and often emphasize speed over accuracy. They often approach tasks incorrectly because they do not wait until all the directions are provided.

DEVELOPMENTAL CONSIDERATIONS AND ASSOCIATED FEATURES

For children with ADHD, the core features of overactivity, impulsivity,

DON'T FORGET

Children with Hyperactive-Impulsive Type ADHD are at risk socially. Their inability to wait their turn does not make them very popular with their peers. Socially, children with ADHD often present with poor social skills and experience difficulty making and maintaining friendships. Often these children will gravitate toward other troubled children, and they may engage in various forms of rule breaking and other behavioral problems.

DON'T FORGET

According to the current DSM-IV-TR diagnostic criteria, children who meet the criteria for both ADHD Inattentive Type and ADHD Hyperactive-Impulsive Type meet the criteria for a diagnosis of ADHD Combined Type.

and inattention will impact on learning and relationships based on the nature of developmental tasks emphasized at each stage of development.

Early Precursors to ADHD Hyperactive-Impulsive Type

Although ADHD is very difficult to diagnose prior to 3 years of age, retrospective parent interviews have identified a number of early precursors to the Hyperactive-Impulsive type of ADHD. As infants, children with difficult temperaments tend to be at greater risk for developing ADHD later on. Other early risk factors include excessive activity, poor sleep patterns, and irritability. Parents also report that these infants are more difficult to soothe when upset than their non-ADHD peers (Barkley, 1998). During the toddler period (1–2.5 years), children with ADHD demonstrate higher levels of underregulated behaviors (lack of self-control), and in the transition to preschool (3 to 6 years) lack of self-control persisted, at a time when non-ADHD peers were demonstrating increased maturity and greater self-control. During the preschool period, children with ADHD are described by parents and teachers as being more demanding, stressful, and problematic than their non-ADHD peers, especially in "free play" or unsupervised activities (Campbell, March, Pierce, Ewing, & Szumowski, 1991).

ADHD and the School-Aged Child (6 to 11 Years)

In the Putting It into Practice scenario, Leonard and Jeremy demonstrate many of the characteristic difficulties that ADHD children exhibit during the school age period. School-aged children are faced with the developmental task of increasing their sense of competence and mastery. However, children with ADHD face significant challenges in meeting increased academic and social demands. Although all children with ADHD are academically vulnerable, the nature of academic problems varies depending on how the symptoms of ADHD manifest.

School-aged children with the Hyperactive-Impulsive Type of ADHD also experience academic difficulties, but the nature of their academic problems relates more to these children's impulsivity and their inability to inhibit responses that may compete with effective learning. Learning problems are evident in tendencies to jump into tasks prior to listening to all the directions and to rush through assignments, sacrificing accuracy for speed. These children often demonstrate

CAUTION

Children with the Inattentive Type of ADHD are often misunderstood. Frequently, inattention is misinterpreted as lack of motivation. Problems sustaining their attention, poor organizational skills, and ease of distractibility contribute to poor educational outcomes. These children often seem to be one step behind and regularly drift off into daydreaming when the task is monotonous or boring. Homework and seatwork assignments are often poorly attempted and often incomplete. These children often do poorly on tests, not only because of their tendency to miss important details but also because they have a very poor concept of time and manage time poorly. Many ADHD children do not complete tests in the allotted time, and lack of organizational skills also contributes to academic difficulty.

low frustration tolerance and tend to abandon tasks that do not have an immediate solution. Their impulsive behaviors also place this group of children at greater risk for accidental injury (Barkley, 1998).

DON'T FORGET

Children with the Hyperactive-Impulsive Type of ADHD are also socially at risk. Often these children experience social problems because of their intrusive behaviors and tendencies to let their behavior escalate out of control.

ADHD and the Adolescent (12–19)

At least half of the children diagnosed with ADHD will continue to meet the criteria for the disorder throughout adolescence. Adolescents with ADHD are poorly equipped to meet the challenges of managing the curriculum in middle school and high school, with its emphasis on increased workload and independent study skills. These students find that their poor work habits, lack of organizational skills, and poor follow-through often result in significant academic difficulties during this period.

Other social and emotional con-

CAUTION

A major developmental task in adolescence is the formation of a sense of personal identity, which includes the consolidation of a self-concept built on a foundation of peer acceptance and competence. Teens who have a history of poor academic outcomes and concomitant social problems are at increased risk for development of comorbid internalizing problems, such as anxiety and depression (Biederman, Faraone, & Lapey, 1992), and externalizing problems, such as aggression, defiance, and forms of delinquent behavior (Barkley, Fischer, Edelbrock, & Smallish, 1990).

cerns prevalent at this developmental stage include increased risk for reckless driving accidents and participation in other high-risk behaviors such as substance use that are reported to be higher in ADHD populations (Barkley, 1998).

PREVALENCE AND COURSE

According to the *DSM-IV-TR,* estimates of ADHD in school-aged children range from 3% to 7% of the total population. Ninety percent of children identified with ADHD will be diagnosed with the Hyperactive-Impulsive Type. However, this figure may be somewhat misleading in terms of actual prevalence statistics, since many more children with the Inattentive Type can go undiagnosed because of the subtle nature of this subtype.

ADHD and Gender

Ratios of male to female frequency have been reported from 2:1 to 9:1. Currently, the question of whether there are gender differences in the prevalence rates for particular subtypes of ADHD symptoms continues to be an area of debate.

Course

According to Barkley (1998), the earliest age at which a diagnosis of ADHD might be possible is approximately 3 years, although symptoms of inattention are not likely to be noticed until much later. Approximately two thirds of elementary school–aged children who are diagnosed with ADHD have an additional diagnosable disorder (Cantwell, 1994). High rates of comorbidity with both internalizing and externalizing disorders make the course of this disorder particularly prone to poor outcomes. Given the comorbid nature of the disorder, the course of ADHD is best

---

DON'T FORGET

Prevalence rates may vary widely among different reports. The variation in rates can result from several factors, including: whether the samples refer to a clinical or general population; the methods used to classify the disorder; and the assessment instruments used. Unless otherwise stated, all prevalence data reported in this text will refer to data noted in the DSM (APA, 2000).

CAUTION

Although gender and disorder subtyping continues to be a controversial area of debate, a recent review of clinical data for 143 Inattentive and 133 Combined Type with ADHD revealed that children who had the Inattentive Type were more likely to be female (Weiss, Worling, & Wasdell, 2003).

understood within the context of the different developmental pathways that might result based on the comorbid features.

ADHD and Comorbidity

Academic and learning problems.   Academic problems are common in children with ADHD.

ADHD and specific learning disabilities. Prevalence rates for comorbid ADHD and specific learning disabilities (SLDs) are difficult to predict accurately, due to wide variations among published studies regarding how SLDs are defined and measured. Controversies surrounding the definitions and measurement of SLDs will be addressed at length in Chapter 12. Comorbid rates have been estimated to be between 16 and 21% for these two disorders (Frick et al., 1991).

ADHD and internalizing problems. As will be discussed at greater length in Chapter 6, symptoms of depressive disorder and Bipolar Disorder present differently in children and adults. In children, symptoms of depression and Bipolar Disorder often overlap with symptoms of ADHD, making differential diagnosis difficult. One of the major symptoms of depression in children is irritability. Irritable behaviors often manifest in restlessness, agitation, short attention span, problems concentrating, and impulsive responses, which resemble symptoms of ADHD. Unlike the lengthy highs and lows of adult bipolar disorder, children with Bipo-

> **DON'T FORGET**
>
> As many as 30% of children with ADHD will repeat a grade; as many as 40% will be placed in special education programs; and as many as 30% may never finish high school (Barkley, 1998).

> **DON'T FORGET**
>
> Some children with ADHD demonstrate more cognitive or learning problems while others demonstrate more behavioral problems. Some authors have suggested subtyping ADHD on the bases of these two problem areas. Under this system, the two subtypes would be Cognitive ADHD, for predominantly inattention and learning problems, and Behavioral ADHD, for cases where hyperactivity, impulsivity, and behavior problems dominate (August & Garfinkel, 1989; Halperin et al., 1990).

> **DON'T FORGET**
>
> Internalizing problems represent the continuum of overcontrolled responses indicating "problems within the self, such as anxiety, depression, somatic complaints without known medical basis, and social withdrawal from contacts" (Achenbach & Rescorla, 2001, p. 93).

lar Disorder often experience rapid cycles of shifting moods (elation to irritability), with brief and multiple mood swings. Bipolar symptoms of pressured speech (incessant talking), distractibility, and overactivity can be easily mistaken for symptoms of ADHD. Symptoms of anxiety (distractibility, nervous agitation, restlessness, poor concentration) are also similar to symptoms of ADHD.

In one study, Biederman and colleagues (1995) found that up to 70% of depressed children also had comorbid ADHD. In another study, approximately 90% of the younger (prepubertal) children and 30% of the adolescent population referred for Bipolar Disorder had comorbid ADHD (Geller & Luby, 1997). Other studies have found higher rates of comorbidity for overanxious disorder and somatic complaints (e.g., headaches, stomach aches) than children without ADHD. In addition, many children who have ADHD also suffer from problems falling asleep and staying asleep.

CAUTION

Differential diagnosis between ADHD and the internalizing disorders can be a complex process since the three core features of ADHD (inattention, overactivity, and impulsivity) share many of the same characteristics as symptoms of depression, Bipolar Disorder, and anxiety. In addition, there are high rates of comorbidity among these disorders.

CAUTION

One concern regarding the treatment of children with ADHD through the use of stimulant medication has been the underlying fear that this will lead to an increased rate of substance use later on. However, research does not support this concern. In fact, successful treatment of ADHD actually serves as a protective factor for later substance abuse, since adults who were not treated for ADHD are associated with much higher rates of substance abuse (Biederman et al., 1999).

ADHD and externalizing disorders. Children and adolescents with comorbid ADHD and Disruptive Behavior Disorders (ODD and CD) are more seriously maladjusted (Moffit, 1990) and have significantly worse outcomes compared to children with ADHD alone (Barkley et al., 1990). Studies show that as many as 35 to 60% of children with ADHD will also have ODD, while as many as 50% of children with ADHD will go on to develop CD (Szatmari, Boyle, & Offord, 1989).

It has been suggested that a diagnosis of ADHD in childhood can be as strong a predictor for substance use as having a family history of substance abuse. Barkley and colleagues (1990) found that hyperactive teens with ADHD were significantly more likely to use cigarettes and alcohol than their nonhyperactive peers.

ADHD and social relationship problems. At least half of children with ADHD will also have problems in their relationships with peers. There can be a significant discrepancy between social skills and cognitive ability. Using this discrepancy criterion, Greene, Biederman, Faraone, Sienna, and Garcia-Jetton (1997) labeled this subtype "socially disabled" (ADHD+SD). Compared to children who have ADHD alone, Green and colleagues found that children with ADHD+SD demonstrate higher levels of substance abuse, family problems, anxiety, mood problems, and conduct problems.

ETIOLOGY (CAUSES)

Although ADHD is one of the most prevalent childhood disorders, significant controversy remains regarding the exact cause of ADHD. It is most likely that the etiology involves a complex interaction between biological and environmental factors (Wolraich, 2000).

BIOLOGICAL AND NEUROLOGICAL FEATURES

Increased research into the potential neurobiological basis for ADHD has focused on four potential sources of information: structural regions of the brain, genetic transmission, neurotransmitter functions, and neurocognitive processing.

Brain Structures

With the advent of functional resonance imaging (FMRI) and single photon emission computed topography (SPECT), brain scans have revealed less activity in the frontal brain regions and more activity in the cingulate gyrus in children with ADHD compared to children without ADHD.

While the frontal system is responsible for executive functioning, the cingulate gyrus is involved in focusing of attention and in directing response selection.

Genetic Transmission

Approximately 50% of children with ADHD have a parent who also has the disorder (Biederman et al., 1995).

DON'T FORGET

The executive functions are responsible for initiating and maintaining problem solving behaviors that serve to manage, direct, and control the course of brain activity.

Neurotransmitters

Research has identified low levels of catecholamines (dopamine, norepinephrine, epinephrine) in children with ADHD. The catecholamines are associated with attention and motor activity. Medications prescribed for ADHD, such as Dexedrine (dextramphetamine), Ritalin (methylphenidate), and Cylert (pemoline), increase the number of catecholamines in the brain (Barkley, 1998).

Neurocognitive Processing

There has been increasing interest in examining how executive functioning and arousal levels in children with ADHD contribute to cognitive, emotional, and behavioral processing deficits. Inherent in executive functioning processes is the need to be flexible and readily shift focus between tasks when required and to adapt strategies as needed. Another important factor in problem-solving success is the ability to monitor, evaluate, and revise strategies. Ultimately, the task of being able to hold information in memory while performing these problem-solving tasks involves the use of *working memory*.

Developmentally, increased self-regulatory functions are evident as toddlers transition to the preschool stage. Increased self-control results from the child's ability to internalize good role models provided by parents and the increased utilization of inner language, which serves to guide and direct appropriate behavior and inhibit inappropriate responses.

DON'T FORGET

Executive functioning tasks include initiation or inhibition, flexibility in shifting focus, and monitoring, evaluating, and adapting strategies as needed. In addition to organizing and managing cognitive functions, executive functions are also involved in the management and control of other regulatory functions, including behavioral and emotional control.

DON'T FORGET

The central feature of this model is the concept of behavioral inhibition. Barkley conceptualizes behavioral inhibition as the ability to inhibit a response (to refrain from responding or institute a delay) or stop an active response, and to maintain the delay over time. The delay (or termination) of the response is necessary as a manner of interference control, in order that goal directed behavior can be initiated and maintained (Barkley, 1997).

Barkley's Model of ADHD

Barkley's (1997) model of ADHD focuses on understanding ADHD through the executive functions. The model is built around the concept of *behavioral inhibition,* a central feature of the disorder, and the ways deficits in behavioral inhibition relate to other executive functioning deficits and problems with sustained attention. Barkley is clear in delineating that this model was developed specifically to address deficits in processing that apply to the Hyperactive-Impulsive Type of ADHD. Barkley emphasized that this model does not attempt to explain the Inattentive Type of ADHD.

In Barkley's model, the child's degree of success in behavioral inhibition is central to determining the nature of outcomes of four central executive functioning tasks: working memory (permits tasks of sequential ordering and planning), self-regulation (modulates activity states to initiate goal-directed behavior and sustain effort), internalization of speech (slows down reactivity and promotes inner reflection), and reconstitution (analyzes and synthesizes information). Deficits in behavioral inhibition result in poor problem-solving strategies based on an inability to integrate and coordinate information generated by the four central processes.

Barkley addresses the role of inattention in his model by distinguishing between two forms of inattention that are qualitatively distinct: sustained attention and selective attention. While Barkley attributes deficits in selective attention (inability to filter essential from nonessential details) to the Inattentive Type of ADHD, he contends that children who have the Hyperactive-Impulsive Type of ADHD have problems with sustaining their attention over time. Barkley further distinguishes be-

DON'T FORGET

Barkley considers behavioral inhibition as the necessary first step in problem solving. Developmentally, behavioral inhibition is a precursor to the development of the other higher-order functions. The behavioral delay allows sufficient time to develop skills in the four major areas that are in turn focal points for the development and refining of other essential skills.

CAUTION

Barkley has emphasized that the behavioral inhibition model was developed to explain the Hyperactive-Impulsive Type of ADHD, not the Inattentive Type.

Putting It Into Practice

Josh cannot concentrate on his homework and has to be continually monitored in order to stay seated, stop fidgeting, and get to work (sustained attention for effortful task). When he is playing video games, Josh is riveted to the screen and can play for an hour at a time (sustained attention for self-rewarding task).

tween sustained attention for essentially effortful tasks and what he calls "contingency based attention" or self-rewarding attention.

DIAGNOSIS AND ASSESSMENT OF ADHD

Although an exhaustive review of assessment instruments is beyond the intention of this book, it is essential that clinicians obtain an accurate clinical picture of ADHD in order to rule out competing hypotheses. As has been discussed, ADHD shares many characteristic features with other disorders (Depression, Bipolar Disorder, Anxiety, Posttraumatic Stress Disorder) and other problems of childhood and adolescence (abuse, maltreatment).

Detailed Clinical and Developmental History

A semistructured interview, such as the ones discussed in Chapter 3, should be conducted with the parent(s) or caregiver(s) to obtain information about the child's developmental history, including birth history, developmental milestones, medical history, educational history, social-emotional history, and family dynamics (including family stressors, clinical features, sibling relationships, and extended family). Obtaining parental expectations and impressions about the child's presenting problem is also important.

CAUTION

When conducting an assessment of suspected ADHD, clinicians must ask several key questions, including whether symptoms can be better accounted for by another disorder and whether comorbid disorders are also present.

DON'T FORGET

Assessment involves using multiple methods to obtain information from multiple sources and across multiple situations.

Parent, Teacher, and Youth Rating Scales

An important criterion of ADHD (APA, 2000) is that the disorder manifest across situations (home, school, etc.). Therefore, it is very important to obtain input from home and school to determine how symptoms present across different situations. In addition, given the high rates of comorbidity with other disorders, it is also essential to obtain information concerning other areas of potential diagnostic concern. Thus, an important part of the assessment process involves taking a comprehensive look at other major dimensions of child and adolescent psychopathology.

There are a number of behavioral rating scales that provide measures of ADHD characteristics in addition to other diagnostic categories. The ratings scales have parallel forms that can be completed by parents, teachers, and older children, allowing for a comparison across informants. Three of the more popular behavioral rating scales are the ASEBA (Achenbach & Rescorla, 2001), the CRS-R (Conners, 1996), and the BASC (Reynolds & Kamphaus, 1992). The scales included in each of these rating scales are summarized in Rapid Reference 4.1.

The ASEBA and CRS-R scales provide information from both a dimensional and categorical approach to the classification of ADHD as well as evaluating several other major problem areas. The BASC scales provide an index of functioning based on a dimensional classification system.

In addition to the behavioral rating systems, there are also scales designed to evaluate executive functioning. The Brown Attention-Deficit Disorder Scales (Brown ADD Scales; 2001) are available as parent and teacher questionnaires (3–12 years) and a self-report form (8 years to adult). The scales measure executive functioning in six areas: organization, attention, sustained effort, modulating emotions, working memory, and monitoring or evaluation. A comprehensive diagnostic form is also available to assist clinicians in integrating information from clinical history and to provide guidance in screening for comorbid disorders.

The Behavior Rating Inventory of Executive Function (BRIEF; Gioia, Isquith, Guy, & Kenworthy, 2000) is also available in parent and teacher rating forms. This measure provides a rating of executive functions in two broad areas: behavioral regulation (inhibit, shift, emotional control) and meta-cognition (initiate, working memory, plan/organize, organize materials, monitor). The instrument is available in school-age (5–18) and preschool versions (2–5:11).

Other Areas of Assessment

Academic difficulties are often part of the profile of children with ADHD. Therefore, individual intellectual and academic assessments may also be an important part of the assessment process in order to rule out other potential diagnostic categories (e.g., mental retardation) or to

CAUTION

The individual assessment session can mask symptoms of ADHD because of the inherent "contingent attention" involved in the novelty of the testing process (Barkley, 1998).

≡ *Rapid Reference 4.1*

Behaviors and Disorders Evaluated by the ASEBA, CRS-R, and BASC Scales

ASEBA	CRS-R	BASC
DSM-Oriented Scales	**DSM-IV Diagnostic Categories**	**Dimensional Scales**
Affective Problems	ADHD Inattentive Type	Externalizing Problems: Aggression, Hyper-activity, and Conduct Problems
Anxiety Problems	ADHD Hyperactive-Impulsive Type	Internalizing Problems: Depression, Anxiety, Somatization
Somatic Problems	ADHD Total (Combined Type)	School Problems: Attention, Learning
Attention-Deficit/Hyperactivity Problems		Adaptive Behaviors: Social Skills, Leadership, Study Skills
Oppositional Defiant Problems		Other Behaviors: Withdrawal, Atypicality
Conduct Problems		
Other Problems That May Be Evaluated (Syndrome Scales)	**Other Problems That May Be Evaluated**	
Anxious/depressed	Anxiety or Shyness	
Withdrawn/depressed	Perfectionism	
Somatic Complaints	Social Problems	
Social Problems	Psychosomatic Complaints	
Thought Problems	Family Problems	
Attention Problems	Emotional Problems	
Rule-breaking Behavior	Conduct Problems	
Aggressive Behavior	Cognitive Problems	
Total Internalizing	Anger Control Problems	
Total Externalizing	Hyperactivity	
Total Problems	Adhd Index	

Note. References for all instruments can be found in Appendix B.

assist in identifying comorbid features (e.g., learning disability). Cognitive assessment may also be helpful in evaluating processing deficits in areas of cognitive efficiency, processing speed, or working memory.

TREATMENT ALTERNATIVES

Treatment alternatives for ADHD will vary depending upon associated targets (comorbid features), symptoms, and the nature and extent of functional impairment. Interventions can be applied at home (parent training and family interventions), at school (behavior management and increasing on-task behaviors), and in interactions with peers (social skills training). Evidence-based research has for the most part focused on the effects of stimulant medications.

Stimulant Medications

A recent large-scale investigation of stimulant medications versus behavior therapy revealed that stimulant medication is more effective in alleviating the core symptoms of the disorder (MTA Cooperative Group, 1999).

Stimulant medications can be found in various forms, including short-acting (Dexedrine and Ritalin) and slow-release forms (Ritalin-SR), and longer-acting forms (Ritalin-LA). Numerous studies have demonstrated positive effects of stimulant medication in controlling the core symptoms of ADHD in areas of impulsivity-hyperactivity (increased sustained attention, reduced restlessness) and inattention (increased attention, decreased off-task behavior, increased academic output; Elia & Rappaport, 1991; Pelham & Milich, 1991). In addition, behavioral benefits of stimulant medication have been demonstrated in reduced ag-

DON'T FORGET

There are three main classes of stimulants currently in use for ADHD: amphetamines (Dexedrine, Adderall, Dextrostat), methylphenidates (Ritalin, Focalin, Concerta, Metadate, Methylin), and pemoline (Cylert). Recently, the Food and Drug Administration (FDA) has approved the first nonstimulant medication for ADHD: Strattera, a selective norepinephrine reuptake inhibitor.

CAUTION

Although there has been considerable research support for medical intervention in the treatment of ADHD, there is some indication that this form of treatment may not be equally effective for all types of comorbid associations. In one large-scale study, anxious youth with ADHD receiving behavior therapy responded as well as anxious youth who received medications alone (MTA Cooperative Group, 1999).

gressive behaviors (Hinshaw, Heller, & McHale, 1992) and improved parent-child interactions (Barkley & Cunningham, 1978).

Behavior Management Programs and Functional Behavioral Assessments

While results of the MTA Cooperative Group studies (1999) revealed that medication was the single most effective treatment for ADHD, behavioral treatment did provide benefits in improving symptoms in other key areas, such as social skills, aggressive responses, and parent-child interactions.

Interventions in the Home and School Environments

Empirically, studies have demonstrated that parent training (PT) programs can be an effective method of improving parenting skills while reducing parent stress, core symptoms of ADHD, and noncompliance (Sonuga-Barke, Daley, Thompson, Laver-Bredbury, & Weeks, 2001). Successful interventions in the home and school environments often involve the use of contingency management programs based on information provided from a functional behavioral assessment. Treatment manuals are available to assist clinicians in developing programs for parents of children with oppositional behaviors, social problems, and parent-child conflict (Barkley, 1997; Bloomquist, 1996).

While PT programs have demonstrated improved functioning at home, including teacher consultation in the PT program can also be helpful. Combining PT programs with teacher consultation allows for generalization of behaviors from the home to school environment. One of the more positive outcomes of parent and teacher collaboration is the enhanced communication between home and school that is monitored through the use of daily communication (often a student agenda can serve as the daily report for notes between parent and teacher). Studies have revealed that this combined approach can result in significant improvement in home and school behaviors (Pelham, Wheeler, & Chronis, 1998).

> **DON'T FORGET**
> ....
> Contingency management programs are developed to address specific systems of positive and negative consequences to insure behavioral change. Children with ADHD respond best to programs that have immediate reinforcers for good behavior and that have clearly defined goals and specific target behaviors.

✒ TEST YOURSELF ✒

1. **Historically, it was thought that ADHD symptoms were associated with**
   - (a) poor parenting practices.
   - (b) trauma to the frontal lobe.
   - (c) problems with visual motor integration.
   - (d) poor teaching.

2. **Which of the following is true about ADHD?**
   - (a) More males than females are identified.
   - (b) Ninety percent of children with ADHD will be diagnosed with the hyperactive-impulsive type.
   - (c) ADHD can be identified as early as 3 years of age.
   - (d) All of the above.

3. **Which of the following disorders is least likely to be associated with ADHD?**
   - (a) Bipolar Disorder
   - (b) Oppositional Defiant Disorder
   - (c) Anxiety Disorder
   - (d) Eating Disorder

4. **According to Barkley, the difference between the Inattentive Type of ADHD and the Impulsive-Hyperactive Type is that**
   - (a) those with Inattentive Type have deficits in sustained attention.
   - (b) those with Impulsive-Hyperactive Type have problems with sustained attention for self-rewarding tasks.
   - (c) those with Inattentive Type have deficits in selective attention.
   - (d) both a and c are correct.

5. **Which of the following is *not* one of Barkley's four executive functioning components?**
   - (a) Reconstitution
   - (b) Externalization of speech
   - (c) Self-regulation
   - (d) Working memory

6. **Results of the MTA Cooperative Group Study (1999) revealed that**
   - (a) PT groups were as effective as medication in reducing ADHD symptoms.
   - (b) anxious youth with ADHD receiving behavior therapy responded as well as anxious youth taking medications alone.
   - (c) medications were least effective for children with impulsivity.
   - (d) behavior therapy did not assist with other symptoms such as poor social skills.

(continued)

7. Which of the following is *not* an executive function?

(a) Ability to shift between tasks

(b) Ability to monitor and revise strategies

(c) Rigidity

(d) Working memory

8. Contemporary theories of ADHD believe that ADHD is most likely caused by

(a) heredity.

(b) environment.

(c) a complex interaction between biological and environmental factors.

(d) frontal lobe trauma.

Answers: 1. b; 2. d; 3. d; 4. c; 5. b; 6. b; 7. c; 8. c

Five

ANXIETY DISORDERS

Internalizing problems result from behaviors that are *overcontrolled,* compared to externalizing or *undercontrolled* behaviors (Achenbach, 1966; Cicchetti & Toth, 1991). Internalizing behaviors are "problems within the self, such as anxiety, depression, somatic complaints, without known medical cause, and withdrawal from social contact" (Achenbach & Rescorla, 2001, p. 93). By definition, internalizing problems are more covert in their nature and therefore often more difficult to detect and assess.

INTERNALIZING DISORDERS

There are several practical reasons for discussing anxiety, depression, and somatic problems from an internalizing perspective, including high rates of comorbidity, shared features of negative affectivity, shared assessment difficulties, and common problem areas associated with these disorders, such as social withdrawal, peer neglect, poor self-efficacy, and low self-esteem.

Prevalence Rates for Internalizing Disorders

Although younger boys and girls have similar prevalence rates for internalizing disorders (7–9%), in adolescent populations (12 to 16 years), females are approximately four times more likely to have internalizing disorders (15.7%) than males (3.9%; Offord, Boyle, & Szatmari, 1989). The following patterns have also emerged:

DON'T FORGET

Anxiety Disorders, Mood Disorders (Depressive Disorders and Bipolar Disorder), and Somatoform Disorders share internally oriented symptoms: depressed mood states, anxious and inhibited responses, and tendencies to express emotional distress as physical discomfort. Factor analysis of syndrome scales of the ASEBA (Achenbach & Rescorla, 2001) yielded an internalizing dimension comprising three syndrome scales: Anxious/Depressed, Withdrawn/Depressed, and Somatic Complaints.

Putting It Into Practice

Kerry is a very quiet little girl and a marginal (C) student. Kerry's thoughts often drift away from the task at hand, and her teacher feels that Kerry is probably a slower learner who is readily overwhelmed by task demands. On occasion, Kerry complains of stomachaches and headaches, and she misses about 4 days of school a month because she is not feeling well. Robby is in Kerry's class, but unlike Kerry, Robby is a disruptive force in the class. Robby is also a C student, but his teacher feels that he would get better grades if he would just focus on his work. Robby can be bossy and often interrupts class lessons and routines. When the teacher is asked to bring children's names for discussion to the next team meeting, she immediately thinks of Robby and two other boys who are disruptive and disturbing. Kerry's name does not come to mind.

Two years later, Kerry is referred to the school psychologist because she is in danger of failing the fifth grade. An assessment at that time reveals that Kerry is actually a bright girl who is overwhelmed by worries, fears, and her own feelings of inadequacy. Furthermore, Kerry has developed a number of avoidance behaviors due to her growing anxiety and depression, resulting in increased fears, somatic complaints, and frequent absenteeism.

- As many as 10–15% of children and youth will experience symptoms of depression (Smucker, Craighead, Craighead, & Green, 1986).
- In any one year, 13% of children will be diagnosed as having an Anxiety Disorder (Costello et al., 1996).
- Approximately one-fourth of children attending clinics for headaches or low energy have a somatoform disorder (Garber, Walker, & Seman, 1991).

Given the high rates of comorbidity between anxiety and depression, there has been significant debate over the past two decades whether anxiety and depression represent distinct diagnostic categories or whether symptoms might be better explained by a broad band notion of negative affectivity. In 1991, Clark and Watson proposed the tripartite model of anxiety and depression, in which *negative affectivity* (emotional distress) is conceptualized as a common underlying symptom shared by both anxiety and depression, while low positive affectivity is considered to be unique to depression and physiological arousal is considered to be unique to anxiety.

Subsequent research has sup-

DON'T FORGET

Comorbidity rates as high as 60–70% have been reported between anxiety and depression. Developmentally, onset of anxiety is a precursor to depression (Kovacs & Devlin, 1998).

ported only the first two hypotheses, since physiological arousal was not evident in all forms of anxiety. Research has demonstrated that low positive affectivity (anhedonia) can discriminate between children with Depressive Disorders and Anxiety Disorders (Lonigan, Carey, & Finch, 1994), while negative affectivity is a feature shared by both anxiety and depression (Chorpita, 2002; Chorpita, Plummer, & Moffit, 2000).

> **DON'T FORGET**
>
> The tripartite model suggests a three-part solution to the depression and anxiety debate: a feature common to both anxiety and depression (negative affectivity), a feature unique to depression (low positive affectivity), and a feature unique to anxiety (physiological arousal).

THE ANXIETY DISORDERS OF CHILDHOOD AND ADOLESCENCE

Anxiety Disorders are common in childhood and adolescence, with 1-year prevalence rates estimated to be as high as 13% (Costello et al., 1996). Anxiety Disorders share features of chronic worry about current or future events and can involve a number of common response patterns: behavioral (escape and avoidance), cognitive (negative self-appraisals), and physiological (involuntary arousal: increased heart rate, rapid breathing, tremors, and muscle tension).

Although the *DSM-III* recognized three anxiety disorders of childhood (Separation Anxiety Disorder, Avoidance Disorder, and Overanxious Disorder), currently Separation Anxiety Disorder (SAD) is the only anxiety disorder to appear under the category of childhood onset disorders (*DSM-IV-TR*). What was previously called Overanxious Disorder of Childhood is currently located within the major section of the *DSM-IV* under Generalized Anxiety Disorder (GAD). The current list of *DSM-IV-TR* anxiety disorders can be found in Rapid Reference 5.1.

Anxiety Disorders from a Developmental Perspective

The Specific Phobias and Separation Anxiety Disorder are the earliest-occurring Anxiety Disorders. Generalized Anxiety Disorder (GAD) is likely to have onset within the age

> **DON'T FORGET**
>
> Spence (1997) has verified the existence of six separate but correlated forms of anxiety that can exist in children: panic-agoraphobia, Social Phobia, separation anxiety, obsessive-compulsive problems, generalized anxiety, and physical fears.

Rapid Reference 5.1

The Major *DSM-IV* Categories of Anxiety Disorders

Generalized Anxiety Disorder (GAD)	Pervasive, excessive worry and anxiety, e.g., "free-floating anxiety."
Panic Attack	Intense and sudden onset of feelings of terror, fear, or apprehension, accompanied by physical (shortness of breath, heart palpitations, physical discomfort) and cognitive/emotive responses (wanting to escape, fear of losing control, fear of going crazy)
Agoraphobia	Fear of situations or places that might evoke/sustain a panic attack
Specific Phobias	Specific anxiety and fear elicited by an object or situation and resulting in avoidant behaviors
Social Phobia	Fear of anxiety regarding specific situations involving social or performance expectations
Obsessive-Compulsive Disorder (OCD)	Preoccupation with obsessions (anxiety-provoking thoughts/desires) and/or compulsions (driven to act to neutralize the anxiety)
Acute Stress Disorder	Immediate response to an extremely traumatic event causing heightened arousal and avoidance of arousing situations/events, lasting up to 4 weeks
Posttraumatic Stress Disorder (PTSD)	Re-experiencing thoughts, feelings, or distress associated with an extremely traumatic event, resulting in increased arousal and numbing/avoidance of thoughts/feelings/situations associated with the traumatic event, lasting at least 1 month
Substance-Induced Anxiety Disorders	Anxiety symptoms resulting directly from the use of a substance: e.g., inhalants, alcohol, stimulants, medications
Separation Anxiety Disorder (SAD)	Excessive worry about separation from significant caregivers or home, lasting at least 4 weeks, and causing significant distress and impairment

DON'T FORGET

High rates of comorbidity exist among the anxiety disorders. Children diagnosed with a primary anxiety disorder frequently present with other anxiety disorders.

range from 8 to 10 years of age, while onset in adolescence seems most likely for Social Phobia, Panic Disorder (with or without Agoraphobia), and Obsessive-Compulsive Disorder (see Saavedra & Silverman, 2002, for a review).

≡*Rapid Reference 5.2*

The Developmental Nature of Children's Common Fears

Developmental Age	Common Fears
Toddler stage	Strangers, toileting activities, personal injury
Preschool	Imaginary creatures, monsters, the dark, animals
Elementary school	Small animals, the dark, lightning and thunder, threats to personal safety
Middle school	Health (dental treatment), being sent to the principal's office
Adolescence	Physical illness, medical procedures, public speaking, sexual matters, political/economic conditions and catastrophies (war)

Source: Adapted from Barrios and Hartmann, 1997.

PHOBIAS AND FEARS

Although fears are common in childhood, the nature and number of fears change with age. Some common fears of various developmental stages are reported in Rapid Reference 5.2. The majority of studies report that the number of fears declines with age.

A *Specific Phobia* is a persistent, significant fear of an object or place that does not have a reasonable basis (*DSM-IV-TR*). Adults and older children will be aware that this fear is unreasonable, although very young children may not. Avoidance of the feared object or event is frequent. Exposure to the feared object may elicit significant physiological responses, such as dizziness, shortness of breath, increased heart rate, and even fainting.

The focus of the fear is anticipation of harm in some way (e.g., fear of dogs is a fear of being bitten). Responses of heightened anxiety increase as the child moves closer to the feared object. Often a strong desire to escape is imminent, and inability to escape may result in heightened arousal (panic). Having a Specific Phobia increases the likelihood of

CAUTION

A diagnosis of Specific Phobia is not made unless the phobia interferes with functioning to a significant degree. In child and adolescent populations (under 18 years of age), the phobia must be present for at least 6 months (*DSM-IV-TR*).

CAUTION

Childhood is a time when many immunizations are needed. The most common phobic response to the sight of blood or receiving an injection is fainting.

DON'T FORGET

The development of anxiety disorders in children can be associated with a wide range of influences, including genetic factors, temperament (behavioral inhibition), parent psychopathology, and other family factors, such as communication styles, parenting practices, and attachment history.

Putting It Into Practice

Gloria is very fearful of thunderstorms. On one particular stormy night, an enormous clap of thunder roars through the house with such intensity that the furniture seems to shake. Just at that moment, the phone rings. Each ring is accompanied by another thunder clap. Now each time the phone rings, Gloria jumps, fearing that thunder will follow. Gloria has acquired a conditioned fear of telephone rings.

having another phobia, and Specific Phobias are often comorbid with other Anxiety Disorders and with Mood Disorders.

Prevalence

Approximately 15% of children who are referred for anxiety have Specific Phobias, with girls reportedly more fearful overall than boys (Silverman & Nelles, 2001).

In addition to Specific Phobias, two broader types of phobias have been associated with onset most likely in midadolescence: Social Phobia and Panic Disorder with Agoraphobia. The phobias (specific, social, and agoraphobia) elicit fears in response to an imminent threat, while GAD refers to a more free-floating and nonspecific worry.

Etiology and Behavioral Explanations for Phobias

The etiology of Specific Phobias has most commonly been linked to individual *conditioning experiences* (Muris et al., 1998). Classical conditioning provides a framework for understanding how people develop phobic responses. For example, a very turbulent flight might result in future fear of flying. However, in addition to providing an explanation for how phobias might develop, classical conditioning can also provide the solution. Behavioral techniques can be applied to successfully decondition phobic responses. The nature of these systematic desensitization programs will be discussed in the section on treatment.

In addition to classical conditioning, other behavioral explanations also exist, such as observation, modeling, and operant conditioning. Studies have linked anxious and fearful responses in some children to fearful maternal models (Pickersgill, Valentine, Pincus, & Foustok, 1999). Behaviorists also use *operant conditioning* to explain how fears can result in the development of a host of avoidant behaviors. In the example in the Putting It into Practice box, if Gloria pulls the phone plug out of the wall, she will be able to avoid her acquired fear of phone ringing. However, avoidant behaviors can compromise adaptive behavior (Gloria will not get any phone calls), and fears can take on a life of their own as they generalize to other similar stimuli (e.g., phone ringing on the TV, alarm ring).

DON'T FORGET

Developmentally, phobias and separation anxiety are the earliest forms of anxiety.

CAUTION

Insecure attachment can develop from inconsistent or overprotective parenting responses to stressful situations. In both situations, the infant does not learn to internalize information on how to cope with distressing circumstances. Over time, the child may interpret many external cues as potentially threatening, setting the stage for the development of specific fears and generalized anxiety (Kendall & Ronan, 1990).

Parenting and Attachment Theory

Investigations of the influence of attachment on the development of anxiety in children have revealed that adolescents who were anxiously attached as infants (anxious-resistant attachment) were significantly more likely to develop Anxiety Disorders than their peers who were not anxiously attached (Warren, Huston, Egeland, & Sroufe, 1997).

Biological and Genetic Components

The etiology of Specific Phobias is probably best understood in terms of multiple pathways, including temperament, family characteristics, and exposure to conditioning experiences. Parents of children with Anxiety Disorders report that their children had more difficult temperaments as infants (crying and being fussy, irritable, and difficult to soothe), experienced more fears as toddlers, and experienced more problems adjusting to changes in routines than children without Anxiety Disorders (Rapee, 1997).

THE ASSESSMENT OF CHILDHOOD ANXIETY DISORDERS

In their review of assessment and diagnostic instruments, Silverman and Saavedra (2004) review the main instruments used in evidence-based treatment studies. The authors stress the importance of using structured or semistructured interviews, rather than unstructured interviews, to insure higher validity rates.

When assessing children for Anxiety Disorders, based on their review of kappa scores, the authors recommend using the Anxiety Disorders Interview Schedule for *DSM-IV:* Child and Parent Versions (ADIS for DSM-IV:C/P; Silverman & Albano, 1996; Silverman et al., 2001). In their evaluation of Parent Rating Scales, the authors recommend the Achenbach scales for internalizing disorders such as anxiety and mood.

A list of some of the more common measures for assessing anxiety in childhood and adolescence is presented in Rapid Reference 5.3. The list is not exhaustive but provides a general list of instruments that may be helpful in assessing the Anxiety Disorders. From this list, Silverman and Saavedra (2004) recommend three instruments for use in evidence-based practice: the Revised Children's Manifest Anxiety Scale (RCMAS), the Stait-Trait Anxiety Inventory for Children (STAIC), and the Fear Survey Schedule for Children—Revised (FSSC-R).

Treatment

In their review of empirically supported treatments for children with phobic disorders, Ollendick and King (1998) suggest *participant modeling* and *reinforced practice* as two well-established treatment methods. Modeling as a treatment intervention is based upon principles of observational learning (Bandura, 1977). Studies have demonstrated that participant modeling is superior to filmed models or participation alone. The technique of reinforced practice also has its roots in behavioral theory, specifically operant conditioning and contingency management. Studies have demonstrated that practice that is reinforced positively and practice plus self-instruction are superior to self-instruction alone or modeling plus practice. (See Ollendick and King, 1998, for a review.)

In their investigation, Ollendick and King (1998) also found several techniques that were in the "probably efficacious treatment methods" category, including imaginal desensitization, in vivo desensitization, filmed modeling, and cognitive behavioral interventions using self-instruction training. The technique of *systematic desensitization* is often used to reduce an individual's fear by gradually exposing the person to the feared object or event and breaking the association between the event and the emotion (fear) by substituting an emotion that is incompatible with fear (relaxation). The technique and its variants can be very helpful tools to assist young children in overcoming irrational fears and phobias, such as school phobia. There are several variations to the systematic desensitization paradigm,

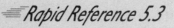

Rapid Reference 5.3

Some Common Assessment Instruments for the Evaluation of Anxiety in Children and Adolescents

Instrument	Ages	Brief Description
Revised Children's Manifest Anxiety Scale (RCMAS; Reynolds & Richmond, 1994)	6–17 years	Scales include Total Anxiety, Physiological Anxiety, Worry/Oversensitivity, Social Concerns/Concentration, and Lie Scale.
Anxiety Scale of the Beck Inventories for Youth (Beck & Beck, 2001)	7–12 years	One of five 20-item scales, measuring, self-concept, depression, anxiety, anger, and disruptive behavior.
The Children's Yale Brown Obsessive Compulsive Scale (CY:BOCS; Goodman, Rasmussen & Price, 1988)	6–18 years	Rates severity of obsessions and compulsions: time spent, distress, and interference in daily functioning.
The Multidimensional Anxiety Scale for Children (MASC; March, 1997)	8–19 years	Scales and subscales (in parentheses) include Physical Symptoms (Tense/Somatic), Harm Avoidance (Perfectionism/Anxious Coping), Social Anxiety, and Separation/Panic.
Fear Survey Schedule for Children—Revised (FSSC-R; Ollendick, 1983)	7–18 years	Five fear scales: Fear of Failure/Criticism, Fear of Unknown, Fear of Danger/Death, Fear of Injury, and Fear of Medical Situations.
Stait-Trait Anxiety Inventory for Children (STIAC; Spielberger et al., 1973).	6–18 years	Two 20-item scales measuring state (situational) and trait (generalized) anxiety.
Social Phobia and Anxiety Inventory for Children (SPAI-C; Beidel, Turner & Fink, 1996)	8–17 years	Scales include Assertiveness, General Conversation, Physical and Cognitive Symptoms, Avoidance, and Public Performance.
Anxiety Disorders Interview Schedule for *DSM-IV*: Child and Parent Versions (ADIS-IV; Silverman & Albano, 1997)	7–17 years	Available in parent and child versions. Assesses anxiety and related disorders.

Note. References for all instruments can be found in Appendix B.

DON'T FORGET

Wolpe (1958) developed procedures of systematic desensitization to progressively countercondition feared responses. Based on the underlying premise that relaxation and anxiety are incompatible responses, the program provides systematic steps to reduce anxiety.

Step 1: Clients are instructed in how to perform deep muscle relaxation.

Step 2: A fear hierarchy is constructed from the least to most feared aspect of a given situation (e.g., a hierarchy of fear-inducing thoughts regarding fear of flying might start with packing luggage and end with boarding the plane).

Step 3: The items from the fear hierarchy are gradually presented while the clients produce a deep muscle relaxation response.

distinguished by the way the feared stimulus and relaxation response can be paired. The pairing can occur *in vivo* (in reality) or be imagined. Studies have suggested that in vivo techniques are superior to merely imagining a situation, while imaginal desensitization has been found to be more effective than no treatment.

SEPARATION ANXIETY DISORDER

Children who experience SAD experience intense feelings of distress that are developmentally inappropriate and endure at least 4 weeks. Although SAD is recognized as one of the disorders first evident in childhood or adolescence, occurrence prior to age 6 is considered early onset. The disorder manifests before 18 years of age (*DSM-IV-TR*).

The need to remain in close proximity to the caregiver often results in significant impairment in social and academic functioning. Children with SAD may experience significant discomfort if asked to leave familiar territory. Symptoms of distress may be evident in physical and somatic complaints such as pronounced stomachache and vomiting. Parents often find the child with SAD to be very demanding and intrusive.

DON'T FORGET

The *DSM-IV-TR* diagnostic criteria for SAD require excessive worry about separation from the caregiver to be manifested in at least three of the following ways: fears of the caregiver succumbing to an accident or harm, excess worry about an anticipated separation at some future time, school refusal, fear of being alone without the caregiver (or adult substitute), reluctance to sleep alone or sleep away from home, nightmares about separation, and repeated physical complaints (headaches, stomachaches) if separation occurs or is anticipated.

Prevalence, Comorbidity, and Course

Although prevalence rates for SAD are relatively low in the general population (approximately 4%), rates can be as high as 10% in clinical populations. Separation Anxiety Disorder is more frequent in females than males and is often comorbid with GAD, depression, and somatic complaints (Last, Hersen, Kazdin, Orvaschel, & Perrin, 1991). Symptoms of SAD tend to reappear under stressful conditions. This disorder may be a precursor to increased risk for later depression and Anxiety Disorders and for the onset of panic attacks and Agoraphobia for females in adulthood (Albano, Chorpita, & Barlow, 1996).

Etiology

The Role of Biological, Genetic, and Temperament Factors

At least one study found that over 80% of children with SAD or GAD had mothers with a history of Anxiety Disorders (Last, Hersen, Kazdin, Finkelstein, & Strauss, 1987).

Parenting and Behavioral Modeling

Overprotectiveness and reinforcement of the child's avoidance behaviors can influence the maintenance of SAD. In some families, maternal depression and family dysfunction may result in the overparenting of the child who does not want to leave home for fear that he or she will not be able to protect the parent.

Treatment

Treatments for SAD can be accomplished using the same methods outlined for GAD.

Cognitive Behavioral Interventions

The use of cognitive behavioral interventions can be successful in treating SAD (see Ollendick & King, 1998,

---

DON'T FORGET

Seventy-five percent of children with SAD demonstrate school refusal; however, only one third of children who refuse to attend school have SAD (Black, 1995). School refusal may occur for many reasons, including reluctance to attend school following a lengthy absence (e.g., period of illness), a change of schools, or fears of victimization and bullying.

DON'T FORGET

Parents who demonstrate warmth and structure produce the best child outcomes in terms of child self-confidence and self-reliance (Baumrind, 1991). On the other hand, children of parents who are low on warmth and high on control (authoritarian parenting style) demonstrate more fearfulness, low self-esteem, and low initiative (Hudson & Rapee, 2000).

DON'T FORGET

Treatment of school refusal can be an important component of treating SAD in children. Structured contingency management programs with firm rules (expectations) that provide appropriate rewards for successful separation and remove reinforcement for avoidant behaviors can provide successful intervention for school refusal (Black, 1995).

Putting It Into Practice

During the interview, Jason seems unsettled and restless. When asked why he wasn't doing well in school, Jason said that it was hard to keep his mind on his work. He said he worried about a lot of things. He was worried that a robber might come and break into the house. He also worried that someone might steal his bike. He worried about whether he would make the baseball team this spring. He said it was like his head was always thinking of more things to worry about. Sometimes, before a test, he would actually get sick to his stomach because he was afraid he would not remember what he had studied.

DON'T FORGET

The *DSM-IV-TR* recognizes the physical or somatic nature of anxious symptoms in children and GAD in this population as excessive/pervasive worry plus one of the following symptoms: restlessness, easily fatigued, irritability, problems with concentration, muscle tension, or sleep disturbance (problems falling or staying asleep). Given these symptoms, it is not difficult to see why many children with GAD may be misdiagnosed as having ADHD.

for a review). The Coping Cat program, which has been successful for children who have GAD (see an explanation of the program in the section on GAD), has also assisted children with SAD.

GENERAL ANXIETY DISORDER IN CHILDREN AND ADOLESCENTS

Unlike the phobias and separation anxiety, children who experience GAD do not have a specific focus for their worries; instead, these children report pervasive worries that generalize across concerns about family, friends, school, health, and performance issues.

Excessive worry and anxiety coupled with an inability to control the worry are the cardinal features of GAD.

The *DSM-IV-TR* does not distinguish between GAD in adults and children. However, while adults require three additional symptoms of excessive worry, children require only one additional symptom.

The mood must be a pervasive mood (more days than not) over the course of 6 months. In addition, the disorder must be responsible for significant adaptive functioning deficits in the academic, social, or familial relationship areas.

Due to their overly conforming and hard-working nature, children with GAD are rarely referred for treatment by school personnel (Last et al., 1991). In addition to school- and peer-related problems, children with GAD may also worry about health-related issues or vague global concerns (Strauss, Lease, Last, & Francis, 1988).

Prevalence, Comorbidity, and Course

> **CAUTION**
>
> Children with GAD may be overly conforming and hesitant to participate in activities. Perfectionistic tendencies may require excessive reassurance from others regarding their performance. Worries about the world at large may also be evident in tendencies to ruminate regarding the potential for catastrophic events.

Between 2 and 5% of the population will be diagnosed with GAD in the course of their lifetime. Onset for GAD can be relatively early (8 to 10 years) with about one third developing other Anxiety or depressive disorders (Last, Perrin, Hersen, & Kazdin, 1996). Strauss and colleagues (1988) found that 70% of young children had comorbid GAD and SAD, while adolescents with GAD often had depression (47%) or Specific Phobia (41%).

Etiology

The Role of Biological, Genetic, and Temperament Factors

Twin studies suggest that as much as 30 to 40% of anxiety transmission may be due to genetic factors (Eley, 1999). Although the neurotransmitter GABA (gamma-amniobutyric acid) may send messages to increase excitatory responses to threat, a malfunction may deter GABA's responsibility to send messages to inhibit responses (cease fire) when necessary. Continued firing and excitation may result (Lloyd, Fletcher, & Minchin, 1992).

Information Processing and Cognitive Biases for Emotional Information

According to cognitive theory, anxious individuals anticipate and interpret ambiguous events in a negative way. Compared to their peers, anxious children interpret events more negatively, tend to engage in self-blame more readily, and focus on the negative rather than positive aspects of events (Silverman & Ginsburg, 1995).

> **CAUTION**
>
> Although anxious children and children with ODD share tendencies to interpret ambiguous information in a negative and threatening way, children with ODD respond with aggression, while children with Anxiety Disorders respond with avoidance tactics (Barrett, Rappee, Dadds, & Ryan, 1996).

Parenting and Behavioral Modeling

Studies have shown that anxious parents may actually increase their children's tendencies to engage in anxious and avoidant behaviors (Barrett et al., 1996). Furthermore, children of anxious parents may not benefit from cognitive behavioral training (CBT) to reduce anxiety unless parents are included in the CBT program (Cobham, Dadds, & Spence, 1998).

Treatment

The Coping Cat program (Kendall, 2000) has been demonstrated to be an effective way to reduce anxiety in children in randomized clinical trials of individual CBT training (Kendall, 1994) and more recently in group training (Flannery-Schroeder & Kendall, 2000). The program focuses on the development and practice of coping skills. The program also relies heavily on more behaviorally oriented components such as imagined and in vivo exposure to the fear-producing situations using systematic desensitization.

DON'T FORGET

The Coping Cat program assists children to reduce anxiety by understanding and recognizing physical responses and developing problem-solving strategies to cope, using the following FEAR mnemonic:

F   Feel frightened?

E   Expect the worst?

A   Attitude/Actions that can help

R   Results and Rewards

Putting It Into Practice

Esther had an overwhelming fear that her classmates would see her hand tremble as she took down notes from the board. She began to cover her hand with her left hand so that no one could see her taking notes. If anyone looked at her, Esther was sure they would notice the tremors. One day, filled with panic, Esther dropped her pen and ran out of the classroom. Her heart was pounding in her chest, and she felt that she would surely die. Esther called in sick the next day.

SOCIAL PHOBIA (SOCIAL ANXIETY)

A pervasive fear of embarrassment that often leads to avoidance of social or performance situations is at the center of Social Phobias.

Older children may realize that the fear is unreasonable but be unable to control it. Embarrassment may be associated with eating, drinking, or writing in public. Fears center around others' ability to detect their nervous tremors, blushing, or problems breathing. A diagnosis of Social Phobia in children and adolescents requires that the condition must be evident for at least 6 months and interfere significantly with functioning.

Children and adolescents may respond to Social Phobia with avoidant reactions (school attendance issues), escape behaviors (going to a library cubicle instead of the lunch room), negative self-appraisals, and increased physiological arousal (discomfort and somatic complaints). Understandably, social skills are often poor.

Developmental Features

Social Phobia and Younger Children

Compared to children with simple or specific phobias, children with social phobias tend to be older, have higher levels of severity, and are significantly more likely to become depressed later on (Last et al., 1992). Despite this finding, there has been significant controversy regarding whether Selective Mutism (persistent failure to speak in certain social situations) should be retained as a separate category of childhood disorders or conceptualized as an Anxiety Disorder, particularly a form of Social Phobia.

Social Phobia and Adolescence

It is not surprising that onset of Social Phobia has been most consistently linked with adolescence, given the nature of adolescent concerns regarding peer acceptance and social pressure (Beidel et al., 1999).

Disorder Subtypes

There are two subtypes of Social Phobia: a generalized form (pervasive across most social situations) and a more specific, situational Social Phobia (e.g., a fear of public speaking). In their study, Hoffman and colleagues (1999) found that almost half of adolescents had the generalized type of Social Phobia and that this type was more severe and evidenced higher levels of psychopathology than the situational type.

> **DON'T FORGET**
>
> In younger children, symptoms may include tantrums, crying, freezing, or refusal to engage in social situations with unfamiliar people. The *DSM-IV-TR* also requires (1) evidence of normal social interaction with familiar people and (2) pervasive fear across adult and peer situations (p. 456).

> **DON'T FORGET**
>
> As noted by Elkind, *personal fable* (tendencies to feel that no one has ever experienced what they are experiencing) and *imaginary audience* (everyone is looking at them) are two factors that may be particularly relevant to the development of a Social Phobia at this time.

Prevalence and Comorbidity

The lifetime prevalence for Social Phobia is estimated to be between 3 and 13%. However, prevalence rates for children have been estimated to be much lower (1–2%; Beidel, Turner, & Morris, 1999). One clinic study found that 27% of children with GAD and 5% of children with SAD had Social Phobia (Bernstein & Borchardt, 1991).

Etiology

Biederman and colleagues (1993) have found increased risk for Anxiety Disorders in general, and Social Phobia in particular, in children who have a *behaviorally inhibited* temperament. As discussed previously, parent communication, attachment, and parenting style have all been implicated in the development of fearfulness and phobic reactions in children. Genetically, there is an increased risk for Social Phobia in first-degree relatives who have the disorder (Fryer, Mannuzza, Chapman, Liebowitz, & Klein, 1993).

Treatment

In addition to techniques previously discussed for Specific Phobias, social skills training may also be a valuable component of any intervention program. Social skills interventions have been developed specifically to address concerns of children with Social Phobias (Francis & Ollendick, 1988; LeCroy, 1994) by focusing on skill awareness, situational awareness, practice and role play, and eventual in vivo application using participant modeling techniques.

PANIC DISORDER WITH AND WITHOUT AGORAPHOBIA

Panic attacks result from an intense, overwhelming, and inescapable fear that permeates thoughts, feelings, and sensations. Attacks are sudden and acute, lasting about 10 minutes. Because symptoms can include a number of somatic symptoms (palpitations, sweating, trembling, shortness of breath, feelings of smothering or dying, chest pain, dizziness), the attacks are often mistaken for heart attacks in adults. Cognitively, there can be a fear of losing control, depersonalization, or going crazy and a strong urge to escape. Attacks are accompanied by at least 4 and up to 13 somatic and cognitive symptoms. Panic attacks can be unexpected or triggered by situations (e.g., crowds, heights, confined spaces, etc.).

Because of its association with the Anxiety Disorders, the heightened arousal

Putting It Into Practice

The mall was very crowded, and Sara was becoming tired of shopping. All of a sudden, Sara felt like the floor was slipping out from under her. She was immediately overcome by a feeling of panic and dread. She felt like she was going to explode. Her heart started pounding, and her ears were ringing. She could see the ceiling start to spin, and she felt like she was going to faint. All of a sudden, she thought she was going crazy; it was as if the walls were going to close in on her and squeeze the life out of her. Someone tried to talk to her, but Sara ran out of the store into the parking lot in a frenzied attempt to escape. She needed some air. She felt like she was choking; she couldn't breathe. Five minutes later, everything seemed to come back into focus, as if she had just returned from another planet. Had she been abducted by aliens?

of a panic attack can be triggered by a Specific Phobia or can be the response of a severely distressed child with SAD who is not able to see his or her caregiver.

If someone experiences repeated panic attacks and becomes preoccupied with the fear of having a panic attack, then a diagnosis of Panic Disorder may be appropriate. Panic Disorder can occur without Agoraphobia but is often accompanied by Agoraphobia. Agoraphobia is a fear of venturing out into public places, especially alone. Agoraphobia, in itself, is not a codable disorder according to the *DSM-IV-TR* but occurs in conjunction with Panic Disorder, which is coded with or without Agoraphobia as a feature.

Although there is little research available concerning Panic Disorder with Agoraphobia in children and adolescents, family transmission of the disorder from parent to child is suspected (Last et al., 1991). Kearney, Albano, Eisen, Allan, and Barlow (1997) found that in youth aged 8 to 17 some of the most common symptoms experienced were nausea, heart palpitations, shortness of breath, shaking, and extremes in temperature (hot or cold flashes). In addition, youth with Panic Disorder were also more likely to have symptoms of depression and heightened sensitivity to anxiety.

Prevalence

Lifetime prevalence for Panic Disorder in community samples can be as high as 3.5%, with onset between late adolescence and the early 30s. Women are twice as likely to have a Panic Disorder than men. In a study of over 600 adolescents, King, Ollendick, Mattis, Yang, and Tonge (1997) found that 16% reported at least one panic attack (4 of 13 symptoms). In this study, females reported twice as many attacks (21.3%) as males (10.8%).

Etiology

Biological, Genetic, and Neurotransmitter Function

Those in whom panic attacks occur before the age of 20 are 20 times more likely to have a first-degree relative who also has a Panic Disorder. Twin studies also suggest a genetic link (*DSM-IV-TR*).

Irregular activity of the neurotransmitter norepinephrine has been implicated in the onset of panic attacks. The locus ceruleus, an area high in norepinephrine usage, which sends messages to the amygdale, which is known to trigger emotional reactions, has also been investigated.

Cognitive Distortions

Cognitive theorists suggest that panic attacks can result from a misinterpretation of bodily sensations. Heightened awareness in panic-prone individuals is also often associated with *anxiety sensitivity,* evident in faulty assessments and a tendency to overreact to bodily sensations, which ultimately result in illogical conclusions.

Treatment

Pharmacological Treatment

Antidepressant drugs (most of which work to restore appropriate levels of norepinephrine) can be successful in alleviating panic attacks. At least one study has suggested that the selective serotonin reuptake inhibitors (SSRIs) can alleviate panic symptoms in children and youth (Renaud, Birmaher, Wassick, & Bridge, 1999).

Cognitive Behavioral Treatment

One cognitive behavioral treatment program, the Panic Control Treatment for Adolescents (PCT-A; Hoffman & Mattis, 2000), has been successful in helping adolescents develop coping skills to fend off future panic attacks, including cognitive appraisals, educational awareness, and situational exposure to reduce panic responses.

OBSESSIVE-COMPULSIVE DISORDER

Obsessive-Compulsive Disorder (OCD) involves recurring and intrusive obsessions (irrational thoughts) and/or compulsions (uncontrollable behaviors) that occupy at least an hour daily and interfere with normal day-to-day functioning.

Developmental Considerations

Normally, children engage in rituals and superstitions that peak in the preschool years (2 to 4 years) and then progressively decline. However, for children with OCD, rituals and compulsions increase as the child gets older (Zohar & Bruno, 1997). In children with OCD, obsessions and compulsions often center on four primary areas: contamination (hand washing), safety (checking), preoccupations with orderliness and symmetry (aligning), and counting or touching rituals. Younger children may engage in compulsive motor symptoms such as walking in a particular design or finger licking (Swedo, Rapoport, Leonard, Leanane, & Cheslow, 1989). In younger children, compulsions often occur without obsessions, while adolescents often report multiple obsessions and compulsions (Kashani & Orvaschel, 1988).

Children and adolescents are also more likely to include family members in their rituals and can be demanding of adherence to rituals and rules. Often rituals are undetected and children just appear slow at doing their work. Children with OCD may do poorly in school because of preoccupations or perfectionistic tendencies. Piacentini, Bergman, Keller, and McCracken (2003) found that almost 50% reported significant problems at home, at school, and socially. School problems included concentration and homework. A list of the most common obsessions, compulsions, and rituals can be found in Rapid Reference 5.4.

Prevalence and Comorbidity

Approximately 2–4% of children and adolescents meet diagnostic criteria for OCD (*DSM-IV-TR*). Approximately 75% of children with OCD have a comorbid disorder. Studies have shown that between 5 and 7% have Tourette's disorder, while between 47% to 57% (depending on age) have a behavior disorder (Geller et al., 2001). Acute flare-ups of OCD symptoms in young children may often be accompanied by separation anxiety (Grados, Labuda, Riddle, & Walkup, 1997).

≡≡*Rapid Reference 5.4*

Obsessive-Compulsive Disorder: Common Rituals, Obsessions, and Compulsions

Often rituals can go undetected and can be performed in secret (Wever & Philips, 1994) by children who are embarrassed about their need to rigorously adhere to a repetitive schedule. Some common OCD obsessions and compulsions are listed here.

- Cleaning and washing compulsions: excessive hand washing, showering, teeth brushing to remove contaminants (obsessions about toxicity)
- Obsessive need for symmetry: aligning objects perfectly, obsessive neatness
- Obsessive hoarding or saving: collecting useless items (e.g., rubber bands, papers)
- Repetitive rituals: rereading, rewriting, repeating phrases
- Obsessive fears of aggression or violence: fears of performing a violent act
- Checking compulsions: repeated checking for locked doors, turning stove off, checking calculation errors
- Compulsive list making: making and altering lists

Etiology

Biological, Genetic, and Neurotransmitter Function

Reported risk for OCD can be as high as 8% in relatives with early onset OCD (Bellodi, Sciuto, Diaferia, Ronchi, & Smeraldi, 1992). Low levels of the neurotransmitter serotonin have been detected in patients with OCD, and the tricyclic antidepressants clomipramine (Anafranil) and the SSRI fluoxetine (Prozac), which serve to increase serotonin levels, have been effective in treating symptoms of OCD.

CAUTION

An acute onset of OCD or tic disorder has been reported in cases of Pediatric Autoimmune Neuropsychiatric Disorder (PANDAS), a stretococcal infection resulting in abrupt onset of OCD and/or tic disorder. Antibiotics were effective in treating the throat infections and eliminating the OCD symptoms, both initially and upon relapse (Murphy & Pinchinero, 2002).

Behavioral Theories

Despite increasing support for biological and neurological etiology, many adhere to behaviorist explanations that suggest that compulsive behaviors can develop by associations that are random in nature.

Behaviorists reason that hand-washing rituals become associated with a reduction in anxiety and are repeated on that basis. While some associations are random, there are also other associations that might link OCD symptoms to traumatic incidents.

Parenting and Family Environment

There has been increased interest in family influences on negative thought patterns in anxious children. Studies suggest that over 80% of children with OCD have families who are highly critical and overinvolved (high on expressed emotion), while adolescents with OCD describe their families as having less warmth, support, and closeness (Valleni-Basile et al., 1995).

Putting It Into Practice

Lotty rubs her lucky penny just before it is her turn to serve on the volleyball court. Lotty hammers a great serve and aces a key point for her team. When it is her turn to serve again, Lotty will again rub the lucky penny. At the last game she could not find her lucky penny, so she was very anxious, and her serves were off. Today, she is back on the game, and she attributes it all to the power of the lucky penny.

CAUTION

Up to 50% of child onset OCD can be attributed to traumatic events, resulting in OCD symptoms organized around themes of serious illness, loss of a family member, or school-related stress, such as high school entry (Geller et al., 1998).

Cognitive Theories

Maladaptive thinking results in feelings of an inability to control the risk factors (e.g., harm) while causing the patient to feel somehow responsible for their occurrence (e.g., thoughts about harming) and driving the need to cleanse the thought by repeating compulsive behaviors (Rachman, 1993).

Treatment

Psychopharmacology

Randomized controlled trials have determined that SSRIs can be an effective treatment for OCD in children and adolescents (McClellan & Werry, 2003).

DON'T FORGET

Common SSRIs include paroxetine (Paxil), fluoxetine (Prozac), fluvoxamine (Luvox), and sertraline (Zoloft).

Behavioral Therapy: Exposure and Response Prevention

Most methods follow Rachman's (1993) procedure, which involves repeated exposure to the anxiety-producing situation or object (e.g., contamination or dirt) while refraining from performing the anxiety-reducing compulsion (e.g., hand washing).

Cognitive Behavioral Therapy (CBT)

Based on their review of 11 CBT studies, Barrett, Healey-Farrell, Piacentini, and March (2004) suggest that these studies collectively provide preliminary evidence for the effectiveness of CBT for OCD. The authors have developed a 14-week program called the FOCUS program (Freedom from Obsessions and Compulsions Using Special tools) for youth and families. The FOCUS program uses principles of CBT, exposure and response prevention, disorder awareness, and relapse prevention.

POSTTRAUMATIC STRESS DISORDER AND ACUTE STRESS DISORDER

Although Posttraumatic Stress Disorder is an Anxiety Disorder, it will be discussed in Chapter 13.

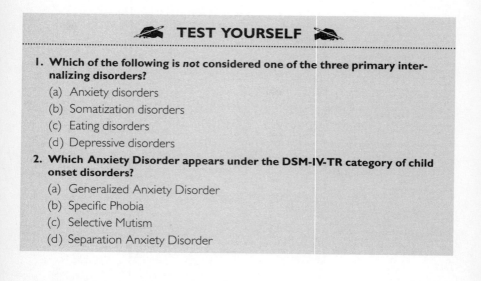

✐ TEST YOURSELF ✐

1. **Which of the following is *not* considered one of the three primary internalizing disorders?**

   (a) Anxiety disorders

   (b) Somatization disorders

   (c) Eating disorders

   (d) Depressive disorders

2. **Which Anxiety Disorder appears under the DSM-IV-TR category of child onset disorders?**

   (a) Generalized Anxiety Disorder

   (b) Specific Phobia

   (c) Selective Mutism

   (d) Separation Anxiety Disorder

3. **A therapist creates a fear hierarchy and presents selective images paired with instructions to engage in deep muscle relaxation. This technique is called**

   (a) Rachman's procedure.

   (b) systematic desensitization.

   (c) Coping Cat program.

   (d) in vivo sensitization.

4. **Fear of having repeated panic attacks can often lead to fear of venturing out into open places, which is known as**

   (a) free-floating anxiety.

   (b) arachnophobia.

   (c) Social Phobia.

   (d) Agoraphobia.

5. **Which of the following is an example of an obsession?**

   (a) Praying

   (b) Counting

   (c) Hand washing

   (d) Fear of contamination

6. **Which of the following anxiety disorders appears first, developmentally?**

   (a) Specific Phobia

   (b) Panic Disorder

   (c) Social Phobia

   (d) Obsessive-Compulsive Disorder

7. **Which is the most common symptom of separation anxiety disorder?**

   (a) Reluctance to sleep alone

   (b) Fear of the dark

   (c) School refusal

   (d) Eating problems

8. **Excessive and pervasive worry that is free floating is a description that best applies to**

   (a) Separation Anxiety Disorder

   (b) Social Phobia

   (c) Obsessive-Compulsive Disorder

   (d) Generalized Anxiety Disorder

Answers: 1. c; 2. d; 3. b; 4. d; 5. d; 6. a; 7. c; 8. d

Six

THE MOOD DISORDERS: DEPRESSION AND BIPOLAR DISORDER

I t is not uncommon to feel irritable, unhappy, or upset at times, or to feel elated when we receive exciting news. However, for individuals suffering from Mood Disorders, depressed or elated states can be extreme and long lasting, causing problems with day-to-day functioning.

There are two main mood states: depression, a state of low positive affectivity, and the polar opposite, mania, a state of euphoria. Individuals who suffer from depression can experience an intense form of the disorder, called *Major Depressive Disorder* (MDD), or a milder but chronic form called *Dysthymia*. Individuals may relapse after recovery. Those who experience the negative mood state without any manic intervals are considered to have *Unipolar Depression*. When individuals experience a fluctuation between depressed states and elated moods, they are considered to have *Bipolar Disorder*, previously referred to as *manic depressive disorder*. The *DSM-IV-TR* divides Mood Disorders (those disorders whose predominant feature is a disturbance of mood) into two major subtypes of mood disorders: the Depressive Disorders (major depression and dysthymia) and the Bipolar Disorders.

DON'T FORGET

Depression is not listed as a childhood disorder in the *DSM-IV-TR*, although special criteria for children (irritability instead of depressed or sad mood and different time lines for disorder duration) are included under the discussion and criteria for adult Mood Disorders.

DON'T FORGET

The Depressive Disorders are distinct from the Bipolar Disorders since the Bipolar Disorders include an elevated mood component (manic, hypomanic) as well as a depressed mood state, the combination of which is reflected in the prefix *bi*, meaning *dual states*. The Depressive Disorders, in contrast, manifest a single (unipolar) emotional state of low positive affectivity.

Putting It Into Practice

Christy was referred to the school social worker due to high absenteeism. When the social worker made a home visit, Christy's mother stated that her daughter's absences resulted from frequent complaints of feeling sick to her stomach. The mother disclosed that Christy had been involved in a bicycle accident over 2 years ago, resulting in a separation of her cartilage from the rib cage when her chest hit the handle bars. Due to this painful condition, Christy missed over a month of school and subsequently had to repeat the grade 3 program. Christy's mother enrolled her in a private school for that year.

Christy re-enrolled at her home school this year; however, her friends are all in the next grade level. Since the accident, Christy often complains of not feeling well. She is very thin, and her teacher has noticed that her lunch is often left on her plate, barely touched. At home, Christy is often irritable and moody. She doesn't seem to have much interest in doing anything. The family is under considerable financial strain and lived with extended family until recently. Christy has had to share a bedroom with her younger sister, who is in the same grade as Christy. They do not get along.

Last week, after a brutal argument with her sister, Christy ran out of the house crying and saying she was going to kill herself. Her mother wondered if she was doing this just to get attention, because she did not believe that someone as young as Christy could actually be depressed. She was hoping Christy would just get over it.

MAJOR DEPRESSIVE DISORDER (MDD)

Duration

With adults, a major depressive episode requires that the mood be pervasive for a 2-week period. The average duration in adults and children is 4 months. A diagnosis of MDD requires either (1) a depressed mood state, evident in anhedonia (low positive affect) in adults or irritability in children, or (2) loss of interest or pleasure in day-to-day activities (*DSM-IV-TR*). In addition to one of these criteria, the *DSM-IV-TR* stipulates four additional symptoms required for the diagnosis, from a list of seven potential symptoms: significant weight gain or loss (in children, failure to make expected gains), insomnia or hypersomnia, psychomotor retardation or agitation, fatigue, feelings of worthlessness, inability to concentrate, and recurrent suicide ideation. The feeling is pervasive and symptoms are intense, with some symptoms often occurring on a daily level.

A *Dysthymic Disorder* (minor depression) is diagnosed if the following conditions hold:

1. A pervasive depressed mood (loss of interest, anhedonia) or irritability (in children) is evident for at least 2 years (at least 1 year in child populations).
2. Depression is accompanied by at least two of the seven symptoms previously noted.
3. During the course of the 2 years (adult) or 1 year (child) there has not been symptom relief for a period greater than 2 months.
4. There has been no evidence of a Major Depressive Disorder during the 2 years (1 year for children).

Clinical Symptoms, Associated Features, and Developmental Adaptations

Although the core clinical features of MDD are similar in children, adolescents, and adults, there are some differences in how these symptoms manifest at different age levels. In addition, variations would also be expected in the nature of environmental stressors at different developmental stages. With the 1994 revision of the *DSM,* the criterion symptom of irritability was added as a cardinal marker for the expression of depression in child populations.

The *DSM* revision also altered time requirements for symptom presentation in children (1 year for dysthymia in children compared with 2 years for adults) and elaborated a number of associated features that might be typical at different developmental levels.

Symptoms and characteristics of depression differ depending on the child's developmental level. Therefore, a discussion of characteristics that might be associated with depression in children and adolescents will follow a developmental focus.

Toddlers and Preschool Period

Recently, investigators have determined that preschool children as young as 3 years of age can demonstrate some classic symptoms and

DON'T FORGET

For diagnostic purposes, irritability is described as a cranky mood in children and may be evident in angry outbursts and low frustration tolerance.

DON'T FORGET

Spitz (1946) observed institutionalized infants who seemed to waste away in the absence of affectionate care despite having their physiological needs met (a condition called *morasmus*). Due to the extreme nature of their listlessness and chronic sobbing, Spitz called the reaction *anaclitic depression*.

characteristics of MDD (anhedonia, sadness or irritability, neurovegetative signs). Toddlers can display symptoms of depression in loss of appetite, lack of sleep (vegetative symptoms), delays in the acquisition of developmental milestones (walking, talking, toilet training), and in their experiences of nightmares and night terrors. At this stage, more agitated expressions might include ex-

> **DON'T FORGET**
> ....
> As a result of their investigations of MDD in preschool children, Luby and colleagues (2003) have advocated for modifications of the *DSM-IV-TR* criteria for MDD in very young children. Their findings suggest that the current criteria are too stringent for preschool children, leading to underdiagnosis at this age level.

cessive head banging or rocking behaviors. Investigators have also found that thematic play can also provide useful information regarding the nature of depressive symptoms in children at this age level (Luby et al., 2003).

Childhood

While genetic transmission may be a strong factor in adolescent depression, childhood (prepubertal) depression may be more environmental than genetic (Thapar, Harold, & McGuffin, 1998). Environmental stressors at this age level might include family conflict, problematic parenting style, and peer rejection. In childhood, symptoms of depression might be evident in somatic complaints, irritability, and social withdrawal. Common comorbid clusters within this age range include behavior disorders, ADHD, and Anxiety Disorders (*DSM-IV-TR*). Depressed children often have low self-esteem and can be very self-critical. At this stage, depression will probably manifest in poor academic achievement and poor social relationships. Often behaviors may vacillate between acting out (anger) and withdrawal (sadness). Low frustration tolerance is likely.

Adolescence

In adolescents, there is a higher rate of the endogenous/melancholic subtype of depression, and there are higher rates of suicide attempts and fatalities than in prepubertal children (Ryan et al., 1987). Adolescent depression is continuous with adult depression (Ryan et al.), and as with adult depression, there is stronger evidence of a genetic component. Some of the more common symptoms in adolescence include psychomotor retardation/hypersomnia and delusions (especially auditory hallucinations). Common comorbid clusters at this age range include behavior disorders, ADHD, Anxiety Disorders, substance disorders, and Eating Disorders (*DSM-IV-TR*).

CAUTION

Given the high level of sensitivity to body image at this age level, negative thoughts may turn to negative self-appraisals based on physical features considered ugly or unattractive and body type (the adolescent may consider him- or herself overweight). Negative thought patterns may generalize to low self-esteem, poor school achievement, social withdrawal, or heightened risk taking evident in delinquent behavior, sexual acting out, or substance abuse. Youth with MDD have higher rates of pregnancy and increased risk of suicide (Ryan et al., 1987).

CAUTION

Suicide was the third leading cause of death in youth and young adults (10 to 19 years of age) in 1997 (Shafer & Craft, 1999). Between 1979 and 1997, the suicide rate for 10- to 14-year-olds doubled, while the rate for adolescents in the 15–19-year range increased by 13% (Guyer, MacDorman, Martin, Peters, & Strobino, 1998).

DON'T FORGET

Three times as many females attempt suicide than males; however, four times as many males succeed in completed suicides than females.

Depressive Syndromes and Symptoms

Not everyone who experiences a depressed mood will meet clinical criteria for a depressive disorder, as indicated in the *DSM-IV-TR.* Children, adolescents, and adults can all experience depressed moods or feel depressed on occasion. Sometimes these feelings are reactive to particular stressors. At other times, nostalgia or melancholy might trigger feelings of sadness, while on other occasions mood can be influenced by physiological (hormonal) changes or changes that are substance induced (e.g., alcohol is a depressant).

Suicide and Substance Abuse

Children and adolescents with suicide ideation experience intense feelings of depression, anger, hopelessness, anxiety, and worthlessness. They often feel helpless and ineffective to change circumstances that cause overwhelming psychological pain. Children and adolescents who contemplate suicide have suicidal thoughts or what is called *suicidal ideation.* Not all children who have thoughts of suicide will engage in a suicide attempt, however, and fortunately not all attempts will result in a completed suicide. While females are more likely than males to attempt suicide, males are more likely to succeed in completed suicides.

The reason for the disparity between attempts and completions is in the lethality of the methods used. Females tend to attempt suicide through drug overdose, while males use guns (60% of males die of self-inflicted gunshot wounds), hanging, and other more violent means (Garland & Zigler, 1993).

Risk Factors for Suicide

Substance abuse, aggressive or disruptive behaviors, and depression have all been cited as the strongest predictors of suicide attempts in children and youth.

Since substance abuse and alcohol are implicated in approximately 50% of suicides, it has been suggested that increasing rates of suicide among adolescents may be related to increased rates of alcohol abuse (Brent, 1995). Lewinsohn, Clarke, Seeley, and Rohde (1994) found that youth with previous suicide attempts were 18 times more likely to attempt suicide again than youth who had not attempted suicide.

Further information from Shaffer and colleagues (1996) revealed that 66% of those who completed suicides had at least one of three main risk factors: prior suicide attempt, substance or alcohol abuse, and evidence of a mood disorder. In addition, the authors found that a life stressor usually precipitated the suicide attempt.

CAUTION

Having a mood disorder is one of the major risks for suicide. As many as 7% of adolescents who develop an MDD will commit suicide prior to reaching middle adulthood (Weissman et al., 1999).

CAUTION

One of the strongest predictors of a future suicide attempt is a previous suicide attempt. Shaffer and colleagues (1996) found that 30% of adolescents who committed suicide had at least one previous attempt.

CAUTION

Common precipitating life stressors for suicide attempts in adolescents include loss of a relationship, teen pregnancy, physical or sexual abuse, disciplinary crisis or trouble with school or the law, conflict with parents or conflict in the home between parents, exposure to suicide (which can cause a contagion effect), and a recent move (Shaffer et al., 1996).

Suicide and Protective Factors

Borowsky, Ireland, and Resnick (2001) investigated protective factors that might guard against suicide attempts in Black, Hispanic, and White adolescents. Results revealed that common protective factors that cut across all ethnic groups were academic achievement and connectedness to parents, family, and school. Additionally, emotional well-being (for all females) and high grade point average (for all males) were also safeguards. Further analysis revealed that the presence of three protective factors reduced suicide risk by 70% to 80%. Based on their findings, Borowsky and colleagues suggest the need to evaluate the role of suicide prevention programs using multisystemic therapy (MST) to focus on improving parenting skills, decreasing negative and coercive parenting practices, and strengthening family cohesion and connectedness.

Prevalence and Comorbidity

Approximately 5% of the general population of children and adolescents will suffer from depression. Studies have demonstrated that boys and girls are equally likely to develop depression at younger ages. In adolescence, however, depression is almost twice as common in adolescent females than males (Fleming & Offord, 1990). Comorbidity is especially high between depression and the Anxiety Disorders, although many other comorbid relationships exist.

Course

The course of depression can be long and enduring. Although only 2 weeks' duration is required for a major depressive episode, the average length of an MDD is approximately 4 months. Kovacs, Akiskal, Gatsonis, and Parrone (1994) found that 76% of children with early onset dysthymia develop MDD later on.

In addition to the long-term impact of the Depressive Disorders on future interpersonal and psychosocial problems, there is also an increased risk for developing other disorders. In one follow-up study of 6- to 12-year-olds with MDD, 30% developed Bipolar Disorder on follow-up (Geller et al., 1995).

> # CAUTION
>
> He thought it was a light at the end of the tunnel, but it turned out to be another train coming at him ... Double Depression. Often at the end of a lengthy bout of dysthymia the cloud does not lift but becomes even darker. When dysthymia develops into MDD, it is called *Double Depression*.

> # DON'T FORGET
>
> While both genetic and environmental influences have been implicated in the development of MDD, environmental influences are likely to be more instrumental in childhood depression, while genetic factors are more prominent in the development of MDD in adolescence.

Etiology

Genetic Background and Neurotransmitter Functions

Children, adolescents, and adults who have a family history of depression are at higher risk for depression. However, other factors that also operate in the home, such as parenting style, may be as significant as genetic transmission. Results from twin studies suggest that a genetic link is stronger for adults and adolescents than for children, who are better accounted for by environmental factors.

Neurotransmitter functions. Although evidence for neuroendocrine imbalance (hormone cortisol) has been related to depression in adults, this has not been substantiated in children. Antidepressants that have been instrumental in increasing low levels of the neurotransmitter serotonin in adult depression have had mixed results with children. Some studies have found antidepressants not to be effective in reducing symptoms of depression in children (Fischer & Fischer, 1996).

Risks and Protective Factors

A number of risk factors have been linked to the development of Depressive Disorders in childhood and adolescence: abuse or neglect, stress, loss of a parent or loved one, comorbid disorders (ADHD or conduct or learning disorders), breakup of a romantic relationship, having a chronic illness (e.g., diabetes), and other trauma, such as a natural disaster (NIMH, 2000b).

Family Risk Factors

A high prevalence rate for alcoholism among first-degree relatives of prepubertal children and adolescents with mood disorders has been reported (Puig-Antich, Geotz, & Davies, 1989). Family poverty and conflict between parents have also been cited as increasing the risk for depression in children as well as their parents (Hammen, 1991).

CAUTION

The FDA issued a public health advisory (March 22, 2004) and asked manufacturers of several antidepressant drugs to include warnings on the label regarding the recommendation to closely monitor adults, children, and adolescents for a potential worsening of depression and suicidality in patients being treated with antidepressant medications.

DON'T FORGET

Younger children responded to the trauma of a natural disaster (an Australian bushfire) with depressed symptoms, while older (middle school) children responded with emotional distress more similar to symptoms of PTSD (McDermott & Palmer, 2002).

DON'T FORGET

Children of depressed mothers are twice as likely to be depressed over their lifetime than peers whose mothers are not depressed. Over 40% of children whose mothers are depressed are diagnosed with childhood depression.

In their study of the parenting style of depressed mothers, Malphurs and colleagues (1996) found that depressed mothers were more withdrawn (emotionally unavailable for their children) and intrusive (controlling, irritable, and impatient). Other studies have demonstrated that infants and young children of depressed mothers are at higher risk for developing insecure attachments and poor emotion regulation and that daughters are at increased risk for becoming depressed (Cicchetti & Toth, 1998).

Peer Influence
Lack of social competence, low peer support, and rejection or peer neglect are all risk factors for child and adolescent depression (Harter & Marold, 1994). Children who are depressed are often irritable, have fewer acquired social skills, and are more likely to engage in negative or aggressive interactions.

Theoretical Models of Depression

Cognitive Behavioral Model
Theorists who support a cognitive model link unipolar depression to maladaptive thought processes, which interpret events in negative ways. The two most influential cognitive explanations are the models of *negative thinking* and *learned helplessness*.

Negative thinking.   According to Beck (1997), negative thinking colors our perceptions of the world. Negative thoughts are pessimistic, viewing the glass as half empty rather than half full. Negative schemas eventually develop into what Beck refers to as the *negative triad,* whereby individuals interpret their experiences, their selfhood, and their future in negative ways.

Several errors of thinking can occur as a result of negative schemas that serve to perpetuate the negative thought process, including minimizing the positive and magnifying or overgeneralizing the negative.

Learned helplessness.   Seligman (1975) originally articulated the concept of learned helplessness to describe the reactions of experimental animals that were repeatedly shocked on one day and then provided with a barrier they could jump over to reach safety on the following day. However, most of the dogs did not flee; they gave up. Seligman reasoned that the dogs had learned that the shocks were not

DON'T FORGET

The cognitive triad comprises the three pervasive thoughts of hopelessness, helplessness, and worthlessness.

Putting It Into Practice

Sally and Jenna take the same psychology quiz. Sally does well, but Jenna fails the quiz. According to attribution theory, Sally can make a positive attribution (pat herself on the back and say "I did well because I am smart" (internal or global attribution) and "I always expect to get good grades because I study hard" (stable). However, Jenna might need to save face, so she might reason that the test was unfair (external attribution) and that furthermore this professor always gives unfair tests (stable), or that something must have distracted this professor because she usually gives fair tests (unstable).

In this scenario, Sally has responded positively, while Jenna has developed a defensive maneuver to protect herself from thinking negatively about herself: Jenna writes her failure off as a bad test.

within their control and did not engage in problem-solving behaviors because they felt helpless to influence the outcome.

More recently, *attribution theory* (linking of thoughts to outcomes) has added a new twist on learned helplessness to help explain why only some people respond to stressors with defeat.

Family and Peer Influence Models

The role of family processes on depression.   In their analysis of the role of family processes in adolescent depression, Sheeber, Hops, and Davis (2001) suggest four potential areas in which family dynamics may influence their adolescent's vulnerability to developing depression: the adversarial family climate (high stress or low support), the negative reinforcement model, the self-fulfilling prophecy, and poor modeling for emotion regulation.

Peer influences in mediating depression. While Sheeber and colleagues (2001) looked at the influence of family processes on adolescent depression, Patterson and Capaldi (1990) developed a model that looks at much earlier influences. The authors suggest that children who are reared in a negative family environment enter the social arena with low self-esteem, poor interpersonal skills, tendencies to respond aggressively (verbally or physically), and a negative cognitive style.

CAUTION

Aggression can become depression. In their model, Patterson and Capaldi (1990) suggest that the children who tend to be verbally or physically aggressive ultimately seal their own fate as they are increasingly rejected by their peers. Other children respond to rejection with increased oppositional behaviors and heightened rejection, which leads to low self-esteem and ultimately depression.

An Ecological Transactional Model

In discussing their model, Cicchetti and Toth (1998) emphasize the need to consider the concepts of *multifinality* and *equifinality* in discussing the potential course and outcomes of depression in children and adolescents. The authors discuss the need to consider the "potentiating and compensatory" processes across all levels of influence from early ontogenic development (early development of physiological systems of regulatory arousal and attachment relationships) through the micro-, exo-, and macrosystem influences on the development of depression. It is within such a model, the authors suggest, that interventions can be developed to target stage-specific needs and family influences as well as social-contextual influences.

Assessment

The use of structured and semistructured interview schedules in the assessment of internalizing disorders has been previously discussed (see Chapter 3 for a review). In addition, many of the general behavioral rating scales and individual personality scales also include measures of depression. A number of common instruments for measuring depression are listed in Rapid Reference 6.1.

Treatment

Medication

The role of medication in the treatment of depression has previously been discussed, as well as the recent warnings issued, and will not be reviewed again at this time.

Empirically Supported Treatments

In their review of clinical treatments for depression in children and adolescents, Kaslow and Thompson (1998) discussed a child and an adolescent program that met criteria for probably efficacious treatments as outlined by the American Psychological Association. The programs, which both use CBT, were a child-based program developed by Stark, Swearer, Jurkowski, Sommer, and Bowen (1996) and an adolescent program developed by Lewinsohn, Clarke, Rhode, Hops, and Seeley (1996).

Cognitive Behavioral Treatment

The use of CBT for the reduction of depressive symptoms in adults has met with significant success. Beck (1997) has developed a structured 20-session program that is aimed at gradually increasing activities and elevating mood through challenging automatic thoughts, identifying negative thinking, and restructuring

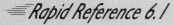

Rapid Reference 6.1

Common Assessment Instruments for Evaluation of Depression in Children and Adolescents

Instrument	Ages	Brief Description
The Depression Scale of Beck Youth Inventories (Beck & Beck, 2001)	7 to 14	20-item scale assesses depression based on *DSM-IV* criteria. Four-choice format measures negative thoughts related to self, life, and future expectations.
The Hopelessness Scale for Children (Kazdin, 1986)	6 to 13	True/false response format. 17 questions assess hopelessness, which correlates highly with depression and suicide ideation.
Child Depression Inventory (Kovacs, 1992)	6 to 17	Score for Total Depression, as well as five subscales: Negative Mood, Interpersonal Problems, Ineffectiveness, Anhedonia, and Negative Self-Esteem.
Depression and Anxiety in Youth Scale (Newcomer et al., 1994)	6 to 18	Identification of MDD and over-anxious disorder based on the *DSM-III-R* classification. Self-report, parent, and teacher versions, available.
Reynolds Adolescent Depression Scale (Reynolds, 1987)	13 to 18	Self-report measure based on four-choice format yields a score for Total Depression.
Reynolds Child Depression Scale (Reynolds, 1989)	Grades 3 to 6	Self-report measure provides graphic choice format (five faces ranging from happy to sad) for young children. Score for Total Depression.

Note. References for all instruments can be found in Appendix B.

CAUTION

Remember that, as an internalizing disorder, depression may be more difficult to assess on the basis of observational reports and measures. Youth may also not be aware that what they are feeling is depression, or they may not be able to articulate their feelings adequately. It is also very important to remember that depression in children is often expressed as irritability, which may manifest in verbal and physically aggressive responses and may be misdiagnosed as problems of conduct.

thoughts from maladaptive to adaptive thinking. Lewinsohn and colleagues (1996) have developed a CBT program for adolescence that was adapted from Beck's program and includes a parent component.

Stark and colleagues (1996) have developed a CBT program for depressed children and their parents. Initially the program was used as a school-based treatment approach, but Stark has modified the program to include individual and group formats. The program focuses initially on the development of positive mood and ultimately seeks to teach children to reframe their negative thought patterns.

BIPOLAR DISORDERS

The *DSM-IV-TR* provides criteria for manic, mixed, and hypomanic episodes of a bipolar disorder. A manic episode is described as a "distinct period" of abnormally elevated, expansive, or irritable mood, lasting for at least a week, causing significant impairment, and accompanied by at least three of the following seven symptoms:

- Heightened sense of self-esteem or grandiosity
- Little need for sleep
- Pressured speech
- Flight of ideas
- Distractibility
- Heightened goal-directed activity (psychomotor agitation, sexualized behaviors, social contacts)
- Excessive involvement in risky behaviors (spending spree, theft, sexual behavior)

DON'T FORGET

In addition to the low positive affect associated with unipolar depression, children and adolescents who have Bipolar Disorder also experience the highs of manic states.

CAUTION

The difference between a *manic episode* (1 week) and a *hypermanic episode* (4 days) is in the duration and severity. A hypermanic episode is a less severe episode (which does not cause significant impaired functioning) of heightened and expansive mood lasting for at least 4 days. Both episodes require three symptoms from the list. Bipolar II is diagnosed in cases of major depressive episodes with a hypermanic episode.

Bipolar I is diagnosed if one or more manic or mixed episodes (both major depressive episode and a manic episode overlapping within a 1-week period).

Cyclothymic Disorder, a chronic fluctuating mood disturbance (*DSM-IV-TR*), is diagnosed when the prevailing mood for the past 2 years has involved hypomanic symptoms and depressive symptoms (not meeting criteria for MDD).

In their review of literature over the previous 10 years concerning child and adolescent Bipolar Disorder, Geller and Luby (1997) suggest that childhood-onset Bipolar Disorder may be more severe, be more chronic, and have rapid-cycling features similar to the more severe types and often treatment-resistant forms of adult bipolar disorder. The mixed manic and rapid-cycling patterns may manifest as brief and multiple episodes, which may cycle numerous times within a single day (Geller et al., 1995).

CAUTION

Although the *DSM-IV-TR* has added many associated and symptom features for childhood depressive disorders (MDD, Dysthymic Disorder), there is virtually no mention of how the bipolar disorders might manifest differently in children. However, one specifier for the Bipolar Disorders that may be particularly relevant to childhood-onset bipolar is the *rapid cycling* specifier, used when four or more mood episodes occur within a 12-month period. Although this specifier is seen in approximately 10–20% of adult populations, current literature suggests that this may be a predominant feature of Bipolar Disorder in children.

In their literature review, Geller and Luby (1997) provide examples of how the core features of a manic episode might be evident in childhood and adolescence. The following summary is based upon their review.

In childhood, rather than discrete episodes, there are more likely to be rapid mood shifts between elation and irritability. A sense of childhood grandiosity or

Putting It Into Practice

Arthur was giggling wildly and running down the hall when his fifth-grade teacher cited him for breaking a school rule. When Arthur got to his desk, he immediately threw his books on the floor and stamped his feet in protest. Time out did little to change his mood, and Arthur glared at the other students while he huffed in the corner. During this time out, unknown to the teacher, Arthur managed to stab himself in the arm with a pencil. Two minutes later, Arthur asked if he could rejoin the class activity and began laughing hysterically at an animated picture the teacher was showing on the overhead projector. Arthur could not resist making remarks about the lesson and challenged the teacher on her interpretation of the facts. When he was sent to the principal's office because of his disruptive and disrespectful attitude, Arthur openly confronted the principal for hiring a teacher who couldn't teach and stated furthermore that he could teach the class better himself.

In this scenario, Arthur displays many of the symptoms typical of childhood-onset Bipolar Disorder.

inflated self-esteem that defies logic may result in children's believing that they are being taught incorrectly or that they are above the law. Some students may have grandiose aspirations in manic periods of being a famous athlete or musician while having minimal talent, or becoming an astronaut while failing in school. Problems with sleep may be evident: Younger children may watch television all night in their rooms or rearrange their furniture instead of sleeping, and adolescents may engage in late-night partying. Pressured speech and fight of ideas are similar to adult symptoms but with content specific to child or adolescent interests. Children and adolescents may also get caught up in high levels of motor and goal-directed activity and multitasking (making telephone calls while making illustrations, sorting card collections, etc.). Dangerous and risk-taking behaviors may be evident in sexual promiscuity, fast driving, spending sprees, and theft.

Prevalence

Prevalence rates are relatively unknown in child populations; however, adolescent prevalence has been suggested to be around 1% of the population.

Etiology

Biological and Genetic Background
Family history is strongly associated with Bipolar Disorder.

DON'T FORGET
....
Aggressive behavior can be a common characteristic of Bipolar Disorder. According to Steiner (2000), aggression associated with Bipolar Disorder is often of the escalating type.

DON'T FORGET
....
Heredity is strongly associated with bipolar disorder. Studies have found a 30–40% risk of inheriting Bipolar Disorder in those with one bipolar parent and as high as a 50–70% risk if both parents have a major affective disorder (Levine, 1999).

Assessment: Differential Diagnosis

Bipolar disorder can often be confused with ADHD and CD due to the existence of overlapping symptoms. Children or adolescents who seem depressed and also demonstrate symptoms that resemble those of ADHD but are more severe (excessive temper outbursts, rapid mood swings) should be evaluated for the existence of Bipolar Disorder, especially if family history is positive for the disorder (NIMH, 2000).

According to Geller (2001), the

biggest problem in the diagnosis of bipolar disorder in children is how to tell a child with mania from a child with ADHD (p. 4). When one reviews the diagnostic criteria for mania, it is readily apparent that almost half of the criteria (decreased need for sleep, excessive talking, distractibility, irritable mood) are symptoms shared by ADHD. Geller and colleagues (2001) have responded to the challenge by going back to the *DSM-IV* definition of mania and finding the two cardinal features of mania (elation and grandiosity), then combining these two features into one necessary criterion. Geller and colleagues believe that, using this criteria, they can distinguish between Bipolar Disorder and ADHD. Additionally, the manic symptom of hypersexuality was found in 43% of the bipolar sample in the absence of any reported history of sexual abuse.

Treatment

Due to the complex nature of Bipolar Disorder in children and adolescents, a multimodal treatment plan that combines medications and psychotherapeutic interventions and places emphasis on relapse prevention has been recommended (AA-CAP, 1997). In their review of lithium, a mood stabilizer that has been used in the treatment of Bipolar Disorder in children and youth, Tueth, Murphy, and Evans (1998) suggest that lithium is well tolerated by children and adolescents. However, there are a number of reported side effects that may make compliance difficult to maintain in adolescent populations: stomach upset, nausea, overeating, weight gain, tremor, enuresis, and acne. In studies of adolescent noncompliance, 90% of youth who were noncompliant with lithium relapsed in an 18-month time span (Strober, Morrell, Lanpert, & Burroughs, 1990).

DON'T FORGET

Mania, unlike the euphoric states of adult bipolar symptoms, may present as irritable and destructive outbursts in children. Early-onset Bipolar Disorder (prior to puberty) is often characterized by rapid cycling and irritability and may often co-occur with CD and ADHD or have symptoms that closely mimic these two disorders. Later-onset (adolescence) Bipolar Disorder tends to have a sudden and acute onset, often starting with a manic episode and showing less cormorbidity with ADHD and CD (NIMH, 2001).

CAUTION

The use of antidepressants to treat depression in an individual with Bipolar Disorder may precipitate manic symptoms if taken without a mood stabilizer. Furthermore, stimulant medication for ADHD-like symptoms in a child with Bipolar Disorder can exacerbate manic symptoms (NIMH, 2001).

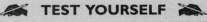
TEST YOURSELF

1. **Depressed mood in children is often expressed as**
   (a) crying.
   (b) irritability.
   (c) pervasive sadness.
   (d) fatigue.

2. **Double Depression refers to**
   (a) having depression for twice as long as normal.
   (b) dysthymia developing into major depression.
   (c) two bipolar episodes back to back.
   (d) a unipolar episode followed by a bipolar episode.

3. **According to *DSM-IV-TR* dysthymia in children requires symptoms to be present for**
   (a) 2 months.
   (b) 2 years.
   (c) 1 month.
   (d) 1 year.

4. **Currently, it is believed that childhood depression is caused by _____ and adolescent depression is due to _____.**
   (a) situational influences, genetic influences
   (b) genetic influences, situation influences
   (c) situational influences, situation influences
   (d) genetic influences, genetic influences

5. **Although more _____ attempt suicide, more _____ are successful.**
   (a) males, females
   (b) females, males
   (c) children, adolescents
   (d) males, males

6. **Cognitive theorists attribute depression to the cognitive triad. Which of the following components is not part of the triad?**
   (a) Hopelessness
   (b) Helplessness
   (c) Uselessness
   (d) Worthlessness

7. **Cicchetti and Toth developed a model of depression based on the**
   - (a) cognitive attributions model.
   - (b) ecological transactional model.
   - (c) psychodynamic model.
   - (d) internalizing-externalizing model.

8. **Compared to adults, children with Bipolar Disorder tend to have cycles that are**
   - (a) longer and less intense.
   - (b) shorter and less intense.
   - (c) brief, intense, and rapid cycling.
   - (d) the same as adult Bipolar Disorder.

Answers: 1. b; 2. b; 3. d; 4. a; 5. b; 6. c; 7. b; 8. c

Seven

SOMATOFORM DISORDERS

I t is not uncommon for children to complain of aches and pains that do not have a medical basis. In fact, functional somatic complaints, with medically unexplained symptoms, account for approximately 20% of child visits to pediatric clinics (Robinson, Greene, & Walker, 1988). Whereas children and youth with serious physical illness often demonstrate a progressive decline in school performance, health, and physical well-being, children who are somatizers often have a more rapid onset, tend to have families with similar symptom presentations, and have no physical basis for the somatic complaints.

In their investigation of child and youth somatization, Garber and colleagues (1991) collected responses to the Children's Somatization Inventory (CSI) from 540 school-aged children and adolescents in Tennessee. Responses indicated that 50% of children and youth surveyed reported at least one somatic complaint, 15% reported four or more symptoms, and 1% had 12 or more symptoms. There was increased reporting of multiple symptoms with increasing age. In this survey, approximately 11% of adolescent boys and 15% of adolescent girls reported multiple somatic complaints.

The Somatoform Disorders collectively represent physical and somatic complaints that *do not* have a medical or organic basis. In individuals with somatoform disorders, emotional distress is experienced as physical or somatic discomfort and pain. Most often, a relationship can be established between the onset of the somatic complaint and the introduction of a psychosocial stressor. Indi-

CAUTION

Although the majority of somatic complaints precipitated by environmental stressors are transient and usually dissipate as the stress subsides, for some children somatization can become a recurrent and debilitating condition that may eventually manifest as a Somatization Disorder. In children with a Somatization Disorder, somatic symptoms become the focal point and often interfere with relationships (at home and school) and academic performance.

viduals with these disorders do not pretend to be ill or fake illness (as in Factitious Disorder or Malingering) but genuinely believe that they are ill. The physical or somatic complaints cause significant distress and interfere with daily functioning. The pain and distress that individuals with somatoform disorders feel is not under their voluntary control, and responses occur at a subconscious level. Often these individuals seek medical assistance due to the somatic nature of their complaints. There are six different subtypes of disorders subsumed under the Somatoform Disorders category. The Somatoform Disorders are summarized in Rapid Reference 7.1.

≡Rapid Reference 7.1

Somatoform Disorders Listed in the *DSM-IV-TR*

Hysterical Disorders	Actual loss or change in physical functioning
• Somatization Disorder	Long-standing and recurring; pattern of multiple somatic complaints that refer to at least four different anatomical sites (head, back, joints, stomach, chest, etc.) and are manifested in eight different pain symptoms, involving gastrointestinal, sexual, and pseudoneurological sites.
• Undifferentiated Somatization Disorder	One or more physical complaints (fatigue, loss of appetite, gastrointestinal problems, etc.) that endure for at least 6 months, are without medical cause, and cause significant distress and impaired functioning.
• Conversion Disorder	Loss of function (motor or sensory) without medical basis. Criteria state that a psychosocial stressor or psychological factor must be linked to the disorder onset.
• Pain Disorder	Significant pain in the absence of medical reasons.

Preoccupation Disorders	Excessive concern about physical status or well-being
• Hypochondriasis	Preoccupation with the belief that one has a serious disease.
• Body Dysmorphic Disorder	Preoccupation with an imagined or exaggerated defect in physical appearance.

SOMATIZATION AND DEVELOPMENTAL ISSUES

In a study of the use of health care service by children and youth, Schor (1986) found that children's responsiveness to stressful life events peaked at two transition periods: transition to elementary school and entry into junior high school. Furthermore, physical complaints resulted in an increased use of health care services during these times to investigate the nature and causes of somatic complaints. Studies have demonstrated that stress can impact on emotional well-being in children, resulting in numerous somatic complaints (Garber et al., 1991).

Somatic complaints have also been associated with depression and anxiety in children and youth; however, since many of the measurements developed to assess anxiety and depression also include items with somatic content (headaches, stomachaches, nausea, etc.), the nature of the association is not clear. The situation is further complicated by the fact that depression in young children is more likely to be precipitated by stressful environmental determinants than genetic factors (Thapar et al., 1998). Somatic complaints (not feeling well, headaches, stomachaches) can be the presenting symptoms or comorbid symptoms of depression and anxiety in children.

The *DSM-IV-TR* category of Somatoform Disorders is characterized by disorders that have physical or somatic symptoms without any known medical, organic, or neurological basis. Symptoms are often precipitated by environmental stressors. Children undergoing stressful situations report higher rates of somatic symptoms than children who are not experiencing stressful circumstances (Campo & Fritsch, 1994).

Garber and colleagues (1991) found a number of common somatic complaints in their pediatric population, including headaches, fatigue, sore muscles, abdominal and back pain, and blurred vision. The most frequently reported symptoms were headaches, low energy, sore muscles, nausea or stomach upset, and back and stomach pain. Children who were high somatizers (i.e., who responded with the most symptoms) tended to endorse the following somatic categories: headaches (25%), low energy (21%), sore muscles (21%), and abdominal discomfort (17%). Factor analysis of the CSI responses revealed a four-factor solution: pseudoneurologic, cardiovascular, gastrointestinal, and pain/weakness.

A review of studies on pain symp-

DON'T FORGET

The association between symptoms of anxiety, depression, and somatic complaints has been well established in the literature, as symptoms from these syndromes all cluster under the dimension of internalizing problems (Achenbach & Rescorla, 2001).

toms in children reveals a developmental course that can predict the nature of children's somatic complaints. Initially, children present with a *predominant symptom* (rather than multiple symptoms). The most commonly reported somatic complaints in prepubertal children are headaches and abdominal pain (Garber et al., 1991).

Studies have also demonstrated a continuity between these unexplained symptoms in childhood and symptoms experienced in adulthood (Hotopf, 2002). Later-occurring symptoms (adolescence) include pain in the extremities, muscle aches, fatigue, and neurological symptoms (Walker, Garber, & Greene, 1991).

Although children often translate symptoms of stress into physical complaints, it is important to differentiate between feigning illness to avoid a laborious task (homework, school tests), and symptoms of "true" somatization. If a child is intentionally producing symptoms of illness to assume a "sick role" then the disorder is more appropriately categorized as a *Factitious Disorder*. If illness is feigned to avoid a task, the label is more appropriately *Malingering*. Individuals with Factitious Disorder often are reinforced by unconscious secondary gain; that is, attention provided because they appear ill. However, Malingering is motivated by primary gain: There is an ulterior motive to appearing ill.

> ### DON'T FORGET
> Developmentally, abdominal pain seems to precede complaints of headaches. Studies have found that recurrent abdominal pain (RAP) is frequently related to emotional symptoms in children and their parents (Garber, Zeman, & Walker, 1990).

> ### DON'T FORGET
> Developmentally, young children usually present with one symptom (*monosymptomatic*) and with increasing age report multiple symptoms (*polysymptomatic*).

> ### CAUTION
> The difference between Factitious Disorder and Malingering is one of motivation. Although both conditions involve an intention to appear ill, in Factitious Disorder the intent is to assume a sick role, with no primary gain. In Malingering, on the other hand, although illness may also be feigned, the motivation would be for primary gain.

SOMATIZATION DISORDER

Clinical and Associated Developmental Features

Despite the fact that children commonly respond to psychosocial stressors with reported physical and somatic complaints, a diagnosis of Somatization Disorder in children is rare. The *DSM-IV-TR* criteria for Somatization Disorder were developed for adult populations. In addition to onset prior to age 30 and a history of several years' duration, eight symptoms are required:

- Pain related to at least four different areas (head, abdomen, back, etc.) or functions (menstruation, sexual activity, urination)
- Two gastrointestinal symptoms (e.g., nausea, vomiting, food intolerance, diarrhea)
- One sexual symptom
- One pseudoneurological symptom (double vision, amnesia, fainting, problems swallowing, paralysis, conversion symptoms, balance problems)

Somatization Disorder, a hysterical pattern of multiple symptoms without medical cause, was initially called *Briquet's syndrome.* The disorder is relatively rare, with as high as 2% of women and less than 0.2% of men having the disorder (*DSM-IV-TR*). In reviewing the symptoms for Somatization Disorder, it is not difficult to see how a diagnosis would be rare in childhood, especially if no modifications were made to the criteria. Reviewing the literature concerning the nature and

DON'T FORGET

The symptoms of Somatization Disorder must have no medical basis, or if there is a medical problem, symptoms must be in excess of that which would be expected.

Putting It Into Practice

Sara was very difficult to manage at home. In fact, Sara was so demanding that her mother, Grace, sent Sara to live with grandparents in New York when Grace returned to Georgia with her new husband. Sara missed a lot of school because of illness, which never could be diagnosed (headaches, stomachaches, body aches, and fatigue). Her grandparents ultimately could not handle the constant doctor appointments and medical bills, and eventually they returned Sara to her mother. Despite being very bright and an A student until middle school, Sara had spent the last 2 years in Special Education programs because she was too emotionally distracted and had missed too much school. Diagnosed with anxiety and depression, Sara was on a number of different medications. The school was calling Grace on a daily basis, saying that Sara was falling asleep in class and complaining of fatigue, headaches, and stomach problems. Sara spent most afternoons sleeping in the nurse's office because she was "too tired" to lift her head. Despite numerous trips to the doctor and numerous medical tests, the doctors could find no physical cause for Sara's somatic complaints.

history of somatic complaints in children, Fritz, Fritsch, and Hagino (1997) suggest that the rarity of diagnosis of the disorder in children and youth most likely reflects the "developmentally inappropriate" nature of the criteria rather than the disorder's having an adult onset. Support for this suggestion can be found in reports of adult patients who have severe Somatoform Disorder. Often these patients disclose a history of illness reverting back to childhood onset (Hotopf, 2002).

Prevalence and Course

Given the difficulties associated with diagnostic criteria, little is known about the prevalence rates for the disorder in childhood and adolescence (Fritz et al., 1997). However, in their study of somatization complaints, Offord and colleagues (1987) found that between 11% of females and 4% of males (12 to 16 years) were identified as having recurrent and distressing somatic complaints. Available data concerning adolescent populations suggest that symptoms associated with Somatization Disorder, such as headaches, stomachache, dizziness, and pain, are a relatively frequent occurrence (Taylor, Szatmari, Boyle, & Offord, 1996). In their study of 1,035 adolescents (12 to 17 years of age) residing in Bremen, Germany, Essau and colleagues (2000) found that 11% of their sample reported criteria that matched Undifferentiated Somatoform Disorder.

In their study, Essau and colleagues found that at least two thirds of their sample reported having one symptom, which lasted for 6 months. The most commonly reported symptoms were headaches (15.5%), lump in the throat (14.4%), and abdominal pain (12.4%). They also found gender differences, which supported other findings. Boys report more headaches at a younger age, while girls report more headaches as teens (Abu-Arefeh & Russell, 1994). The disorder seems to have a familial and gender course, with up to 10–20% of females developing the disorder in families in which a close relative also had the disorder (*DSM-IV-TR*). Females tend to endorse more somatic complaints than males (Garber et al., 1991).

Comorbidity

Females with Somatization Disorder also tend to have either anxiety or depression, while males with the disorder are also at risk for Substance Use

DON'T FORGET

Undifferentiated Somatoform Disorder requires only one major symptom, without medical cause, for at least 6 months' duration, and causing serious distress.

Disorders (Essau et al., 1999). There are high rates of association between reporting somatic complaints, anxiety, and depression. It has been suggested that Somatization Disorder, in its pervasiveness, endurance, and persistent course, may align more closely with Axis II personality disorders (lifelong disorders) than with Axis I disorders.

Etiology

Studies have investigated several risk factors for Somatization Disorder, including parental divorce (Zoccolillo & Cloniger, 1985), parent illness (Hotopf, 2002), and child sexual abuse (Kinzl, Trawegert & Biebl, 1995). Children can respond to stress in various ways based on their temperament and the extent and nature of family support systems. Often children convert stress into physical symptoms. Some precipitating situations that can be particularly stressful in childhood include transitions to new school programs, parent divorce, a relocation or move, and being overwhelmed academically. Somatization can become a child's way of attempting to cope with life's stresses, which can have maladaptive consequences.

Biological and Genetic Factors

Wender and Klein (1981) found that higher risk for Somatization Disorder occurred in families with Antisocial Personality Disorder, ADHD, alcoholism and Somatization Disorder. Twin studies have been inconclusive. Studies of temperament have increased our understanding of how inhibited (shy or wary) children may be less able to cope with severe environmental demands. These children may be more sensitive emotionally and prone to internalizing disorders due to their low threshold for uncertainty and their poor coping mechanisms.

Psychodynamic Perspective

Psychodynamic theorists discuss hysteria in terms of primary and secondary gain. In psychodynamic terms, somatic complaints can represent unconscious conflicts, so that physical pain represents psychic pain. Being unable to deal with someone who is a pain in the neck might literally translate into neck stiffness, while being sick to the stomach might reflect being unable to stomach a situation any longer. Primary and secondary gain can be explained in the following way. At a primary level, hysterical or physical symptoms keep conflicts out of conscious awareness. The person is able to focus on the physical problem rather than the psychic pain. On a secondary level, the debilitation caused by the physical problem usually removes the person from the responsibility of having to confront a distasteful task.

Behavioral Perspective

A behavioral explanation for the development of a Somatoform Disorder would be linked to reinforcements received for being ill and/or learned behaviors through modeling a family member who was also chronically ill. Some of the secondary gains for being ill might be increased attention and reduced expectations.

Cognitive Perspective

The cognitive perspective would explore how maladaptive thoughts might translate into physical symptoms. Clinical practice suggests that children often express their desire for attention by communicating with parents through physical symptoms.

Family and Parenting

Having a parent who has a chronic physical illness may predispose children to somatization disorder later in

---

CAUTION

Out of psychic awareness, out of mind. A supervisor who did not want to fire his best friend had developed a paralysis in the hand when he awoke the next morning. As a result, he was unable to sign the termination papers (Conversion Disorder).

Putting It Into Practice

Wanda is having a great afternoon chatting with an old college roommate who she hasn't seen for years. The conversation has gone on for quite some time, and 5-year-old Amy, Wanda's daughter, has had enough of this boring afternoon tea party. After several unsuccessful attempts to get her mother's attention, Amy does the inevitable. She complains to her mother that she is "not feeling well." Her stomach hurts, she says, and asks if they can please go home now.

---

life (Garber et al., 1990; Hotopf, 2002). Furthermore, family systems theory might predict that having a child with an apparent illness could help deflect family focus from other family problems. Within this framework, family members can redefine their roles to focus on the sick child while averting emphasis from other potentially conflicted areas of family or marital life. Children who somaticize often have families that also share anxious and depressive features (Garber et al.).

Culture

According to the *DSM-IV-TR* adult populations worldwide reveal many differences in the types and rates of somatic symptoms. The *DSM-IV-TR* mentions symptoms specific to Africa and South Asia, including burning sensations in the hands and feet and the sensation of "worms crawling in the head or ants crawling under the skin" (p. 487). Although research is definitely lacking concerning child and adolescent cross-cultural comparisons, with children cultural differences have been reported in the rates (but not necessarily types) of somatic complaints

(Bird, 1996). One cross-cultural study revealed that Russian children had higher scores on the Somatic Complaint scale of the Achenbach Child Behavior Checklist than American children (Carter, Grigorenko, & Pauls, 1995). However, regardless of differential rates of reporting across cultures, several studies have reported that strong associations between somatic complaints and symptoms of anxiety and depression are universal (Carter et al., 1995; Garber et al., 1991).

CONVERSION DISORDER

Clinical and Associated Developmental Features

Of all the Somatoform Disorders, Conversion Disorder is the most frequently and commonly researched area in children (Regan & Regan, 1989). Conversion Disorder was initially called *Hysterical Neurosis (Conversion Type)* in the second revision of the *DSM* (APA, 1968) and is referred to as Dissociative (Conversion) Disorder in the tenth revision of the *International Classification of Diseases (ICD-10,* 1992). Conversion Disorder is a condition that consists of a single somatic symptom that impacts on normal motor or sensory function. Considered one of the hysterical Somatoform Disorders, it occurs when psychological conflicts manifest dramatically in physical symptoms that cause debilitating results but have no medical or organic basis. Symptoms suggest a medical or neurological basis (pseudoneurological), but upon investigation results are negative. Although the Somatoform Disorders as a category represent physical symptoms that are precipitated by psychosocial stressors, criteria for Conversion Disorder (*DSM-IV-TR*) require that the associated stressor be determined (e.g., family conflict, marital discord, trauma, etc.). The disorder may appear immediately after the stressful event or after a delay.

CAUTION

Although the individual may claim paralysis, as in hand paralysis (glove anesthesia) or foot paralysis (foot anesthesia), symptoms will not follow the normal neurological pathway (e.g., paralysis will stop at the wrist or ankle, which is anatomically impossible). Conversion symptoms are also inconsistent, with the patient being able to move the purportedly paralyzed limb if distracted.

The symptom or deficit is not intentionally produced but is induced by stressors or psychosocial conflicts that can initiate and exacerbate the condition. Some of the manifestations of the disorder include problems with balance or localized weakness, paralysis, difficulty swallowing (lump in the throat), loss of sensitivity (touch), double vision, blindness or deafness, convulsions (seizures), and hallucinations.

The *DSM-IV-TR* also suggests several associated features that represent extreme variations of an individual's reaction to the loss of function ranging from *la belle indifference* (lack of concern about the symptoms) to displaying symptoms in a dramatic or histrionic manner. The *DSM-IV-TR* suggests that in children under 10 years of age, conversion symptoms are most likely to be expressed as seizures or problems of gait. Symptoms that have been reported more frequently by children and adolescents include pseudoseizures, disturbances of gait, and paralysis (Leslie, 1988).

Prevalence, Comorbidity, and Course

Conversion Disorder is rarely diagnosed prior to 10 years of age and is generally diagnosed in late childhood to early adulthood (*DSM-IV-TR*). In children and youth the disorder may peak in the middle school years. One common preschool-aged phenomenon is a tendency for young children to develop a pseudoparesis or limp after a minor injury. The limp may last for a few hours or continue for days (Fritz et al., 1997). The most likely explanation for prolonging this behavior seems to be the attention received as secondary gain. The most common form of Conversion Disorder is pseudoseizures, which represent between 15% and 50% of all Conversion Disorders (Fritz et al.). Although pseudoseizures look very much like real seizures, electro-encephalograms (EEGs) reveal no actual seizure activity.

Etiology

Based on limited data, research seems to indicate that risk for Conversion Disorder might be familial; however, support has been limited to monozygotic but not dizygotic twins (*DSM-IV-TR*). Although there is limited support for genetic transmission, environmental risk factors, such as family factors, have been implicated in contributing to how the disorder is expressed and maintained.

Risks and Protective Factors

Stressors

Although it would be assumed that the vast majority of children with Conversion Disorder have experi-

DON'T FORGET

Diagnostic criteria stipulate the necessity of identifying the precipitating stressor (*DSM-IV-TR*); therefore, investigations of possible etiological factors have focused on the types of stressors and conditions that might place children at greater risk for Conversion Disorders.

> **DON'T FORGET**
> ....
> Families of children with Conversion Disorders often share many of the same characteristics: preoccupation with illness, communication focused on disease and loss, and hyperawareness of and sensitivity to bodily functions or dysfunction.

enced stressful circumstances, Siegel and Barthel (1986) found that as many as 90% of children with Conversion Disorder had encountered a recent and significant stressor at home or school. Some of the most common stressors identified are peer relationship difficulties, family discord or marital problems, academic difficulties, and economic hardship or unemployment in the family (Lehmkuhl, Blanz, Lehmkuhl, & Braun-Scharm, 1989).

Family Characteristics

Studies have shown that children whose family members have a chronic illness are more likely to model similar symptoms themselves (Siegel & Barthel, 1986). Selter (1985) outlines several possible family types as determined by their response to having a child with Conversion Disorder: anxious families (preoccupied with illness), chaotic families (in which somatization is a source of nurturance and attention), and compensating families, who, according to the family systems model, use the sick child to deflect family problems.

Previous Illness

Investigators report that Conversion Disorder develops in some children following a legitimate illness. Fritz and colleagues (1997) report that between 10% and 60% of children who have a Conversion Disorder had a previous illness.

PAIN DISORDER

Clinical and Associated Developmental Features

Pain Disorder is marked by a clinically significant level of pain that causes distress and a functional impairment. The disorder is thought to be precipitated by psychosocial factors, and the pain is not due to Malingering. Pain is a difficult condition to measure due to its subjective nature. In children, the situation of measurement becomes even more complex because of limitations in the use of self-report at younger ages. Although very young children can demonstrate awareness of pain or hurting initially in themselves and eventually in others, it is not until school age that children can articulate the intensity (level) of pain and associated feelings.

Recurrent Abdominal Pain

Recurrent Abdominal Pain (RAP) is clinically defined as having three or more episodes of reported pain over a 3-month period, with the pain being severe enough to interfere with normal functioning. Although the etiology is unknown, medical review often is unable to determine an organic cause for the pain in the majority of RAP cases.

In pediatric populations, RAP is a high-incidence and potentially seriously disabling condition. Garber and colleagues (1991) found that between 10% and 30% of children and adolescents present with RAP. Studies have also suggested that RAP can be a durable and long-term condition. Children who reported RAP at 4 years of age were likely to continue patterns and 3 times more likely than their peers to demonstrate RAP 6 years later (Borge, Nordhagen, Botten, & Bakketeig, 1994).

HYPOCHONDRIASIS

Clinical and Associated Developmental Features

Individuals who suffer from Hypochondriasis believe, erroneously, that they have a serious medical illness. Lacking physical evidence to substantiate the multiple symptoms that they present, these individuals will often engage in so-called doctor shopping, seeking out someone to support their claims. The belief that they are seriously ill is not within their control, nor are they malingering.

DON'T FORGET

The measurement and monitoring of intensity of pain can be accomplished successfully in children as young as 5 years of age by having children select intensity levels using graduated scaling techniques presented in graphic form: for example, a series of facial expressions, or rising thermometer (Biere, Reeve, Champion, & Addicoat, 1990).

CAUTION

There has been some speculation that children with RAP may have heightened somatic awareness, or hypersensitivity. Absenteeism is high in children and adolescents with RAP and has been reported to be as high as 10% of the academic year (Liebman, 1978).

DON'T FORGET

Similar to results of investigations of other Somatoform Disorders, family factors seem to play key a role in the presence of RAP in children. Investigators have found increased rates of depression and anxiety in children with RAP and in their mothers (Garber et al., 1990). Walker, Garber, and Greene (1993) found that, compared to controls, child characteristics for RAP included significantly more emotional and somatic complaints, while family characteristics included increased emphasis on family illness.

BODY DYSMORPHIC DISORDER

Clinical and Associated Developmental Features

Body Dysmorphic Disorder is one of the preoccupation Somatoform Disorders and occurs when an individual dwells on an imagined imperfection or defect to the extent that it causes significant clinical distress and interferes with normal functioning (*DSM-IV-TR*). Although retrospective clinical interviews suggest that the disorder onset is in adolescence, there is a lack of empirical research to confirm this hypothesis. However, clinical insight would suggest that adolescence, with its natural preoccupation with personal appearance and fitting in with peer groups, might be a logical time for the onset of this disorder.

> ### CAUTION
>
> The preoccupation and obsession with their pseudo-serious medical disease may have the same underlying dynamics as the symptoms of individuals with OCD. The comorbidity between these two disorders has been rated as high as 8% (Barsky, 1992). However, while people with OCD are often painfully aware of the unreasonableness of their obsessions and compulsions, individuals with Hypochondriasis truly are convinced that they are seriously ill.

> ### DON'T FORGET
>
> Elkind and Bowen (1979) described two common adolescent preoccupations: *imaginary fable* (thoughts about one's own uniqueness) and *imaginary audience* (preoccupation with being the center of scrutiny and others' observations).

The etiology of Body Dysmorphic Disorder is still unknown. However, links have been made to OCD due to some similarities in serotonin malfunction and thought preoccupation (Phillips, 1996).

ASSESSMENT AND TREATMENT OF SOMATOFORM DISORDERS

Due to the nature of the Somatoform Disorders, assessment will often require considerable medical input to rule out organic causes. In addition, because somatizers believe the pain is related to medical reasons, they may not be willing or able to understand the need for therapeutic intervention. Due to high rates of comorbidity among the child and adolescent disorders, and because investigations have reported comorbid associations between somatizing and depression, anxiety, and OCD, differential diagnosis should be undertaken whenever Somatoform Disorders are suspected.

Assessment

Very little has been documented regarding assessment and intervention of Somatoform Disorders in children and adolescents. Clinical experience would suggest the use of the structured and semistructured interviews as a start. Also, a number of rating scales and personality inventories include a somatic scale as a component. A list of these instruments can be found in Rapid Reference 7.2.

Treatment

In the absence of empirically based findings regarding treatment for somatoform disorders in children and adolescents, once again clinical experience would suggest the use of behavioral or cognitive behavioral methods that integrate components of systematic desensitization and educational awareness of the disorder. At least one study has reported success for a cognitive behavioral program combined with an SSRI regime for the treatment of adolescents with Body Dysmorphic Disorder (Albertini, Phillips, & Guevremont, 1996).

≋ Rapid Reference 7.2

Some Common Instruments That Contain Scales That Measure Somatic Complaints.

Instrument	Ages	Scale
Personality Inventory for Youth (PIY; Lachar & Gruber, 1995)	7 to 17	The PIY Somatic Concerns scale has three subscales: Psychosomatic Syndrome, Muscular Tension and Anxiety, and Preoccupation with Disease.
ASEBA (Achenbach & Rescorla, 2001)	6 to 18	The Somatic Complaints syndrome scale and the Somatic Problems (*DSM*-oriented scales) are available on all three versions of the ASEBA (parent, teacher, and self-report).
CPRS-R:L (Conners, 1998)	3 to 17	Parent rating scale contains a Psychosomatic subscale.
BASC (Reynolds & Kamphaus, 1992)	3 to 17	All three versions of the BASC (parent, teacher, self-report) contain a Somatization scale.

Note. References for all instruments can be found in Appendix B.

🪶 TEST YOURSELF 🪶

1. **Diagnosis of Somatization Disorder is rare in childhood because**
   (a) children do not experience somatic symptoms.
   (b) children cannot articulate their somatic symptoms.
   (c) children do not recognize somatic concerns at a conscious level.
   (d) current *DSM-IV-TR* criteria are developmentally inappropriate.

2. **Somatization Disorder was originally called**
   (a) hysteria nervosa.
   (b) St. Vitus' dance.
   (c) Briquet's syndrome.
   (d) Pseudopsychoillness.

3. **Which of the following is true regarding somatization disorder (SD)?**
   (a) Males with SD are at greater risk for substance abuse.
   (b) Females with SD report greater memory problems.
   (c) SD is linked to anxiety but not depression.
   (d) Family links to SD have not been investigated or substantiated.

4. **According to the *DSM-IV-TR*, the difference between Somatization Disorder and Undifferentiated Somatoform Disorder is that Undifferentiated Somatoform Disorder requires**
   (a) half as many symptoms.
   (b) only five generalized symptoms.
   (c) only one physical complaint for at least 6 months.
   (d) only one physical complaint for at least 1 year.

5. **Somatic symptoms in children and adolescents differ. Which of the following statements is true?**
   (a) Younger children present with multiple symptoms, while adolescents present with one primary symptom.
   (b) Teens usually have fewer somatic complaints than younger children.
   (c) The most commonly reported symptoms in younger children are headaches and stomach pain.
   (d) Recurrent abdominal pain (RAP) in children has no relationship to parent or family medical symptoms.

6. **Intentionally producing symptoms of illness in order to gain secondary rewards, such as increased attention, would be referred to as**
   (a) Malingering.
   (b) Factitious Disorder.
   (c) Conversion Disorder.
   (d) illness by proxy.

7. John is planning to run in a marathon when he discovers that one of the competitors is a former lover, whom he cannot face or run against. When he wakes up on the morning of the race he cannot move his foot below the ankle. John would likely be diagnosed with

(a) neurasthenia.

(b) pseudopedia.

(c) Conversion Disorder.

(d) Body Dysmorphic Disorder.

8. At 20 years of age, Rory is convinced that his nose is gigantic. The problem has escalated since adolescence. Rory refuses to go out in public and cannot even face himself in the mirror. Like Pinocchio, every day he feels his nose is growing to larger proportions. He recently quit his day job as a bank teller to work as an all-night disc jockey at a radio station so that he will not have to expose his gigantic profile. It is likely that Rory is suffering from

(a) Conversion Disorder.

(b) Pain Disorder.

(c) Body Dysmorphic Disorder.

(d) imaginary audience.

Answers: 1. d; 2. c; 3. a; 4. c; 5. c; 6. b; 7. c; 8. c

Eight

PROBLEMS OF CONDUCT

While internalizing disorders are often difficult to diagnose and assess due to their covert and internal nature, externalizing problems are often intrusive, disruptive, and frequently involve aggressive responses that can be physically and verbally intimidating. By the time that parents or teachers appeal for help from professionals in managing these very difficult behaviors, the situation is often one in which the child is *out of control . . . and in control.*

Longitudinal studies (Tremblay et al., 1999) have demonstrated that, normally, overt acts of aggression peak in the second year and diminish with age as children become more socialized. However, not all children follow this preferred developmental path. For some children, overt aggression is a stable pattern of behavior lasting from middle school well into adolescence. This pattern or developmental trajectory of increased aggressive responses seems particularly durable for early starters (Aguilar, Sroufe, Egeland, & Carlson, 2000). In the first three years of development, Aguilar and colleagues found that the following family characteristics placed children at the greatest risk for developing disruptive behavior disorders: avoidant attachment, caregiver depression, stress, low SES, caregiver sensitivity, and quality of caregiving.

THE DISRUPTIVE BEHAVIOR DISORDERS

The *DSM-IV-TR* lists two Disruptive Behavior Disorders under the category of Disorders Usually First Diagnosed in Infancy, Childhood, or Adolescence: Oppositional Defiant Disorder (ODD) and Conduct Disorder (CD). In addition to sharing aggressive features, both disorders have been classified as externalizing disorders in factor analytic studies based on clusters of specific behavioral symptoms (ASEBA; Achenbach & Rescola, 2001).

Oppositional Defiant Disorder and Conduct Disorder: Two Unique Disorders or One?

Initially there was much debate regarding whether ODD and CD represented a continuum of severity, with ODD being a milder form or precursor to CD. More recently, several arguments have been raised in support of retaining the two disorders as distinct. One reason is that age of onset for ODD (typically 4- to 8-year range) is earlier than for CD (childhood onset, one symptom prior to age 10; adolescent onset, no conduct problem prior to age 10). Another reason is that 75% of children with ODD do not develop CD. Although ODD and CD share aggressive features, studies have revealed that these two disorders present with qualitatively distinct forms of aggressive behavior.

In their meta-analysis of 60 factor analytic studies, Frick and colleagues (1993) identified four quadrants of behaviors aligned along two dimensions: overt versus covert behaviors and destructive versus nondestructive behaviors. The four resulting behavior subtypes can be viewed in Rapid Reference 8.1.

The study was important because it revealed that items that distinguished between ODD and CD clustered along overt (ODD: aggressive and oppositional) versus covert (CD: status and property violations) dimensions.

Putting It Into Practice

David has always been difficult to manage. From the earliest of times, David would rather take the path of most resistance. Before he could even talk, David would just stubbornly sit on the ground, rather than follow his mother's lead. With the advent of language, David evolved from "No, I won't" into a pattern of constant arguing, and defending himself. However, despite his great vocabulary, compliance was not a word that David ever learned. Every request resulted in a losing battle for his mother, and every battle ended in a war of the wills.

DON'T FORGET

Arguments in favor of retaining separate categories for ODD and CD include age of onset (ODD earlier than CD); discontinuity rather than continuity (majority of children with ODD do not develop CD); and qualitatively distinct forms of aggressive behavior (ODD aggressive/nondestructive; CD destructive and rule violations).

DON'T FORGET

The behavioral items in the study by Frick and colleagues (1993) map on to the two syndromes that make up the Externalizing scale on the Achenbach scales (Achenbach, 1991): Aggressive scale behaviors fitting best with ODD and the Delinquent scale fitting behaviors of CD.

≡ *Rapid Reference 8.1*

Four Quadrants of Aggressive Behaviors

Conduct Disorder	Oppositional Defiant Disorder
Covert Nondestructive Status violations: Truancy, running away, rule violations, swearing	**Overt Nondestructive** Oppositional: Touchy, stubborn, argumentative, defiant, annoying
Covert Destructive Property violations: Vandalism, theft, fire setting	**Overt Destructive** Aggression: Bullies, fights, blames others, is cruel or spiteful

Source: Frick et al., 1993.

OPPOSITIONAL DEFIANT DISORDER (ODD)

Clinical Description and Associated Features

The cardinal feature of ODD is a "persistent, hostile, defiant, disobedient and negative pattern of behaviors directed towards authority figures" (APA, 2000). Given this constellation of behaviors, it is not surprising that children with ODD create significant stress in any environment where compliance and rule-governed behavior are expected. The oppositional behavior pattern is persistent, relentless, and durable (must be evident for at least 6 months). Children with ODD display a number of behavioral symptoms that make them extremely difficult to manage because of their confrontational nature. A diagnosis of ODD (APA, 2000) requires four of the following eight symptoms, occurring on a frequent basis (often):

- Loss of temper
- Argumentative with adults/confrontational
- Defiant/refuses to comply with requests
- Deliberately annoying
- Blames others for mistakes or problems
- Touchy and easily irritated
- Angry and resentful
- Spiteful and vindictive

The behaviors must occur more frequently and in excess of what would be expected given the child's age and developmental level. As would be anticipated, given the types of behaviors demonstrated and the frequency and intensity with which they are expressed, significant impairment would be expected at home (family relationships), school (social and academic) and employment (part-time work, etc.).

In the initial case study, David demonstrates many of the clinical and associated features of ODD. Children with ODD are often stubborn and noncompliant. They can be very contrary and argumentative with others; however, they are quick to shift the blame to other people, defending their actions as necessary given others' unreasonable demands. These children may also appear to be passively aggressive, as they systematically ignore repeated requests to follow directions. They will not compromise, refusing to bend even a little, and often adhere stubbornly to a refusal to negotiate.

Oppositional Defiant Disorder behaviors initiate in the home and often carry over to familiar adults with whom they will push the boundaries and test the limits. These children may deliberately annoy others, especially well-known peers and siblings, who may also be a constant source for intimidation and verbal aggression.

Children with ODD may present with either a low self-concept or a

DON'T FORGET

A diagnosis of ODD must occur before age 18, and symptoms must not be better accounted for by either Conduct Disorder or Antisocial Personality Disorder. In other words, the clinician is required to make a *differential diagnosis* between ODD and CD. Because CD is the more severe disorder, it would take precedence over ODD in the pecking order in making a differential diagnosis if symptoms met criteria for CD.

CAUTION

It is always important to consider the influence of age and developmental stage when making a diagnosis. Remember that oppositional behavior is normal at some stages of development. Therefore, transient oppositional behavior often demonstrated by toddlers and teenagers (the two terrible Ts) would not warrant a diagnosis of ODD unless the intensity and duration were atypical (APA, 2000).

CAUTION

ODD behaviors may not be evident in the school or community and are not likely to be evident in the clinical interview. These children seem to be most comfortable with pushing the boundaries in *familiar territory*. ODD behaviors may extend into the school situation if they are very ingrained or automatic and if reinforced by teachers or peers.

sense of inflated self-esteem. Often, like David, children with ODD will engage parents in battles that escalate into a high level of emotional turmoil on both sides. Parents often ultimately employ a coercive and negative parenting style in response to their children's aggressive and defiant behaviors. However, it has been well documented that these negative and coercive practices often serve to perpetuate the problem (Patterson et al., 1991).

Prevalence

Prevalence rates have been estimated between 2% to 16% of the population (APA, 2000). Prior to puberty, more males than females are diagnosed with ODD; however, the rates equalize in adolescence. High rates of comorbidity have been established for ODD with CD, learning disorders, and ADHD. Over 80% of children diagnosed with ODD have comorbid ADHD while 65% of children with ADHD will have ODD.

Developmental Course

Path analysis suggests a sequence of maladaptive behaviors that begins with ADHD, progresses to ODD, and ultimately culminates in CD (Loeber, Green, Lahey, Christ, & Frick, 1992). However, there is also evidence that discontinuity can exist (behaviors dissipate with age) in the milder forms of the maladaptive behaviors (Loeber & Stouthamer-Loeber, 1998).

CAUTION

Coercion theory (Patterson et al., 1991) would predict that parents who engage in highly charged hostile and negative interchanges with their children actually serve to escalate their child's aggressive and defiant behaviors. Patterns of hostile and negative interactions serve to actually reinforce and maintain increasing levels of aggressive and defiant behaviors.

DON'T FORGET

While ODD is associated with overt and nondestructive behaviors, CD is linked with covert behaviors that can be destructive and violate the rights of others.

CONDUCT PROBLEMS AND CONDUCT DISORDER (CD)

Literature often uses the term *conduct problems* (CP) to refer to behaviors associated with the more serious end of the disruptive behavior spectrum. The diagnostic category used by the *DSM-IV-TR* (APA, 2000) for the more severe disruptive behavior disorder is conduct disorder.

Clinical Description and Associated Features

According to the *DSM-IV-TR* (APA, 2000), the main clinical feature of CD is "a repetitive and persistent behavioral pattern" that involves the "violation of social norms or the rights of others."

Criteria for CD are based on symptoms that fall into four categories of aggressive behaviors and violations of rules and age-appropriate norms:

- Acts of aggression toward others and animals
  bullying, threatening
  initiating fights
  use of a weapon to cause harm
  cruelty to others
  cruelty to animals
  theft while confronting (e.g., mugging)
  forced sexual activity
- Destruction of property
  fire setting with intent to harm
  property destruction
- Deceit or theft
  committing break-ins (e.g., house, car)
  conning others
  theft (e.g., shoplifting, forgery)
- Rule violations
  staying out all night*
  running away
  frequently playing truant*

A diagnosis of CD requires at least 3 of the preceding 15 criteria. The criteria must be present for the past 12 months, with evidence of at least one symptom within the previous 6 months. If the youth is older than 18 years, then CD can only be diagnosed if Antisocial Personality Disorder is not the more appropriate diagnosis. For items with the asterisk, behaviors should have evidence of occurring prior to 13 years of age.

Youth with CD often initiate aggressive acts and will often engage in physical altercations or threaten, bully, and intimidate others. Often these youth can manipulate others through skillful ability to con others through lying, deceit, and a failure to follow through on promises and

DON'T FORGET

According to diagnostic criteria of the *DSM-IV-TR*, in order of severity, the most severe disorder takes precedence in diagnosis. From the least to most severe, the disorders are ODD, CD, and Antisocial Personality Disorder. However, Antisocial Personality Disorder cannot be given as a diagnosis to persons under 18 years of age.

obligations. Rule violations begin at an early age (prior to 13 years of age). Youth may run away from home (at least twice) for a lengthy duration.

Youth with CD may show little remorse or empathy and demonstrate minimal concern for the feelings and thoughts of others. Aggressive tendencies may be heightened in situations that are more ambiguous, as they may have a bias toward reading hostile intent into the motives of others and react accordingly.

Often youth with CD may feign feelings of guilt or remorse in order to avert a harsher punishment or to divert blame to their companions. Other associated features include engaging in high-risk behaviors, which may include increased risk of accidents, substance use or abuse, sexually transmitted diseases, and teen pregnancy (APA, 2000).

There are two subtypes of the disorder based on age of onset (childhood versus adolescence) as well as specifiers for the disorder severity (*mild:* few criteria and minor harm; *moderate;* and *severe:* many criteria causing significant harm to others).

DON'T FORGET

Social cognitive theorists suggest that aggressive acts in some children may be activated by a *hostile attribution bias:* a tendency to interpret ambiguous actions or expression as having a hostile intent and then responding to the perception of threat.

CAUTION

CD with *Childhood-Onset Type* applies if at least one criterion symptom was present prior to 10 years of age, while CD with *Adolescent-Onset Type* is used if no symptoms were evident prior to 10 years of age.

DON'T FORGET

In a factor analysis of criteria associated with ODD and CD, Frick and colleagues (1993) found four quadrants of potential responses based on overt/covert and destructive/nondestructive behaviors. A table of these behaviors can be seen in Rapid Reference 8.1.

More Data on Subtypes of CD

Using the clusters of overt/covert and destructive/nondestructive behaviors and information from their longitudinal study of problem behaviors in children and youth, Loeber and Keenan (1994) suggest a number of potential subtypes of CD:

- *Authority conflict pathway.* As with ODD, behaviors are defiant and involve rule violations. Defiance does not result in harm to others (e.g., truancy, running away).
- *Covert pathway.* Violations include rule violations (e.g., shoplifting, vandalism) but do not include acts of violence toward others.
- *Overt pathway.* Youth are aggressive at a young age and

continue to engage in more serious acts of aggression and violence toward others.

- *Dual overt/covert (combination of two previous pathways).* Youth engage in rule violations and aggressive acts.
- *Triple pathway.* Youth demonstrate behaviors from all three clusters.

Results of their study revealed the following outcomes: the triple-pathway youth had the worst overall future outcomes, while the dual overt/covert youth were most likely to engage in delinquent behaviors. For youth on the overt pathways, unless intervention was successful, aggression led to increasing violence, crimes, and increasingly poor adolescent outcomes. Those youth on an exclusive authority conflict pathway continued to engage in battles with authority figures; however, they had the best overall outcomes of all subtypes.

Prevalence

Prevalence rates for CD have been estimated to be between 1% and 10%. There are indications that the prevalence rate for CD has increased over the past (APA, 2000). Conduct disorder is one of the most frequent presenting concerns of youth who are referred to mental health settings. Males outnumber females; however, gender differences have been reported for different behavioral outcomes. Males tend to exhibit symptoms of vandalism, physical altercations, theft, and have more school discipline issues. Females with CD manifest symptoms in running away, substance use, truancy, and prostitution (APA, 2000).

Comorbidity

As with ODD, high rates of comorbidity exist for CD. Due to increasing age of the population, in addition to those areas of comorbidity already mentioned for ODD, youth with CD also have high comorbid associations with substance abuse and depression. Half of youth with CD have substance abuse problems (Reebye, Moretti, & Gulliver, 1995).

Developmental Course (Pathways and Progressions)

Within the realm of disruptive behavior disorders, CPs represent the most serious, complex, and problematic behaviors. Considerable research focus has been placed on the major pathways delineated by the onset of conduct problems: childhood onset, also called *early starters;* and adolescent onset, also referred to as *late starters.*

CAUTION

Aggregating youth with severe behavior problems into groups for treatment purposes can have adverse effects. It has also been noted that children on this developmental path tend to have poor social relationships and tend to gravitate toward other youth with similar developmental trajectories and engage in deviancy training among disordered peers (Dishion, Spracklen, Andrews, & Patterson, 1996).

Early-Onset Pathway: Early Starters

Longitudinal studies suggest that overt aggression should desist in a downward progression after the age of two. However, young children who evidence conduct problems at a very early age often persist and develop more serious conduct behaviors over time that generalize across situations, reaching further out into the community at large (Patterson & Yeorger, 2002).

Outcomes for children and youth in this category are poor, and ingrained behaviors can be highly resistant to intervention.

Late-Onset Pathway: Late Starters

There is less research information available about this subgroup, who seem to have less deviance and end up getting into trouble by association with the more deviant peer group, often due to inadequate parental monitoring (Patterson, Capaldi, & Bank, 1991). This group may be more resilient because they have developed more adequate coping skills (socially and behaviorally) at earlier levels.

THE CATEGORY OF DISRUPTIVE BEHAVIOR DISORDERS

As previously discussed, research supports the existence of ODD and CD as two unique disorders (Frick et al., 1993). However, as Disruptive Behavior Disorders, ODD and CD *share many common features,* such as defiance, aggression, and rule breaking behaviors, and have much in common regarding etiology, assessment, and treatment. Furthermore, although 75% of children with ODD will not be diagnosed with CD, 90% of youth with CD had an initial diagnosis of ODD (Rey, 1993). The following sections (etiology, assessment, and treatment) will be used to apply to both ODD and CD unless otherwise specified.

Etiology: Risk Factors and Protective Factors

Biological, Neurological, and Genetic Factors

Neurological investigations have found less frontal lobe activity in the brains of youth with CD (Moffit & Henry, 1989). Twin and adoption studies have also indicated that CD can be influenced by both genetic and environmental factors. Increased risk for Disruptive Behavior Disorders has been noted in families where the biological or adoptive parent has Antisocial Personality Disorder or when biological parents suffer from alcohol dependence, Mood Disorders, Schizophrenia, or a history of ADHD (APA, 2000).

Based on findings from studies conducted with adult populations, elevated levels of the hormone testosterone (Dabbs & Morris, 1990) may be implicated in the genetic transmission of aggressive impulses. In addition, low levels of DBH (which converts dopamine to noradrenaline) may produce higher thresholds for sensation-seeking behaviors in some children (Quay, 1986).

> ## DON'T FORGET
> Decreased activity in frontal lobe functioning has been associated with poor ability to inhibit behavioral responses and weaknesses in planning ability. This association may help explain why there are such high rates of comorbidity between ADHD and the Disruptive Behavior Disorders.

> ## DON'T FORGET
> Child noncompliance can be an effective means of avoidance or escape from doing undesirable tasks such as in requests to comply (e.g., picking up toys or cleaning a bedroom). Coercion theory would predict that in these situations, the parent will often respond with escalating and coercive responses (yelling, screaming, hitting) likely due to their occasional success.

Psychodynamic Theories

A *psychodynamically* oriented therapist might interpret aggressive and defiant behaviors as a manifestation of deep-seated feelings of lack of parental love, absence of empathy, and inability to trust (Gabbard, 1990).

Behavioral Theories

Within a behavioral framework, noncompliant and aggressive behaviors would develop in response to a prescribed set of learning principles. A clinician from a *behaviorist perspective* would attempt to isolate the factors in the environment responsible for reinforcing and sustaining the behavior. Within the family context, *coercion theory* (Patterson et al., 1991) might be used to explain how patterns of noncompliance and aggression have been sustained by the parents' repeated giving in to demands.

Cognitive Theories

Looking at hostile and aggressive behaviors from the vantage point of the *cognitive perspective*, emphasis would be placed on determining how maladaptive thoughts influence hostile and defiant behaviors. Studies by Dodge and colleagues (Dodge, 1991) have revealed that aggressive children often have a *hostile attribution bias* and misread ambivalent cues as being inherently hostile (e.g., a half smile is interpreted as a sneer) or rejecting. In these instances, children may respond in a hostile and defensive manner because they attribute hostile or rejection intentions to others.

Family Patterns, Attachment, and Parenting

A *family systems* clinician might focus on the parent-child relationship and childhood aggression may be interpreted as the child's attempt to shift the balance of power due to inconsistent, or extreme boundaries and or limit setting by parents. With respect to theories of attachment and parenting, research evidence has linked insecure attachment to aggressive preschool behaviors (Greenberg, 1999), while Baumrind (1991) would suggest that an *authoritarian parenting style* could set the stage for latent aggression giving way to expression in the adolescent years.

Assessment

In addition to the general structured and semi-structured interview schedules, the general behavioral rating scales discussed previously provide several scales devoted to conduct problems. The behavioral scales also provide information regarding possible comorbid relationships among the various behaviors sampled.

The following specific scales would be anticipated to have clinical or borderline clinical elevations for ODD and CD populations. On the ASEBA (Achenbach & Rescorla, 2001) children with ODD and CD will likely have elevated scores on the following syndrome scales: Social Problems, Rule-Breaking Behavior, Aggressive Behavior, Externalizing Problems, and Total Problems. The *DSM*-oriented scales of the ASEBA will likely show elevations on ODD and CD. Conner's parent and teacher scales (CPSR, CTSR, 1998) would have elevations on the Oppositional and Social Problem scales, while the Conners-Wells' Adolescent Self-Report Scale (CASS, 1997) would likely indicate Family Problems, Conduct Problems, and problems with Anger Control. On the Behavior Assessment System for Children (BASC; Reynolds & Kamphaus, 1992), the scales that would be elevated would likely include the Aggression, Conduct Problems, and Composite Externalizing Problems scales.

Treatment

Empirically Supported Treatments for Disruptive Behavior Disorders

One of the problems in finding evidence-based treatments specifically for ODD or CD has been that many findings are grouped under the broad category of Disruptive Behavior Disorders. Brestan and Eyberg (1998) reviewed and evaluated 82 studies involving more than 5,000 youth (with Disruptive Behavior Disorders: ODD and/or CD) according to criteria established by the APA Task Force of the American Psychiatric Association (1995) on evidence-based treatments. The authors found that the majority of programs reviewed were based on cognitive behavioral methods, with or without a parent component. The authors found two parent training programs that met the higher criteria: a parent training program developed to reduce behavior problems in young children (Webster-Stratton, 1984) and a behavioral parent training program based on a manual called *Living with Children: New Methods for Parents and Teachers* produced by Patterson and Gullion (1968). The manual provides lesson plans for parents directed toward improving skills in areas of prioritizing and targeting behaviors for intervention and developing reinforcement programs to reduce unwanted and increase desirable behaviors.

Brestan and Eyberg (1998) highlighted two programs as probably efficacious: a children's problem-solving skills program (Kazdin, Esveldt-Dawson, French, & Unis, 1987) and a program targeting anger control (Lochman, Burch, Curry, & Lampton, 1984). Both programs focus on skill training over a relatively large number of sessions. The Problem-Solving—Skills-Training (PSST; Kazdin, 1996) program is a 20-session program developed to teach children how to solve problems in a highly predictable and logical manner. The Coping Power (Larson & Lochman, 2002) program is a 33-session program developed to promote anger control.

Specific Interventions for Oppositional Defiant Disorder

Intervention programs for ODD have met with difficulties due to the highly resistant nature of the disorder (Rey, 1993) and have been highly criticized for not considering contextual factors that impact on high-risk families (Kazdin, 1996). However, programs specific to ODD have recently begun to attract increased attention.

In their review of existing interventions for ODD, Greene, Ablon, Goring, Fazio, and Morse (2003) criticize the majority of existing programs for targeting interventions almost exclusively at parenting practices in families that are often highly stressed and who drop out of programs at high rates. The authors suggest that the results of many of these studies present a bias picture of only the most-motivated families who completed the program. The authors suggest the need to target cognitive distortions and deficiencies evident in children with ODD. Greene and colleagues (2003) have developed an alternative intervention program, Collaborative Problem Solving (CPS; Greene & Ablon, 2004) to address deficiencies in the ODD child's processing in areas of emotion regulation, frustration tolerance, problem-solving, and flexibility. The CPS program is designed to increase parent awareness of the underlying parent/child characteristics that propel the ODD behavior through the development of three strategies to manage behaviors. Empirical investigations comparing the CPS program to parent training (PT) using Barkley's defiant-youth program (Barkley, 1997) revealed superior short-term and long-term improvement for ODD children, which was statistically and clinically significant.

Conduct Disorder

Children and youth with serious emotional and behavioral disorders have been serviced by a continuum of care from the least-restrictive (outpatient) to most-restrictive (residential treatment centers [RTC]) alternatives. Until recently, the majority of empirical support for treatment effectiveness has come mainly from clinic-based studies. Despite the extensive use of RTC placements for the most severely disordered youth, empirical evidence has been minimal and lacking in experimental controls (U.S. Department of Health and Human Services, 1999).

Home-based alternatives, such as family preservation programs, also have suffered from a lack of empirical support or have demonstrated inconsistent outcomes (Meezan & McCroskey, 1996). Yet studies of the effectiveness of multisystemic therapy (MST) have demonstrated that providing services in the community can be successful for juvenile offenders (Henggeler & Borduin, 1990) compared to hospitalization as an alternative (Schoenwald et al., 2000). Success of the MST approach, which focuses on multiple determinants of deviant behavior, has been attributed to ecological validity (community outreach) and cognitive behavioral methods.

Other community-based alternatives that have been supported empirically include comparisons by Chamberlain and Reid (1991, 1998) of the success of juveniles placed in specialized foster care programs (SFC) using methods developed by Patterson, Reid, Jones, and Conger (1975) compared to juveniles assigned to RTCs. In another study, Wilmshurst (2002) found that youth with severe emotional and behavioral disorders (EBD) who were randomly assigned to a community-based family preservation program (using cognitive behavioral methods) made significant gains (statistically and clinically) compared to peers assigned to a 5-day residential alternative.

In their review of treatment programs for youth with conduct problems, McMahon and Kotler (2004) stress the need to include family in the assessment and intervention process due to significant influence of the family in precipitating and maintaining the conduct problems. The authors select several programs for discussion, including programs in Oregon designed by Patterson and colleagues: functional family therapy and MST. (For a more extensive review, see McMahon & Kotler, 2004.)

Oregon Social Learning Center (OSLC) PT Programs

The program developed by Gerald Patterson and colleagues (Patterson et al., 1975) was one of the *well-established programs* identified by Brestan and Eyberg's (1998) extensive review. The program has been extensively researched and replicated and found to be successfully modified as an intervention for families with younger children (2.5- to 6.5-year-olds), older children (6.5- to 12.5-year-olds), and adolescents and in conditions that reduced family treatment time from 31 hours to 13 to 16 hours. The program focuses on assisting parents to target and track specific behaviors and then develop reinforcement systems (point systems, contingency plans) to increase positive and decrease negative behaviors. Parents are trained to improve problem-solving and negotiation strategies.

Multisystemic Therapy (MST)

Henggeler and colleagues (1998) have developed a manualized multidimensional program for working with juveniles in their community, involving family, schools, and peers. The multimodal program is a strengths-based approach to family empowerment and uses a wide variety of techniques: family therapy and cognitive and behavioral approaches (contingency management, anger management, etc.). The MST approach has been researched extensively, and there is wide empirical support for the use of MST across a wide variety of serious juvenile problems: sexual offenders, chronic offenders, violent offenders, and youth with comorbid substance use and abuse (Henggeler & Borduin, 1990; Schoenwald et al., 2000).

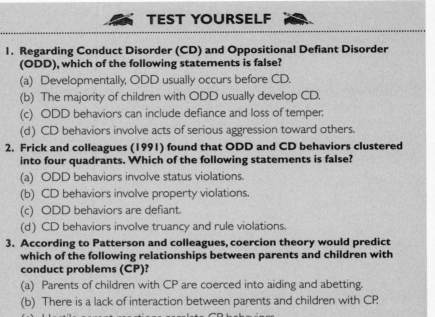

🐟 TEST YOURSELF 🐟

1. **Regarding Conduct Disorder (CD) and Oppositional Defiant Disorder (ODD), which of the following statements is false?**

    (a) Developmentally, ODD usually occurs before CD.

    (b) The majority of children with ODD usually develop CD.

    (c) ODD behaviors can include defiance and loss of temper.

    (d) CD behaviors involve acts of serious aggression toward others.

2. **Frick and colleagues (1991) found that ODD and CD behaviors clustered into four quadrants. Which of the following statements is false?**

    (a) ODD behaviors involve status violations.

    (b) CD behaviors involve property violations.

    (c) ODD behaviors are defiant.

    (d) CD behaviors involve truancy and rule violations.

3. **According to Patterson and colleagues, coercion theory would predict which of the following relationships between parents and children with conduct problems (CP)?**

    (a) Parents of children with CP are coerced into aiding and abetting.

    (b) There is a lack of interaction between parents and children with CP.

    (c) Hostile parent reactions escalate CP behaviors.

    (d) Parents of children with CP are too passive.

4. **Jason interprets an ambiguous facial expression as an angry face, and he retaliates with an aggressive response. This is an example of**

    (a) an early-starter response.

    (b) a late-starter response.

    (c) learned helplessness.

    (d) hostile attribution bias.

5. **Studies suggest that aggregating youth with severe behavior problems for the purposes of treatment can result in**

    (a) significant positive outcomes.

    (b) increased opportunities to develop social skills.

    (c) increased empathic awareness.

    (d) deviancy training.

6. **Greene and colleagues (2003) criticize the majority of treatment programs for ODD because most programs**

    (a) do not include a parent training component.

    (b) do not retain parents for the entire program.

    (c) do not motivate parents.

    (d) fail to target cognitive distortions and deficits in the children.

7. Studies concerning the effectiveness of residential treatment centers (RTC) compared with community-based treatment (CBT) programs for youth with severe conduct problems have found that

(a) CBT alternatives are often superior to RTCs.

(b) RTCs are superior to CBTs.

(c) there is no difference in treatment effectiveness between the programs.

(d) no research has compared alternative programs.

Answers: 1. b; 2. a; 3. c; 4. d; 5. d; 6. d; 7. a

Nine

EATING DISORDERS

The *DSM-IV-TR* classifies eating disorders into two broad categories: Feeding and Eating Disorders of Infancy or Early Childhood, characterized by persistent eating and feeding disturbances (Pica, Rumination Disorder, and feeding disorder); and Eating Disorders, characterized by severe disturbances in eating behaviors (Anorexia Nervosa and Bulimia Nervosa). The reason for the separation of the Eating Disorders into these two broad areas is based upon age of onset and symptom similarities. The Feeding and Eating Disorders of Infancy or Early Childhood appear under Disorders Usually First Diagnosed in Infancy, Childhood or Adolescence, while the onset for Anorexia Nervosa and Bulimia Nervosa occur much later (11 years to young adult). Although the International Classification of Diseases (ICD-10) includes obesity as a general medical condition, it is not considered a disorder in the *DSM-IV-TR* (APA, 2000). However, the *DSM-IV-TR* does specify that if psychological factors are relevant to a particular case of obesity, these factors should be noted under psychological factors affecting a medical condition (APA, 2000, p. 731).

Putting It Into Practice

At 16 years of age, Sara is 5'4" tall, and she weighs 125 pounds today. Last week, Sara weighed 130 pounds, and next week she will probably weigh 120 pounds. Although her weight is approximately where it should be on the height and weight chart, Sara compares herself to models in the magazines, and she is convinced that she looks fat.

Sara is constantly dieting, but she is not good at it. She has starved herself for the past 2 days. Today, she is irritable and upset. That is usually the feeling that starts the cycle. Now she will binge to ease the tension. In a 2-hour period, Sara will consume an entire cheesecake, a large coke, a cheeseburger, a large helping of fries, a box of chocolate chip cookies, and a half quart of ice cream. After the binge, Sara will feel guilty, depressed, upset, and angry with herself until she purges the food through self-induced vomiting. In a few days, the entire bulimic cycle will begin again. Sara has Bulimia Nervosa.

ANOREXIA NERVOSA AND BULIMIA NERVOSA

Individuals with Anorexia Nervosa and Bulimia Nervosa share a number of common features. Onset of the eating disorder will often occur after a period of intense dieting. People with both disorders will most likely be females (90%) who are preoccupied with being thin and at the same time are preoccupied with food. Both share a fear of becoming obese and have a distorted sense of body shape and weight.

Despite a number of common features, individuals with Anorexia Nervosa and Bulimia Nervosa also have personality differences. The major defining feature that separates individuals with Anorexia Nervosa from individuals with Bulimia Nervosa is that those who have Anorexia Nervosa will ultimately be successful in their refusal to maintain a normal body weight. As a result, anorexics will weigh less than 85% of their expected weight (APA, 2000).

> ### DON'T FORGET
>
> The news media will often report stories of celebrities who have disclosed having an eating disorder, such as Princess Diana. In the early 1980s, when few people knew about the prevalence of eating disorders, the country was shocked to find out that Karen Carpenter, a famous singer and entertainer, had died from medical complications resulting from Anorexia Nervosa.

> ### CAUTION
>
> Young girls in the 11–13-year-old range become increasingly weight conscious and try to lose weight, just at the time when weight gain is normal due to puberty. Early-maturing girls are at greater risk for developing eating disorders than later-maturing girls (Swarr & Richards, 1996).

> ### DON'T FORGET
>
> Despite the term *anorexia*, which means loss of appetite, the anorexic is preoccupied with food and is constantly hungry because of their self-induced starvation.

ANOREXIA NERVOSA

Clinical and Associated Developmental Features

The diagnostic feature of Anorexia Nervosa is the refusal to maintain a minimally acceptable weight. Individuals with the disorder will maintain their weight at least 15% below what is considered normal (based on one of several available versions of the Metropolitan Life Insurance tables or pediatric growth chart). The ICD-10 diagnostic criteria define this minimum in terms of a body mass index (BMI) equal to or lower than $17.5 \, \text{kg}/\text{m}^2$. Anorexics' intense fear of gaining weight is the focal point of their motivation to monitor their food intake to the extent that the disorder can be fatal.

Putting It Into Practice

Tracy finally felt good about herself. She had been weighing herself three times a day, and today she finally found that she had lost over 20 pounds in the previous three months. Tracy had learned to curb her appetite by cooking for others and then rushing off, not having time to eat. She was obsessed with food but was even more obsessed with having the willpower to stop herself from eating. Tracy finally knew she had won the battle when her period stopped. That was her benchmark. Now she knew she had lost enough weight. Now if she could only lose a little more from her buttocks, she would be happy.

Driven by a fear of gaining weight and a distorted perception of their body size and shape, individuals with Anorexia Nervosa usually begin to lose weight initially through restricting higher calorie foods. Ultimately, with increased restrictions, their diet becomes limited to a few low-calorie foods, such as celery. Diagnostic criteria for Anorexia Nervosa, according to the *DSM-IV-TR* (APA, 2000), includes the following symptoms: maintaining of weight less than 85% of minimum expected; intense fear of gaining weight or becoming fat; distorted sense of body shape; and absence of three consecutive menstrual cycles (a condition referred to as *amenorrhea*).

Individuals with anorexia will often feel a sense of power in being able to control their desire to eat. Other associated features include feelings of ineffectiveness, perfectionism, inhibited emotional expression and spontaneity, rigid thinking patterns, and a strong need to control environmental influences.

Inherently, for individuals with Anorexia Nervosa, self-concept and self-esteem are virtually synonymous with body image. They view weight loss as an achievement and self-starvation as strength of character. Their distorted sense of body proportion does not allow them to perceive how their bones might protrude from their bodies or that their malnutrition has caused them to appear like walking skeletons. Physiologically, their restricted diets can cause significant health problems. Refusal to eat may result in the necessity for medical interventions, such as tube feeding, in order to avert a fatality.

Subtypes of Anorexia Nervosa

There are two subtypes of Anorexia Nervosa. When most people think about Anorexia Nervosa, they think about the *restricting subtype.* The restricting subtype maintains the low weight by restrictive dieting, fasting, or excess exercise. Individuals of this subtype do not normally engage in the binge and purge process. Individuals with the *binge-eating/purging subtype* of Anorexia Nervosa may engage in the binge and purge process by eating more than they typically would eat and then follow eating with a purge activity (self-induced vomiting, laxatives). Some individuals with this subtype may not binge in the true sense of the word, but even if they eat a small amount, they will follow eating with a purge activity to rid the body of the food. Usually binge and purge activities likely take place on a regular (weekly) basis.

Prevalence and Course

Approximately 1% of the population will be diagnosed with Anorexia Nervosa in a lifetime, although there is concern that this rate is increasing. The disorder is found primarily in females (approximately 90%). The disorder is most pronounced in female adolescents from middle- to upper-class Caucasian families (Pate, Pumariega, Hester, & Gaarner, 1992). However, a preoccupation with thinness has not only resulted in overall increased prevalence rates but also has seen the disorder become more pervasive across all social strata and ethnic groups. The typical age of onset is between 14 to 18 years of age. Better prognosis is associated with earlier adolescent onset. Recovery rates are low, with only approximately 10% fully recovering from the disorder, while almost 50% achieve partial recovery (Herzog et al., 1993). Approximately half of females who are anorexic go on to develop bulimia at some later stage.

The course of Anorexia Nervosa is somewhat unpredictable; however, the disorder can be precipitated by a stressful event. While some individuals succumb to a single episode, others will follow a more chronic course evident in fluctuating weight loss and gain, relapse, and increasing health problems. Within the first 5 years, many individuals with the restricting subtype of Anorexia Nervosa will develop an eating pattern that is more typical of the binge-eating/purging subtype. If this shift is accompanied by sufficient weight gain, then the diagnosis may also change from Anorexia Nervosa to Bulimia Nervosa. Unchecked, chronic starvation and weight loss can result in severe dehydration and electrolyte imbalance that may require hospitalization. Of those requiring hospitalization, the mortal-

> **DON'T FORGET**
>
> The anorexic cycle begins with fear of obesity and a distorted body image. This leads to self-starvation. Starvation leads to preoccupation with food. Ultimately anxiety and depression are woven into the cycle at each stage.

> **DON'T FORGET**
>
> Rosen, McKeag, Hough, and Curley (1986) surveyed female athletes and found that many were at high risk for eating disorders. In their survey of college gymnasts, approximately 62% admitted to engaging in self-destructive weight control techniques: diet pills (24%), self-induced vomiting (26%), laxatives (7%), and diuretics (12%).

ity rate is high (10%) due to either suicide, starvation, electrolyte imbalance, or other medical complications (APA, 2000).

Comorbidity

Anorexia Nervosa is associated with depression, irritability, anxiety, social withdrawal, and insomnia. Obsessive-compulsive characteristics are also common, as anorexics are preoccupied with food (APA, 2000). Lack of impulse control is common in the binge-eating/purging subtype, which may also be evident in comorbid disorders of substance abuse. Anxiety (75%), depression (73%), and Personality Disorders (74%) are highly comorbid disorders (Deep, Nagy, Weltzin, Rao, & Kaye, 1995; Herzog, Schellberg, & Deter, 1997).

BULIMIA NERVOSA

Clinical and Associated Developmental Features

The cardinal feature of Bulimia Nervosa is the bulimic cycle that involves binge eating followed by compensatory methods designed to prevent weight gain.

The diagnostic criteria for Bulimia Nervosa include recurrent episodes of binge eating and recurrent use of compensatory strategies to prevent weight gain. The binge and compensatory behaviors occur at least twice a week for at least 3 months, and self-worth is evaluated through weight and body proportion.

Subtypes of Bulimia Nervosa

There are two subtypes of Bulimia Nervosa based on the compensatory methods used: the *purging type* (self-induced vomiting, laxatives, diuretics, enemas) and the *nonpurging type* (fasting, excessive exercise).

Because of the guilt and shame associated with eating and purging, individuals with bulimia can go undetected for some time. Binges are usually done in private, and food is often consumed at a rapid pace. Precipitating circumstances surrounding a binge episode might include feelings of depression, environmental stressors, irritability, tension, and hunger (fasting).

Although bulimics engage in compensatory behaviors to remove calories from their bodies, the practice of repeated vomiting has several adverse side effects. Physically, acids from the stomach can cause deterioration of the esophagus over time and erode enamel on teeth. Studies have also determined that repeated vomiting results in people feeling more hungry and less satiated than if they had not engaged in bouts of vomiting (Wooley & Wooley, 1985). Therefore, bulimics are often caught in cycles that produce more intense feelings of hunger and are at higher risk for repeat binge-purge episodes.

DON'T FORGET

There are two subtypes for each eating disorder. Anorexia Nervosa has subtypes based on how weight is kept to the minimum (restricting types and binge-eating/purging type). Subtypes of Bulimia Nervosa are classified on the nature of the compensatory strategy used to eliminate what has been consumed (purging and nonpurging types). Among the subtypes, similarities exist between the binge-eating/purging type of anorexia and the purging type of bulimia. Similarities are also evident in the restricting type of anorexia and nonpurging type of bulimia in the use of fasting and excessive exercise to control weight gain.

DON'T FORGET

The bulimic cycle begins with a feeling of tension or irritability that produces a strong desire to eat. The urge leads to a loss of control and a binge episode. Following the binge episode, the bulimic feels guilty, depressed, uncomfortably full, and compensates by getting rid of the food (purging or nonpurging). Following the compensatory behaviors, the bulimic feels in control once again.

Prevalence, Course, and Comorbidity

The lifetime prevalence is approximately 1 to 3%, and the male to female ratio is 1 male for 10 females. Onset is later than for Anorexia Nervosa, and bulimia usually begins in late adolescence or early adulthood. The course is often chronic, with high rates of relapse. Most individuals with Bulimia Nervosa have fluctuating weight loss but primarily remain within the average weight range for their height.

Throughout the course of development, many adolescent girls engage in experimental diets and compensatory weight loss behaviors. One survey of college students found that 50% engaged in binges on a periodic basis, while a number of students reported using compensatory behaviors of vomiting (6%) or laxatives (8%) at least once (Mitchell, Pyle, & Miner, 1982). Attie and Brooks-Gunn (1995) suggest that Eating Disorders tend to develop in response to two stressful life transitions: onset of adolescence and onset of young adulthood.

ETIOLOGY OF EATING DISORDERS

There are several possible explanations that have been suggested concerning the development of Eating Disorders. In likelihood, etiology is a complex interaction between biological, psychological and environmental (family and peer stressors) factors. Similarities and differences between Anorexia Nervosa and Bulimia Nervosa have been discussed throughout this chapter.

Although the two eating disorders share many of the same features, there are also important differences between Anorexia Nervosa and Bulimia Nervosa. A summary of the differences can be found in Rapid Reference 9.1.

Onset of anorexia occurs earlier than bulimia and studies have shown that family characteristics and personality characteristics seem to differ in females with anorexia and bulimia, especially when comparing the two more contrasting and unique types of these disorders, for example, Anorexia Nervosa (restricting type) and Bulimia Nervosa (binge-eating/purging type). While individuals with anorexia (restricting type) tend to be more rigid, perfectionistic, and obsessive in their quest for thinness, those with the binge-eating/purging type of bulimia tend to be more outgoing and sociable. However, while anorexics are more likely to be sexually immature, bulimics tend to have greater difficulties with impulse control and can be more sexually active (Halmi, 1995).

Studies of family characteristics have also noted differences in these two eating disorder groups, with more pathology evident in families of those suffering from bulimia.

DON'T FORGET

Similarities between the two eating disorders include the following:

- Onset after intense dieting
- Fear of obesity
- Preoccupation with thinness and food
- Distorted sense of body shape and weight

Biological, Genetic, and Neurotransmitter Functions

The risk for developing an eating disorder is six times as great if the person has a relative with an eating disorder (Strober, Freeman, Lampert, Diamond, & Kaye, 2000). At least

≡Rapid Reference 9.1

Differences Between Anorexia Nervosa (restricting type) and Bulimia Nervosa

Anorexia Nervosa (restricting type)	Bulimia Nervosa
Earlier age of onset: 14 to 18 years	Later age of onset: 15 to 21 years
Amenorrhea (absence of menstrual cycle) as a consequence of low body weight	Amenorrhea less likely; irregularities in menstrual cycle more common
Greater denial of parent-child conflict; less demonstration of open conflict	Greater tendencies for more intense, hostile, and open parent-child conflict
Less family history of obesity	Greater family history of obesity
Tendencies toward introverted behaviors such as social withdrawal and decreased interest in sex over time	Tendencies toward extroverted behaviors manifested in substance abuse and promiscuity or heightened interest in sex
High tendencies of comorbidity with depression and Obsessive-Compulsive Personality Disorder or traits	High tendencies of comorbidity with anxiety, as well as depression, substance abuse, obsessive-compulsive traits, and Borderline Personality Disorder

one twin study found that if one monozygotic twin has bulimia, then there is a 23% chance that the other twin will develop the disorder (Walters & Kendler, 1995). Low levels of serotonin (Carrasco, Diaz-Marsa, Hollander, Cesar, & Saiz-Ruiz, 2000) have also been associated with Eating Disorders, similar to other disorders previously discussed.

DON'T FORGET

Low serotonin levels have also been linked to depression and Obsessive-Compulsive Disorder.

Garner, Garfinkel, and O'Shaughnessy (1985) suggest that early eating patterns and inheritance combine together to define an individual's *weight set point*. The authors use the theory of weight set point to explain why dieting in isolation does not work. In order to lose weight, restricted eating must also be accompanied by increasing the metabolic rate (exercise) to offset the internal regulating functions. Genetically, there seems to be a history of maternal obesity in families of bulimics.

DON'T FORGET

The authors suggest that the weight set point is the body's internal weight regulator that responds to messages sent by the hypothalamus. When activated, the lateral hypothalamus (LH) sends a message of increased hunger; stimulation of the ventromedial hypothalamus (VH) sends a message of decreased hunger. If weight drops below the ideal set point, the LH is activated to increase hunger, and the metabolic rate is lowered to preserve the set point; if weight is above the set point, the VH is stimulated to depress appetite, and the metabolic rate is raised.

Temperament and Personality

Approximately half of anorexics will be restrictive, while the other half will demonstrate characteristics of the binge-eating/purging type. Personalities among these two types differ, with the binge-eating/purging type sharing many features of bulimia. The restrictive subtype tend to be more inhibited, perfectionistic, insecure, conforming, and capable of high levels of self-control. By comparison, those with the binge-eating/purging type tend to be more outgoing, extraverted, and have problems with impulse control (Casper, Hedeker, & McClough, 1992).

Family Influences

Family dynamics can play a major role in the precipitation and maintenance of Eating Disorders. Mothers of females with Eating Disorders tend to be perfectionistic and also prone to dieting themselves. Hilde Bruch (1991) maintains that while *effective parents* are sensitive to their child's needs and respond appropriately to biological (hunger) and emotional (nurturing) needs, *ineffective parents* respond inappropriately by providing comfort food at times when their children are not hungry but when they are anxious or irritable. In this case, inappropriate responses serve two functions: They preempt the child's establishment of their own set of internal signals to activate hunger, and they link food to comfort.

Salvador Minuchin, Rosman, and Baker (1978) described four characteristics of *anorexic families,* including enmeshment, overprotectiveness, rigidity, and denial of conflict. They saw these families as overly concerned about outward appearances and very controlling in their influence. Given little room to develop independence within this controlling and enmeshed environment, anorexia provides these girls with the ability to control their own food intake, while at the same time delaying their maturation (lack of onset of womanhood) and remaining dependent.

In contrast, *bulimic families* tend to have more psychopathology (depression and substance abuse) compared to controls. Fairburn, Welch, Doll, Davies, and O'Connor (1997) found that compared to families of anorexics where open confrontation is avoided, families of bulimics engage in more open hostility, parent-child conflict, and confrontation. Families of bulimics also tended to engage in more relational aggression intent on blaming and attempting to control each other.

Socioenvironmental Influences

Surveys regarding how people perceive their body image, relative to the ideal image, reveal that dissatisfaction with body image has increased signif-

icantly in the past 25 years. Compared to responses collected in 1972, women's dissatisfaction ratings for their overall body image obtained in 1997 doubled the number dissatisfied (25% to 56%). Although women were less content than men about their body image, males also increased their sense of dissatisfaction about their body image substantially in the interim, from 15% to 43% (Garner, Cooke, & Marano, 1997). In one study of 9- and 10-year-old girls, researchers found that between 31% to 81% of 9-year-old girls and between 46% to 81% of 10-year-old girls expressed fears of being fat and had engaged in dieting and binge-eating episodes (Mellin, Irwin, & Scully, 1992).

Cognitive and Behavioral Theories

Cognitive distortions are evident in the thought processes of individuals with Eating Disorders. Tendencies toward negative self-appraisals and obsessional preoccupation with food are the prominent features of this pattern of maladaptive thinking. Behaviorally, the anorexic cycle and the bulimic cycle are negatively reinforcing and self-perpetuation.

ASSESSMENT OF EATING DISORDERS

In addition to the broad assessment instruments discussed previously, the Eating Disorder Inventory-2 (EDI-2, Garner, 1991) is a self-report instrument that assesses common psychological and behavioral traits associated with bulimia and anorexia. There are eight subscales: Drive for Thinness, Bulimia, Body Dissatisfaction, Ineffectiveness Scale, Perfectionism, Interpersonal Distrust, Interoceptive Awareness, and Maturity Fears.

Intervention and Treatment of Anorexia Nervosa

Medical Intervention

Close contact with the primary care physician is very important in cases of Eating Disorders due to the seriousness of the physical complications that can develop. In anorexia, three goals of treatment are monitored very closely: weight gain; resolution of underlying maladaptive thoughts, behaviors, and interpersonal relationships; and maintenance of weight gain.

Behavioral Interventions

Behavioral interventions target positive behaviors to replace and intervene in the anorexic cycle. Within the hospital setting, anorexics are often placed on behavioral plans that offer tangible rewards (access to telephone, television, makeup, etc.) for eating.

Cognitive Behavioral Therapy

Several cognitive behavioral programs have been developed to assist anorexics. One program that combined cognitive therapy and family therapy obtained a 64% success rate (reached ideal weight) at the end of a 16-month treatment program. Follow-up revealed that 82% maintained gains 1 year later (Robin, Bedway, Diegel, & Gilroy, 1996). Components of a cognitive-based program would provide promoting eating disorder awareness, developing appropriate weight goals and attitudes, linking privileges to goal attainment, monitoring of eating behaviors by an adult (to avoid purging), fostering awareness of maladaptive thought patterns (perfectionism, negative thinking), developing relaxation techniques, and focusing on relapse prevention. In addition, individual therapeutic sessions would address psychosocial stressors (family, peers) and therapy directed toward any comorbid problems (e.g., anxiety and depression). Cognitive behavioral programs can be provided on an individual or group basis and frequently involve the family.

Family Interventions

Minuchin and colleagues (1978) developed several techniques for working with anorexic families. Observation of family dynamics for Eating Disorders provided the most salient information when the session was conducted during a meal. Family systems interventions focus on issues of enmeshment and the family's tendencies to avoid issues of marital or family conflict by focusing energy on the anorexic child.

Intervention and Treatment of Bulimia Nervosa

Medical Interventions

Although bulimia does not pose the medical threat that anorexia does, there is still a need to monitor medical side effects. In addition, antidepressants (SSRIs) such as fluoxetine (Prozac) may be an effective adjunct to treatment of bulimia in reducing depressive symptoms, elevating mood, and decreasing the need to engage in binge episodes (Bezchlibnyk-Butler & Jeffries, 1997).

Cognitive Behavioral Therapy

Maladaptive thinking such as linking self-esteem to body image can be reframed using cognitive behavioral methods, outlined earlier for Anorexia Nervosa. With the binge-eating/purging type, monitoring would require restricted access to binge-type foods (high-calorie foods, e.g., cake, ice cream). Group therapies often combine anorexics and bulimics in the same eating disorder groups.

Family Interventions

Due to the fact that bulimic families are much more volatile than anorexic families, therapy would likely be directed at more appropriate methods of communication, appropriate conflict resolution, and reestablishing appropriate boundaries.

OTHER EATING DISORDERS

Binge-Eating Disorder

Appendix B of the *DSM-IV-TR* (APA, 2000) contains a number of categories of disorders suggested for possible inclusion in *DSM-IV*; however, insufficient evidence precluded their inclusion. One of these categories includes Binge-Eating Disorder. Binge-Eating Disorder involves impaired ability to control excessive eating episodes that cause significant distress. Unlike anorexia or bulimia, Binge-Eating Disorder is not followed by compensatory strategies (such as self-induced vomiting, laxatives, fasting, or excessive exercise); however, similar to anorexia or bulimia, overindulgence is followed by feelings of guilt, embarrassment, disgust, and depression. There is a controversy whether any compensatory behaviors (e.g., purge on occasion) should be included or excluded from the defining criteria for this proposed category. As might be anticipated, frequent binge-eating episodes in the absence of purge behaviors may result in fluctuating weight problems, including being overweight or obese. Onset is usually in late adolescence or early adulthood. Binge-Eating Disorder is often comorbid with depression.

Feeding and Eating Disorders of Infancy or Early Childhood

As noted in the beginning of this chapter, information on Eating Disorders is available in two separate sections of the *DSM-IV-TR* (APA, 2000). Eating Disorders with onset in adolescence or young adulthood (Anorexia Nervosa and Bulimia Nervosa) and the disorders first diagnosed in infancy, childhood, and adolescence (Pica, Rumination Disorder, and feeding disorder).

Pica

Infants initially explore their world by mouthing objects and can commonly ingest nonnutritive substances, especially if not well supervised. The cardinal feature of Pica, however, is consuming one or more nonnutritive substances on a regular and persistent basis over a period of at least 1 month. The substances ingested differ developmentally with infants and younger children commonly consuming paint, hair, cloth, plaster, and string. Older children typically may eat animal droppings, sand, insects, pebbles, or leaves. Adolescents or adults may consume clay or soil (APA, 2000). Because some cultures sanction ingesting nonnutritive substances, such as soil, a diagnosis of Pica must rule out cultural practice. This eating disorder is most often associated with Mental Retardation or one of the Pervasive Developmental Disorders. The prevalence rate for adults with Severe Mental Retardation can be as high as 15% (APA, 2000).

Rumination Disorder

The characteristic feature of this disorder is the repeated regurgitation and rechewing of food. The disorder is common in infants and those with Mental Retardation. Because the food is regurgitated and not ingested, weight loss, failure to thrive, and even death can result. As many as 25% of infants with Rumination Disorder will die. Precipitating factors associated with the disorder include stressful conditions, lack of stimulation or neglect, and strained parent-child relationship. In older children and adults, Mental Retardation is the predisposing factor (APA, 2000). Onset is usually between 3 and 12 months; however, in cases with Mental Retardation, onset may be later.

Feeding Disorder of Infancy or Early Childhood

The primary feature of this disorder is a failure to eat adequately, resulting in a failure to maintain proper weight or a substantial weight loss. Onset must occur prior to 6 years of age. Associated features include irritability, withdrawal, and developmental delays. Impaired parent-child relationship may exacerbate the condition, while abuse and neglect may be the predisposing factor. Failure to thrive accounts for between 1% to 5% of all infant admissions to hospital. Research has shown that children with feeding disorder often have more attachment problems than their healthy peers (Drotar, 1995).

🐟 TEST YOURSELF 🐟

1. **The word *anorexia* means**
   (a) to waste away.
   (b) to do without.
   (c) loss of appetite.
   (d) loss of desire.

2. **According to the *DSM-IV-TR* (APA, 2000) a diagnosis of Anorexia Nervosa requires a weight maintenance of**
   (a) 75% of the minimum expected.
   (b) 85% of the minimum expected.
   (c) 90% of the minimum expected.
   (d) 95% of the minimum expected.

3. **Which of the following is true regarding Anorexia Nervosa and Bulimia Nervosa?**
   (a) Onset of anorexia is usually earlier than bulimia.
   (b) Bulimia is often associated with the restricting type of diet.
   (c) Anorexics rarely become bulimic.
   (d) Lack of impulse control is often a characteristic of anorexia.

4. **According to the *DSM-IV-TR*, a binge-eating episode must include**
   (a) consuming an excessive amount of food in a discrete period of time.
   (b) ritualistic eating habits.
   (c) a feeling of loss of control resulting from overeating.
   (d) both a and c.

5. **Anorexia Nervosa is**
   (a) universal.
   (b) evident only in the United States.
   (c) more prevalent in industrial societies.
   (d) more prevalent in low SES populations.

6. **Which of the following is *not* an example of a nonpurging type of bulimia?**
   (a) Fasting
   (b) Excessive exercise
   (c) Diuretics
   (d) Restrictive dieting

(continued)

7. Which of the following is not a similarity between anorexia and bulimia?

(a) Fear of obesity

(b) Sexual inhibition

(c) Distorted sense of body shape

(d) Onset after intense dieting

8. Which of the following is not a part of the *anorexic family* described by Salvador Minuchin and colleagues (1978)?

(a) Open hostility

(b) Enmeshment

(c) Overprotectiveness

(d) Rigidity

Answers: 1. c; 2. b; 3. a; 4. d; 5. c; 6. c; 7. b; 8. a

Ten

SUBSTANCE-RELATED DISORDERS

In a recent survey of over 10,000 teenagers in the United States in Grades 7 through 12, more than 9% stated that they had used a weapon in the past year; 25% had smoked cigarettes in the past 30 days, and one in seven 7th and 8th graders had already experienced sex (Blum et al., 2000). Although these results demonstrated improvements in some areas over previous findings, the report suggests that many teens continue to engage in high-risk behaviors. Blum and associates found that the three factors that contributed most to high-risk behaviors in teens included school failure, percentage of unstructured free time, and nature of peer activities.

The *DSM-IV-TR* uses the term *substance* to relate to a drug of abuse, a medication, or a toxin. The substances discussed in the *DSM-IV-TR* (APA, 2000) fall into 1 of 11 categories, including alcohol, amphetamines, caffeine, cannabis, cocaine, hallucinogens, inhalants, nicotine, opioids, phencyclidine (PCP), sedatives, hypnotics, or anxiolytics. In addition to these classes of substances, the *DSM-IV-TR* also notes that many over-the-counter medications and prescription medications can also cause Substance-Related Disorders.

The *DSM-IV-TR* (APA, 2000) groups Substance-Related Disorders into two broad categories: *Substance Use Disorders* (Substance Dependence and Abuse) and *Substance-Induced Disorders* (Intoxication, Withdrawal). Following a discussion of general guidelines for establishing the existence of each of the four broad areas noted previously—Dependence, Abuse, Intoxication, and Withdrawal—the *DSM-IV-TR* then provides specific substance-related information. The current chapter will follow the same direction. Other than the *DSM-IV-TR* criteria that were established for adults, there is no clear agreement on how to define when alcohol or drug use becomes problematic or criteria that might be used to more appropriately define abuse and dependence in adolescents and youth (Winters, Latimer, & Stinchfield, 2001).

SUBSTANCE USE DISORDERS

Substance Dependence

Compulsive use of a substance on a repeated basis, despite adverse effects, is a characteristic feature of Substance Dependence. Within a 12-month period, at least three other conditions must be met in order to determine dependence on a substance:

1. Tolerance.
2. Withdrawal symptoms following abstinence.
3. Increased use and increased amounts.
4. Unsuccessful attempts to control the use.
5. Extensive time involved in obtaining or maintaining the use.
6. Forgoing important activities (social, work, etc.).
7. Continued use despite adverse physical or psychological consequences (APA, 2000).

The *DSM-IV-TR* notes that Substance Dependence can be applied to each substance discussed, with the exception of caffeine. Individuals with Substance Dependence usually crave the substance. Tolerance levels differ depending on the substance used, how the central nervous system is affected, and individual differences in sensitivity to the substance (e.g., some first-time drinkers experience little effect, others are significantly impaired with very little alcohol). An individual can still match criteria for Substance Dependence without exhibiting either tolerance or withdrawal; however, it is likely that cases with tolerance and withdrawal are at greater risk for developing associated medical problems and may have higher relapse rates.

DON'T FORGET

Tolerance refers to either needing more of a substance to achieve the desired effect or experiencing less of an effect from continued use of the same amount. *Withdrawal* symptoms are specific physiological or psychological reactions causing discomfort in response to abstinence from the substance. Often those experiencing withdrawal symptoms will reestablish contact with the substance, or similar substance, to alleviate the symptoms.

DON'T FORGET

In order to distinguish whether tolerance and withdrawal are components of the dependency, the *DSM-IV-TR* uses two separate specifiers: *With Physiological Dependence,* to denote tolerance and withdrawal are present; and *Without Physiological Dependence,* to note absence of tolerance and withdrawal.

Substance Abuse

The cardinal feature of Substance Abuse is a pattern of chronic, repeated, and sustained use of a substance despite significant adverse consequences resulting in one or more of the following situations occurring within a 12-month period:

- Failure to fulfil a major obligation (truancy, absenteeism, suspensions, expulsions)
- Engaging in physically high-risk behaviors (driving while impaired; operating machinery)
- Legal problems (arrest)
- Problems in relationships resulting from excessive use (substance induced fights, arguments)

A diagnosis of Substance Abuse is made in the absence of meeting criteria for substance dependence.

SUBSTANCE-INDUCED DISORDERS

Substance Intoxication

An individual becomes intoxicated when ingestion of a substance results in a specific set of symptoms (substance-specific syndrome). Each substance has its own set of syndrome-specific symptoms. The syndrome is considered reversible because once the effect of the substance wears off, then the intoxicated behaviors revert to preintoxication levels. Some examples of intoxicated behaviors include belligerence, mood lability, cognitive impairment, and impaired judgement.

Intoxication can impact on a number of sensory functions, including perception, psychomotor behavior (reflexes), concentration and attention, and cognitive processing. Intoxication can also influence personality and interpersonal behaviors. Although alcohol use may initially be associated with less inhibited social behaviors and an apparent facade of social ease, repeated use may result in social withdrawal. According to the *DSM-IV-TR* (APA, 2000), responses to intoxication are similar among some substances (e.g., amphetamines and cocaine both produce grandiosity and hyperactivity, while alcohol intoxication shares

DON'T FORGET

Intoxication results from the substance's effect on central nervous system (CNS) functioning. Different substances affect the CNS in different ways in different individuals and at different times. For example, alcohol might make one person argumentative and another giddy.

similar features with the sedative, hypnotic, and anxiolytic substances). Common substances used by adolescents and youth are presented in Rapid Reference 10.1. Some of the more common presenting features of intoxication are outlined in the chart.

Substance Withdrawal

Substance Withdrawal refers to a specific set of behaviors (substance-specific syndrome) resulting from abstinence from a substance that has been taken on a chronic, repeated, and prolonged basis. The resulting syndrome impacts significantly to cause distress and impairment in day-to-day functioning in areas of importance. Withdrawal is often accompanied by a high level of discomfort and distress and impacts on physiological and psychological functioning. Often there is a craving for the substance to relieve the symptoms of withdrawal. Substances that are likely to cause withdrawal symptoms include alcohol, cocaine, nicotine, opioids, and sedatives. Most symptoms of withdrawal are the opposite of symptoms noted for intoxication.

Prevalence of Substance Use

Since 1975, the University of Michigan, under a grant from The National Institute on Drug Abuse (NIDA), has collected data on use of illicit drugs in adolescents and youth. Initially, the Monitoring the Future (MTF) Study surveyed substance use in 12th graders; however, since 1991 survey responses have been collected from high school seniors, 8th graders, and 10th graders. The most recent survey, collected in 2003, involved 48,467 students in 392 public and private schools. A comparison of results from 2001 and 2003 can be found in Rapid Reference 10.2. The survey provides significant information regarding current trends in drug use. Although the data reveal a steady decline in reported usage over the years, the rates are still alarmingly high in some areas. In 2003, there was a steady increase in reported usage of any illicit drug with increasing age: 22% of 8th graders, 41% of 10th graders, and 51% of 12th graders. Alcohol use was the most prominent substance reported at all grade levels, with 45% of 8th graders having used alcohol in the past year and 21% within the past 30 days. At the high school level, almost two thirds of 10th graders and three quarters of 12th graders had used alcohol within the past year, while 35% (10th graders) and 47% (12th graders) reported use in the past 30 days. Cigarette smoking and marijuana/hashish usage were also among the heaviest drug use reported. Inhalant use was one of the few areas that noted a decline, rather than an increase, with age.

The majority of drug experimentation in adolescence does not amount to a

Common Drugs Used by Adolescents and Youth and Their Symptoms

Drug name	How used	Slang terms	Symptoms of intoxication
Marijuana	Most common method is smoking the dried grass rolled into marijuana cigarettes (joints)	weed, pot, bud, herb, grass, reefer, ganja, green, Mary Jane, cheeba, dope, smoke	The high generally wears off in about 2–3 hours.
Marijuana + embalming fluid	Usually really Marijuana + PCP	Loveboat: symptoms of paranoia, difficulty concentrating, agitation, and suspicions	Common experiences of intoxication: mood elevation; increased awareness of senses; increased appetite; sleepiness; dizziness; anxiety and paranoia; short-term memory problems.
GHB (gamma-hydroxybutyrate)	A clear odorless substance that can be mixed with drinks	GHB, gamma oh, goop, jib, liquid ecstasy, sleep, soap, booster, Somatomax	Disinhibition, disorientation, and confusion; also known as *date rape drug* Withdrawal: anxiety, tremors, delirium, hallucinations

(continued)

Common Drugs Used by Adolescents and Youth and Their Symptoms (*continued*)

Drug name	How used	Slang terms	Symptoms of intoxication
LSD (D-lysergic acid diethylamide)	Pills, blotter tabs	acid, dots, hits, blotter, purple haze, barrels, sugar cube, Elvis, blue cheer, electric Kool-Aid, Zen	Dilated pupils; tremors; flushing; chills; distorted sense of time; depersonalization Negative bad trip effects: paranoia, delusions, anxiety, and mood swings
PCP (phencyclidine)	Often used to "lace" other drugs (e.g., sold as many other drugs). Snorted, ingested orally, smoked, or injected	*PCP:* angel dust, amoeba, sherms, STP, embalming fluid, peace pills, animal tank *PCP + Marijuana:* wet, greens, killer weed, leak, dippers *PCP + Ecstacy:* elephant flipping, pikachu	Low dose: drowsy; constricted pupils; impaired motor skills Higher dose: erratic behavior

Source: Information adapted from www.justfacts.org, a web site provided by The Center for Substance Abuse Research (CESAR), University of Maryland, College Park, MD.

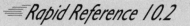

Rapid Reference 10.2

Monitoring the Future Study: A comparison of lifetime prevalence rates for substance use in adolescents and youth in 8th, 10th, and 12th graders in 2001 and 2003

Drug	8th Grade 2001	8th Grade 2003	10th Grade 2001	10th Grade 2003	12th Grade 2001	12th Grade 2003
Any illicit drug	26.8	22.8	45.6	41.4	53.9	51.1
Marijuana	20.4	17.5	40.1	36.4	49.0	46.1
Inhalants	17.1	15.8	15.2	12.7	13.0	11.2
LSD	3.4	2.1	6.3	3.5	10.9	5.9
Cocaine	4.3	3.6	5.7	5.1	8.2	7.7
Crack	3.0	2.5	3.1	2.7	3.7	3.6
Heroin	1.7	1.6	1.7	1.5	1.8	1.5
Tranquilizer	5.0	4.4	9.2	7.8	10.3	10.2
Alcohol	50.5	45.6	70.1	66.0	79.7	76.6
30 day*	21.5	19.7	39.0	35.4	49.8	47.5
Cigarettes	36.6	28.4	52.8	43.0	61.0	53.7
1/2 pack+ per day**	2.3	1.8	5.5	4.1	10.3	8.4
Steroids	2.8	2.5	3.5	3.0	3.7	3.5
MDMA	5.2	3.2	8.0	5.4	11.7	8.3

Source: Reprinted from the National Institute on Drug Abuse web site at http://www.drugabuse.gov.

*Consumed alcohol within the past 30 days.

**Use of cigarettes, at least half a pack daily.

significant and lifelong addiction. In fact, the majority of youth abandon the practice once they enter young adulthood (Kouzis & Labouvie, 1992). However, for some, the developmental pathway is not so positive. Youth who rely on heavy and repeated usage over time develop poor outcomes and are at higher risk for juvenile delinquency, teen pregnancy, and academic failure (Newcomb & Felix-Ortiz, 1992).

Although information about usage is readily available via the NIDA web site, there is far less information available concerning substance abuse. Cohen and colleagues (1993) interviewed 500 adolescents and youth regarding Substance Use and Abuse. Based on their results, alcohol abuse was reported by 4% of males

CAUTION

Frequency of use is not always reported in surveys of substance use. In this survey it is an important component, as experimentation can be high in adolescence, especially for alcohol, cigarettes, and marijuana. For the sake of brevity, only the lifetime prevalence is reported in Rapid Reference 10.1 for the majority of drugs. The reader is encouraged to review the published results, which include annual, 30-day and, at times, daily usage rates.

and 3% of females in the 14- to 16-year-old age range, while in the next age bracket (17 to 20 years), the percentages increased for girls (9%) and were substantially higher for males (20%). Rates for drug abuse were much lower in this study, with less than two% of the younger group reporting drug abuse. However, within the older group, rates again noted an increase for males, with up to 5% disclosing drug abuse compared to less than three% of females.

In addition to reported gender differences, ethnic differences have also been investigated. Abuse of alcohol, barbituates, amphetamines, and hallucinogens is more prominent among Caucasian males, while abuse of heroin, crack, and cocaine is more prevalent in Hispanic youth. Native American youth tend to abuse alcohol (Vik, Brown, & Myers, 1997).

Prevalence, Course, and Comorbidity

Prevalence-of-usage rates based on age level and substance are available in Rapid Reference 10.2. The course of Substance Use and Abuse has been investigated across development. Age of onset has been declining, with most recent estimates suggesting indoctrination into drug use at about 11 to 12 years of age (Fitzgerald, Davies, Zucker, & Klinger, 1994). Retrospective interviews with adolescents who abuse substances have revealed that earlier *Substance Use* (prior to age 15) is more likely to result in later *Substance Abuse* and that as the number of conduct problems increases, the corresponding risk for Substance Abuse increases accordingly (Robins & McEvoy, 1990).

CAUTION

The term *binge drinking* is used to refer to heavy consumption on a single occasion (e.g., five or more drinks during the same drinking session). Prevalence rates for drug usage often refer to frequency of taking drugs rather than quantity of drug consumed. One survey reported that approximately 33% of high school seniors and 25% of sophomores engage in binge drinking at least twice a month (Johnson & Pandina, 2000).

Researchers have also investigated the types of drugs taken relative to increasing severity. Results suggest that the most common progression in drug taking begins with alcohol and cigarettes and then progresses to marijuana. Entry into the hard-drug market, such as the market for cocaine and heroin, is at the later stages of drug use. Investigations of the *gateway phenomenon* (how early drug use sets the stage for later and harder drugs) reveal that the majority of youth who experiment with drugs, such as alcohol, cigarettes, and marijuana, do not go on to take harder drugs (Waldron, 1998). Youth who are at risk for progressing from experimentation to the development of a habitual and compulsive pattern of drug abuse often have other comorbid disorders and associated risk factors (which will be discussed shortly).

Many children and youth who use substances have comorbid disorders. Several other disorders have been linked to Substance Use and Abuse, including depression, anxiety, Disruptive Behavior Disorders, Eating Disorders, and ADHD. Many have ADHD, plus depression, plus Substance Abuse (Kaplan, 1998). Information from the National Comorbidity Study revealed that individuals with Anxiety Disorders are 2 to 3 times more likely to engage in substance use compared to their nonanxious peers (Kendler, Gallagher, Abelson, & Kessler, 1996).

ADHD and Substance Abuse

In their 8-year follow-up of ADHD children in adolescence, Barkley and colleagues (1990) found that hyperactive teens with ADHD were significantly more likely to use cigarettes and alcohol than their nonhyperactive peers. However, a recent study that followed ADHD children into adolescence revealed higher levels of Substance Use (alcohol, tobacco, and illicit drug use) than their non-ADHD peers (Molina & Pelham, 2003). Furthermore, the authors suggest that a diagnosis of ADHD in childhood seems to be as strong a predictor for Substance Use as having a family history of Substance Abuse and that this risk is not substance specific but cuts across alcohol, tobacco, marijuana, and other drugs.

The authors suggest that results may point to a developmental path-

CAUTION

In this study, the remarkable finding was that it was not the severity of hyperactive-impulsive symptoms or ODD/CD symptoms but the *severity of inattention* that predicted the vulnerable population.

CAUTION

A general concern regarding the treatment of children with ADHD through the use of stimulant medication has been the underlying fear that this will lead to an increased rate of substance use later on. However, research does not support this concern. In fact, successful treatment of ADHD actually serves as a protective factor for later Substance Abuse, as adults who were not treated for ADHD are associated with much higher rates of Substance Abuse (Biederman, Wilens, Mick, Spencer, & Faraone, 1999).

way from inattention to Substance Abuse mediated by academic impairment and suggest that executive functioning deficits may be at the basis of this link to Substance Abuse.

Etiology

Biological, Genetic, and Neurotransmitter Function

Early investigations of alcohol abuse among twins determined that if one twin abused alcohol, the likelihood of the second twin to also abuse alcohol was 54% (Kaij, 1960). Further support is also available from studies of children of alcoholics adopted at birth. These children show a higher rate of alcohol abuse than children who did not have biological parents that were alcoholics (Cadoret, Yates, Troughton, Woodworth & Stewart, 1993).

Studies of neurotransmitter function and genetic transmission have found that an abnormal dopamine receptor (D2) can be found in the majority of individuals who have alcohol dependence and in at least half of those addicted to cocaine (Lawford et al., 1997). One of the most popular theories of addiction suggests that recurrent substance use mimics the effect of naturally occurring neurotransmitters and that the body reduces production as a result (Goldstein, 1994). For example, taking alcohol to relax simulates the neurotransmitter GABA's effect of reducing anxiety. Taking alcohol on a repeated basis, the brain has less need for GABA and production declines. As tolerance is increased, the person requires more and more alcohol to achieve the same effect.

Behavioral Perspective

From a behaviorist perspective, the altered states (reduction of tension or elevation of mood) produced by drugs can be a rewarding alternative for those who are taking them. Reduction of tension is an initial side effect of a number of drugs, including alcohol and marijuana. Given a high level of stress and tension, many people may *self-medicate* to reduce tension. Support for this suggestion can be found in studies that have found high levels of depression and anxiety among those who abuse substances.

DON'T FORGET

Increased usage and decreased production of GABA creates a dependency on the drug to simulate what would have been a natural GABA function.

Sociocultural Perspective

Youth whose families and peers sanction drinking are much more likely to become problem drinkers as are those whose families are unsupportive and stressful. In a longitudinal study that tracked approximately 100 youth from preschool to high school, Shedler and Block (1990) found that Substance Use (marijuana) could be clustered into three categories: *frequent users* (used at least once weekly, plus had tried another drug), *abstainers* (had not tried any drugs), and *experimenters* (tried a few times, plus tried one other drug). Results revealed that teens who experimented with marijuana (which was a relatively commonly used drug at that time) were normal well-adjusted teenagers. Frequent users had the worst profiles; starting out as insecure and distressed in elementary school, these troubled teenagers continued to experience problems socially and emotionally, evident in hostile and antisocial behaviors. Abstainers were also maladjusted and tended to be overcontrolled, timid, and withdrawn.

Dishion, McCord, and Poulin (1999), at the University of Oregon, developed a 12-week intervention program focused on 11- to 14-year-old youth who were considered high risk for drug abuse and increasingly more serious delinquent behaviors. The program, called the Adolescent Transitions Program (ATP), involved 158 at-risk youth (83 boys and 75 girls) who were enrolled in Grades 6 through 8. Youth were randomly assigned to one of four groups: peer group, peer plus parent group, parent only group, and control group (no intervention). The ATP focused on improving skills in the following areas: emotion management, relationship building, and limit setting and saying no to drugs. Parent groups focused on communication skills and problem management.

The study provided a dramatic demonstration of how negative peer influences, *deviancy training,* can encourage rule-breaking behaviors and drug use at a time when peer influence is at a peak and the likelihood of experimentation with drugs is the most pronounced. Within this context, adolescents with low self-esteem or those who are alienated may be most vulnerable to drug use to enhance acceptability and peer status.

Diathesis-Stress Model

Given the nature of drug use and abuse, it is highly likely that etiology results from a combination of multiple factors. One model that attempts to incorporate several factors into an explanation of the development of drug abuse is the *diathesis-stress model* (Windle & Tubman, 1999). The

CAUTION

At the end of the 12-week program, all three groups revealed improved skills and parent-child relationships relative to the control group. However, follow-up 3 years later revealed that those who were aggregated with peers during the 12-week period reported 2 times the tobacco use compared to nongrouped peers and 75% reported more delinquent behaviors. Furthermore, those youth who had the least amount of delinquent behaviors initially showed the greatest amount of change but in a negative direction.

model looks at how some individuals might be more vulnerable to drug-related attempts to cope with stress based on individual characteristics (familial alcoholism, genetic transmission, personality/temperament). At the best of times, coping skills might be adequate. However, when environmental factors (family, school, peers, economics) are adverse, resulting stress may make some individuals more likely to respond using drugs to self-medicate and buffer stress.

Risks and Protective Factors

There are several factors that can place youth at risk for Substance Use and Abuse that operate at all levels of influence. At a personal level, genetic links to an alcoholic parent may increase risk to substance use when environmental pressures increase. Poor self-esteem, depression, anxiety, and attentional problems have all been linked with increased risk for Substance Use. Association with peers who use substances and living in a neighborhood where drugs are readily accessible also place youth at risk. On the other hand, having a supportive family, feeling a sense of belonging to school and community, and doing well academically are all protective factors that serve to buffer youth from engaging in frequent substance use.

The National Institute on Drug Abuse (2003) has recently published the second edition of *Preventing Drug Use among Children and Adolescents: A Research-Based Guide for Parents, Educators, and Community Leaders.* The document is also available on the NIDA web site at www.drugabuse.gov. The guide introduces 16 principles of prevention, addressing issues of risks and protective factors, prevention planning, and prevention-program delivery based on the existing research. The first 4 principles address the importance of addressing issues of risks and protective factors in prevention such that programs enhance protective factors and reduce risks. The principles acknowledge several facts concerning risks and protective factors, including age-related changes and family influences having greater impact in the earlier years, while associating with substance-abusive peers may be an important risk later on (Dishion et al., 1999). Domains of influence are also an important factor when considering the influences of risks and protective factors that can cut across individual, family, peer, school, and community settings.

Treatment

In recent years, there has been increasing recognition of the unique features of drug abuse in youth compared to adults and the need to incorporate these features into programs designed specifically for adolescents (Deas, Riggs, Langen-bucher, Goldman, & Brown, 2000).

Twelve-Step Models

The 12-step models have as their origin the 12-step orientation developed by Alcoholics Anonymous (AA) and Narcotics Anonymous (NA), which were founded on the beliefs that addiction is a progressive disease and that treatment requires abstinence (Kassel & Jackson, 2001). Traditionally, 12-step programs involve community-based meetings that are frequented by recovering members who support each other's abstinence through confessions, sharing stories, and often by providing opportunities for connecting with a lifeline buddy for crisis purposes. Due to the anonymity of the individuals involved in the programs, empirical evidence is lacking concerning the outcomes of the majority of 12-step programs. However, Brown (1993) revealed that 12-step groups, such as AA, Cocaine Anonymous, and NA, are supported and widely attended by recovered youth, while investigations of the 12-step Minnesota model found that youth who attended the program had better outcomes than untreated youth (Kassel & Jackson, 2001).

Cognitive Behavioral Therapy (CBT)

Substance programs that use cognitive behavioral therapy (CBT) focus on a number of targets to reframe maladaptive thinking patterns that have developed as conditioned responses to environmental triggers. The underlying premise is based on learning theory and hypothesizes that Substance Abuse develops as a response to environmental cues or triggers and consequences (socially reinforcing events, physiological arousal) that precipitate and maintain abusive habits (Waldron & Kern-Jones, 2004).

Programs that use CBT mainly focus on enhancing skills in self-management through awareness of triggers and developing adaptive ways of responding to these triggers. Important components of these programs include self-monitoring, assertiveness/refusal skills, avoidance of specific triggers, problem solving, relaxation training, and other approaches to adaptive coping (Monti,

DON'T FORGET

Waldron and Kern-Jones (2004) discuss how framing a cognitive perspective within a social learning model (Bandura, 1977) allows for greater consideration of multiple factors in the acquisition and maintenance of Substance Abuse through mechanisms of observation and imitation learning (parents and peers) in such areas as social reinforcement, self-efficacy, and the development of associated belief systems.

Abrams, Kadden, & Cooney, 1989). A key component of the program is a built-in relapse-prevention component. Empirical investigations of CBT programs have studied the efficacy of these programs delivered individually, in groups, or with family.

In their investigations, Liddle and Hogue (2001) found that youth assigned to individual CBT or Family therapy had significant declines in internalizing and externalizing problems and a reduction in drug use. Liddle and Hogue (2001) and Waldron and Kern-Jones (2004) both found a delay factor operating in CBT programs for youth alone. Liddle and Hogue suggested that perhaps time is required to consolidate the CBT skills that were not evident at posttreatment but emerged as delayed positive outcomes on later follow-up. Initial findings from these and other studies of CBT suggest that CBT programs delivered individually, in groups, or with families can be an effective method of treating Substance Use and Abuse in youth. However, as Waldron and Kern-Jones (2004) suggest, investigation of how these programs can be successful must also address the iatrogenic effects found in other studies that aggregated high-risk youth (Azrin, Donohue, Besalel, Kogan, & Acierno, 1994; Dishion et al., 1999). Ultimately, a greater understanding will be obtained regarding how to best deliver treatment that is supportive and not detrimental.

Family-Based Treatment

Investigations including the family in treatment alternatives for Substance Use and Abuse have used CBT (see preceding), MST (Henggeler, Schoenwald, Borduin, Rowland, & Cunningham, 1998), and functional behavioral family (Emery, 2001) approaches. The inclusion of a family component in the treatment program has been demonstrated to increase participant engagement in the process and increase program effectiveness (Stanton & Shadish, 1997). In a study comparing behavioral family therapy to a treatment alternative (process-oriented treatment), Azrin and colleagues (1994) found family therapy to have a 50% success rate for reduction of alcohol and drug use compared to increased usage in the process-oriented group. In another comparison study, Donohue and Azrin (2001) found family behavioral therapy superior to a program using a problem-solving method.

Prevention

In the United States, federal funds have been available since 1994 to assist in the provision of education programs to prevent drug abuse. However, since 1998, due to amendments to the Safe and Drug-Free Schools and Communities Act (SDFSCA), federal grant requirements have included the need to use empirically based programs (evidence-based curriculum). Several programs exist that incorporate features that have been proven effective through research to reduce drug use and abuse, including awareness of the harmful effects of illicit drugs, nicotine, and alcohol and information regarding how to be more assertive and effective in refusing drugs when offered. Empirically based drug abuse prevention programs targeted at middle school students have been successful in significantly reducing early use of tobacco, alcohol, and other drugs.

Despite the availability of funds and the mandate to include evidence-based programs, a survey conducted by Ringwalt and colleagues (2002) found that 75% of middle schools were using programs that were not supported by research. In fact, the curriculum used by the majority of middle schools, the Drug Abuse Resistance Education program (DARE), has been researched extensively and found to be ineffective in the prevention of drug use and abuse. Other than DARE, the two most popular programs used in public and private schools that have research support are Project Alert and Life Skills Training.

The Life Skills Training program (LST) has been demonstrated effective in significantly reducing drug use and abuse in minority students at risk for drug use due to poor academic performance and association with substance-abusing peers (Botvin, 2001; Griffin et al., 2003). Although the LST program was initially tested on White students in suburban schools, this school-based prevention program has since demonstrated effectiveness across minority ethnic populations (Caucasian, African American, and Hispanic) and socioeconomic levels. The portability of the LST program was demonstrated in a controlled investigation of the program's effectiveness in 29 inner-city New York schools. The LST program was delivered to 7th graders by regular education teachers in 15 sessions (45-minute duration). Sessions provided information about social skills, drug refusal, and personal management. Compared to students who received the standard New York City school drug education program, students enrolled in the LST program demonstrated lower rates of alcohol, cigarette, and inhalant abuse than peers not enrolled in the LST program.

Principles of prevention planning (NIDA, 2003) outline several important research-supported areas to tar-

DON'T FORGET

The prevention guidelines (NIDA, 2003) suggest that school programs should focus on age-appropriate behaviors and intervene to reduce risk factors associated with later maladaptive behaviors such as aggression and self-control (preschool). In elementary school, targets should include emotional awareness, social problem solving, increased communication, and academic support. Improved study habits, academic support, drug resistance skills, self-efficacy, and antidrug attitudes are important areas of focus in middle and high school.

get in the family, school, and community. Family programs should include drug awareness, parent skills training, increased monitoring and supervision, and the need for consistent discipline and limit setting.

Combined family and school programs enhance a community's efficacy in promoting cohesiveness and a sense of belonging.

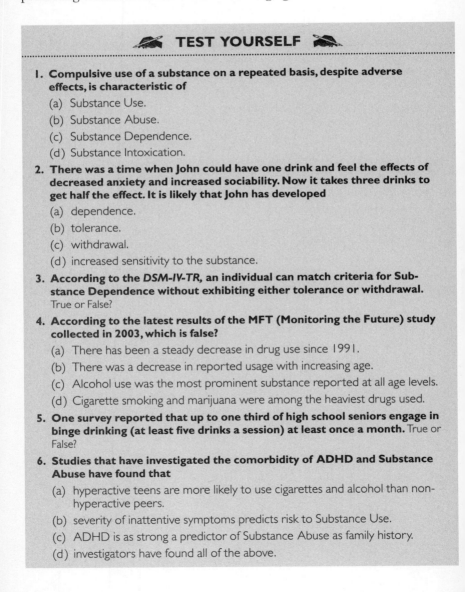

🐟 TEST YOURSELF 🐟

1. **Compulsive use of a substance on a repeated basis, despite adverse effects, is characteristic of**

   (a) Substance Use.

   (b) Substance Abuse.

   (c) Substance Dependence.

   (d) Substance Intoxication.

2. **There was a time when John could have one drink and feel the effects of decreased anxiety and increased sociability. Now it takes three drinks to get half the effect. It is likely that John has developed**

   (a) dependence.

   (b) tolerance.

   (c) withdrawal.

   (d) increased sensitivity to the substance.

3. **According to the *DSM-IV-TR*, an individual can match criteria for Substance Dependence without exhibiting either tolerance or withdrawal.** True or False?

4. **According to the latest results of the MFT (Monitoring the Future) study collected in 2003, which is false?**

   (a) There has been a steady decrease in drug use since 1991.

   (b) There was a decrease in reported usage with increasing age.

   (c) Alcohol use was the most prominent substance reported at all age levels.

   (d) Cigarette smoking and marijuana were among the heaviest drugs used.

5. **One survey reported that up to one third of high school seniors engage in binge drinking (at least five drinks a session) at least once a month.** True or False?

6. **Studies that have investigated the comorbidity of ADHD and Substance Abuse have found that**

   (a) hyperactive teens are more likely to use cigarettes and alcohol than non-hyperactive peers.

   (b) severity of inattentive symptoms predicts risk to Substance Use.

   (c) ADHD is as strong a predictor of Substance Abuse as family history.

   (d) investigators have found all of the above.

7. Although 12-step programs seem to be a viable treatment alternative for adolescents who have Substance Use and Abuse problems, obtaining empirical support has been difficult due to

(a) high dropout rates in these programs.

(b) anonymity associated with the programs.

(c) lack of systematic approach.

(d) lack of interest.

8. Recent investigations of treatment alternatives for youth with Substance Use and Abuse problems have found that including the family in treatment

(a) can increase participation and program effectiveness.

(b) can undermine program success.

(c) is inferior to individual process-oriented treatment.

(d) is virtually impossible.

Answers: 1. c; 2. b; 3. True; 4. b; 5. True; 6. d; 7. b;. 8. a

Eleven

MENTAL RETARDATION AND PERVASIVE DEVELOPMENTAL DISORDERS

T he decision to discuss Mental Retardation (MR) and the Pervasive Developmental Disorders (PDD) within the same chapter was based upon the fact that PDD is most often associated with some degree (mild, moderate, severe or profound) level of MR. It is hoped that understanding the nature of MR will assist the reader in having a better foundation for learning about PDD.

MENTAL RETARDATION

Background

Mental Retardation (MR), which is also known as *learning disability* or *intellectual disability* in other countries, is not actually a medical condition or psychiatric diagnosis and is not really a psychiatric disorder, although it is listed in psychiatric diagnostic manuals (Gillberg & Soderstrom, 2003). In reality, MR is most often used as an administrative label to designate individuals who have subnormal intellectual functioning (usually an IQ below 70) with associated deficits in other areas of adaptive functioning. The *DSM-IV-TR* (APA, 2000) defines MR as *subnormal intellectual functioning* accompanied by *dysfunction or impairment in two adaptive areas,* while the ICD-10 (WHO, 1993) refers to MR as *arrested or incomplete development of the mind* resulting in impairment of skills.

The use of intelligence tests to identify children with below-normal intelligence was introduced at the turn of the century when Alfred Binet was commissioned by the French government to develop an instrument (the Binet Scale) to assist in identifying children with inferior mental ability for purposes of special school placement. Although Binet cautioned against the use of a single score to describe intelligence (Gould, 1981), when the instrument was translated into English by Goddard and subsequently revised by Terman (Stanford-Binet), both authors promoted the strong belief that the IQ score was a valid measure of intelligence and, furthermore, that intelligence was itself fixed and genetically determined.

By the middle of the century, use of the IQ measure as the sole determinant of MR met with increasing disfavor on several fronts. The American Association on Mental Retardation (AAMR) lobbied hard for inclusion of multiple criteria in the determination of MR. However, intelligence testing continued to be the major defining criteria for some years to come. Rampant use of IQ testing to qualify students for special education placement throughout the 1960s and 1970s met with increasing controversy, culminating in the classic case in California of *Larry P. versus Riles*. As a result, severe restrictions were placed on the use of intelligence tests to place African American children in special education programs in California.

Ultimately, lobbying for the rights of all children to have a free and appropriate education, including children with disabilities, resulted in the passing of Bill PL 94-142.

Classification of Mental Retardation

There are currently three primary systems of classification of MR in North America: the *DSM-IV-TR* (APA, 2000); the AAMR, and the Educational System.

The **DSM-IV-TR** *Classification System*

Mental Retardation appears under the Disorders Usually First Diagnosed in Infancy, Childhood, or Adolescence because one of the major criteria is that onset is prior to 18 years of age. Other than Personality Disorders, MR is the only other classification of disorders that appears on Axis II. The reason for Axis II placement is that, like the Personality Disorders, MR is a lifelong problem and, as such, can be mistakenly overlooked when making an Axis I diagnosis.

Significantly subnormal intellectual functioning. The *DSM-IV-TR* defines subnormal intellectual functioning as an IQ of *approximately 70 or less* on a standard individual intellectual assessment instrument (WISC-IV; Stanford-Binet 5th Edition).

DON'T FORGET

Bill PL 94-142 (Education for All Handicapped Children, 1975) emphasized the need to protect the rights of the handicapped and supported the AAMR focus on including adaptive as well as intellectual measures in determining MR in children.

DON'T FORGET

According to the *DSM-IV-TR* (APA, 2000), there are three main criteria required for a diagnosis of MR: significantly subnormal intellectual functioning, impairment in adaptive functioning, and onset prior to eighteen years of age.

The reason that the score is suggested as "approximately 70" is to allow for the standard error of measurement. Intelligence test scores can predict within a 95% accuracy rate. In the case of an IQ score of 70, that would translate into an IQ range of 65 to 75.

The *DSM-IV-TR* (APA, 2000) recognizes four levels of severity of MR based on intellectual functioning and associated expectations: mild, moderate, severe, and profound. The classification of severity is based on intellectual level and provides a number of characteristics and anticipated outcomes associated with each level of impairment. Eighty-five percent of individuals with MR will have a mild level of severity. A summary of the classification and expected outcomes are presented in Rapid Reference 11.1.

Impairment in adaptive functioning. Adaptive functioning covers a wide spectrum of life skills that determine how well an individual is able to function independently in their environment. The *DSM-IV-TR* (APA, 2000) requires identification of adaptive functioning deficits (functioning significantly below age and cultural expectations) in at least two areas, including communication skills, self-care, home living, social/interpersonal skills, use of community resources, self-direction, functional academic skills, work, leisure, health, and safety. The *DSM-IV-TR* (APA, 2000) does not address how to measure deficits in adaptive functioning or the extent of deficit required to meet the criteria for MR.

American Association on Mental Retardation (AAMR)

The AAMR is currently in its 10th revision of *Mental Retardation: Definition,*

DON'T FORGET

The intelligence test produces an IQ score that is a standard score having a mean of 100 and a standard deviation of 15. Sixty-eight% of the population can be expected to score within 1 standard deviation of the mean (IQ score ranges from 85 to 115). A score of 70 represents the threshold of 2 standard deviations below the mean. Two deviations above the mean (IQ 130) is usually the threshold for identifying the gifted range.

CAUTION

Children who lack stimulation or have been deprived of adequate opportunity to develop their cognitive skills may also score very low on IQ tests. It is therefore essential to determine whether deficits are the result of true limitations in capacity or lack of opportunity.

CAUTION

Adaptive functioning may also be influenced by many factors other than intellectual ability, including motivation, comorbid conditions, deprivation, opportunities to access supportive services, and family support.

Rapid Reference 11.1

Severity Levels of Mental Retardation

Degree of Mental Retardation	IQ range	Percent of retarded population	Expected outcome
Mild Mental Retardation (education system: educable MR)	50–55 to 70*	85	Early years may look like delays rather than deficits *Upper limit:* grade 6 academic level Adults: self-support with supervision
Moderate Mental Retardation (education system: trainable retarded)	35–40 to 50	10	*Academic expectation:* grade 2 Adults: supervision and sheltered workshops
Severe Mental Retardation	20–40	3–4	Minimal self-care; group homes
Profound Mental Retardation	Below 20	1–2	Often involves multiple handicaps; supervision and sheltered settings

Source: DSM-IV-TR (APA, 2000).

*The DSM-IV-TR states "approximately 70" to account for the 5% error in intellectual assessments and resulting in the confidence interval of 65 to 75.

> **DON'T FORGET**
>
> Underlying this shift was strong opposition to attempts to fit individuals with MR into existing diagnostic categories (*DSM-IV-TR* categories of severity) with assigned models of service.

> **DON'T FORGET**
>
> While the *DSM-IV-TR* (APA, 2000) does not define how to measure a significant deficit in adaptive functioning, the AAMR is specific in its operational definition of adaptive limitations meeting a threshold of 2 standard deviations below the norm on a standardized measure. The AAMR criterion requires a significant deficit (2 standard deviations below the norm) in any one of the following three adaptive categories: conceptual, social, or practical skills.

Classification and Systems of Support (2002), which builds upon the previous landmark decision (1992) to shift emphasis away from the *DSM-IV-TR* focus on severity of disorder (mild, moderate, severe, and profound) toward greater focus on intensity of intervention required (intermittent, limited, extensive, or pervasive).

The AAMR emphasizes that MR is not a mental disorder or a medical disorder but a state of functioning beginning in childhood that is characterized by limitations in intellectual and adaptive skills. The most recent definition emphasizes the need to consider multidimensional and ecological influences in developing interventions. Therefore, the AAMR is strongly supportive of interventions aimed at individualized supports to enhance productivity.

AAMR criteria for Mental Retardation.   There is consistency between the AAMR and *DSM-IV-TR* regarding age of onset (prior to 18 years), IQ criterion (approximately 70), and the fact that IQ score alone is unacceptable. However, differences do exist between the *DSM-IV-TR* and the AAMR in how adaptive behavior is defined and guidelines regarding how deficits are determined.

The current definition (AAMR, 2002) recognizes nine areas where supports should be evaluated, including human development, education, home living, community living, employment, health and safety, behavior, social, and protection/advocacy issues. Recently, the AAMR introduced the Supports Intensity Scale (SIS; AAMR, 2003), which was developed to evaluate the level of support intensity needed to assist with more effective treatment planning.

Educational Definitions of Mental Retardation

Although the definition of MR used by the educational system was initially in agreement with the definition set by the AAMR, the suggested IQ level to serve as the threshold for MR has changed over the years. In the 1970s, when Bill

PL 94-142 was issued, the IQ level set by the AAMR for MR was 85. The situation is even more complex because, while IDEA provides the general impetus for educational determination, funds for special education programs are allocated by state codes that set cutoff scores to determine eligibility for programs.

Education has seen significant change over the years regarding how disabilities are defined. The initial criteria involved an IQ range of 55 to 80 for classification as EMR, while students with IQs in the 25 to 55 range were classified as TMR.

In their study of classification procedures and consistency of placement within the state of California, Mac-Millan and Forness (1998) found that significant discrepancies existed between criteria for placement and actual placement decisions regarding identification of students with MR and those with specific learning disabilities (SLD). The authors suggest that placement decisions may be made more on compliance issues (allotted placements per category) than on predetermined criteria.

> **DON'T FORGET**
>
> Depending on the district, terms vary as do program titles. Education commonly uses either Educable Mentally Retarded (EMR) or Educable Mentally Handicapped (EMH) and Trainable Mentally Retarded (TMR) or Trainable Mentally Handicapped (TMH) to designate programs and student placement within the MR category.

> **CAUTION**
>
> Although the majority of states accept the MR cutoff at an IQ between 70 and 75, some states, like Iowa, have retained higher cutoff levels, for example, IQ 85 (MacMillan & Forness, 1998). With the reauthorization of IDEA expected in 2004 or early 2005, it is not clear whether more specific and consistent definitions will be required across all states.

Developmental and Associated Features

There are wide variations in the presenting features of MR depending on the severity and associated personality and behavioral characteristics. Developmental delays vary widely with the nature of the retardation. For some individuals, incapacity is limited to impaired academic performance (once called *6-hour retardates*), while adaptive skills are adequate in all other areas. Other individuals have concomitant aggressive features and behavior problems that exacerbate their limitations and reduce their ability to adjust and adapt successfully. Some of the negative features that can predict more serious problems include self-injurious behavior, aggression, stereotypical movements, communication problems, and overactivity (Aman, Hammer, & Rohahn, 1993).

Cognitively, depending on the level of severity, some individuals with mild MR (such as upper level Down syndrome) can be quite capable of adequate functioning at a slower pace with modified goals. Typically, cognitive limitations are less noticeable in predictable and structured environments and most noticeable in novel situations or when abrupt changes disrupt predicted routines.

Prevalence, Comorbidity, and Course

The overall prevalence of MR is approximately 1 to 3%. Males are probably more highly represented in this population. Eighty-five percent of the MR population have Mild Mental Retardation. By definition, onset is before 18 years of age, and earlier identification is associated with more severe forms of MR. Mild delays may not be detected until formal schooling begins.

According to the *DSM-IV-TR* (APA, 2000), individuals with MR are at risk for comorbid disorders at a rate 3 to 4 times higher than the general population. In addition, diagnosis may be more complex, as the common disorder features may be modified by the presence of MR. The *DSM-IV-TR* lists the following disorders as the most common comorbid disorders of MR: ADHD, Mood Disorders, Pervasive Developmental Disorders (PDD), Stereotypic Movement Disorder, and mental disorders due to a medical condition (e.g., head trauma). Comorbidity may also vary with the etiology of MR, for example, Fragile X often has comorbid ADHD and Social Phobia, while Prader-Willi syndrome is often accompanied by anxiety and ADHD.

CAUTION

According to *DSM-IV-TR* (APA, 2000), if criteria are met for MR, then that diagnosis is given on AXIS II. Any other presenting condition is placed on AXIS I. In consideration of comorbid ADHD features, it is important to remember that many children with MR are often inattentive and active. An important distinction regarding MR populations is that a diagnosis of ADHD is only made if these symptoms are excessive for the child's *mental age, not chronological age*.

Etiology

Biological and Genetic Factors

Mental retardation can be the result of *genetic defects*.

One of the most well-known types of MR, Down syndrome, results from a chromosomal abnormality involving chromosome 21 (incorrect number of chromosomes or damaged chromosomes). Down syndrome children usually have classic features, including short stature, round face, almond-shaped eyes, flat facial features, and low muscle tone.

They can be socially engaging and affectionate, but they can also be stubborn. Speech problems are common, and health problems (heart) are also common. Down syndrome children can vary widely in their IQ potential, with some children scoring into the

> **DON'T FORGET**
> ....
> Risk factors for MR may also be related to having another medical condition at birth, such as cerebral palsy or a seizure disorder, such as epilepsy.

upper limits of the low average range (upper-level Down syndrome). The risk for Down syndrome increases with the maternal and paternal age. The risk for women over 45 years of age is 1 in 25 births.

Prader-Willi syndrome is often recognized at birth due to low muscle tone and low reflex responses. A disorder of chromosome 15, Prader-Willi syndrome is recognizable in school-aged children, not only in physical features (short stature, small hands and feet), but by the accompanying problems of impulsivity, temper tantrums, compulsive eating, and some degree of MR (IQ scores generally in the 60 to 80 range).

Environmental Factors

During prenatal development, environmental factors can cause birth defects. Environmental toxins, called *teratogens,* can cause considerable harm to the fetus. Approximately 33% of all babies born to mothers who are heavy consumers of alcohol will be born with *fetal alcohol syndrome (FAS)*. Clinical features of FAS include slow growth, central nervous system dysfunction (MR, hyperactivity, irritability); and unusual facial features (underdeveloped upper lip, flattened nose, widely spaced eyes). Although facial features become less pronounced with age, cognitive deficits remain.

Other causes of MR that may occur postdelivery include premature birth, lack of oxygen at birth (anoxia) due to difficult delivery (cord wrapped around neck); head injuries, encephalitis, or meningitis. Children can also acquire diminished brain capacity due to pollutants in the environment, such as developing lead toxicity due to consuming lead-based paint.

Assessment

Assessment of MR requires a full developmental and medical history in order to determine the potential etiology, onset (prior to 18), and to rule out other competing diagnostic possibilities. Obtaining information regarding when the child achieved developmental milestones is an important part of the interview process for the identification of MR, as many of these children will demonstrate developmental delays in the acquisition of milestones. Individual assessment of intellectual functioning and adaptive functioning are also a necessary part of the identification and diagnostic process.

Intellectual assessment should be conducted using the age- and culture-appropriate instrument. Common intellectual instruments used to assess intelligence in English speaking children are summarized in Rapid Reference 11.2.

Although the *DSM-IV-TR* does not specify the extent of adaptive deficit required, there are several scales that can be used to measure adaptive functioning. These instruments provide information concerning how the individual's level of adaptive functioning compares to developmental expectations. Although information is obtained through structured interview format, results provide standard scores that can be used to directly compare adaptive levels with intellectual expectations. The instruments also provide age-equivalent scores to assist in determining developmental expectations. A list of common adaptive measures is available in Rapid Reference 11.2.

Intervention

Interventions for children and adolescents with MR focus primarily on either behavioral/emotional issues or educational issues.

Behavioral Interventions

Behavioral programs have been very successful in targeting and altering problematic social, emotional, and behavioral concerns. The reason for the success of the behavioral programs can be linked to the program focus on breaking down problem behaviors into component parts (simplicity) and to systematically shaping behaviors into more socially adaptive skills through contingency management.

Empirical support for the use of behavioral methods with MR populations is well documented (Handen, 1998), and several techniques are available to develop programs across the developmental spectrum to suit a number of problem behaviors (behavior chaining, secondary rewards, token economies). Contingency programs can be developed to reduce excess behaviors (aggression, noncompliance) and increase deficit behaviors (compliance, social skills) at school and in the home (Wielkiewicz, 1995).

DON'T FORGET

Adaptive functioning can differ based on environmental demands. The *DSM-IV-TR* also advised that adaptive information be collected from different (home and school) sources.

Parent Training Programs

Research has demonstrated that including a parent component in the behavioral program can enhance suc-

≡ Rapid Reference 11.2

Common Intellectual Assessment Instruments

Instrument/Age level	Assessment	Measures
The Wechsler Preschool and Primary Intelligence Test (WPPSI-III): 2:6 to 7:3	Individual	Full Scale IQ, Verbal IQ, Performance IQ
The Wechsler Intelligence Scale for Children (WISC-IV): ages 6–16:11	Individual	Full Scale IQ: Verbal Comprehension, Perceptual Reasoning, Processing Speed and Working Memory Indexes
The Stanford-Binet, 5th Edition: ages 2 years to 85	Individual	Full Scale IQ, Verbal IQ, Performance IQ
The Differential Abilities Test (DAS) Preschool level: 2:6 to 5:11 School age level: 6 to 17:11	Individual	Verbal Ability, Nonverbal Ability, Spatial Ability, and General Conceptual Ability

Common Adaptive Behavior Instruments

Instrument/Age level	Assessment	Measures
Vineland Adaptive Behavior Scales: Birth to 18:11	Interview Survey Interview Expanded Classroom Edition	Adaptive behavior in four domains: Communication, Daily Living Skills; Socialization, and Motor Skills
AAMR Adaptive Behavior Scales—School, 2nd Edition (ABS-S:2): 3 years through 18:11	Behavior Rating Scale	Five factor scales: personal self-sufficiency, community self-sufficiency, personal-social responsibility, social adjustment, and personal adjustment
Adaptive Behavior Assessment System (ABAS II): Birth to 21	Parent and Teacher Rating Scales	Assesses 10 specific adaptive skills (*DSM-IV-TR*), plus three general areas (AAMR)

(continued)

Common Assessment Measures for Pervasive Developmental Disorders

Instrument/Age level	Assessment	Measures
Gilliam Autism Rating Scale (GARS): 3 years through 22	Behavior Rating Scale	Autism quotient, four scales: stereotyped behaviors, social interaction, communication, and developmental disturbance
Childhood Autism Rating Scale (CARS): 2 years+	Behavior Rating Scale	Classifies autistic symptoms into mild-moderate-severe range
Asperger Syndrome Diagnostic Scale (ASDS): 5 through 18 years	Behavior Rating Scale	Asperger quotient, five scales: cognitive, maladaptive, language, social, and sensorimotor
Gilliam Asperger's Disorder Scale (GADS): 3 through 22 years	Behavior Rating Scale	Four scales

Note. References for all instruments can be found in Appendix B.

cess by increased consistency and transfer of effects between home and school or treatment facility (Handen, 1998).

Educational Programs

The debate regarding whether children with MR are better served within special education programs or the regular class (a practice referred to as mainstreaming or inclusion) has waged over the past 20 years or more. While some studies show minimal effects of special education programming (Hocutt, 1996), other studies suggest that mainstreaming does not sufficiently address academic concerns (Taylor, 1986). With the new reauthorization of IDEA on the horizon, it remains to be seen what future direction will be recommended to best meet the needs of children with MR and all other children with special educational needs.

Prevention

Prevention programs have been instituted at all levels of intervention, from prenatal awareness campaigns (effects of drug abuse and alcohol, genetic counseling) to early intervention programs targeting parenting skills and early stimulation programs, such as Head Start programs. The impact of early intervention programs within the first 5 years of life has been clearly documented in the prevention of increasing cognitive declines (Guralnick, 1998).

PERVASIVE DEVELOPMENTAL DISORDERS (PDD)

As the name would imply, the category of PDD includes disorders that are severe and have pervasive impairments in several areas of functioning, including *restrictive range of activities* (stereotypical behaviors, restricted interests), *lack of reciprocal interaction,* and *limitations in communication skills.* The majority of children with PDD will also have comorbid MR.

There are four disorders that fall under the PDD umbrella: Autistic Disorder, Rett's Disorder, Childhood Disintegrative Disorder, and Asperger's Disorder. Individuals who meet some of the criteria or have atypical features may more appropriately be labeled as PDD, Not Otherwise Specified (NOS). The section on PDD will begin with a discussion of two lesser known and less prevalent disorders that have similar types of onset: Rett's Disorder and Child Disintegration Disorder. Prevalence rates are difficult to obtain for these two disorders. They are described as rare by the *DSM-IV-TR* (APA, 2000).

Rett's Disorder and Childhood Disintegrative Disorder

Rett's Disorder

Children who eventually present with Rett's Disorder experience no problems with prenatal or perinatal development and demonstrate normal motor development throughout the first 5 months of life. At birth, head circumference is normal. Until onset (which may occur anytime between 5 months and 48 months), these children appear to be developing at a normal pace. However, in the 1st or 2nd year of life, deterioration of function begins its predictable, characteristic, and progressive course, involving deceleration of head growth, loss of previous hand function (which is replaced by stereotypical hand wringing), loss of social engagement, loss of coordination, and severely impaired language and psychomotor skills.

Rett's Disorder is usually associated with severe or profound levels of MR and is found only in females. There may be some recovery of social engagement later on.

Childhood Disintegrative Disorder

While onset for Rett's Disorder can be as early as 5 months, for Childhood Disintegrative Disorder, the

---

DON'T FORGET

Children who are eventually diagnosed with Rett's Disorder and Childhood Disintegrative Disorder begin their development in an apparently normal fashion. However, following a period of what looks like normal development, parents are faced with the tragic loss of their normal child as, without warning, children with these disorders begin a rapid decline and deterioration in functioning.

period of normal development is longer, with onset following at least 2 years of normal functioning. Although Rett's Disorder is found only in females, children with Childhood Disintegrative Disorder are more likely to be male. Tragically, after at least 2 years of normal social, cognitive, and motor development, children develop a progressive loss of previous function (prior to age 10) in at least two of the following areas: language, social/adaptive skills, bowel or bladder function, play, or motor skills. Loss of function is accompanied by at least two areas of atypical functioning and qualitative impairment in *social interaction* (lack of reciprocity), *communication* (stereotypical, lack of initiation), and *restricted range of activities* (repetitive and stereotypical patterns of behavior).

Autistic Disorder and Asperger's Disorder

Autism is a pervasive developmental disorder that features a triad of symptoms involving severe *impairment in social interaction* (lack of social engagement and reciprocity), markedly *restricted range of activities and interests* (rigid and inflexible thinking and pervasive need for sameness), and *impaired communication* (lack of communication). Leo Kanner first documented accounts of autism in 1943, when he described seemingly incompatible and atypical characteristics shared in a number of case studies. The children seemed noncommunicative, aloof, and engaged in nonproductive and meaningless activity, including an obsessive need for sameness. Yet they demonstrated what Kanner felt was good cognitive potential in their remarkable rote memory and performance on the Seguin Form Board Test.

According to Rutter (1978), during the next 30 years a number of different diagnostic labels were suggested to account for these atypical features (infantile autism, childhood

CAUTION

Although areas of impaired functioning (social interaction, communication, restricted range of activities) are very similar in children with Rett's Disorder and those with autism, differential diagnosis is relatively simple, as autistic children do not demonstrate a progressive deterioration after a period of normal development.

DON'T FORGET

Although Asperger's Disorder is less well known than autism, Hans Asperger actually published his account of atypical children with similar features in a paper the year following Kanner's publication. However, it was not until Wing (1981) published a paper comparing Kanner's syndrome with Asperger's syndrome that Asperger's Disorder gained recognition in its own right.

psychosis, childhood schizophrenia) and were applied to children who had all, some, or few of the features described by Kanner.

Although autism has been recognized by both the *DSM-IV* (APA, 1994) and the ICD-10 (WHO, 1993) for quite some time, Asperger's Disorder is a relatively new diagnostic category having only been added to both the *DSM-IV* and ICD-10 on their most recent revisions (1993, 1994). Children with autism and Asperger's Disorder share a number of common features (qualitative social impairment, restricted range of activities/interests); however, the diagnostic manuals suggest that a diagnosis of autism requires language delay and/or qualitative impairment in language, while a diagnosis of Asperger's requires no significant language delay.

Controversy surrounding the autism/Asperger's debate has been ongoing. Some theorists have suggested that Asperger's Disorder represents a less severe type of autism (Schopler, 1985), while others (Howlin, 1987; Wing, 1981) have recommended retention of the separate categories, specifically due to the language-based differences noted in the criteria.

Prevalence rates also seem different. For example, Gillberg (1998) found that Asperger's Disorder was 5 times more common than autism.

Recently, Macintosh and Dissanayake (2004) conducted an extensive empirical review in an attempt to resolve the controversy as to whether autism and Asperger's should be considered distinct diagnostic categories or whether both disorders should be considered along the same autistic spectrum. The review focused on all relevant studies, which included individuals diagnosed with Asperger's and individuals diagnosed with high-functioning autism (HFA), in order to evaluate similarities and differences between these two groups (see Macintosh & Dissanayake, 2004, for details). Results of their meta-analysis revealed that initial differences be-

CAUTION

Several studies do not support the current diagnostic criteria. Researchers have found children who meet the criteria for Asperger's who have language problems, (Eisenmajer et al., 1996; Prior et al., 1998); while others have found autistic children who do not demonstrate significant language delay (Eisenmajer et al., 1996; Miller & Ozonoff, 2000).

DON'T FORGET

In their review, Macintosh and Dissanayake (2004) noted that although different language patterns were evident (the HFA group demonstrating more atypical speech patterns [*echolalia, noun reversals, atypical gestures*], while the Asperger's group tended to have more verbal rituals and asked odd questions), studies demonstrated little basis for differentiation on the basis of diagnosis.

tween these two groups diminished with increasing age. Although the HFA group demonstrated later language onset and greater dysfunction in preschool, by adolescence, the only distinguishing feature between these two groups was that teens with Asperger's Disorder engaged in more pedantic dialogues.

Investigations of cognitive patterns produced mixed results: Some studies suggested strengths in verbal intelligence (elevated Verbal IQ) for children with Asperger's and strengths in visual intelligence (elevated Performance IQ) for children with HFA; other studies did not confirm these findings. However, between-group differences were found in studies investigating capabilities for *theory of mind* reasoning (*an individual's ability to comprehend that others have a mental set or belief system that may influence their actions*). A common method of studying theory of mind is through the mechanism of false beliefs. An example of such a technique is presented in the Putting It Into Practice box.

In these investigations, children with autism (even HFA) have significantly more difficulty predicting the correct response compared to normal children or children with Asperger's Disorder.

Putting It Into Practice

Nancy loves chocolate milk. Nancy always brings her chocolate milk to school in a blue container. Today Nancy leaves her container of milk on the desk and leaves the room. Millie loves chocolate milk too, but she only has white milk in her container. While Nancy is out of the room, Millie drinks Nancy's chocolate milk and replaces it with white milk. The container is dark blue, so Nancy cannot see the color of the milk. When Nancy comes back into the room, will she think the milk in the blue container is chocolate or white?

DON'T FORGET

Ultimately, Macintosh and Dissanayake (2004) suggest that best clinical practice might be to consider both disorders as part of the *autism spectrum disorders* and then to specify the subtype of the disorder as either Autistic Disorder or Asperger's Disorder.

Comparative Evaluation of Autism/Asperger's Disorder: A Summation

Based on their meta-analysis, Macintosh and Dissanayake (2004) acknowledge that despite methodological problems (e.g., problems comparing studies due to differences in defining criteria), there seem to be few qualitative differences evident between individuals diagnosed with high-functioning autism and Asperger's Disorder that would warrant two distinct syndromes.

Autistic Spectrum Disorders

Autistic Disorder

According to the *DSM-IV-TR* (APA, 2000) a diagnosis of autism requires

≡Rapid Reference 11.3

DSM-IV-TR Criteria for Autism

Six symptoms are required from the following list.

Qualitative impairment in social interaction: at least two symptoms required	• Nonverbal communication (eye contact, gestures, facial expressions) • Peer relationships • Spontaneous sharing (showing, pointing) • Social/emotional reciprocity
Qualitative impairment in communication: at least one symptom required	• Delayed or lack of language • Impaired conversations skills • Stereotyped and repetitive usage of atypical language patterns (echolalia, pronoun reversal) • Lack of symbolic play or social imitation
Restricted range of activities/interests: at least one symptom required	• Preoccupation with single interest (lining up objects) • Preoccupation with parts of objects (wheel of a car) • Rigid adherence to nonfunctional routines • Repetitive motor mannerisms (self-stimulatory behaviors, handflapping)

evidence of "qualitatively" impaired functioning in two areas: social interaction and communication; plus, marked restriction in activities due to stereotypical and repetitive patterns of behavior. The diagnostic symptoms and *DSM-IV-TR* criteria are outlined in Rapid Reference 11.3. A total of six symptoms are required for a diagnosis of autism, two from the first category and one from each of the remaining two.

DON'T FORGET

The autistic triad of symptoms includes the following:

1. Qualitative impairment in social interaction.

2. Qualitative impairment in communication.

3. Restricted range of activities.

In addition to meeting the six symptom criteria outlined previously, delays or atypical behavior patterns must also be noted in at least one of the following three social areas: *social interaction, social communication,* and *social/imaginative play.*

The onset of Autistic Disorder is prior to 3 years of age.

CAUTION

Cognitive delay is not addressed under the criteria for autism due to the wide variation in cognitive functioning. However, 75% of children with autism have MR, while those with Asperger's Disorder are generally in the average range.

Asperger's Disorder

A diagnosis of Asperger's Disorder (APA, 2000) requires the same criteria as autism for qualitative impairment in social interaction (two symptoms) and restricted range of activities (one symptom). For examples of these behaviors, refer to Rapid Reference 11.3. According to the *DSM-IV-TR* (APA, 2000), Asperger's Disorder must also meet the following criteria:

- There is no clinically significant delay in language (e.g., single word usage by 2 years of age).
- There is no qualitative impairment in communication.
- There is no clinically significant delay in cognitive development (self-help skills or adaptive skills other than social delay).

Associated Features and Developmental Considerations of Autistic Spectrum Disorders

Language and Communication

There is wide variability in the language skills of individuals with Autistic Disorder. Most have some qualitative impairment in speech; however, the degree of severity can vary. Usually there is late onset of speech or minimal communication. Impairment is evident in verbal and nonverbal communication. If they do speak, the voice may be monotone and robotic, with intonation more like that used for asking questions (raising pitch at the end) than for making a statement. Echolalia (tendencies to repeat what is said to them) and pronoun reversals are common. There is an absence of pragmatic speech and they often interpret information literally. Also included within this category is the lack of spontaneous make-believe or socially initiated play.

Children with high-functioning autism, compared to Asperger's, demonstrated later onset of language, experienced problems in two-way conversations, and were more likely to have early repetitive, stereotyped, and idiosyncratic language patterns (Eisenmajer et al., 1996). Although children with Asperger's Disorder have a better developed vocabulary than those with higher functioning autism, they share problems in areas of pragmatics, comprehension, and intonation with their higher functioning autistic peers (Ramberg, Ehlers, Nyden, Johansson, & Gillberg, 1996).

Research findings. Several investigations have provided increased understanding of why difficulties exist in language development and imaginative play. Although children with autism develop syntax (understanding of sentence production) comparable to other children of the same mental age (Tager-Flusberg et al., 1990), children with autism experience problems with relational concepts (short, tall), underlying desire or intention (want, believe), and pronoun reversals (*I* and *you*). Studies have shown that even if gestures are within the repertoire of these children, they do not use gestures spontaneously to communicate (Prior & Werry, 1986). Furthermore, the children demonstrate significant pragmatic problems, tending to talk at someone rather than in a reciprocal interchange (Volkmar, 1987).

> **DON'T FORGET**
>
> Despite the differences between children with higher functioning autism and those with Asperger's concerning language in the early years, studies suggest that by the time these children are in middle school, their language skills will look far more similar.

> **DON'T FORGET**
>
> It has been suggested that deficits in understanding others' mental states (research regarding theory of mind and desire) likely accounts for difficulties in integrating the role of the listener in their communication output (Perner, Frith, Leslie, & Leekam, 1989).

Social Interaction

While children with MR often excel at imitative behavior, children with autism fail to engage in imitative exchanges either socially or in game format. Following routines is accomplished in a mechanical way that preempts any personal engagement in the task. Often, autistic children seem unaware of others in their presence and seem to lack the initiative or inclination to communicate with others socially through sharing interests (pointing, etc.) or enjoyment.

In children with Asperger's Disorder, verbal skills are often much better developed than their lower functioning autistic peers. However, children with Asperger's Disorder often initiate pseudosocial conversations and can talk endlessly about a specific preoccupation in monologue without any interest in their audience's reaction. Unlike their autistic peers, children with Asperger's Disorder often desire to have friendships as they become older; however, they have few social skills and little understanding of the process involved.

Research findings. Studies have established several deficits that contribute to underlying difficulties in social reciprocity, including use of normal eye contact to establish reciprocal exchange (Volkmar & Mayes, 1990), lack of social smile

DON'T FORGET

Developmentally *referential looking* (shifting gaze between caregiver and object of interest) occurs around 6 to 9 months and is followed by the active use of gestures to engage adults in reciprocal interaction.

DON'T FORGET

When their senses are overwhelmed, these children may find solace in hyperfocusing on a repetitive nonfunctional task (spinning wheels on a truck, lining up toys) or in the rigid adherence to the familiar.

(Dawson, Hill, Spencer, Galpert, & Watson, 1990), deficiencies in social imitation (Klinger & Dawson, 1996), and deficiencies in *joint attention behavior* (Mundy, 1995).

Restricted Patterns of Behaviors and Interests

In autistic children, *preoccupation* can be with *sameness* (refusals to change routines), *nonfunctional routines* (lining up objects, spinning tops), or with *object parts* (continually spinning the wheel of a toy truck). Preoccupation can also be evident in a *fixation* with numbers, schedules, and timetables. Some children will memorize every name in a telephone book or every television program in *TV Guide*.

Research investigations have suggested several possible reasons for the need for repetition and sameness. Children with autism have been described by parents as being either hyperresponsive (readily overwhelmed by external input) or hyposensitive (unresponsive to external input).

Prevalence, Comorbidity, and Course

Prevalence rate for Autistic Disorder is approximately 5 cases per 10,000, while the prevalence rate for Asperger's Disorder has been estimated to be as high as 20 to 25 per 10,000 (Gillberg, 1998). Autism and Asperger's Disorder are more common in males than females. Up to 75% of children with autism have an associated diagnosis of MR, although the degree of retardation can range from mild to profound. In children with Asperger's Disorder, MR is less frequent and, if evident, is usually in the mild range. Comorbidity with attention problems, affective disorders, Obsessive-Compulsive Disorder, and Tourette's Disorder is common among children with Autistic Disorder and Asperger's Disorder. Many individuals with Asperger's Disorder also have ADHD and can be vulnerable to depression. Autistic Disorder is also often associated with neurological findings, such as an irregular EEG, and approximately 25% will develop seizures (APA, 2000).

Etiology

As early as the late 1960s, autism was thought to be caused by mothers who shaped their child's future by their cold and nonnurturing ways. The term *refrigerator mother* was used to describe the mothers of autistic children.

Biological, neurological, and neurotransmitter factors. Studies have demonstrated that if one monozygotic twin has autism, then the chances of the second twin also having autism are at least 1 in 3. Furthermore, in families where the second twin does not have autism, the nonautistic twin has autistic features but to a lesser extent (Bailey, Phillips, & Rutter, 1996).

As of yet, no specific genes have been isolated. The neurotransmitter serotonin has been implicated. However, unlike other disorders that were linked to a low level of serotonin (depression, Obsessive-Compulsive Disorder), studies have demonstrated elevated levels of serotonin in approximately 25% of those with Autistic Disorder (Klinger & Dawson, 1996).

> **CAUTION**
>
> There is an increased risk and higher incidence of autism in families of children with Asperger's Disorder and increased risk for Asperger's Disorder in families with autism (Eisenmajer et al., 1996; Gillberg, 1998).

> **CAUTION**
>
> There has been significant controversy and debate regarding whether autism can be caused by a childhood vaccine (particularly the measles-mumps-rubella vaccine [MMR]) or a mercury-containing preservative (thimerosal) used in some childhood vaccines since 1930. A recent report published by the Institute of Medicine (IOM), summarized in *Infection Control Today* (2004), suggests that based on a review of 19 studies on autism and vaccines, the IOM panel found (1) no evidence of thimerosal causing autism, (2) no evidence that the MMR vaccine causes autism, and (3) no support for the theory that vaccines may trigger an immune response that damages the brain.

Assessment

The assessment of autism or Asperger's Disorder can be aided by the use of a number of behavioral rating scales that have been designed specifically to evaluate the likelihood that symptoms represent autism or Asperger's Disorder. Of course, a medical and family history are essential to chart the course of the disorder as well as obtaining information to evaluate potential comorbid disorders. A summary of some of the most commonly used rating scales can be found in Rapid Reference 11.2.

Treatment and Intervention

The autistic spectrum disorders represent a wide range of functioning. Although most children will demonstrate difficulties that conform to the triad of symptoms, how the disorder is manifested and the degree of severity will vary markedly. Therefore, it is very difficult to suggest any one program for all children. The importance of conducting an assessment that targets the areas of need is a crucial precursor to developing an appropriate treatment plan.

Autism was one of the disorders of childhood that was reviewed as part of the APA Task Force on evidence-based treatments. In her extensive review of programs for children with autism, S. J. Rogers (1998) did not find a specific program that matched the more stringent criteria, although the investigation did reveal eight comprehensive programs that obtained positive outcomes. The programs were intensive (involving anywhere from 15 to 40 hours a week), focused on early intervention (5 years or younger), and used behavioral methods. Significant gains were noted in decreased symptoms of autism, enhanced language skills, achievement of developmental goals, and social relations.

Dawson and Osterling (1996) conducted a similar meta-analysis and found that approximately half of the children who participated in the programs were able to bypass special education and enroll in the regular elementary school classroom. The authors suggest a number of characteristics common to successful programs, including targeting specific deficits (attention, compliance, appropriate play), use of a highly structured and predictable program with low pupil to staff ratio, integration of programs across situations (clinic, home, school), engagement of parents as cotherapists, and careful monitoring of transitions between programs.

Although there is some controversy regarding which program is the best for autistic children, there is agreement that beyond early intervention, at a minimum, educational programs should provide opportunities for intense engagement in the process of learning, individualized and systematic instruction, and parental involvement (Hurth, Shaw, Izeman, Whaley, & Rogers, 1999).

Lovaas and the UCLA Applied Behavioral Analysis Program

One pioneering program in the area of intervention programs for autistic children was the program developed by Ivar Lovaas (1987) at UCLA. Modeled on principles of applied behavioral analysis (ABA), the program was intensive (3-year duration, 40 hours a week), pervasive (home and clinic), and relied heavily upon behavioral methods of operant conditioning, imitation, and reinforcement. Initially, the focus was on appropriate behavior (reducing disruptive behavior and increasing compliance and imitation). In the 2nd year, language training (increased use of appropriate expressive language) and social play were emphasized. The 3rd year provided opportunities for fine-tuning skills for integration into the school system (emotional expression, preacademic skills, etc.). Average age on entrance to the program was approximately 2.5 years.

When the children were approximately 7 years of age, outcomes were compared for children enrolled in the most intensive group with those who received less intensive programming. Almost half (47%) of the children in the intensive group increased their IQ scores an average of 37 points (placing them in the average range) and were promoted to the regular second grade. Unfortunately, children who received less intensive services, or only special education, demonstrated minimal gains overall. Gains were maintained at follow-up 6 years later.

TEACCH Program

Another program that has gained increasing popularity is the Treatment and Education for Autistic and Related Communication Handicapped Children program (TEACCH; Schopler, 1994). The program focuses on close collaboration between parents and professionals and is based on the underlying belief that children are motivated to learn language as intentional communication, in a means-end association. For example, a child learns to say the word *eat* or *cookie* to obtain a favorite treat. The pragmatic approach of this program is evident as language becomes contextualized and integrated into ongoing daily activities rather than being taught as a discrete skill. The TEACCH program also translates abstract concepts (e.g., time, space) into visually meaningful alternatives (visual schedules and charts) that provide children with a visible way to track and predict the order of events, thereby alleviating anxiety generated by preoccupations with the need for sameness and rigidity of routines.

The TEACCH program is a functional approach (Schopler, 1994) that has been used internationally to assist in the integration of children with autism into regular classroom activities. Empirically, the TEACCH program has been identified as a successful treatment for reducing self-injurious behaviors (Norgate, 1998), in enhancing skills in individuals with high-functioning autism and Asperger's Disorder (Kunce & Mesibov, 1998), and more effective than a nonspecific educational alternative (Panerai, Ferrante, & Zingale, 2002).

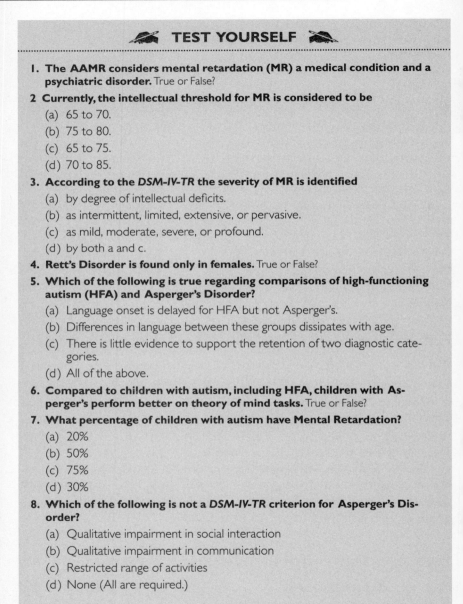

TEST YOURSELF

1. **The AAMR considers mental retardation (MR) a medical condition and a psychiatric disorder.** True or False?

2. **Currently, the intellectual threshold for MR is considered to be**
   (a) 65 to 70.
   (b) 75 to 80.
   (c) 65 to 75.
   (d) 70 to 85.

3. **According to the *DSM-IV-TR* the severity of MR is identified**
   (a) by degree of intellectual deficits.
   (b) as intermittent, limited, extensive, or pervasive.
   (c) as mild, moderate, severe, or profound.
   (d) by both a and c.

4. **Rett's Disorder is found only in females.** True or False?

5. **Which of the following is true regarding comparisons of high-functioning autism (HFA) and Asperger's Disorder?**
   (a) Language onset is delayed for HFA but not Asperger's.
   (b) Differences in language between these groups dissipates with age.
   (c) There is little evidence to support the retention of two diagnostic categories.
   (d) All of the above.

6. **Compared to children with autism, including HFA, children with Asperger's perform better on theory of mind tasks.** True or False?

7. **What percentage of children with autism have Mental Retardation?**
   (a) 20%
   (b) 50%
   (c) 75%
   (d) 30%

8. **Which of the following is not a *DSM-IV-TR* criterion for Asperger's Disorder?**
   (a) Qualitative impairment in social interaction
   (b) Qualitative impairment in communication
   (c) Restricted range of activities
   (d) None (All are required.)

Answers: 1. False; 2. c; 3. d; 4. True; 5. d; 6. True; 7. c; 8. b

Twelve

SPECIFIC LEARNING DISABILITIES

Throughout this text, there has been some discussion of the wide variations in definitions for childhood disorders depending on the nature of the defining source and/or geographical region. Definitions for specific learning disabilities are perhaps the most discrepant in this regard. Since our understanding of prevalence rates and the nature of research outcomes is contingent upon how the disorder is defined, a significant portion of this chapter will be devoted to presenting an overview of the current controversies and trends in defining specific learning disabilities.

DISCREPANCIES IN DEFINITIONS AND CLASSIFICATION OF SPECIFIC LEARNING DISABILITIES

There is considerable controversy regarding how to best define specific learning disabilities and the implications of terms of usage in different parts of the world. The differences in definitions can be found based on the nature of the defining source (e.g., the *DSM-IV-TR* [APA, 2000]; U.S. Federal Educational; National Joint Committee for Learning Disabilities) and on the country of origin. In many countries of the world, the term *learning disability* continues to be equated with Mental Retardation (MR) or intellectual disability. However, *specific learning disability* has also often become equated with *developmental dyslexia* (Demonet et al., 2004), which is primarily used to describe a reading disability.

THE *DSM-IV-TR* DEFINITION OF LEARNING DISORDERS

Formerly called *Academic Skills Disorders,* the *DSM-IV-TR* (APA, 2000) clusters specific learning disabilities under *Learning Disorders* in the subsection entitled Disorders Usually First Diagnosed in Infancy, Childhood, or Adolescence. The *DSM-IV-TR* presents a discussion of four types of learning disorders: Reading Disorder, Mathematics Disorder, Disorder of Written Expression, and Learning

> **DON'T FORGET**
>
> A learning disorder is evident if achievement in one of the above areas (reading, mathematics, writing) is substantially below what would be expected based on age and intellectual potential. Furthermore, *substantially below* is defined as a discrepancy between achievement and intelligence that is in excess of 2 standard deviations.

> **DON'T FORGET**
>
> The *DSM-IV-TR* (APA, 2000) acknowledges that associated processing deficits in areas of visual perception, linguistic processes, attention, and memory may accompany a learning disorder. However, if a sensory deficit is evident, then the learning disorder must be in excess of what would be expected, given that deficit.

> **DON'T FORGET**
>
> A key defining feature in making a differential diagnosis of MR is that in MR academic achievement is low but commensurate with expected IQ, while in the learning disabled population, a significant discrepancy exists between IQ and achievement.

Disorders NOS (not otherwise specified, for atypical variations).

However, the *DSM-IV-TR* adds that discrepancies between 1 and 2 standard deviations may be acceptable, especially if a disorder in cognitive processing compromises the overall IQ score by lowering it.

A Reading Disorder, or *dyslexia* is diagnosed if achievement in reading (accuracy, fluency (speed), or comprehension) is significantly below the expected level. In the United States, the prevalence of Reading Disorder is estimated to be approximately 4% of the school-age population and is far more prevalent in males (60 to 80%). A Mathematics Disorder may be evident in problems understanding or naming mathematical concepts, operations, and functions. Mathematics disorders are less prevalent than reading disorders and appear in 1% of school-aged children. A Disorder of Written Expression beyond spelling is more difficult to assess due to a lack of standardized measures and the difficult and often laborious methods of scoring instruments that are available. Prevalence rates are also lacking for this lesser known disorder. However, disorders of spelling or handwriting alone are not considered sufficient to diagnose a Disorder of Written Expression.

THE FEDERAL DEFINITION OF LEARNING DISABILITY: A WORK IN PROGRESS

The federal definition of *learning disabilities* as it appears in the 1999 reauthorization of IDEA (Individuals with Disabilities Education Act), which was published in the Federal Register, March 12, 1999, is summarized as follows:

'Specific learning disability (SLD) means a disorder in one or more of the basic psychological processes involved in understanding or using language, spoken or written, in which the disorder may manifest itself in an imperfect ability to listen, think, speak, read, write, spell, or to do mathematical calculations. The term SLD is inclusive in subsuming other previously used terms, such as perceptual handicap, brain injury, minimal brain dysfunction, dyslexia, and

> **CAUTION**
>
> One of the major arguments put forward by the committee is that students with higher IQs are more likely to have a significant discrepancy between their IQ and achievement than students with lower IQs. Therefore, the IQ-achievement discrepancy is biased in favor of students with higher IQs getting assistance, while those with lower IQs do not qualify for assistance.

developmental aphasia. However, the term SLD is exclusive in that it excludes children who have learning problems that are primarily a result of visual, hearing, motor handicaps, MR, emotional disturbance, or environmental or cultural disadvantage' (p. 12422). The assessment process is thus one of ruling out or excluding other possible causes for learning problems in order to establish that a child's academic difficulties are due to a specific learning disability.

However, current debates regarding how to determine whether a child has a learning disability focus on the use of the discrepancy criteria. Dr. Robert Paternack, assistant secretary for Special Education and Rehabilitative Services at the U.S. Department of Education, recently (April, 2003) testified before the Subcommittee on Education Reform concerning appropriate methods of identifying learning disabilities. The report stated that the committee was discouraged by the widespread use of the IQ-achievement discrepancy model as the determining factor in whether a child was deemed SLD and proposed instead that a *response to intervention model* (RTI) be applied to service children in need of assistance and evaluate the appropriateness of these interventions. See Appendix C for current status.

THE NATIONAL JOINT COMMITTEE FOR LEARNING DISABILITIES (NJCLD)

The NJCLD uses the term *learning disabilities* to refer to a heterogeneous group of disorders manifested by significant difficulties in the acquisition and use of listening, speaking, reading, writing, reasoning, or mathematical skills. The disorders are considered to be intrinsic to the individual, due to central nervous system dysfunction, and may occur across the life span. Furthermore, the NJCLD also recognizes that associated problems of self-regulatory behaviors, social perception, and social interaction often co-occur with SLD but do not themselves constitute a learning disability. The NJCLD definition states that although other handicapping conditions (sensory, MR, serious emotional disturbance) or environmental influences (cultural, inappropriate instruction) may exist comorbidly, they cannot account for the disability.

CONTROVERSY AND TRENDS IN THE DEFINITION OF LEARNING DISABILITIES

The *DSM-IV-TR* (APA, 2000) definition has been criticized on the grounds that the definition is too narrow, considering only three academically oriented disorders, and in its exclusive orientation that implies that a learning disorder cannot exist in comorbid relationship with another disorder. The federal definition has also been criticized for its vague references to *basic psychological processes* at the basis of the disability and lack of guidelines regarding how to measure the *manifestation of an imperfect ability*. The NJCLD definition improves upon the *DSM-IV-TR* definition by recognizing the heterogeneous nature of disabilities as well as including comorbid disorders and recognizing the likelihood of associated social problems. However, the NJCLD definition does not provide any guidelines regarding how to measure the *significant difficulties* in acquisition of academic skills that result.

The Discrepancy Model

Although the discrepancy criterion is currently receiving widespread interest with the pending reauthorization of IDEA and the committee's recommendation that the criterion be done away with, criticisms regarding the discrepancy model are not new. One of the major difficulties to date is the lack of consistency in how a significant discrepancy is operationally defined. Some studies have arbitrarily applied the 2-year rule to define the discrepancy (e.g., a significant discrepancy between grade attainment and present functioning occurs once there is a 2-year gap, Grade-4-age child functioning at a Grade-2 level). However, this criteria has been criticized on two counts: (1) it is very difficult for a child to be 2 years behind in the early grades, and (2) the model relies on a failure-based criterion. However, Sattler (2002) cautions that comparisons of achievement

> **DON'T FORGET**
> ....
> Kavale, Forness, and MacMillan (1998) suggest that theorists have lost sight of the biophysiological nature of the disorder and that without reference to the nature of the central nervous system impairment, the disorder has been reduced to an empty concept used to refer to academic failure.

grade scores with actual grade scores is not statistically sound and likely to derive invalid conclusions.

A more common practice in defining the discrepancy criterion is to convert academic scores to standard scores and compare these directly with IQ scores. Using this method, discrepancies between 15 to 22 points (1 to 1.5 standard deviations) are most commonly used to determine a significant discrepancy between IQ and academic performance. Although this method works well in the middle ranges, IQ scores at the upper and lower levels tend to bring criticisms such as that made earlier by Dr. Pasternak.

Furthermore, the discrepancy model is also problematic when children's IQ scores are compromised by processing problems underlying the learning disability (Sattler, 2002). Despite the inherent difficulties in applying the discrepancy criteria, there continues to be strong support (Kavale, Forness, & McMillan, 1998; Sattler, 2002) for retaining the model to determine eligibility for SLD programs. According to Sattler (2002) the emphasis, at this time, should be on conducting research to determine the best method of using the model. See Appendix C for an IDEA04 update.

PREVALENCE

It is very difficult to determine prevalence rates for SLDs because there is wide variability among published studies regarding how SLD is defined and measured.

> ### DON'T FORGET
>
> An IQ score is a standard score with a mean of 100 and a standard deviation of 15. Therefore, an individual with an IQ of 100 would have a discrepancy of 1 standard deviation if the academic score was expressed as a standard score of 85, 1.5 standard deviations for a score of 78, or 2 standard deviations for a score of 70.

> ### CAUTION
>
> Using this method, a student with an IQ of 140 would be considered to be significantly behind if the academic score was 125 (which is within the Superior range). However, a student with an IQ of 85 would have to have an academic score of 70 (Borderline range) to qualify as SLD.

> ### CAUTION
>
> Definitions of learning disabilities can vary depending on whether one uses the DSM-IV-TR diagnostic criteria for diagnosing a learning disorder or IDEA04 criteria for determining the presence of a SLD. Although the DSM definition requires that there be a significant discrepancy between expectations and achievement, there is little direction regarding what the difference should be or how to measure it. IDEA04 suggests that children may be identified as SLD based on their lack of response to research-based intervention (RTI).

For example, in studies that have used a *discrepancy criterion* (standard score differences between achievement scores and IQ scores), prevalence figures for comorbid ADHD + SLD have ranged from 16 to 21% (Frick et al., 1991) in a study where a 20 point discrepancy between intelligence (IQ) and achievement was used to a prevalence of 38 to 45% in a study where a 10 point discrepancy was used between the standard reading scores and the IQ (Dykman & Ackerman, 1992; Semrud-Clikeman et al., 1992).

LEARNING DISABILITIES AND SOCIAL SKILLS DEFICITS

For the past 30 years, research has documented that children with learning disabilities encounter more social difficulties than their non–learning disabled peers. The association between learning disabilities and social difficulties is so prevalent that Rourke (1989) has suggested inclusion of the fact that these children have "significant difficulties in mastering social and other adaptive skills" (p. 215) as part of the definition. The Interagency Committee on Learning Disabilities (ICLD) conducted a massive evaluation of available research concerning learning disabilities and social skills and concluded that social skills deficits can represent an SLD (1987). As a result, the ICLD suggested that the NJCLD definition be altered to include social skills among the other areas of skill acquisition deficits (e.g., listening, speaking, reading, writing, reasoning, mathematical abilities, or social skills). However, opposition to potentially defining SLD as a social deficit was voiced about concerns that an individual could have a social SLD and not have an academic deficit (Forness & Kavale, 1991).

In their study of learning disabled children, Stone and La Greca (1990) found that children with SLD not only had significantly lower sociometric scores compared to nondisabled peers but that they also were overly represented in the rejected and neglected sociometric groupings. The authors also found that social skills deficits impacted not only on social competence but also on academic achievement.

Furthermore, social skills deficits may emerge in kindergarten, prior to diagnosis of SLD (Vaughn, Hogan, Kouzekanam, & Shapiro, 1990), and persist into adulthood (Gerber & Reiff, 1994). Gresham and Elliott (1990) out-

DON'T FORGET

Studies of children's social status groups have determined five distinct social classification groups: popular, rejected, neglected, average, and controversial (Coie, Dodge, & Coppotelli, 1982). Children who are neglected are considered to have low social impact scores (low social visibility), while those who are rejected score high on social impact but low on social preference (likability).

line three ways in which social competence can be undermined: *skill deficit*
(individual has not learned required
skill), *performance deficit* (individual has
the skill but does not apply it), and *self-
control deficit* (individual demonstrates
aversive behaviors that compete or interfere with the acquisition and performance of appropriate social skills).

Kavale and Forness (1996) conducted a meta-analysis of 152 studies
concerning social skill deficits in chil-

> # CAUTION
> ....
> The difference between social skills
> and social competence has been dis-
> tinguished based on the following ac-
> cepted criteria. Social competence is a
> trait that determines the probability of
> completing a social task in an accept-
> able way; social skills are the requisite
> behaviors that are exhibited in social
> situations that produce socially ac-
> ceptable outcomes (McFall, 1982).

dren with SLD. Of the 6,353 students involved in the meta-analysis, 72% were
male, and the average IQ was 95. Results revealed that almost .75 of the students
(74%) received negative assessments of their social skills that would clearly discriminate them from their non-SLD peers. The authors found that *teachers* perceived the SLD students to be less academically competent and having less social
interaction than their non-SLD peers. Teachers also rated 70% of the SLD population as demonstrating anxiety. *Peer assessments* (non-SLD peers) revealed that 8 of
10 SLD students were rejected by their peers, with 7 of 10 not considered as
friends by peers. Other findings were that non-SLD peers rated the SLD children
as less popular, competent, communicative, and cooperative than their non-SLD
peers. *Self-assessment* results indicated that 70% of SLD students identified social
skills deficits, while 80% identified lack of academic competence as their biggest
concern. Eighty percent noted social competence deficits in areas of understanding social situations and generating appropriate solutions to social problems. As
might be anticipated, 70% admitted to poor self-concept and lack of self-esteem.
Measures of external-internal locus of control and attributions revealed that the
majority of SLD students were externally driven (attribute outcomes to outside influences rather than their own effort) and attribute their success to luck rather than
effort. Failure was attributed to lack of ability rather than effort.

As a result of their meta-analysis, Kavale and Forness (1996) conclude that although the majority of students with SLD exhibit social skills deficits, due to the
wide variety in deficits found, they could not determine why the deficits occur.
The authors call for further research to investigate the relationship between social and academic deficits as well as the potential contribution of underlying
mechanisms (language, memory, perception, cognition) to the development of
social dysfunction. Given the results of their meta-analysis, the authors suggest
that although social deficits are evident in the majority of children with SLD, and

as such constitute an associated feature of many SLD profiles, inclusion of social deficit as a criterion for SLD is not recommended at this time.

LEARNING DISABILITIES AND SUBTYPES

In addition to subtyping of learning disabilities into areas of academic deficit (APA, 2000), Rourke and colleagues (Harnadek & Rourke, 1994; Rourke, 1989) have described a syndrome that they call *nonverbal learning disability* (NLD). The syndrome has also been referred to in the literature as *developmental right-hemisphere syndrome* (DRHS) and *nonverbal learning disorder* (Gross-Tsur, Shalev, Manor, & Amir, 1995; Strang & Casey, 1994). Predominant symptoms include interpersonal skill deficits, nonverbal problem-solving deficits, visual perceptual disorganization, motoric slowness, and mathematical disability. The Predominantly Inattentive Type of ADHD is often a comorbid disorder.

According to Rourke and colleagues (1989), long-term prognosis for NLD without intervention reveals an increased risk for internalizing disorders, depression, suicide ideation, and increased isolation as adults.

Specific Reading Disability/Developmental Dyslexia

Although learning disabilities are recognized as a heterogeneous group of disorders (NJCLD, 1987), specific reading disability is the most prevalent (80% of learning disabilities) and well-researched disability to date. Therefore, the remaining section of this chapter will focus on the specific reading disability. In general, reading disabilities afflict children who are usually at least of average intelligence, whose reading disability is not related to general cognitive limitations or other environmental factors, such as inappropriate instruction, socioeconomic disadvantage, or sensory deficits. The disability impacts on the acquisition of basic reading skills from simple phonological processing (sound-symbol association) to word identification and passage comprehension.

CAUTION

Difficulties exist distinguishing NLD and Asperger's Disorder and in establishing legitimacy for the NLD subtype within education, which tends to conform to the more traditional concept of learning disabilities as language-based disorders (Thompson, 1997). Traditional SLD profiles often reveal an elevated Performance IQ relative to lower Verbal IQ; the profile of NLD is the reverse, with Verbal IQ often significantly higher than Performance IQ.

Definition of Dyslexia

In a recent paper produced by the International Dyslexia Association

(Lyon & Shaywitz, 2003), the authors present a definition of *developmental dyslexia* that expands on the original working definition developed in 1994. The current definition differs from that derived in 1994 by specifying the disability as neuro-biological in origin and conceptualizing the reading disability as a specific type of disability rather than one of several general disabilities. The definition character-izes the disability manifested in difficulties with accurate and/or fluent word recognition and by poor spelling and decoding abilities as a result of deficits in phonological awareness. The disability is not predicted by either cognitive abili-ties or instructional methods. Associated features may also include problems in reading comprehension and poor vocabulary development resulting from lack of reading. The current definition is clear in its recognition of fluency as a major and long-term outcome of dyslexia. Although many readers with dyslexia will increase their reading accuracy as a result of intervention, lack of fluency will produce long-term problems resulting in effortful, slow, and laborious reading (Shaywitz, 2003).

Etiology

Biological, neurological, and genetic transmission.   Twin studies have found that dys-lexia was evident in 68% of monozygotic twins (DeFries & Alarcon, 1996), and genetic effects seem most pronounced in children with high IQs compared to those with low IQs (Knopik, 2001).

The revised definition of dyslexia proposed by Lyon and Shaywitz (2003) rec-ognizes the neurological basis of the disorder, which has been confirmed through the use of functional magnetic resonance brain imaging (fMRI) and magnetoen-cephalography (MEG). Results have demonstrated that the left-hemisphere pos-terior brain system in dyslexics does not respond appropriately when reading (Frith & Frith, 1999). Studies have determined that two different systems oper-ate to develop reading ability, an initial more laborious system of phonetic aware-ness (parieto-temporal region) and a more rapid decoding system used by more-skilled readers (e.g., sight vocabulary, from the occipito-temporal region). Apparently, dyslexic readers demonstrate underactivation of both these areas with an increased activation of the frontal gyrus (letter to sound decod-ing), which carries the entire decod-ing load for the dyslexic population (Shaywitz, 2003). This functional ex-planation of dyslexia relates pro-cessing deficits to actual locations in the brain. Cognitively, the linguistic

DON'T FORGET

Reading involves *visual recognition* of an array of letters as meaningful, re-calling (*memory*) the meaning of the word, and integrating that word within a greater context (*comprehension*).

and visual coding processes should work together to provide links between the written and spoken word. From a cognitive perspective, both permanent memory and working memory are involved in learning to read.

Increased research effort and technological advances have also confirmed that deficits in the phonological components of language are at the basis of dyslexia. Lyon and Shaywitz (2003) suggest that phonemic awareness is at the basis of understanding how to break the reading code. This deficit in phonology is the most specific factor in predicting dyslexia to date (Morris et al., 1998).

Developmental Dyslexia and the Discrepancy Criterion

In their definition of dyslexia, Lyon and Shaywitz (2003) suggest that unexpected difficulty in learning to read is a preferable criterion to the discrepancy formula, which they state is growing out of favor with more and more professionals. However, the authors suggest assessing the degree of unexpectedness by comparing reading age to chronological age or educational level without reference to intellectual potential. To support their argument, the authors cite delay in identification while waiting for assessments rather than placing effort on remediation and intervention. See Appendix C for further discussion.

ASSESSMENT

Historically, assessment of SLD has involved the process of exclusion; for example, assessment is driven by differential diagnosis to rule out competing hypotheses to explain why the child has a reading disability. Ruling out other possible explanations for a specific learning disability often entails assessment of intellectual, sensory (hearing, vision, language), familial, developmental, emotional, and school history (absenteeism, number of schools attended, interventions attempted, etc.).

Instructional Component

New to the updated definition, the authors (Lyon & Shaywitz, 2003) also include reference to effective classroom instruction. The reason for inclusion of instructional history is because the authors believe that many children with reading problems lack early prereading skills, and early intervention targeting these deficits can alleviate the problem in many cases. They cite research by Torgesen (2000), demonstrating a reduction in reading failure from 18% to less than 6% due to effective early intervention, but caution that even extensive early intervention may not solve the problems of the severely disabled.

INTERVENTION

The cumulative effect of poor reading skills is self-evident. Poor readers lack the exposure to information presented in print and have less opportunity to develop their vocabularies, general knowledge, and language skills.

Aaron and Joshi (1992) suggest that poor readers can be grouped into one of three categories: (1) deficient decoding but adequate comprehension (*fluency problem*), (2) adequate decoding but poor comprehension, and (3) poor decoding and comprehension. It is most likely that children with dyslexia will fall into either category 1 or 3.

Reading Fluency and Repeated Readings

Repeated readings is a technique that has been demonstrated effective in increasing reading fluency (O'Shea, Sindelar, & O'Shea, 1985). Students read a selected passage (curriculum based) and use their own reading rate as a baseline for improved performance. Reading rate (words per minute) is calculated by dividing the number of words read correctly by seconds read and multiplying by 60. Comprehension questions at the end of the reading passage provide an index of rate/comprehension.

Reading Comprehension and Graphic Organizers

Kim and colleagues (2004) reviewed 21 group studies regarding the effectiveness of using graphic organizers to improve comprehension in students with SLD. In their review, the authors acknowledge that studies have demonstrated that graphic organizers are most effective when they are created by the students, positioned after the text, and used for a longer period of time (Dunston, 1992). It has been suggested that the use of graphic organizers might be

DON'T FORGET

Unlike their poor-reader peers, fluent readers read more, increase their vocabularies, and obtain greater exposure to general knowledge and cognitive diversity in areas of problem solving and higher-order thinking (Baker, Decker, & DeFries, 1984). Stanovich (1986) coined the term *Matthew effects* (rich get rich/poor get poorer) to refer to this escalating phenomenon.

DON'T FORGET

Graphic organizers (Ausubel, 1963) are visual and/or spatial methods of highlighting important information to be presented by drawing on a reader's previous knowledge base and providing a framework for facilitating and incorporating new information.

particularly helpful for SLD students because of their documented problems organizing and recalling verbal information (Wong, 1978) and their noted strengths in spatial or visual reasoning (Witelson, 1977).

Results of the meta-analysis by Kim, Vaughn, Wanzek, and Wei (2004) suggest that despite methodological difficulties (lack of standardized reading measures and variety of methods used), the use of graphic organizers seemed to have a beneficial effect for students with dyslexia in enhancing reading comprehension through the use of semantic organizers. The authors conclude that visual displays of information, such as graphic organizers, may assist readers with SLD to organize information, aiding in comprehension and subsequent recall. However, the authors also stress the need for more in-depth and comparative research in this fruitful area that has only produced three studies in the past 10 years.

🔍 TEST YOURSELF 🔍

1. **One of the criticisms against the _DSM-IV-TR_ definitions of Learning Disorders is that**
   (a) the definitions are too broad.
   (b) the definitions cover too many different disabilities.
   (c) the definition is too narrow.
   (d) the definition is written for adults.

2. **According to Kavale, Forness, and McMillan, current definitions of specific learning disabilities fail to acknowledge the role of central nervous system impairment.** True or False?

3. **The discrepancy model has come under current criticism because this model**
   (a) does not work well with the Middle range IQ scores.
   (b) is biased in favor of children with higher IQs.
   (c) is compromised by underlying processing problems.
   (d) has the characteristics of both (b) and (c).

4. **A deficit in social competence is currently considered as one of the SLDs disabilities by the NJCLD.** True or False?

5. **Which of the following is true?**
   (a) Children with SLDs usually do not have problems with peer relationships.
   (b) Children with SLDs are perceived as being too sociable by their teachers.
   (c) Children with SLDs are rated as less socially capable than non-SLD peers.
   (d) Children with SLDs are very capable of understanding social situations.

6. **Children with nonverbal learning disabilities (NLDs)**
   (a) are readily recognized as a specific learning disability by the educational system.
   (b) are more socially adept than traditional types of SLD peers.
   (c) excel at math.
   (d) are at risk for depression and suicide if intervention is not sought.

7. **Studies of children with dyslexia have found that**
   (a) fluency is a major and long-term outcome of dyslexia.
   (b) dyslexic readers exhibit underactivation of the areas of the brain associated with phonetic and visual awareness.
   (c) reading failure can be reduced by intensive and effective early intervention.
   (d) all of the above are true.

8. **Stanovich (1986) coined the phrase *Matthew effects* to refer to**
   (a) the cumulative effect of poor reading skills.
   (b) poor readers tend to compensate by being better listeners.
   (c) the majority of children with dyslexia are male.
   (d) the majority of children with dyslexia come from poverty.

Answers: 1. c; 2. True; 3. d; 4. False; 5. c; 6. d; 7. d; 8. a

Thirteen

CHILDREN AND TRAUMA: POSTTRAUMATIC STRESS DISORDER

Environmental stressors can occur on a daily basis. Some stressors are more intense and prolonged than others and, as a result, can cause more severe emotional repercussions. When stress results in a temporary state of distress, the disorder is described as an "adjustment disorder." However, when the stressor is of a catastrophic nature, then Posttraumatic Stress Disorder (PTSD) may develop in the aftermath.

ADJUSTMENT DISORDERS: A STRESS-BASED TEMPORARY DIAGNOSTIC CATEGORY

Adjustment disorder is defined by the *DSM-IV-TR* (APA, 2000) as a psychological response to an identifiable stressor (or stressors) that results in significantly distressing emotional and behavioral reactions. The response is notably more intense than would be expected, given the circumstances, and causes significant impairment in functioning. Wenar and Kerig (2000) categorize Adjustment Disorders as a bridge between normal behavior and psychopathology. The reaction occurs within 3 months of the stressful situation and lasts no longer than 6 months after the stressor is removed. The stressor may be an isolated event or incident (e.g., loss of job, termination of relationship), recurrent (yearly income tax crisis), or chronic (poverty). Furthermore, the *DSM-IV-TR* requires that bereavement is ruled out. The prevalence of Adjustment Disorders is between 2% and 8%, and there is an equal likelihood of the disorder occurring in boys and girls.

DON'T FORGET

When capacity to cope with existing demands exceeds our ability to cope, then stress becomes distress.

Posttraumatic Stress Disorder

Although Posttraumatic Stress Disorder (PTSD) is also triggered by a

Putting It Into Practice

When Eric's father was transferred, Eric did not want to move. When his parents put the house up for sale, Eric wrote a message on the bulletin board in his bedroom telling prospective buyers that the house was haunted. Eventually his parents were on to Eric's plan, and the house did sell. As a result, the family moved from Chicago to Boston and Eric settled into a period of intense withdrawal. He refused to make friends with his new classmates. Entering middle school was bad enough, but starting in a new school was even worse. Eric blamed his parents continually for his problems with peers, academics, and teachers. However, when basketball season started, Eric, who was a star performer, quickly made the team and developed a set of friendships that changed circumstances drastically as the old Eric was revitalized.

In this example, although a school move and relocation are normal stressful events for children, Eric's response is extreme, debilitating, and causing severe impairment in his family, social, and academic functioning. However, true to its name, Eric's *period of adjustment* to his new circumstances did eventually resolve, and Eric ultimately was able to engage in his new surroundings.

specified stressor, the nature of the stressor is extreme, traumatic, and often life altering.

Description and Associated Features

The *DSM-IV-TR* (APA, 2000) defines PTSD as a cluster of symptoms which develop in the aftermath of exposure to an extremely traumatic episode or event. There are six defining criteria (A through F). The first criterion (A1) defines the relationship between the individual and the event. The person must either directly have experienced or witnessed or been confronted by the event that was either life threatening or resulting in serious injury to the person or others. The second criterion (A2) describes the response to such an event as instilling a sense of "fear, helplessness or horror" in the person. Both criteria (A1 and A2) are required for a diagnosis of PTSD. However, there is a separate notation regarding criterion (A2) when diagnosing children. In this case, the *DSM-IV-TR* states that rather than respond with fear, helplessness, and horror, children may respond with "disorganized or agitated behavior" (p. 467).

The *DSM-IV-TR* provides a list of events as examples to convey the magnitude of such traumatic events that includes but is not limited to natural disasters, wars, victimization (sexual or physical), terrorist attacks, serious automobile accidents, and being diagnosed with a life-threatening disease. In young children, it may be difficult to determine what constitutes a traumatic event, as some events may be

Putting It Into Practice

Juan, a 17-year-old Hispanic youth, was referred to the school psychologist at the end of the first school term because of apparent academic and emotional concerns. His grades were slipping, and it looked like he might not get any credits his first term. The counselor has also explained that Juan was the driver in a fatal car wreck at the end of the previous academic year in which his best friend was killed. Although Juan was hospitalized, the counselor said that he insisted on going to the funeral, even though he could barely move, having suffered several broken ribs.

When the psychologist met with Juan, he was initially reluctant to discuss the accident, but as rapport was established, he admitted to feeling helpless, feeling fatigued due to lack of sleep, and having problems concentrating on his school work. He wanted to quit school because he did not want to be in the same class with students who blamed him for his friend's death, and furthermore he did not see why he should plan for a future. He admitted to having vivid dreams of his friend, seeing him as if he were alive. Often he would wake up, startled. He had no recollection of how the accident happened, as he could not remember the details, even though a witness had said that there was another car involved.

Although he has a girlfriend, he rarely feels like doing anything, and in the past few months he has preferred to be alone. Although he was very close to his deceased friend's family (they were inseparable), he has not seen them since the funeral.

In this case, Juan is faced with the aftermath of a traumatic experience in which he was seriously injured and his friend was killed. He feels helpless because of the accidental nature of the wreck. Undoubtedly for Juan there is significant survivor guilt. Faced with traumatic events of this nature, individuals react with fear, horror, or helplessness. In younger children, these feelings are often expressed in disorganized and agitated behaviors.

CAUTION

There are five symptoms in this cluster: *recurrent intrusive thoughts or images,** *recurrent dreams,** *reliving the experience through flashbacks or vivid experiences,** *intense psychological distress in the presence of triggers or cues,* and *intense physiological distress to cues.*

**There are three exceptions to this cluster noted for child behaviors: Recurrent images may take the form of repetitive play in children, frightening dreams may occur but without insight, and trauma-specific reenactment would likely replace flashbacks.*

nonviolent or nonthreatening, however, still have a traumatic impact developmentally (e.g., inappropriate sexual touching, etc.).

Children and adolescents who experience PTSD can demonstrate flashbacks, numbing, avoidance, heightened physiological arousal, and a sense of foreshortened future. The *DSM-IV-TR* groups the symptoms into three broad criterion clusters: (B) reexperiencing of intrusive thoughts and images, (C) avoidance and numbing, and (D) hyperarousal.

Symptoms from these clusters must be evident for more than a month and cause significantly impaired functioning.

Reexperiencing the trauma is often intrusive, unpredictable, and uncontrollable and causes significant anxiety and distress. The diagnosis of PTSD requires one symptom from this cluster.

Avoidance of people, events, or situations that might trigger associated thoughts or images is often obtained by physical distancing and emotional numbing. There is usually a loss of interest in normal activities and a stunted perspective on the future.

Increased agitation and arousal can be evident in interrupted sleep or nightmares, difficulties concentrating or distractibility, and irritability or anger.

The *DSM-IV-TR* (APA, 2000) also suggests that children may initially react with *disorganized and agitated behaviors,* such as clinging, crying, and so on. Posttraumatic Stress Disorder qualifiers are specified as *acute* if symptoms last less than 3 months and *chronic* beyond that duration. In addition, the disorder is labeled as Acute Stress Disorder if symptoms last less than 1 month.

Other associated features of the disorder may include a sense of increased guilt or survivor guilt. Of particular importance in working with children and adolescents are several associated features that are listed in

DON'T FORGET

Three symptoms are required from this seven symptom cluster that includes *avoidance of conversations associated with the trauma, avoidance of associated activities, inability to recall trauma details, loss of interest in normal activities, feelings of detachment, restricted affect range,* and *sense of foreshortened future.*

DON'T FORGET

Two of the following five symptoms are required: *problems falling or staying asleep, anger or irritable outbursts, problems with concentration or completing tasks, hypervigilance,* and *startle response.*

DON'T FORGET

The disorganized/disoriented pattern of behaviors was also noted in traumatized infants when they were reunited with their parents in the Ainsworth Strange Situation attachment studies.

CAUTION

Despite attempts to modify criteria of PTSD symptoms to better match child characteristics, controversy and debate continue concerning two significant themes: the need for increased understanding of how symptoms manifest at different developmental ages, and the need to adapt the symptoms required in each cluster to better meet child characteristics (AACAP, 1998).

≡ Rapid Reference 13.1

Associated Features of PTSD in Children and Adolescents

Symptoms that might be evident in survivors of sexual or physical abuse or in children who are a witness to violence include the following:

- Difficulties with affect regulation
- Behaviors that are impulsive and self-destructive
- Somatic complaints
- Feelings of shame
- Feelings of hopelessness or despair
- Social withdrawal
- Hostility
- Constantly being on guard, feeling threatened
- Change in personality
- Impaired social relationships
- Feelings of permanent damage
- Dissociative symptoms

Source: DSM-IV-TR (APA, 2000, p. 465).

the *DSM-IV-TR* (APA, 2000). A summary of this list can be found in Rapid Reference 13.1.

The *DSM-IV-TR* (APA, 2000) does provide specific assistance in modifying the features to more appropriately fit younger children. Anxieties and fears may take the form of dreams of monsters, generalized nightmares, or involve themes of rescue. Reliving the experience may take the form of traumatic play. Some children may respond to a sense of helplessness by developing a belief that they can foresee the future (*omen formation*). The *DSM-IV-TR* cautions that it may be difficult to actually observe a restriction in activities in some children and that obtaining information from parents or teachers might be very helpful in this area.

Putting It Into Practice

Several studies have specifically looked at how the *DSM-IV* (APA, 1994) symptoms, which were primarily suited to adults, might manifest in children and adolescents. Although *emotional numbing* is not typically the most prevalent symptom in children with PTSD (Carrion, Weems, Ray, & Reiss, 2002), it has been observed at all levels. Several studies suggest that *reexperiencing* is the most prevalent symptom in school-age children (Carrion et al., 2002; Le Greca, Silverman, Vernberg, & Prinstein, 1996).

In a recent study of child symptoms of PTSD, Weems and colleagues (2003) addressed the underlying relationship between emotional numbing and hyperarousal. The authors were particularly interested in whether theories of the relationship between these two symptom clusters for adult populations (Litz, 1992) would apply to children. The hypothesis is that emotional numbing may result from emotional exhaustion resulting from hyperarousal. In a sample of 59 children who were victims of interpersonal trauma (mean age 10 years, 6 months), the authors found preliminary evidence that the direction of effects between emotional numbing and hyperarousal was in the predicted direction, suggesting that emotional numbing in children may result from emotional exhaustion due to a depletion of cognitive and emotional resources (hyperarousal).

Historical Evolution of PTSD in Childhood and Adolescence

The recognition that children can and do experience significant and, at times, life-altering responses to trauma is a relatively new phenomenon. As was discussed in the introductory chapter, there is often a lag between recognition of a disorder in adult populations and subsequent acknowledgment that the disorder exists in child and adolescent populations. However, in keeping with this theme, initial attempts to document evidence of a new disorder in childhood often rely on the use of adult symptoms as the criterion reference point.

With reference to the *DSM-III-R* (APA, 1987) criteria for PTSD, Pynoos (1990) writes: "PTSD is the only anxiety disorder whose etiology is associated with a known external event. . . . this anxiety disorder can occur at any age; recently, increased attention has been focused on the symptoms of PTSD in children who have experienced extreme stress (and) psychic trauma" (p. 48).

With the advent of this new category of disorders in 1987, clinicians would eventually see a shift in focus from conceptualizing children's responses to traumatic situations as a temporary adjustment (Yule, 1998), filed under the Adjustment Disorders, to a greater understanding of the biological, psychological, and social consequences these responses might have for future development (Pynoos, 1994).

While some studies have looked at how adult PTSD symptoms might manifest in childhood and adolescence, other researchers have looked at how symptom presentations might differ between adults and children and what symptoms might look like across the developmental spectrum.

DON'T FORGET

PTSD as a disorder had a rather late onset, even for adult populations. The disorder first appeared in the *DSM-III* (APA, 1980). By the next revision, the *DSM-III-R* (APA, 1987), there was increasing recognition of the potential relationship of this disorder to child and adolescent populations.

Developmental Adaptations

Although there are common symptoms shared by PTSD victims at all ages, it should not be surprising that children would also have some symptoms that differ from adults, due to the impact of "divergent stressors, developmental themes, family issues and collateral symptoms" (Amaya-Jackson & March, 1995b, p. 294).

Criteria for very young children (under 4 years of age).   The fact that very young children can be traumatized has been recognized in the attachment literature for quite some time. Scheeringa and colleagues (1995) argue that almost half (8 out of 18) of the qualifying criteria of the *DSM-IV* (APA, 1994) for PTSD can only be obtained through verbal descriptions of experiences and internal status, thus rendering the criteria inappropriate for very young children with limited verbal skills. As a result, Scheeringa and colleagues have developed an alternative set of criteria for children under 4 years of age, including dropping reference to fear and horror from criterion (A2) and reduction in the amount and types of symptoms required. The model is currently under investigation.

Characteristics evident in school-age children.   Children's dreams and nightmares may develop into night terrors, while sleep problems, for example, sleepwalking and bedwetting, are not uncommon (Amaya-Jackson & March, 1995b). Reenactment of traumatic events in young children is more likely to occur through repetitive play than reports of flashbacks (Scheeringa & Zeanah, 2001), and in their trauma play, children may alter the stories by creating happy endings in an attempt to achieve mastery over an otherwise helpless situation (Amaya-Jackson & March, 1995b). Children may experience problems at school due to difficulties with attention and concentration (Amaya-Jackson & March, 1995a) and may overreact to school drills and fire alarms, which could trigger the startle response (March, Amaya-Jackson, & Pynoos, 1994).

Developmentally, children may reexperience traumatic events through repetitive traumatic play and reenact-

---

CAUTION

There are several reasons why PTSD may go undiagnosed in childhood. Those involved with the child (parents, teachers, counselors) may minimize the impact of the trauma to reassure themselves that the child is still intact or rationalize that, given the child's age, the trauma impact will be temporary. Some parentified children from chronically traumatic environments may try to protect the caregiver by minimizing the impact of the trauma. In addition, children with PTSD might alternate long periods of reexperiencing with equally long periods of avoidance and numbing, which might be misinterpreted as having resolved PTSD issues (AACAP, 1998).

ing behavioral responses. Distressing dreams may generalize into themes of monsters or rescue, while repetitive play, drawings, and stories may be used to reenact the circumstances surrounding a traumatic event. Play may be subdued and restricted, while anxiety may take the form of vague somatic complaints of headaches or stomachaches.

It has also been noted that for some children, numbing and avoidance may take the form of restlessness, poor concentration, hypervigilance, and behavioral problems (Malmquist, 1986).

Children may avoid thoughts, locations, play themes, and concrete items that may serve to remind them of the event. Traumatic exposure may also lead to a temporary elevation in increased risk-taking behaviors (Pynoos, 1990). With young children, problems may surface particularly around bedtime and can be expressed as fear of the dark or fear of sleeping alone in anticipation of nightmares.

Putting It Into Practice

Ricky is *hyperactive, distractible,* and *impulsive.* His teacher is certain that he has ADHD. However, Ricky's teacher is unaware that he is a witness to severe bouts of domestic violence on a recurrent basis and that being hyperactive, distractible, and impulsive can indicate anxiety and even PTSD in children. There is a high comorbidity rate between PTSD and ADHD, and some children with PTSD present with ADHD symptoms (Cuffe, McCullough, & Pumariega, 1994; McLeer, Deblinger, Henry, & Orvaschel, 1992).

DON'T FORGET

There are many factors that can influence how children will respond to a traumatic event. Response can depend on the degree of exposure, the proximity to the event, the nature of the personal impact, and the age or developmental stage of the child. For example, Pynoos (1994) found in two independent studies (sniper on the school grounds and earthquake) that the closer the child was physically to the actual trauma, the greater the PTSD impact.

The impact of PTSD at different developmental stages. It has been suggested that each developmental stage may have different symptom clusters for PTSD (AACAP, 1998).

In a study of the responses of 2,379 students in Grades 4 to 12 six months after a bushfire disaster, McDermott & Palmer (2002) found important developmental differences in postdisaster psychological responses. In their study, they found that younger children (Grades 4 to 6) were more vulnerable to postdisaster *depressive symptoms,* while middle school children (Grades 7 to 9) reported the most *emotional distress* symptoms, which peaked at the 8th grade. While depression scores were lowest for children in the 8th to 10th grades, depression scores again increased in the 11th and 12th grades.

DON'T FORGET

Comorbidity is a common occurrence with PTSD, and increased risk has been noted for depression, anxiety, and substance abuse (Pfefferbaum, 1997). Some authors have speculated that PTSD might predispose children to the development of Depressive Disorders (Yehuda & McFarlane, 1995). However, developmental level may also influence this predisposition to depression. Based on the results of their study, McDermott and Palmer (2002) suggest that in the aftermath of a trauma, younger children may be more vulnerable to symptoms of depression, while middle school children may be vulnerable to the full-blown emotionally distressing symptoms of PTSD.

CAUTION

Pynoos (1994) discusses how trauma could impact on development in two important ways: proximal and distal. In the more immediate or proximal sense, the trauma can serve to impact on newly acquired skills and competencies. In this way, the trauma could serve to interrupt the solidification process and actually result in regressive behaviors. The more long-term or distal impact could be a future influence on overall personality formation with respect to increased risk taking, heightened threat appraisals, and inappropriate self-attributions.

Pynoos and Nader (1993) suggest that the adolescent years may be particularly vulnerable to the effects of trauma exposure. Developmentally, as children get older there is increased interaction with the environment, which can lead to increased exposure to potential stressors. In addition, adolescents tend to reenact to trauma through risk-taking behaviors that can increase the chances of more stressful consequences. Schools and neighborhoods take on greater influence and risk factors continue to increase under pressures of peer group influence. According to Pynoos (1994), the impact of severe trauma at adolescence can be particularly devastating and life altering, as it can serve to disrupt the trajectory of positive growth and sever the opportunity of integrating past experiences with future expectations. The impact could be significantly negative to alter the adolescent's sense of purpose and future identity.

Often, like the initial case study of Juan, PTSD victims may experience significant survivor guilt, which in Juan's case was particularly strong as he was also responsible for the accident that caused the trauma. As Pynoos and Nader (1993) suggest, if the trauma results in the death of a family member or friend, then the situation becomes even more complex. Often the interaction between trauma and grief reactions will result in continued focus on the traumatic circumstances surrounding the death and serve to block the grieving process and subsequent adaptation.

Prevalence

Unlike the other Anxiety Disorders, estimates of prevalence for PTSD are more difficult to obtain due to the wide variability of populations from which these rates are drawn. The *DSM-IV-TR* (APA, 2000) suggests that according to community-based studies, the lifetime prevalence rate for adult PTSD is approximately 8%, while the prevalence rate for adolescent PTSD (mean age 17 years) from a nonreferred Massachusetts community was reported to be 6.3% (Giaconia et al., 1994). However, in clinic populations and samples of urban populations, substantially higher rates have been reported. In one study of 79 girls (12 to 21 years of age) attending an urban adolescent health clinic, 67% met criteria for a diagnosis of PTSD (Horowitz, Weine, & Jekel, 1995), while 27% of a sample of 97 juniors attending five high schools in a major metropolitan area endorsed clinical PTSD symptom levels. In the latter example, *community violence* was the variable most highly associated with PTSD (Berton & Stabb, 1996). Furthermore, as there is a high risk for PTSD in sexually abused populations, it is highly likely that prevalence rates may even be higher than expected. For example, McLeer and colleagues (1992) found that 43.9% of 92 sexually abused children aged 3 to 16 met criteria for PTSD.

Etiology

Biological, genetic, and neurological correlates. There is evidence that highly stressful events will produce physical changes in the body and brain. Abnormal activity of the neurotransmitter *norepinephrine* and elevated levels of the hormone *cortisol* have both been implicated in the process (Baker et al., 1999). There is also evidence

CAUTION

Reports suggest that females are at higher risk for PTSD and can be up to 5 times more likely to develop PTSD symptoms when exposed to trauma (Breslau, Davis, Andreski, & Peterson, 1991). There has been a suggestion that boys may not manifest symptoms that would be recognized as clearly as girls and may act out rather than present with internalizing symptoms, such as anxiety or depression, which are often tapped by PTSD instruments and interviews (Ostrov, Offer, & Howard, 1989).

DON'T FORGET

Attachment research has found that traumatized infants who respond with disorganized/disoriented responses to their parent's return in Ainsworthe's Strange Situation studies demonstrated elevated levels of cortisol at the reunion (Spangler & Grossmann, 1999). On the other hand, mothers of securely attached infants actually moderate stress by lowering the cortisol responses in their vulnerable (behaviorally inhibited) infants (Nachmias, Gunnar, Mangelsdorf, Parritz, & Buss, 1996).

that enduring heightened arousal over time may alter the *hippocampus's* (portion of the brain that regulates stress hormones) ability to manage future stressful situations (Bremner, 1999).

DON'T FORGET

Environmental conditions such as poverty, parent mental illness, and teen parenthood are known to be high-risk conditions for the development of poor child outcomes (Zeanah, Boris, & Larrieu, 1997). Understandably, parents who are overwhelmed and distressed can often be less supportive to the needs of their children.

DON'T FORGET

Factors have also been identified that increase the *risk for exposure to traumatic events.* Having a low education, being male, extraversion, early conduct problems, and family history of psychiatric problems all increased the chances of exposure to traumatic events (Breslau et al., 1991).

DON'T FORGET

The *DSM-IV-TR* (APA, 2000) outlines three subtypes of PTSD based on onset and duration of symptoms: *Acute* (symptom duration less than 3 months), *Chronic* (symptoms lasting 3 months or longer), and *Delayed Onset* (6 month delay between the traumatic event and the onset of symptoms). A second form of traumatic response, called *Acute Stress Disorder,* is diagnosed if symptom onset is within the month and symptoms do not extend beyond the month.

Risk factors and protective factors: The context of child development. Although some children can and do develop PTSD, there are also many children who do not. There are some factors that can serve to increase a child's vulnerability to trauma (risk factors), and there are other factors that can help buffer the child (protective factors).

Increased vulnerability. Specific factors that tend to *increase vulnerability* for PTSD are a past history of childhood sexual or physical trauma, low self-esteem, separation from parents before age 10, prior psychiatric disorder, psychiatric disorder in a first-degree relative, being female (Davidson, 1993), and preexisting anxiety or depression (Breslau et al., 1991). The *development of chronic PTSD* in childhood has been related to personality variables of locus of control and lack of personal efficacy (Joseph, Brewin, Yule, & Williams, 1993), while preexisting (trait anxiety) or negative emotionality are predictive of the development of *more-severe PTSD symptoms* (Lonigan et al., 1994).

Subtypes of PTSD

In addition to the subtypes of PTSD noted in the preceding, it has also been suggested that a subtyping distinction should be made based on the type of trauma to which an individual has been exposed. According to Terr (1991), there should be a distinction between singular *Type I traumas* (major traumatic event, e.g., vehicle accident, bridge collapse) and repeated *Type II traumas* (such as multiple and long-term physical or sexual abuse). According to Terr, while Type I trauma would be expected to elicit patterns of responses that demonstrate the classic reexperiencing, avoidance, and hyperarousal, Type II traumas might elicit more pervasive symptoms of denial, numbing or dissociation, and rage.

Precipitating Factors: Victimization, Abuse, and Neglect

In addition to motor vehicle accidents, acts of terrorism, and natural disasters (hurricanes, floods, bushfires, etc.), a high percentage of children and adolescents develop PTSD as a direct result of maltreatment and victimization.

In the United States, guidelines for the major types of child abuse and neglect are provided by the Federal Child Abuse Prevention and Treatment Act (CAPTA), although individual states provide the specific details. At a minimum, categories include *neglect* (failure to provide physical, medical, educational, or emotional needs), *physical abuse* (physical injury intended or otherwise), *sexual abuse* (engagement in sexual activities or exploitation), and *emotional abuse* (acts of constant criticism, withdrawal of love resulting in reduced feelings of self-worth and emotional development).

It has been estimated that 896,000 children in the United States were victims of abuse or neglect in 2002 (National Child Abuse and Neglect Data System [NCANDS], 2002).

Children under 3 years of age had the highest rates of victimization, while females were more likely to be victimized than males.

In their sample of 297 adolescents receiving therapy for substance abuse, Deykin and Buka (1997) found that 75% percent of females (40% of female sample) and 76% of males (3.6% of male sample) met criteria for PTSD resulting from rape trauma.

Horowitz and colleagues (1995)

> ## DON'T FORGET
>
> Of the 896,000 children who were victims of abuse or neglect in 2002,
> - 60% were neglected.
> - 20% were physically abused.
> - 10% were sexually abused.
> - 1,400 died as a result of maltreatment.

> ## CAUTION
>
> Exposure to violence or abuse at an early age sets the stage of increased risk of high-risk behaviors in adolescence: teen pregnancy, early sexual activity, Eating Disorders, substance abuse, Anxiety Disorders and Depressive Disorders, suicide attempts, and emotional disorders (Horowitz et al., 1995).

found that 67% of adolescent girls (aged 12 to 21) attending an urban mental health clinic met criteria for PTSD, while one study found that the risk for PTSD in children with a history of sexual abuse was 21% (Deblinger, McLeer, Atkins, Ralphe, & Foa, 1989). Young girls who have been abused sexually are 2 to 3 times more likely to experience repeated victimization in adulthood and be victims of family violence (Cloitre, Tardiff, Marzuk, Leon, & Potera, 1996). Furthermore, Deblinger and colleagues (1989) suggest that the PTSD symptom profile of sexually abused children may differ from other forms of abuse with more symptoms of reexperiencing and inappropriate sexual behaviors.

Witness to violence.   Exposure to violence and abuse in homes and the surrounding community can result in significant PTSD responses to violent trauma and set the stage for future psychopathology. Children who witness domestic violence, even if they were not victimized, reported significantly higher PTSD scores than children who did not witness violence (Kilpatrick & Williams, 1997). Berton and Stabb (1996) found that 29% of high school juniors surveyed in a major metropolitan area had sufficient symptoms to predispose them to PTSD as a result of witnessing community violence. Consequences of childhood exposure to violence and abuse include social avoidance, foreshortened future, and lack of life opportunities.

CAUTION

Pynoos (1994) has also noted that parent reaction to the child's trauma can have a positive or negative influence: acting to soothe and calm the child or exacerbate the emotional responsiveness by inducing the contagion effect.

DON'T FORGET

The long-term impact of PTSD has been studied by various researchers, and the results suggest that for some, the influence can be devastating. Greene and Ablon (1994) followed up children who were exposed to the Buffalo Creek dam collapse. Of the initial 37% who demonstrated PTSD symptoms two years after the incident, follow-up 17 years later revealed 7% continued to meet criteria for PTSD.

Moderating and protective factors.   Level of family stress, the efficacy of child and parent coping styles, and experiences in dealing with stress in the past have all been identified as moderating factors (Martini, 1995). In addition, marital status, stability, education, family support network, and psychological well-being of the parents have also been noted to serve as buffers (Amaya-Jackson & March, 1995a).

Age of onset can also moderate the degree and nature of the impact. Studies have shown that early onset

PTSD (prior to age 14) is often associated with interpersonal problems, while later onset impacts academic problems (Amaya-Jackson & March, 1995a).

Theoretical Models of PTSD

A number of different models have been developed to assist in better understanding the developmental nature of PTSD.

Behavioral and cognitive behavioral models.   Proponents of cognitive behavioral models interpret the child's response to the traumatic event from a learning theory perspective. Within this framework, reexperiencing a traumatic event can be equated to a conditioned fear response. Although the trauma is not likely to be repeated, extinction does not occur because the fear is continually reenergizing through stimulus generalization and increased connections. Emotional processing can alter how future threat is appraised, turning relatively innocuous events into signals of potential threat (Foa & Kozak, 1986). Other cognitive theorists stress the maladaptive cognitive assumptions and appraisals resulting in dysfunctional beliefs about the future (Ehlers & Clark, 2000).

Attachment and parenting models. Studies have determined that parent variables can influence the outcome for PTSD children in several ways.

Scheeringa and Zeanah (2001) recently reviewed 17 studies that simultaneously assessed parent and child responses to trauma using *DSM-IV* criteria. In all but 1 study, the researchers found a significant posttrauma association between less adaptive parent functioning and less adaptive child functioning. Based on their results, the authors have developed a model of the *relational context of PTSD*, which has at its core the belief that the primary caregiving relationship is central to expression of PTSD symptoms throughout development.

> # CAUTION
>
> Brewin, Dagleish, and Joseph (1996) suggest that traumatic memories may become activated as situationally accessible memories (SAMs) that are distinct from other memories because they are not readily accessed by conscious effort but are triggered by environmental cues.

> # DON'T FORGET
>
> Caregivers can influence their child's PTSD by being too attentive or not attentive enough. McFarlane (1987) found that *maternal overprotectiveness* of children with PTSD led to the worst child outcomes, while *parent avoidance* of PTSD resulted in elevation of PTSD. Interventions that target improved parent-child relationships and handling stressful experiences significantly improved child outcomes regarding PTSD (Olds et al., 1998).

Scheeringa and Zeanah (2001) use the concept of *Relational PTSD* to refer to the "compound effect" resulting from the "co-occurrence of post-traumatic symptomatology in an adult caregiver and a young child, when the symptomatology of one partner, usually the adult, exacerbates the symptomatology of the other" (p. 809). Although parent and child may not necessarily experience trauma due to the same event, it is the response to the trauma that influences the other's symptoms in a negative way. The three patterns are summarized in the Rapid Reference 13.2.

The model of Relational PTSD proposed by Scheeringa and Zeanah (2001) gains additional support when viewed within the context of the attachment literature relating to trauma-exposed adults. From an attachment perspective, studies of disorganized attachment in infants have linked this type of attachment to caregivers who have not resolved a previous trauma or who are preoccupied or overwhelmed with their trauma history, resulting in a caregiver who is frightened or frightening to the infant or young child.

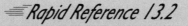 *Rapid Reference 13.2*

Relational PTSD: Response Patterns and Child Outcomes

Parent response pattern	Description/Rationale	Child outcomes
Withdrawn/ Unresponsive/ Unavailable	The parent is emotionally unavailable for the child: Parent's unresolved past trauma, which is reawakened by the child's symptoms, probably leads to the parent's attempts to avoid the child's symptoms.	Worsening of the child's PTSD symptoms.
Overprotective/ Constricting pattern	Parent is prone to reexperiencing the trauma intrusively: Even if the parent were not exposed to the trauma, the parent feels a sense of guilt about not having protected the child from the trauma.	Worsening of the child's PTSD symptoms.
Reenacting/ Endangering/ Frightening pattern	Parent preoccupation with trauma: Parent floods the distressed child with questions and comments specific to the event.	Child may use increased avoidance; caregivers may unconsciously place their children at risk for future trauma.

Source: Scheering and Zeanah (2001).

Even if the attachment relationships are adequate, Lyons-Ruth and Jacobvitz (1999) suggest that if a trauma is severe enough (as would be in cases of PTSD), the potential impact on caregiving could be to impair the process to the extent that it could disorganize the attachment strategy of the child or adult. Caregivers with unresolved trauma may also have a significantly lower threshold for triggers that might reawaken unresolved fears, leading to a perpetuation of disorganized attachment responses, and set the stage for intergenerational transmission of disorganization to occur. Within this "stress-relational-diathesis model," the authors suggest that the impact of early maternal deprivation may remain a latent factor until sufficient stress is introduced and at which time atypical and maladaptive behaviors will again resurface.

Assessment

Richards and Bates (1997) discuss the symptoms of PTSD that are evident in cognitive, affective, behavioral, and somatic responses. The authors suggest that targeting specific treatment strategies to enhance coping in these areas may be an effective approach to managing stress in PTSD children.

In addition to participation in one of the clinically structured or semi-structured interviews, measures of generalized anxiety, depression, and mental status can be obtained using the more general child behavior rating scales discussed earlier. The Personality Inventory for Youth (PIY; Lachar & Gruber,

DON'T FORGET

Main and Solomon (1986) used the term *disorganized/disoriented attachment pattern* for the odd behaviors (apprehension, crying, freezing, conflicting movements, trance-like expressions) displayed by some infants upon their parents return during Ainsworth's Strange Situation procedure. Although normally the need for attachment is elevated at times of stress, for disorganized/disoriented infants, the parent is simultaneously a source of comfort and a source of fear that elicits contradictory attempts to approach and flee the caregiver. This approach/flee response pattern has been linked to *parents who are feared* (victims of abuse) or parents with their own abuse history (Lyons-Ruth & Jacobvitz, 1999), or *frightened,* as in cases where parents have unresolved loss or trauma (Main & Hesse, 1990).

DON'T FORGET

Stress can impact on all levels of functioning, including the following:

Cognitive: (maladaptive thoughts, memory problems, concentration problems, hypervigilance, poor recall for details, foreshortened sense of future)

Affective: (anxiety, irritability, labile affects, restricted affect, traumatic dreams, fear and avoidance, phobias)

Behavioral: (trauma play, hyperactivity, regressive behaviors, anger outbursts, impulsivity, distractibility)

Somatic-Physiological Symptoms: (startle response, headaches, stomachaches, fatigue, sleep deprivation)

1995) contains a number of scales assessing emotional and behavioral adjustment in the home and school environments that would be helpful, including a somatic scale to evaluate vegetative symptoms. The Trauma Symptom Checklist for Children (TSCC; Briere, 1996) is specifically designed to evaluate the impact of traumatic events in children 8 to 16 years of age. Children rate their responses on a 4-point scale that yields five clinical subscales: Anxiety, Depression, Anger, Posttraumatic Stress, and Dissociation. An alternate form contains a sixth scale measuring Sexual Concerns. In addition to the clinical subscales, the instrument also provides measures of avoidance or symptom denial (Underresponse) and heightened responding (Hyperresponse).

Treatment

Cognitive behavioral therapy.   Recently, Cohen, Deblinger, Mannarino, and Steer (2004) evaluated a multisite randomized controlled trial of trauma-focused cognitive behavioral therapy (TF-CBT) for 224 children (ages 8 to 14 years) with PTSD resulting from sexual abuse. The cognitive behavioral program, TF-CBT, and a therapeutic treatment alternative (child-centered therapy [CCT]) were manualized and delivered in 12 weekly sessions to parent and child dyads. The TF-CBT program emphasized skills in feeling expression, emotional management, and cognitive abuse processing. The CCT program was an ego supportive alternative that focused on trust building and empowerment of the parent-child dyad in processing the abuse. Children who participated in the TF-CBT program demonstrated significantly greater improvement of PTSD abuse-associated areas (behavior problems, social problems, shame, depression, and abuse attributions) compared to children in the CCT program. Furthermore, parents also reported less depression and more support of their child as a result of their involvement in the TF-CBT program. The authors conclude that TF-CBT is an effective treatment intervention for children who have experienced sexual abuse.

Guidelines for Treatment

Crisis management.   Working with trauma victims often involves a four-stage approach (Michaelson, 1993), consisting of the following stages:

1. *Normalization:* Education of the victims regarding the symptoms they are experiencing and may experience in the future (sleep, concentration, flashbacks, guilt).
2. *Encourage Verbal Expression:* Engage victims in discussions regarding their feelings of anxiety, frustration, or anger.
3. *Provide Self-Help Information:* Provide handouts on relaxation training and stress management.

4. *Referrals:* Provide information about professionals in the area that they can go to if needed.

Trauma Accommodation Syndrome.   Velkamp and Miller (1994) have developed a five-stage model for conceptualizing how children process stressful responses from inception to resolution. The model provides a good framework for targeting interventions and monitoring progress and is presented in the following box.

Trauma Accommodation Syndrome

Stage 1: Traumatic or life-threatening event

Stage 2: Fear, helplessness, horror

Stage 3: Reenactment: repetitious play, frightening dreams, and/or avoidance that leads to a recurrence of intrusive thoughts or images, resulting in disorganized and agitated behavior

Stage 4: Reevaluation and reexperiencing

Stage 5: Cognitive reappraisal, resolution, accommodation, and adaptation

Source: Adapted from Velkamp and Miller (1994).

🐊 TEST YOURSELF 🐊

1. **According to the *DSM-IV-TR*, criteria for PTSD *must* include**

   (a) direct experiencing or witnessing of an event that is life threatening or causes serious injury to the self or others.

   (b) sense of fear, helplessness, or horror.

   (c) recurring flashbacks.

   (d) both a and b.

2. **In children, repetitive images may take the form of repetitive play.** True or False?

3. **Which of the following is *not* a typical symptom of PTSD?**

   (a) Recurrent need to revisit the site of the PTSD event

   (b) Interrupted sleep/nightmares

   (c) Emotional numbing

   (d) Anger or irritation

(continued)

4. All of the following are probable symptoms of PTSD in children, *except*

(a) disorganized and agitated behaviors.

(b) clinging.

(c) crying.

(d) flashbacks.

5. PTSD was one of the first disorders ever included in the original *DSM*. True or False?

6. According to Scheeringa and colleagues (1995), use of *DSM-IV* criteria for PTSD in very young children is

(a) inappropriate because almost half of the criteria require verbal descriptions.

(b) appropriate because criteria can be observed.

(c) inappropriate because very young children do not experience PTSD.

(d) appropriate for children 4 years of age and up.

7. Which of the following findings did McDermott and Palmer (2002) reveal as a result of their investigation of children's responses to the bushfire disaster?

(a) Middle school children (Grades 7 to 9) reported the most emotional distress.

(b) Younger children (Grades 4 to 6) reported the most emotional distress.

(c) Adolescents reported the most emotional distress.

(d) There were no significant age-related findings.

8. Which of the following is a risk factor for developing PTSD, posttrauma?

(a) Being female

(b) A history of sexual abuse

(c) Exposure to violence and abuse in the home

(d) All of the above

Answers: 1. d; 2. True; 3. a; 4. d; 5. False; 6. a; 7. a; 8. d

Fourteen

CHILDREN OF DIVERSE CULTURES

INTRODUCTION

The importance of understanding how behavioral and developmental expectations may differ across and within various cultures is fundamental to an appreciation of whether behaviors seen as deviant in North America are also viewed as deviant in other cultures. Within this framework, Bronfenbrenner's (1979) ecological model is well suited to providing increased understanding of how systems (family, social, economic, political) interact with culture to provide opportunities or barriers for youth at various stages of development. The ecological/developmental framework provides an excellent vantage point for assessing the impact of poverty, immigration, and ethnicity on psychosocial development and adjustment.

Issues in How Culture is Defined

Prior to discussing the role of cultural influences in shaping behavior, it is important to address how the term *culture* will be used in this text. The explicit and implicit nature of culture is evident in defining *culture* as the *values, beliefs,* and *practices* that represent a given ethnocultural group (Betancourt & Lopez, 1993). The importance of recognizing the impact of values and beliefs on subsequent practices and behaviors provides a definition that is indicative of a given cultural focus,

> **DON'T FORGET**
>
> Culture is defined as the *values, beliefs,* and *practices* that represent a given ethnocultural group.

> **DON'T FORGET**
>
> High rates of somatization in African American males and high rates of depression in Asian women may be illustrations of unique aspects of how *distress* is expressed by these diverse cultures.

while at the same time recognizing the potential role of individual differences within that grouping.

Cultural attitudes and beliefs will influence how mental illness is accepted and understood, coping strategies, inclinations to access services and service utilization, as well as responses to intervention and treatment programs. The recent supplement to the surgeon general's report *Mental Health: Culture, Race and Ethnicity* (U.S. Department of Health and Human Services [USDHSS], 2001) emphasizes that *distress* may be expressed differently by different ethnic groups.

In the past 10 years, there have been several movements to increase awareness of cultural influences in psychopathology.

Cultural Psychopathology and the *DSM-IV*

The fourth edition of the *DSM* (APA, 1994) now includes "specific *culture,* age, and gender features" for each disorder, as well as an appendix providing guidelines for applying *DSM-IV* diagnoses in a multicultural setting. The guidelines stress the need to document cultural identity, any existing cultural explanations for the disorder, and influence of culture on potential support systems as part of the treatment plan and case formulation. The *DSM-IV* also added 25 "culture-bound syndromes" to refer to maladaptive and aberrant behavior patterns that apply to different minority groups. Culture Bound Syndromes that apply to the four major cultures to be discussed further are presented in Rapid Reference 14.1.

The World Mental Health Report

This report (Desjarlais et al., 1996) focuses on the prevalence of mental health issues in low-income countries in Africa, Latin America, Asia, and the Pacific. The report documents high rates of domestic violence toward women (between 50% to 60% had been beaten) and high rates of substance abuse among youth who had migrated from rural to urban communities in search of employment.

Rapid Reference 14.1

Examples of Some Culture Bound Syndromes

Culture Bound Syndrome	Description	Culture
Ataque de nervios: Precipitated by stressful life events	Being out of control: trembling, crying, shouting, verbal/physical aggression Dissociative experiences: seizure-like or fainting spells	Latino
Bilis and colera (muina): Precipitated by extreme anger	Acute nervous tension, headache, trembling, screaming, stomach-ache; severe form can result in loss of consciousness	Latino
Brain fag: Precipitated by school challenges	Difficulties concentrating, thinking, remembering Somatic complaints: head, neck, blurred vision	West African
Falling-out or blacking-out	Collapse (may be preceded by dizziness); eyes are open, but inability to see; unable to move; similar to conversion disorder	Southern U.S. Caribbean
Ghost Sickness	Preoccupation with death and deceased; nightmares, weakness, loss of appetite, anxiety, hallucination, fainting, confusion, suffocation	American Indian
Hwa-byung: Precipitated by suppressing anger	Anger syndrome; insomnia, fatigue, panic, fear of death, depression, anorexia, palpitations, lump in throat, body aches	Korean
Locura: Chronic psychosis	Incoherence, agitation hallucinations; unpredictable and possibly violent	Latino
Mal de ojo (evil eye)	Children are at risk; crying fits, diarrhea, vomiting, and fever	Spanish

(continued)

Examples of Some Culture Bound Syndromes (*continued*)

Culture Bound Syndrome	Description	Culture
Nervios: Precipitated by stressful life events	Wide range of vague symptoms of stress: headaches, tearfulness, irritability, sleep and eating disturbances, trembling, somatic disturbance, etc.	Latino
Qi-gong psychotic reaction: Precipitated by involvement in folk health practices	Acute psychotic, paranoid, or delusional response	Chinese
Rootwork: Precipitating cause: Under a spell or hex, witchcraft	Generalized anxiety, gastrointestinal complaints, weakness, dizziness, and paranoia	Southern U.S., African American
Spell	Trance-like state and communication with deceased	Southern U.S., African American
Susto: Precipitated by frightening event	Fright or Soul loss, unhappiness and sickness. Resembles PTSD, depression, and Somatoform Disorder	Latino, Mexican
Taijin kyofusho	Phobia regarding body (appearance, odor, expression) causing intense fear of humiliation	Japanese

Source: *DSM-IV* (APA, 2000).

Mental Health: Culture, Race and Ethnicity—A Supplement to Mental Health: A Report of the Surgeon General

This report (USDHSS, 2001) is a supplement to the surgeon general's Report on mental health (USDHSS, 1999). Results revealed that approximately 21% of adults and children in the United States suffer from a diagnosable mental disorder. However, while prevalence rates for Whites are similar to those for racial and ethnic minorities based on data from those living in the community (excludes those incarcerated, institutionalized, or homeless), significant disparities exist in the services provided for those in need.

The report suggests that in addition to barriers faced due to low income, minorities also face barriers to service due to mistrust, fear of racism and discrimination, and barriers in communication. Furthermore, *lack of trust* and *problems with communication* can significantly undermine the patient-clinician relationship and nullify any possible therapeutic benefit.

DON'T FORGET

The surgeon general's report reveals that, compared to Whites, minorities

- have less access and availability of services;
- are less likely to receive services;
- receive poorer quality of care; and
- have less representation in mental health research.

CAUTION

Although prevalence rates for mental health disorders may be similar for Whites and minorities, the outcomes are not. Minorities experience the greater burden of having a disorder in the aftermath of poor quality of care. Disproportionate numbers of minorities do not recover from mental illness and experience continued downturn in economic disadvantage.

THE IMPACT OF CULTURE ON CHILD PSYCHOPATHOLOGY

Adult Perceptions of Mental Illness and Behavior Problems

Reluctance of parents to accept a mental health explanation for their child's behavior may be based on unique cultural explanations (physical or spiritual cause) and/or fears that labeling may result in further discrimination based on ethnicity and race (Walker, 2002). As a result, differences in religious, cultural, social, and moral values may cause significant misunderstandings between parent and teacher or clinician. Although there has been increased awareness of the poor quality of mental health services available for minorities in the past 10 years, recognition of mental health issues of children and adolescents from diverse cultures has received less attention (Walker, 2002).

Children and Adolescents of Minority Populations: An Overview

Understanding the underlying attitudes, practices, and values of a given culture also requires an understanding that variations in cultural features will exist within a given culture. Without this premise, the danger of stereotyping is imminent. Therefore, although the remainder of this chapter will be devoted to discussing four minority groups in greater detail, it is important to stress the need to balance knowledge of common cultural practices with an appreciation of within-culture diversity.

Prevalence and Risks

It has been predicted that nonwhite and Hispanic-speaking youth under 18 years of age will comprise over 45% of the population of youth in the United States by the year 2020 (U.S. Bureau of the Census, 1996). Currently, minority youth represent over 50% of the student body in at least five states (NSELA, 2003). Low-income minority children and adolescents are at greater risk for mental health and behavioral disorders due to their low SES, stressful family environments, and poor access to supportive services.

CAUTION

The impact of culture and ethnicity on prevailing or presenting problems must always be considered within the greater context of other environmental influences, including the degree to which this child or family adheres to practices, attitudes, and values of the minority culture.

DON'T FORGET

Minority youth often experience feelings of alienation, cultural conflicts with their families, academic failure, and peer victimization (USDHSS, 2001). In their report on youth suicide prevention with culturally and linguistically diverse populations, Lazear and colleagues (2003) report the following:

- 64% of all Native American suicides were committed by youth 15 to 24 years of age.
- Asian Pacific Islander females aged 15 to 24 years have the highest suicide rate in the country.
- Suicide rates by African American youth (10 to 14 years) increased 233% between 1980 and 1995.
- Rates for depression reported among girls in Grades 5 to 12 vary according to ethnicity: Asian American (30%), Hispanic (27%), non-Hispanic White (22%), and African American (17%).
- Reports of suicide attempts within the previous 12 months were highest for Hispanic males (12.8%) and females (18.9%), compared with all other youth.

Risk of suicide among all teenagers has been increasing. The suicide rate for White teens, 10 to 14 years of age increased 120% between 1980 and 1995 (Lazear, Doan, & Roggenbaum, 2003). However, among minority youth the trend toward suicide and depression is even more pronounced.

On an average day, 109,000 teens are in juvenile detention. More than 60% of all youth who are incarcerated in juvenile justice facilities are racial or ethnic minorities from low-income families. Teplin, Abram, McClelland, Dulcan, and Mericle (2002) found that 66% of males and 75% of females in juvenile detention had at least one psychiatric disorder: half of males and almost half of females had Substance Abuse disorders, over 40% had Disruptive Behavior Disorders, while 20% of females met criteria for Major Depressive Disorder. Results of this and other surveys on minority youth and the juvenile justice system suggest that minority youth are overrepresented in the justice system and underrepresented in the mental health system.

In their recent literature review of studies concerning youth exposure to violence (ETV), Buka, Stichick, Birdthistle, and Earls (2001) report that ETV is greater among ethnic (African American and Latino) minorities and highest in lower-SES youth living in inner cities. Youth who witness high levels of violence on a repeated basis are at serious risk for developing negative outcomes in all facets of psychological, social, emotional, and academic functioning and are at greater risk for engaging in violent behaviors.

The influence of cultural diversity on family attitudes and parenting practices has received increasing interest in the literature (see Kotchick & Forehand, 2002, for review). According to Ogbu (1981), parenting practices are driven by cultural forces that exist by necessity to insure survival and success of the family and preservation of cultural attitudes, values, and practices. Within this framework, parenting practices are developed based upon the availability of resources within the community to develop competencies in keeping with prescribed cultural values. Ogbu (1981) also states that often in these circumstances, childrearing is often guided by folk theories that have been developed to foster behavior in children that is culturally valued.

The following discussion will focus on four major minority groups: African American, Latino/Hispanic Americans; Asian Americans/Pacific Islanders, and Native American Indians. Unless otherwise cited, demographics reported have been obtained from *Mental Health: Culture,*

DON'T FORGET

A probable outcome of chronic ETV is the development of PTSD. In one study, as many as 27% of African American youth had PTSD (Fitzpatrick & Boldizar, 1993).

Race and Ethnicity: A Supplement to Mental Health: A Report of the Surgeon General (USDHSS, 2001).

AFRICAN AMERICANS

Demographics and Sociocultural Background

While approximately 12% of the population in the United States is African American, it is important to understand that the Black population is also increasing in its own diversity as immigrants continue to arrive from as far away as Africa and as close as the neighboring Caribbean Islands. In addition, there is considerable disparity between African Americans who are at higher economic and educational advantage compared with the majority who are disadvantaged (McAdoo, 1997). The majority (53%) of African Americans reside in the southern United States and represent 57% of the population living in large urban inner-city areas noted for high crime, poor housing, poor employment opportunities, and access to fewer support services.

There are a disproportionate number of African Americans living in poverty (22%) compared to the U.S. population at large (13%). Infant mortality is twice that of White infants, while Black preschoolers are 3 times more likely to have HIV/AIDS than their White peers (Willis, 1998).

Familial Influences and Parenting Practices

Despite what seems like overwhelming odds and a history marked with racism and oppression, African Americans have demonstrated a remarkable ability to survive. Over the years, investigators have come to appreciate the role of family and culture in building a foundation for coping based on a supportive network of extended family and kin through sharing resources, housing, and tasks. In addition to extended family networks, survival has also been attributed to flexibility of male and female roles and non-gender-specific role functions. Within the African American community, in addition to religious practices, the church often occupies a central focus for social, civic, and educational activities (Allen & Majidi-Ahi, 2001).

> **DON'T FORGET**
>
> Inner-city living is associated with increased risk of homicide, which is the leading cause of death among young African American adult males. Risk for homicide is 6 to 10 times higher for Black compared to White males, with an increase in murder rate among 15- to 19-years-olds rising from less than 600 in 1984 to over 1,200 in 1987.

The impact of the kinship network, however, may take its toll on those who are ultimately supported by the system. McAdoo (1997) explains that often the family will collectively work together (older children leaving school to help financially) so that the youngest member of the family (often a female) can have the benefits of a higher education and escape the poverty level. However, the burden of the family sacrifice continues to weigh heavily on the recipient, who may be conflicted to either return the resources to the family or isolate herself in self-preservation.

One important value that is stressed by African Americans is the value of independence. By achieving independence, family members are able to be self-sufficient as well as being able to provide temporary assistance to other family members as needed (Willis, 1998). The role of the family and extended family in preserving a sense of cultural heritage can also be seen in the oral tradition as communication of expression often takes verbal or musical form.

Looking at African American parenting practices from the perspective suggested by Ogbu's model (1981), it becomes increasingly clear how these practices are geared toward survival of heritage and culture and preservation of the family based on limited resources and high-risk environments. The common thread that unites these families is the desire to instill pride in their cultural heritage while recognizing racial discrimination and a history of oppression of people of color (Willis, 1998).

Although initial investigations of parenting practices focused on cross-cultural comparisons, more recent studies have begun to concentrate on how various parenting practices within cultures relate to different child outcomes. Recent studies of *authoritative* parenting practices (high warmth, negotiated control) versus *authoritarian* parenting style (low warmth, high control) have revealed that use of authoritarian practices by African Americans can have a positive effect for minority youth. In this case, use of more punitive physical discipline may serve to protect children from engaging in high-risk behaviors in an environment fraught with opportunities for deviant behavior and actually may increase their chances of survival and success (Kelley, Power, & Wimbush, 1992).

African American families are less likely to seek psychiatric help for their children and more likely to approach family doctors, ministers, or friends for advice (Willis, 1998).

CAUTION

Baumrind's (1971) model has been widely cited in research on parenting practices, with most positive outcomes for children attributed to parent use of an *authoritative* rather than *authoritarian* parenting style. However, far fewer studies have considered how well these models fit ethnic minority youth.

CAUTION

In their review of psychiatric disorders and service usage, Angold et al., (2002), found that overall usage rates of service were well below prevalence rates for disorders in African American youth.

CAUTION

It is also important to note that because symptoms of suicidal behavior in African American youth may be more evident in acting out and aggressive and high-risk behaviors, that detection of suicide intent may be misdiagnosed (Weddle & McKenry, 1995).

Prevalence Rates of Psychological and Behavioral Disorders

Although less likely to suffer from depression, African Americans are more likely to experience phobias than non-Hispanic Whites. Among the mental disorders, Somatization Disorder (15%) and Schizophrenia (Black males) have disproportionately higher prevalence rates and poorer outcomes in African American populations. There is a significantly higher prevalence rate reported for Schizophrenia in second-generation African Caribbeans living in the United Kingdom (APA, 2000).

Although African Americans represent only 12% of the population of the United States, they are overrepresented in 40% of the homeless population. They comprise almost 40% of all juveniles in legal custody, and they constitute 45% of all children in public foster care. Exposure to violence is high, with over 25% of African American youth meeting diagnostic criteria for PTSD.

Psychiatric hospitalization rates for severe disorders, such as Schizophrenia, have been reported to be 2 to 3 times higher than for White youth. African American youth are also more likely to be referred to juvenile justice rather than a treatment facility.

While alcohol consumption is lower than that of White youth, drug use among lower-income African American youth is often related to a drug culture of delinquency, selling drugs, and the use of cocaine and heroin. High rates of teen pregnancy among African American girls is associated with high dropout rates, unemployment, and future welfare use (Rosenheim and Testa, 1992).

LATINO/HISPANIC AMERICANS

Demographics and Sociocultural Background

There are approximately 35 million Hispanic Americans living in the United States, with the vast majority (two thirds) represented by Mexican Americans. The remaining Hispanic Americans have Puerto Rican, Cuban, South American,

Central American, Dominican, and Spanish roots. The majority of Latinos live in California, Arizona, New Mexico, Colorado, and Texas.

Education varies among the subgroups, however, with a little over half of young adults having completed a high school education. Poverty rates range from a low of 14% (Cuban Americans) to highs between 31% (Puerto Ricans) to 37% (Mexican Americans). As a comparison, 13.5% of the American population at large are at or below the poverty line.

Familial Influences and Parenting Practices

Although the Hispanic population is very diverse, the following summary will outline some of the common underlying values and beliefs. At the foundation of the Mexican American family is the kinship network promoting a mixture of traditional and more contemporary approaches. The extended family system, including *compadres* (godparents), provide for each other in terms of emotional, social, and financial support. The collective nature of the family network fosters an attitude of cooperation, affiliation, and interdependence, as opposed to more individualistic values of independence, competition, and confrontation (Ramirez, 2001).

Mexican American parents may seem less intent on children achieving milestones in the required time frame and more accepting of a child's individual limitations. Although young children are usually treated with permissiveness and indulgences, in later years they are expected to help out with family duties such as cleaning, cooking, and child care. Gender roles are traditional, with female children expected to be more homebound, while males are given more latitude and encouragement to explore their environment. Both roles are seen as preparatory for their future roles as mothers and fathers (Ramirez, 2001).

Prevalence Rates of Psychological and Behavioral Disorders

Compared to White youth, Latino youth demonstrate more anxiety-related and delinquency-related behavior problems, depression, and drug abuse. In their study of minority youth in the California system of care, Mak and Rosenblatt (2002) found that Hispanic youth were more

DON'T FORGET

The surgeon general's report (US-DHSS, 2001) suggests that use of mental health services by Hispanics and Latinos is poor, with fewer than 20% contacting health care providers. Families may be more inclined to seek assistance from natural healers than from medical professionals.

likely to have been diagnosed initially with Disruptive Behavior Disorder and Substance Abuse despite later indications (parent and clinician rating scales) that this was not the case. As a result, the authors suggest that clinicians may make misdiagnoses at admission based on preconceived notions and that these errors could seriously undermine treatment effectiveness.

ASIAN AMERICANS AND PACIFIC ISLANDERS

Demographics and Sociocultural Background

Asian Americans or Pacific Islanders (AA/PIs) represent approximately 4% of the population of the United States. Approximately half of the AA/PI population is located in the west, most notably in California and Hawaii. Asian Pacific Americans are the fastest growing ethnic minority in the United States, having doubled their population each decade since 1970. The terms *Asian American* and *Pacific Islander* are used to refer to over 60 different ethnic groups that have emigrated to the United States from Asia, the Pacific Rim, and the Pacific Islands. Asian Americans are often referred to as the *model minority* due to their visible success; however, they have also been subjected to anti-immigration sentiment, and ethnic distinctions between ethnic groups are often blurred (Chan, 1998).

In this chapter, discussion will be limited to Chinese and Japanese Americans.

Chinese Americans

Some Chinese Americans have been in the United States for over six generations, while others are recent immigrants. The beliefs, attitudes, and values of the Asian culture are highly influenced by the philosophies contained in the three teachings of Confucianism, Taoism, and Buddhism. At the basis of Confucianism is family piety found in respect for one's parents and elders. Taoism speaks to the individual character rather than the family and focuses on living in tune with nature (yin and yang) and focuses on building inner strength through meditation, asceticism, and self-discipline. Buddhism teaches that life's suffering can be avoided by eliminating earthly desires.

While the majority of Chinese speak Mandarin, the remainder speak multiple variations or dialects that have evolved into distinct languages. Newer immigrant communities are often formed around Chinatowns that provide employment for the unskilled working class and the more wealthy entrepreneurs. This situation often results in two distinct classes (Wong, 1995).

Japanese Americans

The Japanese use different words to categorize immigrant generations. The *Issei* were the first generation to arrive in the United States in the early 1900s, and their children born in the United States are referred to as *Nisei*. Third-generation Japanese are called *Sansei,* while fourth and fifth generations are called *Yonsei* and *Gosei,* respectively. The majority of Japanese Americans settled in Hawaii and California. Japanese Americans in Hawaii are more closely aligned with other Asian Americans and, as such, have maintained a greater extent of their culture than those who remained on the mainland (Nagata, 2001).

Educationally, more than half of Japanese American young adult males and almost half of young adult females have their bachelor's degree or higher. While other Asian groups are increasing in size, Japanese Americans have registered an increasing decline in population.

Familial Influences and Parenting Practices

Adolescence is a period of transition in most cultures; however, in a North American climate, the period is marked by goals of increased independence from family and forging of a unique identity. For Asian American youth, this period can be fraught with extreme pressure resulting from a divided sense of self that straddles two different cultural frameworks. Studies have demonstrated that Asian minority youth can experience culture shock, evident in disappointment, depression, and anger, that is often intense and complicated by conflicted relationships with families who prioritize dependency and submission rather than independence and confrontation (Yeh & Huang, 2000).

Traditionally, Asian families have functioned along prescribed guidelines with privileges assigned to specific roles. The male head of household had unchallenged authority and was responsible for the family's economic status and respect within the community. The mother was responsible for nurturing the children, and working outside of the home was not encouraged. The firstborn male was

> ## DON'T FORGET
>
> Cultural differences along the dimension of *individualism* and *collectivism* (I/C) predict the extent to which a given culture fosters the goals of the *individual* (autonomous, independent) versus the *group* (connection and cooperation) (Hofstede, 1980). While families in North America encourage development of the individual (competition, independence), Asian families traditionally have been motivated by goals to support the group (cooperation and dependency).

DON'T FORGET

Contemporary forces have softened rigid adherence to prescribed roles of the past, as have increases in marriages to non-Asian partners. However, there continues to be strong cultural emphasis on emotional restraint, and not expressing emotions continues to be a valued trait. Piety to family continues to be a significant factor with shame and loss of face as the ultimate punishment for not maintaining appropriate conduct that might reflect badly on one's family (Nagata, 2001).

CAUTION

It has been reported that 1-year prevalence rates for depression among Chinese Americans is between 3% and 7%. In addition, Chinese Americans are more likely to demonstrate depressive symptoms as somatic complaints to a greater extent than African Americans or non-Hispanic Whites.

given preferential treatment, and male children were esteemed relative to females.

Prevalence Rates of Psychological and Behavioral Disorders

Historically, knowledge of the mental health needs of the Asian and Pacific Islanders has been limited. In addition to language barriers, the apparent shame and stigma attached to seeking mental health resources may also be an important contributor to the extremely low utilization rates of mental health services. According to the surgeon general's supplementary report (USDHSS, 2001), only 17% of those with mental health issues seek assistance, and then it is usually when the symptoms reach crisis proportions.

Although suicide rates for Chinese, Japanese, and Filipino Americans are lower than for White Americans, rates for Native Hawaiian adolescents are higher than any other adolescent group in Hawaii (USDHSS, 2001), while rates for Asian Pacific Islander females (15 to 24) are consistently the highest in that age group (Lazear et al., 2003).

In their review of racial/ethnic literature, McCabe and colleagues (1999) found few studies that have investigated Asian/Pacific Islander American youth in juvenile justice or mental health and no studies reporting on these youth in SED sectors. However, despite the fact that Asian/Pacific Islander Americans have been underrepresented, McCabe and colleagues (1999) found that Asian/Pacific Islander Americans were present at rates comparable to other minority groups in alcohol and drug treatment sectors and juvenile justice. The authors suggest that because these youth primarily were from Southeast Asia, a history of refugee-related traumas might account for the vulnerability of this population compared to other Asian/Pacific youth studied previously.

NATIVE AMERICAN INDIANS

Demographics and Sociocultural Background

The Native American population (including Alaska natives) is approximately 1.5% of the total population in the United States. The population is extremely diverse, with over 561 officially recognized tribes. As might be expected, linguistic diversity is also high, with over 200 different languages.

Historically, the majority of Native Americans lived on reservations (80%); however, due to reductions in federal funding, only 20% of the population can be found on reservations today. Native American Indians suffer from chronic unemployment. Mortality rates are high and are attributed to alcoholism, cirrhosis of the liver, homicide, and suicide.

While the national average for high school graduation is 75%, the Native American average is 66%. Twice as many Native Americans are unemployed compared to White Americans. Approximately 26% of the population live in poverty. Native American peoples constitute 8% of the total population of homeless. In the criminal justice system, 4% of all inmates are Native American.

Familial Influences and Parenting Practices

American Indian families support a collective rather than individualistic perspective. However, in sharp contrast to values placed on dependence versus independence in Asian cultures, the Native American culture values independence and autonomy over dependence. There is a wide range of acculturation that exists within Native American communities, with some communities assimilating the dominant American culture, while others focus on preserving their traditional heritage (Joe & Malach, 1998). As a collective society, their involvement can often extend outside the family to the tribe at large. Roles and responsibilities of family members differ among the various tribes. Elders are often seen as the purveyors of wisdom and pass down the tradition through storytelling in the oral tradition (LaFramboise & Graff Low, 2001).

Communication is indirect rather than direct and is designed to protect

DON'T FORGET

Although children's early accomplishments are often a reason for celebration, parents do not share the White American urgency or pressure regarding the timing of meeting important milestones, believing more in readiness being the master of performance. In addition, time settings aligned to a present-time orientation or an event-timed orientation (first laugh, first smile) may also prove problematic (Joe & Malach, 1998).

the immediate family members from being directly involved in punishment for mis-deeds (protects family bonds) or rewards for accomplishments (insures family hu-mility). Messages are often navigated through a chain of family and kin until ultimately being delivered to the source. Messages designated to guide the youth's development or provide guidance in determining restitution for wrongdoing are delivered to the designated source, while behaviors worthy of accolade are routed to the community town crier who will announce the event (LaFramboise & Graff Low, 2001).

Prevalence Rates of Psychological and Behavioral Disorders

Indian Health Service (IHS) clinics are mainly on reservations where only 20% of the American Indian population reside. The surgeon general's supplementary report (USDHSS, 2001) states that little is known about usage rates of services in this population. However, the report does state the following: 50% of adolescents in a juvenile justice facility of a Northern Plains reservation had a substance abuse or mental health disorder while many had multiple disorders (USDHSS, 2001). Prevalence rates for substance/drug abuse were estimated to be as high as 70% in some populations sampled, while exposure to trauma/violent victimization was reported to be as high as twice the national average.

Substance Abuse is a predominant cause for concern, especially among 13-year-old American Native children. In addition, as high as 70% of American Indians among Northern Plains and southwestern Vietnam veterans admitted to alcohol- or drug-related problems. Violent victimization among this population is more than twice the national average, with a rate of 22% of the population experiencing symptoms of PTSD compared to 8% in the general population (USDHSS, 2001).

ASSESSMENT

Cultural Competence

Within the past 10 years, there has been increasing recognition that professionals and communities need to work together toward greater understanding of the needs of diverse cultural populations. Culturally competent service delivery should be pervasive and include legal and ethical issues, school culture and edu-cational policy, psychoeducational assessment, and working with interpreters and research (Rogers et al., 1999). With respect to assessment, several key areas are highlighted for consideration when working with culturally and linguistically di-verse (CLD) students, including prior educational history, SES, racism, accultur-ation, and language acquisition.

It is also important to consider whether normed tests are valid for use with CLD students based on fairness of content, educational background, and product versus process orientation. In many areas, children are deemed to be language competent and eligible for formal assessment using IQ and other standard measures once they have been in the country for 2 years. However, evidence suggests that at least 5 to 7 years are required for academically oriented language development.

The situation is further complicated if tests are not available in bilingual versions, as the use of an interpreter to administer an English version of a test would invalidate the results.

Lynch (1998) suggests several cautions and guidelines for working with interpreters and translators. It is important that the interpreter not only be language proficient (including dialect) but also have an understanding of the available resources. Ideally, the interpreter not only provides a medium for verbal communication but also interprets the underlying cultural message in order to bridge the two cultures. Given the professional requirements of the interpreter, Lynch (1998) cautions against the use of family members as interpreters. Given many of the family dynamics discussed throughout this chapter, parents may be very reluctant to discuss private issues with extended family members present. The use of older children as family interpreters can be especially problematic, placing a psychological burden on these children to act as pseudoparents in their role as interpreter with professionals serving the family.

Treatment

Several papers have been developed to provide guidelines for professionals in developing greater cultural competence (National Mental Health Information Center [NMHIC, 1996]; *American Psychological Association (APA) Guidelines for Providers of Psychological Services to Ethnic, Linguistic and Culturally Diverse Populations*). In discussing a training guideline for psychiatric residences working with children and adolescents, Kim (1995) highlights five essential components of a culturally competent service delivery:

CAUTION

Cummins (1984) suggests that English language proficiency is initially acquired through basic interpersonal communication skills (BICS). The expected time line in developing BICS, which is roughly equivalent to social communication, is approximately 2 to 3 years. However, in the classroom, academic learning requires the development of cognitive academic language proficiency skills (CALPS), which involve reading, writing, and curriculum content. Learning adequate CALPS requires anywhere from 5 to 7 years.

- Recognition and acceptance of cultural differences
- Cultural self-awareness
- Appreciation of the dynamic nature of cultural differences
- Commitment to acquiring a basic understanding of the child's cultural background
- Modification and adaptation of practice skills to address the cultural context of the child and family

---

🐊 TEST YOURSELF 🐊

1. **Compared to Whites, minorities have**
   - (a) greater access to services.
   - (b) more representation in mental health research.
   - (c) higher quality services.
   - (d) less access to services.

2. **The highest rate of suicide among adolescents is held by which minority group?**
   - (a) Native American females
   - (b) African American males
   - (c) Asian Pacific Islander females
   - (d) Hispanic males

3. **Which of the following ethnic minorities values the quality of dependence in their children?**
   - (a) Native American
   - (b) Asian American
   - (c) African American
   - (d) Hispanic American

4. **The term *model minority* has been used to describe which minority group?**
   - (a) Asian American
   - (b) African American
   - (c) Native American
   - (d) Hispanic American

5. **Which of the following minority youth would be most likely to suffer from PTSD?**
   - (a) Asian American
   - (b) African American
   - (c) Native American
   - (d) Hispanic American

6. **Which of the following results from the supplement to the surgeon general's report on culture, race, and ethnicity (USDHSS, 2001) is *false*?**

   (a) Approximately 21% of children and adults in the United States have a mental disorder.

   (b) Prevalence rates of disorders did not differ appreciably between Whites and minorities living in the community.

   (c) African American males had the highest rates of Schizophrenia.

   (d) Outcomes for having a mental disorder are similar for Whites and minorities.

7. **Buka and colleagues' (2001) report on exposure to violence (ETV) revealed that**

   (a) ETV is higher among minority youth.

   (b) ETV is highest in inner-city neighborhoods.

   (c) chronic ETV is associated with higher risk for PTSD.

   (d) all of the above are true.

8. **According to research, which of the following parenting styles would be most appropriate for ethnic minority youth living in low SES environments?**

   (a) Authoritative

   (b) Authoritarian

   (c) Permissive

   (d) Independent

9. **Which of the following youth would be expected to experience the most difficult transition from adolescence to adulthood based on bridging their two cultures?**

   (a) African American

   (b) Asian American

   (c) Hispanic

   (d) Native American

10. **According to studies of English language proficiency, how many years does it normally take to acquire English proficiency for academic subjects?**

   (a) 2 to 3 years

   (b) 1 to 3 years

   (c) 4 to 5 years

   (d) 5 to 7 years

Answers: 1. d; 2. c; 3. b; 4. a; 5. b; 6. d; 7. d; 8. b; 9. b; 10. d

Appendix A

Codes of Ethical Conduct

American Counseling Association. (1995). *The American Counseling Association code of ethics.*

The American Counseling Association (ACA) was founded in 1952 and has over 52,000 members. The ACA Code of Ethics defines principles of ethical behavior to serve as guidelines and standards of practice for its members. The ethics code is available on the ACA website at www.counseling.org.

American Psychological Association. (2002). *Ethical principles of psychologists and code of conduct.*

The newly adopted ethics code went into effect June 1, 2003, and represents the ninth revision since 1953. The American Psychological Association has over 150,000 members and is the largest association of psychologists in the world, with 53 professional divisions currently. The ethics code provides a common set of principles and standards to guide psychologists in their professional and scientific work. The ethics code was published in the December 2002 edition of American Psychologist *(vol. 57, no. 12) and is available on the association website at www.apa.org /ethics.*

American School Counselors Association. (1998). *Ethical standards for school counselors.*

The American School Counselors Association (ACSA) formed in 1952 and currently has 15,000 members. The Ethical Standards *provide principles of ethical behavior required in the provision of school counseling services. The ethics code is available on the ASCA website at www.schoolcounselor.org.*

National Association of School Psychologists. (2000). *Professional conduct manual and principles for professional ethics: Guidelines for the provision of school psychological services.*

The National Association of School Psychologists (NASP) was founded in 1969 and is the largest association of school psychologists world-wide. NASP has developed a comprehensive set of standards to guide school psychologists in their professional conduct in the provision of school psychological services practice. Copies of the standards are available through NASP Publications, 4340 East West highway, Suite 402, Bethesda, MD, 20814 or the NASP website: www.naspweb.org.

Appendix B

References for Assessment Instruments and Resources

Structured and Semistructured Clinical Interviews

Ambrosini, P. J. (2000). Historical development and present status of the Schedule for Affective Disorders and Schizophrenia for School-Age Children (K-SADS). *Journal of the American Academy of Child and Adolescent Psychiatry, 39,* 49–58.

Reich, W., Welner, Z., Herjanic, B., & MHS Staff. (1997). *Diagnostic Interview for Children and Adolescents computer program (DICA-IV).* North Tonawanda, NY: Multi-Health System.

Shaffer, D., Fisher, P., Lucas, C., Dulcan, M. K., & Schwab-Stone, M. E. (2000). NIMH diagnostic interview schedule for children, version IV (NIMH DISC IV): Description, differences from previous versions, and reliability of some common diagnoses. *Journal of the American Academy of Child and Adolescent Psychiatry, 39,* 28–38.

Silverman, W. K., & Albano, A. M. (1996). *Anxiety disorders interview schedule for children for DSM-IV (child and parent versions).* San Antonio, TX: The Psychological Corporation.

Rating Scales and Self-Report Measures

Achenbach, T. M. (1991). *Manual for the Child Behavior Checklist 4–8 and the 1991 Profile.* Burlington: University of Vermont, Department of Psychiatry.

Achenbach, T. M., & Rescorla, L. A. (2001). *Manual for the ASEBA School-Age Forms and Profiles.* Burlington, VT: ASEBA.

Beck, A., & Beck, J. (2001). *The Beck Youth Inventories.* San Antonio, TX: The Psychological Corporation.

Beidel, D., Turner, S. M., & Fink, C. M. (1996). Assessment of childhood social phobia: Construct, convergent and discriminative validity of the Social Phobia and Anxiety Inventory for Children (SPAI-C). *Psychological Assessment, 8,* 235–240.

Briere, J. (1996). *Trauma symptom checklist for children: Professional manual.* Florida: Psychological Assessment Resources.

Brown, T. E. (2001). *Brown Attention-Deficit Disorder Scales manual.* San Antonio, TX: The Psychological Corporation.

Conners, C. K. (1998). *Conners Rating Scales—Revised technical manual.* North Tonawanda, NY: Multi-Health Systems.

Gardner, D. M. (1991). *The Eating Disorder Inventory—2.* Odessa, FL: Psychological Assessment Resources.

Gioia, G. A., Isquith, P. K., Guy, S. C., & Kenworthy, L. (2000). *Behavior Rating Inventory of Executive Function (BRIEF) professional manual.* Odessa, FL: Psychological Assessment Resources.

Gilliam, J. E. (1995). *Gilliam Autism Rating Scale (GARS).* Austin, TX: Pro-ed.

Goodman, W., Rasmussen, S., & Price, L. (1988). *The Children's Yale Brown Obsessive-Compulsive Scale (CY-BOCS).* New Haven: Connecticut Mental Health Center, Clinical Neuroscience Research Unit.

Kazdin, A. E., Rodgers, A., & Colbus, D. (1986). The Hopelessness Scale for Children: Psychometric characteristics and concurrent validity. *Journal of Consulting and Clinical Psychology, 54,* 241–245.

Kovacs, M. (1992). *Child Depression Inventory.* North Tonawanda, NY: Multi-Health Systems.

Lachar, D., & Gruber, C. P. (1995). *Personality Inventory for Youth (PIY) manual.* Los Angeles: Western Psychological Services.

March, J. S. (1997). *The Multidimensional Anxiety Scale for Children (MASC).* North Tonawanda, NY: Multi-Health Systems.

Myles, B. S., Bock, S. J., & Simpson, R. L. (2001). *Asperger Syndrome Diagnostic Scale (ASDS) examiner's manual.* Austin, TX: Pro-ed.

Newcomer, P. L., Barenbaum, E. M., & Bryant, B. R. (1994). *DAYS: Depression and Anxiety in Youth Scale.* Austin, TX: Pro-ed.

Ollendick, T. H. (1983). Reliability and validity of the Revised Fear Survey Schedule for Children (FSSC-R). *Behavior Research and Therapy, 21,* 234–245.

Reynolds, C. R., & Kamphaus, R. W. (1992). *BASC: Behavior Assessment System for Children manual.* Circle Pines, MN: American Guidance Service.

Reynolds, C. R., & Richmond, B. O. (1994). *Revised Child Manifest Anxiety Scale.* Los Angeles: Western Psychological Services.

Reynolds, W. M. (1987). *Reynolds Adolescent Depression Scale (RADS).* Odessa, FL: Psychological Assessment Resources.

Reynolds, W. M. (1989). *Reynolds Child Depression Scale (RCDS).* Odessa, FL: Psychological Assessment Resources.

Reynolds, W. M. (1998). *Adolescent Mental Health Questionnaire (APS).* Odessa, FL: Psychological Assessment Resources.

Schopler, E., Reichler, R., & Renner, B. R. (1993). *Childhood Autism Rating Scale (CARS).* Los Angeles: Western Psychological Services.

Spielberger, C. D., Edwards, C. D., Lushene, R. E., Montouri, J., & Platzek, D. (1973). *Manual for the State-Trait Anxiety Inventory for Children (STAIC).* Palo Alto, CA: Consulting Psychologists Press.

Intellectual/Cognitive Functioning and Adaptive Behavior

Elliott, C. D. (1990). *Differential Ability Scales.* San Antonio, TX: The Psychological Corporation.

Harrison, P., & Oakland, T. (2003). *Adaptive Behavior Assessment System (ABAS) and the ABAS—Second Edition with downward extension.* San Antonio, TX: The Psychological Corporation.

Lambert, N., Nihira, K., & Leland, H. (1993). *ABS-S:2: The Adaptive Behavior Scale—School, 2nd Edition.* Austin, TX: Pro-ed.

Sparrow, S. S., Balla, D. A., & Cicchetti, D. V. (1984). *Vineland Adaptive Behavior Scales.* Circle Pines, MN: American Guidance Service.

Roid, G. H. (2003). *Manual for the Stanford Binet Intelligence Scales, 5th Edition.* Itasca, IL: Riverside Publishing Company.

Wechsler, D. (2002). *Manual for the Wechsler Preschool and Primary Scale of Intelligence, Third Edition (WPPSI-III).* San Antonio, TX: The Psychological Corporation.

Wechsler, D. (2003). *Manual for the Wechsler Intelligence Scale for Children—Fourth Edition (WISC-IV).* San Antonio, TX: The Psychological Corporation.

Resources

Sattler, J. M. (2001). *Assessment of children: Cognitive applications, 4th edition.* La Mesa, CA: Jerome M. Sattler.

Sattler, J. M. (2002). *Assessment of children: Behavioral and clinical applications, 4th edition.* La Mesa, CA: Jerome M. Sattler.

Appendix C

Individuals with Disabilities Education Improvement Act of 2004 (IDEA04)

Children with disabilities were initially granted opportunities for federally funded special education programs under Public Law 94-142, which was passed in 1975 as the *Education of All Handicapped Children Act (EHA)*. The law was renamed *the Individuals with Disabilities Education Act,* (IDEA) in 1990 and has been amended several times over the years. In November, 2004, Congress passed the Individuals with Disabilities Education Improvement Act of 2004, which President George W. Bush signed into law on December 3, 2004. The law goes into effect July 2005. The entire congressional report can be accessed on the web at http://thomas.loc.gov/ under H.R. 1350. Parts of the law reproduced in this Appendix were accessed from the above website.

IDEA 2004 mandates special education and related services for children with disabilities who may qualify for services under one of the 13 specific categories of disabilities listed, including: mental retardation, hearing impairments (including deafness), speech or language impairments, visual impairments (including blindness), serious emotional disturbance, orthopedic impairments, autism, traumatic brain injury, other health impairments, and specific learning disabilities. An exhaustive review of the changes in the law is not the intention of this discussion which will focus on how the law impacts on the identification of children and youth with specific learning disabilities.

Among the several changes to the law which has aligned itself more closely with No Child Left Behind (NCLB), is that the law has redefined how States may determine whether a child has a specific learning disability. This represents a dramatic shift in how specific learning disabilities may be determined compared with IQ-achievement discrepancy formulas used for the past thirty years.

It is important to note that the law has not changed how a learning disability is defined, which remains virtually unchanged from the 1997 version of IDEA (see page 211 for a comparison). According to IDEA04, the definition for a specific learning disability which can be found in Section 602 (29) of the law is stated as follows (changes to the new version are presented in italics with replaced word in brackets):

"602(29) SPECIFIC LEARNING DISABILITY—

(A) IN GENERAL—The term 'specific learning disability' means a disorder in *1* [one] or more of the basic psychological processes involved in understanding or in using language, spoken or written, which disorder may manifest itself in *the* [an] imperfect ability to listen, think, speak, read, write, spell, or do mathematical calculations.

(B) DISORDERS INCLUDED—Such term includes such conditions as perceptual disabilities, brain injury, minimal brain dysfunction, dyslexia, and developmental aphasia.

(C) DISORDERS NOT INCLUDED—Such term does not include a learning problem that is primarily the result of visual, hearing, or motor disabilities, of mental retardation, of emotional disturbance, or of environmental, cultural, or economic disadvantage."

As was discussed in Chapter 12, there has been considerable controversy in the past, concerning the use of the IQ-achievement discrepancy formula for determining whether a child has a specific learning disability, under IDEA. Among the criticisms are the length of time required to substantiate a two-year lag between IQ and achievement, and the potential for cultural bias using the IQ discrepancy model. IDEA04 has made a significant change to the law by addressing how to identify children with specific learning disabilities.

In Section 614 of the law, IDEA04 has added sections on eligibility determination that include the following:

"5) SPECIAL RULE FOR ELIGIBILITY DETERMINATION—In making a determination of eligibility under paragraph (4)(A), a child shall not be determined to be a child with a disability if the determinant factor for such determination is—

(A) lack of scientifically based instruction in reading;

(B) lack of instruction in mathematics; or

(C) limited English proficiency.

(6) SPECIFIC LEARNING DISABILITIES—

(A) IN GENERAL—Notwithstanding section 607(b), when determining whether a child has a specific learning disability as defined in section 602(29), a local educational agency shall not be required to take into consideration whether a child has a severe discrepancy between achievement and intellectual ability in oral expression, listening comprehension, written expression, basic reading skill, reading comprehension, mathematical calculation, or mathematical reasoning.

(B) ADDITIONAL AUTHORITY—In determining whether a child has a specific learning disability, a local educational agency may use a process that determines if the child responds to scientific, research-based intervention as a part of the evaluation procedures described in paragraphs (2) and (3)."

As was discussed in Chapter 12, the vast majority of individuals with SLD (80% of those with SLD) have problems primarily in reading. Research also suggests that compared to their fluent-reading peers, poor-readers can have life-long learning deficits due to the cumulative impact of reading fluency on accessing information, vocabulary development and higher order learning (*Matthew effects* discussed in Chapter 12).

IDEA04 has addressed controversies regarding the use of the achievement-IQ discrepancy model to identify children with learning disabilities by encouraging the use of the *response to intervention* (RTI) model, in place of the discrepancy model (see page 211). This model allows for the use of empirically based interventions to combat reading difficulties, while at the same time, serving as a benchmark for identification of those who do not respond to the intervention as children with specific learning disabilities.

Those who support the changes to IDEA04 argue that the majority of students with SLDs are readily identifiable due to their obvious problems with reading and that the RTI model will be the most efficient and effective way of addressing these problems. They feel that children will obtain more immediate and appropriate interventions without having to wait for a formal evaluation, while those who benefit from the interventions can avoid further involvement in the identification process.

Those who oppose the changes in law voice their concerns about the loss of distinction between children who do not make adequate academic progress due to lower ability, compared to those who struggle academically as a result of neurological impairments associated with specific learning disabilities.

References

Aaron, P. G., & Joshi, R. M. (1992). *Reading problems: Consultation and remediation.* New York: Guilford Press.

Abu-Arefeh, I., & Russell, G. (1994). Prevalence of headache and migraine in school children. *British Medical Journal, 309,* 765–769.

Achenbach, T. M. (1966). The classification of children's psychiatric symptoms: A factor analytic study. *Psychological Monographs, 80*(7, whole no. 609).

Achenbach, T. M. (1991). *Manual for the Child Behavior Checklist/4–18 and 1991 profile.* Burlington: University of Vermont, Department of Psychiatry.

Achenbach, T. M., McConaughy, S. H., & Howell, C. T. (1987). Child and adolescent behavioral and emotional problems: Implications of cross-informant correlations for situational specificity. *Psychological Bulletin, 101,* 213–232.

Achenbach, T. M., & Rescorla, L. A. (2001). *Manual for the ASEBA School-Age Forms and Profiles.* Burlington: University of Vermont, Research Center for Children, Youth, and Families.

Aguilar, B., Sroufe, L. A., Egeland, B., & Carlson, E. (2000). Distinguishing the early-onset/persistent and adolescent-onset antisocial behavior types: From birth to 16 years. *Development and Psychopathology, 12,* 109–132.

Albano, A. M., Chorpita, B. F., & Barlow, D. H. (1996). Childhood anxiety disorders. In E. J. Mash & R. A. Barkley (Eds.), *Child psychopathology.* New York: Guilford Press.

Albertini, R. S., Phillips, K. A., & Guevremont, D. (1996). Body Dysmorphic Disorder. *Journal of the American Academy of Child and Adolescent Psychiatry, 35,* 1425–1426.

Allen, L., & Majidi-Ahi, S. (2001). African American children. In J. T. Gibbs & L. N. Huang (Eds.), *Children of color* (pp. 143–170). San Francisco: Jossey-Bass.

Aman, M. G., Hammer, D., & Rohahn, J. (1993). Mental Retardation. In T. H. Ollendick & M. Hersen (Eds.), *Handbook of child and adolescent assessment* (pp. 321–345). Needham Heights, MA: Allyn & Bacon.

Amaya-Jackson, L., & March, J. (1995a). Posttraumatic Stress Disorder in adolescents: Risk factors, diagnosis, and intervention. *Adolescent Medicine, 6,* 251–269.

Amaya-Jackson, L., & March, J. (1995b). Posttraumatic Stress Disorder. In J. S. March (Ed.), *Anxiety Disorders in children and adolescents* (pp. 276–300). New York: Guilford Press.

American Academy of Child and Adolescent Psychiatry (AACAP). (1998a). Practice parameters for the assessment and treatment of children and adolescents with Depressive Disorders. *Journal of the American Academy of Child and Adolescent Psychiatry,* (10 Suppl), 63S–83S.

American Academy of Child and Adolescent Psychiatry (AACAP). (1998b). Practice parameters for the assessment and treatment of children and adolescents with Posttraumatic Stress Disorder. *Journal of the American Academy of Child and Adolescent Psychiatry,* (10 Suppl), 4S–26S.

American Academy of Child and Adolescent Psychiatry (AACAP). (1998c). Summary of the practice parameters for the assessment and treatment of children and adolescents with Posttraumatic Stress Disorder. *Journal of the American Academy of Child and Adolescent Psychiatry, 37,* 997–1001.

American Academy of Child and Adolescent Psychiatry (AACAP) Official Action. (1997). Practice parameters for the assessment and treatment of children and adolescents with

Bipolar Disorder. *Journal of the American Academy of Child and Adolescent Psychiatry, 36,* 138–157.

American Association on Mental Retardation (AAMR). (2002). *Mental retardation: Definition, classification, and systems of support* (10th ed.). Washington, DC: Author.

American Psychiatric Association (APA). (1958). Diagnostic and statistical manual of mental disorders (1st ed.). Washington, DC: American Psychiatric Press.

American Psychiatric Association (APA). (1980). *Diagnostic and statistical manual of mental disorders* (3rd ed.). Washington, DC: American Psychiatric Press.

American Psychiatric Association (APA). (1987). *Diagnostic and statistical manual of mental disorders* (3rd Rev. ed.). Washington, DC: American Psychiatric Press.

American Psychiatric Association (APA). (1994). *Diagnostic and statistical manual of mental disorders* (4th ed.). Washington, DC: American Psychiatric Press.

American Psychiatric Association (APA). (2000). *Diagnostic and statistical manual of mental disorders* (4th ed., Text Revision). Washington, DC: American Psychiatric Press.

American Psychological Association Task Force on Psychological Intervention Guidelines. (1995). *Template for developing guidelines: Interventions for mental disorders and psychological aspects of physical disorders.* Washington, DC: Author.

Angold, A., Erkanli, A., Farmer, E. M. Z., Fairbank, J. A., Burns, B. A., Keeler, G. S., & Costello, E. J. (2002). Psychiatric disorder, impairment, and service use in rural African American and white youth. *Archives of General Psychiatry, 59,* 893–901.

Angold, A. E., Costello, E. J., & Erkanli, A. (1999). Comorbidity. *Journal of Child Psychology and Psychiatry, 40,* 57–87.

APA Guidelines for Providers of Psychological Services to Ethnic, Linguistic, and Culturally Diverse Populations. (1996). American Psychological Association. Retrieved October, 2004 from http://www.apa.org/divisions/div45/resources.html.

Attie, I., & Brooks-Gunn, J. (1995). The development of eating regulation across the life span. In D. Cicchetti & D. J. Cohen (Eds.), *Developmental psychopathology: Vol. 2. Risk disorder and adaptation* (pp. 332–368). New York: Wiley.

August, G. J., & Garfinkel, B. D. (1989). Behavioral and cognitive subtypes of ADHD. *Journal of the American Academy of Child and Adolescent Psychiatry, 28,* 739–748.

Ausubel, D. P. (1963). *The psychology of meaningful verbal learning.* New York: Grune & Stratton.

Azrin, N. H., Donohue, B., Besalel, V. A., Kogan, E. S., & Acierno, R. (1994). Youth drug abuse treatment: A controlled outcome study. *Journal of Child and Adolescent Substance Abuse, 3,* 1–16.

Bailey, A., Phillips, W., & Rutter, M. (1996). Autism: Toward an integration of clinical, genetic, neuropsychological, and neurobiological perspectives. *Journal of Child Psychology and Psychiatry, 37,* 89–126.

Baker, D. G., West, S. A., Nicholson, W. E., Ekhator, N., Kasckow, J., Hill, K. K., Bruce, A. B., Orth, D. N., & Geracioti, T. D. (1999). Serial CSF corticotropin-releasing hormone levels and adrenocortical activity in combat veterans with Posttraumatic Stress Disorder. *American Journal of Psychiatry, 156,* 585–588.

Baker, L. A., Decker, S. N., & DeFries, J. C. (1984). Cognitive abilities in reading-disabled children: A longitudinal study. *Journal of Child Psychology and Psychiatry, 23,* 111–117.

Bandura, A. (1977). *Social learning theory.* Englewood Cliffs, NJ: Prentice Hall.

Bandura, A. (1985). A model of causality in social learning theory. In M. Mahony & A. Freeman (Eds.), *Cognition and therapy* (pp. 81–99). New York: Plenum Press.

Bandura, A. (1986). *Social foundations of thought and action: A social cognitive theory.* Englewood Cliffs, NJ: Prentice Hall.

Barkley, R. A. (1997). Behavior inhibition, sustained attention, and executive function. *Psychological Bulletin, 121,* 65–94.

Barkley, R. A. (1998). *Attention Deficit Hyperactivity Disorder: A handbook for diagnosis and treatment, 2nd edition.* New York: Guilford Press.

Barkley, R. A., & Cunningham, C. E. (1978). Do stimulant drugs improve the academic performance of hyperkinetic children? A review of outcome research. *Clinical Pediatrics, 17,* 85–92.

Barkley, R. A., Fischer, M., Edelbrock, C. S., & Smallish, L. (1990). The adolescent outcome of hyperactive children diagnosed by research criteria: 1. An 8-year perspective follow-up study. *Journal of the American Academy of Child and Adolescent Psychiatry, 32,* 233–256.

Barrett, P. M., Healey-Farrell, I., Piacentini, J., & March, J. S. (2004). Obsessive-Compulsive Disorder in childhood and adolescence: Description and treatment. In P. M. Barrett & T. H. Ollendick (Eds.), *Handbook of interventions that work with children and adolescents* (pp. 187–216). West Sussex, U.K.: Wiley.

Barrett, P. M., Rappee, R. M., Dadds, M. M., & Ryan, S. M. (1996). Family enhancement of cognitive style in anxious and aggressive children. *Journal of the American Academy of Child and Adolescent Psychiatry, 24,* 187–203.

Barrios, B. A., & Hartmann, D. P. (1997). Fears and anxieties. In E. J. Mash & R. A. Barkley (Eds.), *Treatment of childhood disorders* (pp. 249–337). New York: Guilford Press.

Barsky, A. J. (1992). Hypochondriasis and Obsessive-Compulsive Disorder. *Psychiatry Clinical North America, 15,* 791–801.

Batsche, G. M., & Knoff, H. M. (1995). Linking assessment to intervention. In A. Thomas & J. Grimes (Eds.), *Best practices in school psychology III* (pp. 569–586). Washington, DC: NASP.

Baumrind, D. (1971). Current pattern of parental authority. *Developmental Psychology Monographs, 4*(1, part 2).

Baumrind, D. (1991). The influences of parenting style on adolescent competence and substance use. *Journal of Early Adolescence, 11,* 56–95.

Beck, A. T. (1976). *Cognitive therapy and emotional disorders.* New York: International University Press.

Beck, A. T. (1997). Cognitive therapy: Reflections. In J. K. Zeig (Ed.), *The evolution of psychotherapy: The third conference.* New York: Brunner/Mazel.

Beidel, D. C., Turner, S. M., & Morris, T. L. (1999). Psychopathology of childhood social phobia. *Journal of the American Academy of Child and Adolescent Psychiatry, 38,* 643–650.

Bellodi, L., Sciuto, G., Diaferia, G., Ronchi, P., & Smeraldi, E. (1992). Psychiatric disorders in the families of patients with Obsessive-Compulsive Disorder. *Psychiatry Research, 42,* 111–120.

Bernstein, G. A., & Borchardt, C. M. (1991). Anxiety disorders of childhood and adolescence: A critical review. *Journal of the American Academy of Child and Adolescent Psychiatry, 30,* 519–532.

Berton, M. W., & Stabb, D. D. (1996). Exposure to violence and Post-Traumatic Stress Disorder in urban adolescents. *Adolescence, 31,* 489–498.

Betancourt, H., & Lopez, S. R. (1993). The study of culture, race, and ethnicity in American psychology. *American Psychologist, 48,* 629–637.

Bezchlibnyk-Butler, K. Z., & Jeffries, J. J. (1997). *Clinical handbook of psychotropic drugs.* Toronto: Hogrefe & Huber.

Biederman, J., Faraone, S. V., Mick, E., Moore, P., & Lelon, E. (1996). Child Behavior Checklist findings further support comorbidity between ADHD and major depression in a referred sample. *Journal of the American Academy of Child and Adolescent Psychiatry, 35,* 734–742.

Biederman, J., Wozniak, J., Kiely, K., Ablon, S., Faraone, S., Mick, E., et al. (1995). CBCL clinical scales discriminate prepubertal children with structured interview-derived diagnosis of mania from those with ADHD. *Journal of the American Academy of Child and Adolescent Psychiatry, 34,* 464–471.

Biederman, J., Mick, E., Faraone, S. V., & Lapey, K. (1992). Comorbidity of diagnosis in Attention Deficit Hyperactivity Disorder. *Child and Adolescent Psychiatric Clinics of North America, 1*(2), 335–360.

Biederman, J., Rosenbaum, J. F., Boldue-Murphy, E. A., Faraone, S. V., Chaloff, J., Hirshfeld, D. R., & Kagan, J. (1993). A 3-year follow-up of children with and without behavioral inhibition. *Journal of the American Academy of Child and Adolescent Psychiatry, 32,* 814–821.

Biederman, J., Wilens, T., Mick, E., Spencer, T., & Faraone, S. V. (1999). Pharmacotherapy of Attention-Deficit/Hyperactivity Disorder reduces risk for Substance Use Disorder. *Pediatrics, 104,* e20.

Biere, D. F., Reeve, R. A., Champion, G. D., & Addicoat, L. (1990). The Faces Pain Scale for the self-assessment of the severity of pain experienced by children: Development, initial validation, and preliminary investigation for ration scale properties. *Pain, 4,* 139–150.

Bird, H. (1996). Epidemiology of childhood disorders in a cross-cultural context. *Journal of Child Psychology and Psychiatry, 37,* 35–49.

Bird, H. R., Gould, M. S., & Staghezza, B. (1992). Aggregating data from multiple informants in child psychiatry epidemiological research. *Journal of the American Academy of Child and Adolescent Psychiatry, 31,* 78–85.

Black, B. (1995). Separation Anxiety Disorder and Panic Disorder. In J. S. March (Ed.), *Anxiety Disorders in children and adolescents.* New York: Guilford Press.

Bloomquist, M. L. (1996). *Skills training for children with behavior disorders: A parent and therapist guidebook.* New York: Guilford Press.

Blum, R. W., Beuhring, T., Shew, M., Bearinger, L., Sieving, R., & Resnick, M. (2000). The effects of race/ethnicity, income, and family structure on adolescent risk behaviors. *American Journal of Public Health, 90,* 1885–1891.

Borge, A., Nordhagen, B., Botten, G., & Bakketeig, L. S. (1994). Prevalence and persistence of stomach ache and headache among children: Follow-up of a cohort of Norwegian children from 4 to 10 years of age. *Acta Pediatrics, 83,* 433–437.

Borowsky, I. W., Ireland, M., & Resnick, M. D. (2001). Adolescent suicide attempts: Risks and protectors. *Pediatrics, 107,* 485–495.

Botvin, G. J., Griffin, K. W., Diaz, T., & Ifill-Williams, M. (2001). Preventing binge drinking during early adolescence: One- and two-year followup of a school-based preventive intervention. *Psychology of Addictive Behaviors, 15,* 360–365.

Bremner, J. D. (1999). Does stress damage the brain? *Biological Psychiatry, 45,* 797–805.

Brent, D. S. (1995). Risk factors for adolescent suicide and suicidal behavior: Mental and Substance Abuse Disorders, family environmental factors, and life stress. *Suicide Life-threatening Behaviors, 25,* 52–63.

Breslau, N., Davis, G., Andreski, P., & Peterson, E. (1991). Traumatic events and Posttraumatic Stress Disorder in an urban population of young adults. *Archives of General Psychiatry, 48,* 218–222.

Brestan, E. V., & Eyberg, S. M. (1998). Effective psychosocial treatments of conduct-disordered children and adolescents: 29 years, 82 studies, and 5,272 kids. *Journal of Clinical Child Psychology, 27,* 180–189.

Brewin, C. R., Dagleish, T., & Joseph, S. (1996). A dual representation theory of Posttraumatic Stress Disorder. *Psychological Review, 103,* 670–686.

Bronfenbrenner, U. (1979). *The ecology of human development.* Cambridge, MA: Harvard University Press.

Bronfenbrenner, U. (1989). Ecological systems theory. *Annals of Child Development, 6,* 187–249.

Brown, S. A. (1993). Recovery patterns in adolescent substance abusers. In J. S. Baer, G. A. Marlatt, & R. J. McMahon (Eds.), *Addictive behaviors across the lifespan: Prevention, treatment, and policy issues* (pp. 161–183). Newbury Park, CA: Sage Publications.

Bruch, H. (1991). The sleeping beauty: Escape from change. In S. I. Greenspan & H. L. Pollock (Eds.), *The course of life: Vol. 4. Adolescence.* Madison, CT: International Universities Press.

Buka, S. L., Stichick, T. L., Birdthistle, I., & Earls, F. (2001). Youth exposure to violence: Prevalence, risks, and consequences. *American Journal of Orthopsychiatry, 71,* 298–310.

Cadoret, R., Yates, W. R., Troughton, E., Woodworth, G., & Stewart, M. A. (1995). Adoption study demonstrating two genetic pathways to drug abuse. *Archives of General Psychiatry, 52,* 42–52.

Campbell, S. B., March, C. L., Pierce, E. W., Ewing, L. J., & Szumowski, E. K. (1991). Hard-to-manage preschool boys: Family context and the stability of externalizing behavior. *Journal of Abnormal Child Psychology, 19,* 301–318.

Campo, J. V., & Fritsch, S. L. (1994). Somatization in children and adolescents. *Journal of the American Academy of Child and Adolescent Psychiatry, 33,* 1223–1235.

Cantwell, D. P. (1994). *Therapeutic management of Attention Deficit Disorder: Participant workbook.* New York: SCP Communications.

Carol, L. (1865/1992). *Alice's adventures in wonderland.* Toronto, Ontario: Tor Books.

Carrasco, J. L., Diaz-Marsa, M., Hollander, E., Cesar, J., & Saiz-Ruiz, J. (2000). Decreased platelet monoamine oxidase activity in female Bulimia Nervosa. *European Neuropsychopharmacology, 10*(2), 113–117.

Carrion, V. G., Weems, C. F., Ray, R., & Reiss, A. L. (2002). Towards an empirical definition of pediatric PTSD: The phenomenology of PTSD symptoms in youth. *Journal of the American Academy of Child and Adolescent Psychiatry, 41,* 166–173.

Carter, A. S., Grigorenko, E. L., & Pauls, D. L. (1995). A Russian adaptation of the Child Behavior Checklist: Psychometric properties and associations with child and maternal affective symptomatology and family functioning. *Journal of Abnormal Child Psychology, 23,* 661–684.

Casper, R. C., Hedeker, D., & McClough, J. F. (1992). Personality dimensions in eating disorders and their relevance for subtyping. *Journal of the American Academy of Child and Adolescent Psychiatry, 31,* 830–840.

Chamberlain, P., & Reid, J. (1991). Using a specialized foster care community treatment model for children and adolescents leaving the state mental hospital. *Journal of Community Psychology, 19,* 266–276.

Chamberlain, P., & Reid, J. (1998). Comparison of two community alternatives to incarceration for chronic juvenile offenders. *Journal of Consulting and Clinical Psychology, 66,* 624–633.

Chan, S. Families with Asian roots. (1998). In E. W. Lynch & M. J. Hanson (Eds.), *Developing cross-cultural competence* (2nd ed., pp. 251–354). Baltimore: Paul H. Brookes.

Chorpita, B. F. (2002). The tripartite model and dimensions of anxiety and depression: An examination of structure in a large school sample. *Journal of Abnormal Child Psychology, 30,* 177–190.

Chorpita, B. F., Plummer, C. P., & Moffitt, C. (2000). Relations of tripartite dimensions of emotion to childhood anxiety and mood disorders. *Journal of Abnormal Child Psychology, 28,* 299–310.

Cicchetti, D., & Rogosh, F. A. (1996). Editorial: Equifinality and multifinality in developmental psychopathology. *Development and Psychopathology, 8,* 597–600.

Cicchetti, D., & Toth, S. L. (1991). A developmental perspective on internalizing and externalizing disorders. In D. Cicchetti & L. Toth (Eds.), *Internalizing and externalizing expressions of dysfunction* (pp. 1–19). Hillsdale, NJ: Erlbaum.

Cicchetti, D., & Toth, S. L. (1998). The development of depression in children and adolescence. *American Psychologist, 53*(2), 221–241.

Clark, L. A., & Watson, D. (1991). Tripartite model of anxiety and depression: Psychometric evidence and taxonomic implications. *Journal of Abnormal Psychology, 100,* 316–336.

Cloitre, M., Tardiff, K., Marzuk, P. M., Leon, A. C., & Potera, L. (1996). Childhood abuse and subsequent sexual assault among female inpatients. *Journal of Traumatic Stress, 9,* 473–482.

Cobham, V. E., Dadds, M. R., & Spence, S. H. (1998). The role of parental anxiety in the treatment of childhood anxiety. *Journal of Consulting and Clinical Psychology, 66,* 893–905.

Cohen, J. A., Deblinger, E., Mannarino, A. P., & Steer, R. A. (2004). A multisite, randomized controlled trial for children with sexual abuse–related PTSD symptoms. *Journal of the American Academy of Child and Adolescent Psychiatry, 43,* 393–402.

Cohen, P., Cohen, J., Kasen, S., Velez, C. N., Hartmark, C., Johnson, J., Rojas, M., Brook, J., & Streuning, E. L. (1993). An epidemiological study of disorders in late childhood and adolescence. I: Age- and gender-specific prevalence. *Journal of Child Psychology and Psychiatry, 34,* 851–867.

Coie, J. D., Dodge, K., & Coppotelli, H. (1982). Dimensions and types of social status: A cross-age perspective. *Developmental Psychology, 18,* 557–570.

Comer, R. J. (2001). *Abnormal psychology* (4th ed.). New York: Worth Publishers.

Costello, E. J., Angold, A., Burns, B. J., Stangel, D. K., Tweed, D. L., Erkanli, A., & Worthman, C. M. (1996). The Great Smoky Mountains Study of Youth: Goals, design, methods, and the prevalence of *DSM-III-R* disorders. *Archives of General Psychiatry, 53,* 1129–1136.

Cuffe, S. P., McCullough, E. L., & Pumariega, A. J. (1994). Comorbidity of Attention-Deficit/Hyperactivity Disorder and Posttraumatic Stress Disorder. *Journal of Child and Family Studies, 3,* 327–336.

Culbertson, J. L. (1991). Child advocacy and clinical child psychology. *Journal of Clinical Child Psychology, 20*(1), 7–10.

Cummins, J. (1984). *Bilingual special education: Issues in assessment and pedagogy.* San Diego: College-Hill.

Dabbs, J., & Morris, R. (1990). Testosterone, social class, and antisocial behavior in a sample of 4,462 men. *Psychological Science, 1,* 209–211.

Davidson, J. (1993). Issues in the diagnosis of Post-Traumatic Stress Disorder. In R. S. Pynoos (Ed.), *Posttraumatic Stress Disorder: A clinical review* (pp. 1–15). Lutherville, MD: Sidran Press.

Dawson, G., Hill, D., Spencer, A., Galpert, L., & Watson, L. (1990). Affect exchange between young autistic children and their mothers. *Journal of Abnormal Child Psychology, 18,* 335–345.

Dawson, G., & Osterling, J. (1996). Early intervention in autism: Effectiveness and common elements of current approaches. In M. J. Guralnick (Ed.), *The effectiveness of early interventions: Second-generation research* (pp. 307–326). Baltimore: Paul H. Brookes.

Deas, D., Riggs, P., Langenbuncher, J., Goldman, M., & Brown, S. (2000). Adolescents are not adults: Developmental considerations in alcohol users. *Alcoholism: Clinical and Experimental Research, 24,* 232–237.

Deblinger, E., McLeer, S. V., Atkins, M. S., Ralphe, D., & Foa, E. (1989). Posttraumatic stress in sexually abused, physically abused, and nonabused children. *Child Abuse and Neglect, 13,* 403–408.

Deep, A. L., Nagy, L. M., Weltzin, T. E., Rao, R., & Kaye, W. H. (1995). Premorbid onset of psychopathology in long-term recovered Anorexia Nervosa. *International Journal of Eating Disorders, 17,* 291–297.

DeFries, J. C., & Alarcon, M. (1996). Genetics of specific reading disability. *Mental Retardation & Developmental Disabilities Research Reviews, 2,* 39–48.

Demonet, J., Taylor, M. J., & Chaix, Y. (2004). Developmental dyslexia. *Lancet, 363,* 1451–1460.

Desjarlais, R., Eisenberg, L., Good, B., & Kleinman, A. (1996). *World mental health: Problems and priorities in low-income countries.* Oxford: Oxford University Press.

Deykin, E. Y., & Buka, S. L. (1997). Prevalence and risk factors for Posttraumatic Stress Disorder among chemically dependent adolescents. *American Journal of Psychiatry, 154,* 752–757.

Diller, L. H. (1996). The run on Ritalin: Attention Deficit Disorder and stimulant treatments in the 1990's. *Hastings Center Report, 26,* 12–18.

Dishion, T. J., McCord, J., & Poulin, F. (1999). When interventions harm: Peer groups and problem behavior. *American Psychologist, 54,* 755–764.

Dishion, T. J., Spracklen, K. M., Andrews, D. W., & Patterson, G. R. (1996). Deviancy training in male adolescent friendships. *Behavior Therapy, 27,* 373–390.

Dodge, K. A. (1991). The structure and function of reactive and proactive aggression. In D. J. Pepler & K. H. Rubin (Eds.), *The development and treatment of childhood aggression* (pp. 201–218). Hillsdale, NJ: Erlbaum.

Dodge, K., Bates, J., & Pettit, G. (1990). Mechanisms in the cycle of violence. *Science, 250,* 1678–1683.

Donahue, B., & Azrin, N. (2001). Family behaviour therapy. In E. F. Wagner & H. B. Waldron (Eds.), *Innovations in adolescent substance abuse interventions* (pp. 205–227). Oxford: Elsevier Science.

Drotar, D. (1995). Failure to thrive (growth deficiency). In M. C. Roberts (Ed.), *Handbook of pediatric psychology* (2nd ed., pp. 516–536). New York: Guilford Press.

Dunston, P. J. (1992). A critique of graphic organizer research. *Reading Research and Instruction, 31,* 57–65.

Durlak, J. (1998). Common risk and protective factors in successful prevention programs. *American Journal of Orthopsychiatry, 68,* 512–520.

Dykman, R. A., & Ackerman, P. T. (1992). Attention Deficit Disorder and specific reading disability: Separate but often overlapping disorders. In S. Shaywitz & B. Shaywitz (Eds.), *Attention deficit disorder comes of age: Toward the twenty-first century* (pp. 165–184). Austin, TX: Pro-Ed.

Edelbrock, C. S., & Costello, A. J. (1988). Structured psychiatric interviews for children. In M. Rutteer, A. H. Tuma, & I. Lann (Eds.), *Assessment diagnosis in child psychopathology* (pp. 87–112). New York: Guilford Press.

Ehlers, A., & Clark, D. M. (2000). A cognitive model of Posttraumatic Stress Disorder. *Behavior Research and Therapy, 38,* 319–345.

Eisenmajer, R., Prior, M., Leekam, S., Wing, L., Gould, J., Welham, M., & Ong, B. (1996). Comparison of clinical symptoms in autism and Asperger's disorder. *Journal of the American Academy of Child and Adolescent Psychiatry, 35,* 1523–1531.

Eley, T. C. (1999). Behavioral genetics as a tool for developmental psychology: Anxiety and depression in children and adolescents. *Clinical Child and Family Psychology Review, 2,* 21–36.

Elia, J., & Rapoport, J. L. (1991). Ritalin versus dextroamphetamine in ADHD: Both should be tried. In L. L. Greenhill & B. B. Osmon (Eds.), *Ritalin: Theory and patient management* (pp. 69–74). New York: Mary Ann Liebert.

Elkind, D. (1967). Egocentrism in adolescence. *Child Development, 38,* 1025–1034.

Elkind, D., & Bowen, R. (1979). Imaginary audience behavior in children and adolescents. *Developmental Psychology, 15,* 38–44.

Emery, R. E. (2001). Behavioral family intervention: Less "behavior" and more "family." In A. Booth, A. C. Crouter, & M. Clements (Eds.), *Couples in conflict* (pp. 241–249). Mahwah, NJ: Erlbaum.

Essau, C. A., Conradt, J., & Petermann, F. (1999). Prevalence, comorbidity, and psychosocial impairment of somatoform disorders in adolescents. *Psychology, Health, and Medicine, 4,* 169–180.

Essau, C. A., Conradt, J., & Petermann, F. (2000). Frequency, comorbidity, and psychosocial impairment of Specific Phobia in adolescents. *Journal of Clinical Child Psychology, 29,* 221–232.

Fabrega, H. (1990). Hispanic mental health research: A case for cultural psychiatry. *Hispanic Journal of Behavioral Science, 12,* 339–365.

Fairburn, C. G., Welch, S. I., Doll, H. A., Davies, B. A., & O'Connor, M. E. (1997). Risk factors for Bulimia Nervosa: A community-based case-control study. *Archives of General Psychiatry, 54,* 509–517.

Federal Register. Vol. 64, No. 48, March 12, 1999. Education Department [FR Doc 12405-12672] p. 12422. Retrieved October, 2004 from http://www.admin@gpo.gov.

Fischer, R. L., & Fischer, S. (1996). Antidepressants for children: Is scientific support necessary? *Journal of Nervous and Mental Disease, 184,* 99–102.

Fitzgerald, H. E., Davies, W. H., Zucker, R. A., & Klinger, M. T. (1994). Developmental systems theory and substance abuse: A conceptual and methodological framework for analyzing patterns of variation in families. In L. L. Abate (Ed.), *Handbook of developmental family psychology and psychopathology* (pp. 350–372). New York: Wiley.

Fitzpatrick, K. M., & Boldizar, J. P. (1993). The prevalence and consequences of exposure to violence among African American youth. *Journal of the American Academy of Adolescent Psychiatry, 32,* 424–430.

Flannery-Schroeder, E., & Kendall, P. C. (2000). Group and individual cognitive-behavioral treatments for youth with Anxiety Disorders: A randomized clinical trial. *Cognitive Therapy and Research, 244,* 251–278.

Fleming, J. E., & Offord, D. R. (1990). Epidemiology of childhood depressive disorders: A critical review. *Journal of the American Academy of Child and Adolescent Psychiatry, 29,* 571–580.

Foa, E. B., & Kozak, M. J. (1986). Emotional processing of fear: Exposure to corrective information. *Psychological Bulletin, 99,* 220–235.

Fonagy, P., & Target, M. (1996). A contemporary psychoanalytical perspective: Psychodynamic developmental therapy. In E. D. Hibbs & P. S. Jensen (Eds.), *Psychosocial treatments for child and adolescent disorders: Empirically based strategies for clinical practice* (pp. 619–638). Washington, DC: American Psychological Association.

Forness, S. R., & Kavale, K. A. (1991). Social skill deficits as a primary learning disability: A note on problems with the ICLD diagnostic criteria. *Learning Disability Research and Practice, 6,* 44–49.

Francis, G., & Ollendick, T. H. (1988). Social withdrawal. In M. Hersen & C. G. Last (Eds.), *Child behavior therapy casebook* (pp. 31–41). New York: Plenum Press.

Frick, P. J., & Kamphaus, R. W. (2001). Standardized rating scales in the assessment of children's behavioral and emotional problems. In C. E. Walker & M. C. Roberts (Eds.), *Handbook of clinical child psychology* (pp. 190–204). New York: Wiley.

Frick, P. J., Kamphaus, R. W., Lahey, B. B., Loeber, R., Christ, M. A. G., Hart, E. L., & Tannenbaum, L. E. (1991). Academic underachievement and the disruptive behavior disorders. *Journal of Consulting and Clinical Psychology, 59,* 289–294.

Frick, P. J., Lahey, B. B., Loeber, R., Tannenbaum, L., Van Horn, Y., Christ, M. A., Hart, E. L., & Hanson, K. (1993). Oppositional Defiant Disorder and Conduct Disorder: A meta-analytic review of factor analyses and cross validation in a clinic sample. *Clinical Psychology Review, 13,* 319–340.

Frith, C. D., & Frith, U. (1999). Interacting minds—A biological basis. *Science, 286,* 1692–1696.

Fritz, G. K., Fritsch, S., & Hagino, O. (1997). Somatoform Disorders in children and adolescents: A review of the past 10 years. *Journal of the American Academy of Child and Adolescent Psychiatry, 36,* 1329–1338.

Fryer, A. J., Mannuzza, S., Chapman, R. F., Liebowitz, M. R., & Klein, D. F. (1993). A direct interview family study of Social Phobia. *Archives of General Psychiatry, 50,* 286–293.

Gabbard, G. O. (1990). *Psychodynamic psychiatry in clinical practice.* Washington, DC: American Psychiatric Press.

Garber, J., Walker, L. S., & Seman, J. (1991). Somatization symptoms in a community sample of children and adolescents: Further validation of the Children's Somatization Inventory. *Journal of Consulting and Clinical Psychology, 199,* 588–595.

Garber, J., Zeman, J., & Walker, L. S. (1990). Recurrent abdominal pain in children: Psychiatric diagnoses and parental psychopathology. *Journal of the American Academy of Child and Adolescent Psychiatry, 29,* 648–656.

Garland, A. F., & Zigler, E. (1993). Adolescent suicide prevention: Current research and social policy implications. *American Psychologist, 48,* 169–182.

Garner, D. M., Cooke, A. K., & Marano, H. E. (1997). The 1997 body image survey results. *Psychology Today,* (Jan.–Feb.), 30–44.

Garner, D. M., Garfinkel, P. E., & O'Shaughnessy, M. (1985). The validity of the distinction between bulimia with and without Anorexia Nervosa. *American Journal of Psychiatry, 142,* 581–587.

Gerber, P. J., & Reiff, H. B. (1994). *Learning disabilities in adulthood: Persisting problems and evolving issues.* Boston: Andover Medical.

Geller, B. (2001). A prepubertal and early adolescent Bipolar Disorder phenotype has poor one-year outcome. *The Brown University Child and Adolescent Psychopharmacology Update, 3,* 1–5.

Geller, B., Fox, L. W., & Clark, K. A. (1994). Rate and predictions of prepubertal bipolarity during follow-up of 6- to 12-year-old depressed children. *Journal of the American Academy of Child and Adolescent Psychiatry, 33,* 461–468.

Geller, B., & Luby, J. (1997). Child and adolescent Bipolar Disorder: A review of the past 10 years. *Journal of the American Academy of Child and Adolescent Psychiatry, 36,* 1168–1176.

Geller, B., Sun, K., Zimerman, B., Luby, J., Frazier, J., & Williams, M. (1995). Complex and rapid-cycling in bipolar children and adolescents: A preliminary study. *Journal of Affective Disorders, 34,* 259–268.

Geller, D. A., Biederman, J., Farapme, S., Agranat, A., Cradlock, K., Hagermoser, L., Kim, G., Frazier, J., & Coffey, B. (2001). Disentangling chronological age from age of onset in children and adolescents with Obsessive-Compulsive Disorder. *International Journal of Neuropsychopharmacology, 4,* 169–178.

Geller, D. A., Biederman, J., Jones, J., Park, K., Schwartz, S., Shapiro, S., & Coffey, B. (1998). Is juvenile Obsessive-Compulsive Disorder a developmental subtype of disorder? A review of the pediatric literature. *Journal of the American Academy of Child and Adolescent Psychiatry, 37,* 420–427.

Giaconia, R. M., Reinherz, H. Z., Silverman, A. B., Pakiz, B., Frost, A. K., & Cohen, E. (1994). Ages of onset of psychiatric disorders in a community population of older adolescents. *Journal of the American Academy of Child and Adolescent Psychiatry, 33,* 706–717.

Gibbs, J. T., & Huang, L. (2001). A conceptual framework for the psychological assessment and treatment of minority youth. In J. T. Gibbs & L. A. Huang (Eds.), *Children of color* (pp. 1–32). San Francisco: Jossey-Bass.

Gillberg, C. (1998). Asperger syndrome and high-functioning autism. *British Journal of Psychiatry, 172,* 200–209.

Gillberg, C., & Soderstrom, H. (2003). Learning disability. *Lancet, 362,* 811–821.

Goenjian, A. K., Karayan, I., Pynoos, R., Steinberg, A., Najarian, L., Asarnow, J., Ghurabi, M., & Fairbanks, L. (1997). Outcome of psychotherapy among early adolescents after trauma. *American Journal of Psychiatry, 154,* 536–542.

Goldstein, A. (1994). *Addiction: From biology to drug policy.* New York: W. H. Freeman.

Gould, S. J. (1981). *The mismeasure of man.* New York: W. W. Norton.

Grados, M., Labuda, M. C., Riddle, M. A., & Walkup, J. T. (1997). Obsessive-Compulsive Disorder in children and adolescents. *International Review of Psychiatry, 9,* 83–98.

Greenberg, M. T. (1999). Attachment and psychopathology in childhood. In J. Cassidy & P. R. Shaver (Eds.), *Handbook of attachment* (pp. 469–496). New York: Guilford Press.

Greene, R. W., & Ablon, J. S. (2004). *The collaborative problem-solving approach: Cognitive-behavioral treatment of Oppositional Defiant Disorder.* New York: Guilford Press.

Greene, R. W., Ablon, J. S., Goring, J. C., Fazio, V., & Morse, L. R. (2003). Treatment of Oppositional Defiant Disorder in children and adolescents. In P. M. Barrett & T. H. Ollendick (Eds.), *Handbook of interventions that work with children and adolescents* (pp. 369–393). Chichester, England: Wiley.

Greene, R. W., Biederman, J., Faraone, S. V., Sienna, M., & Garcia-Jetton, J. (1997). Adolescent outcome of boys with Attention-Deficit/Hyperactivity Disorder and social disability: Results from a 4-year longitudinal follow-up study. *Journal of Consulting and Clinical Psychology, 65,* 758–787.

Gresham, F. M., & Elliott, S. N. (1990). *Social skills rating system.* Circle Pines, MN: American Guidance Service.

Griffin, K. W., Botvin, G. J., Nichols, T. R., & Doyle, M. M. (2003). Effectiveness of a universal drug abuse prevention approach for youth at high risk for substance use initiation. *Preventive Medicine, 36,* 1–7.

Gross-Tsur, V., Shalev, R. S., Manor, O., & Amir, N. (1995). Developmental right hemisphere syndrome: Clinical spectrum of the nonverbal learning disability. *Journal of Learning Disabilities, 28,* 80–86.

Guralnick, M. J. (1998). Effectiveness of early intervention for vulnerable children: A developmental perspective. *American Journal of Mental Retardation, 102,* 319–345.

Guyer, B., MacDorman, M. F., Martin, J. A., Peters, K. D., & Strobino, D. M. (1998). Annual summary of vital statistics—1997. *Pediatrics, 102,* 1333–1349.

Halmi, K. A. (1995). Current concepts and definitions. In G. Szmukler, C. Dare, & J. Treasure (Eds.), *Handbook of eating disorders: Theory, treatment, and research* (pp. 5–27). Chichester, England: Wiley.

Halperin, J. M., Newcorn, J. H., Sharma, V., Healey, J. M., Wolf, L. E., Pascualvaca, D. M., & Schaartz, S. (1990). Inattentive and noninattentive ADHD children: Do they constitute a unitary group? *Journal of Abnormal Child Psychology, 18,* 437–449.

Hammen, C. (1991). The family-environmental context of depression: A perspective on children's risk. In D. Cicchetti & S. L. Toth (Eds.), *Rochester symposium on developmental psychopathology, 4,* 251–281.

Handen, B. L. (1998). Mental retardation. In E. J. Mash & R. A. Barkley (Eds.), *Treatment of childhood disorders* (pp. 369–415). New York: Guilford Press.

Harnadek, M. C., & Rourke, B. P. (1994). Principal identifying features of the syndrome of nonverbal learning disabilities in children. *Journal of Learning Disabilities, 27,* 144–153.

Harter, S., & Marold, D. (1994). Psychosocial risk factors contributing to adolescent suicidal ideation. In G. G. Noam & S. Borst (Eds.), *Children, youth, and suicide: Developmental perspectives* (pp. 71–92). San Francisco: Jossey-Bass.

Haynes, S. N., & O'Brien, W. H. (1990). Functional analysis in behavior therapy. *Clinical Psychology Review, 10*(6), 649–668.

Henggeler, S. W., & Borduin, C. M. (1990). *Family therapy and beyond: A multisystemic approach to treating the behavior problems of children and adolescents.* Pacific Grove, CA: Brooks/Cole.

Henggeler, S. W., Melton, G. B., & Smith, L. A. (1992). Family preservation using multisystemic therapy: An effective alternative to incarcerating serious juvenile offenders. *Journal of Consulting and Clinical Psychology, 60,* 953–961.

Henggeler, S. W., Schoenwald, S. K., Borduin, C. M., Rowland, M. D., & Cunninghan, P. B. (1998). *Multisystemic treatment of antisocial behavior in youth.* New York: Guilford Press.

Herzog, D. B., Sacks, N. R., Keller, M. B., Lavori, P. W., von Ranson, K. B., & Gray, H. N. (1993). Patterns and predictors of recovery in Anorexia Nervosa and Bulimia Nervosa. *Journal of Child Psychology and Psychiatry, 32,* 962–966.

Herzog, W., Schellberg, D., & Deter, H. C. (1997). First recovery in Anorexia Nervosa patients in the long-term course: A discrete-time survival analysis. *Journal of Consulting and Clinical Psychology, 65,* 169–177.

Hinshaw, S. P., Heller, T., & McHale, J. P. (1992). Covert antisocial behavior in boys with Attention Deficit Hyperactivity Disorder: External validation and effects of methylphenidate. *Journal of Consulting and Clinical Psychology, 60,* 274–281.

Hocutt, A. M. (1996). Effectiveness of special education: Is placement the critical factor? *The Future of Children, 6,* 77–102.

Hoffman, E. C., & Mattis, S. G. (2000). A developmental adaptation of panic control treatment for Panic Disorder in adolescence. *Cognitive and Behavioral Practice, 7,* 253–261.

Hoffman, S. G., Albano, A. M., Heimberg, R. G., Tracey, S., Chorpita, B. F., & Barlow, D. H. (1999). Subtypes of Social Phobia in adolescents. *Depression and Anxiety, 9,* 15–18.

Hofstede, G. (1980). *Culture's consequences: International differences in work-related values.* Beverly Hills: Sage Publications.

Holmbeck, G. N., Greenley, R. N., & Franks, E. A. (2004). Developmental issues in evidence-based practice. In P. M. Barrett & E. H. Ollendick (Eds.), *Handbook of interventions that work with children and adolescents: Prevention and treatment* (pp. 27–48). Chichester, England: Wiley.

Horn, M. (1989). *Before it's too late: The child guidance movement in the United States, 1922–1945.* Philadelphia, PA: Temple University Press.

Horowitz, K., Weine, S., & Jekel, J. (1995). PTSD symptoms in urban adolescent girls: Compounded community trauma. *Journal of the American Academy of Child and Adolescent Psychiatry, 34,* 1353–1361.

Hotopf, M. (2002). Childhood experience of illness as a risk factor for medically unexplained symptoms. *Scandinavian Journal of Psychology, 43,* 139–146.

Howlin, P. (1987). Asperger's syndrome—Does it exist and what can be done about it? In *Proceedings of the First International Symposium on Specific Speech and Language Disorders in Children.* London: AFASIC.

Hudson, J. L., & Rapee, R. M. (2000). The origins of Social Phobia. *Behavior Modification, 24,* 102–129.

Hurth, J., Shaw, E., Izeman, S., Whaley, K., & Rogers, S. (1999). Areas of agreement about effective practices among programs serving young children with autism spectrum disorders. *Infants and Young Children, 12,* 17–26.

Interagency Committee on Learning Disabilities. (1987). *Learning disabilities: A report to the U.S. Congress.* Bethesda, MD: National Institutes of Health.

Joe, J. R., & Malachy, R. S. (1998). Families with Native American roots. In E. W. Lynch & M. J. Hanson (Eds.), *Developing cross-cultural competence* (2nd ed., pp. 127–164). Baltimore: Paul H. Brookes.

Johnson, V., & Pandina, R. (2000). Alcohol problems among a community sample: Longitudinal influences of stress, coping, and gender. *Substance Use and Misuse, 35,* 669–686.

Jones, M. B., & Offord, D. R. (1989). Reduction of antisocial behavior in poor children in nonschool skill development. *Journal of Child Psychology and Psychiatry, 30,* 737–750.

Joseph, S. A., Brewin, C. R., Yule, W., & Williams, R. (1993). Causal attributions and post-traumatic stress in adolescents. *Journal of Child Psychology and Psychiatry, 34,* 247–253.

Kagan, A. E. (1992). Yesterday's promises, tomorrow's promises. *Developmental Psychology, 28,* 990–997.

Kaij, L. (1960). *Alcoholism in twins: Studies on the etiology and sequels of abuse of alcohol.* Stockholm: Almquist & Wiksell.

Kaplan, A. (1998). Practice parameters offer guidance on Substance Use Disorders in children, adolescents. *Psychiatric Times, XV*(4).

Kashani, H. H., & Orvaschel, H. (1988). Anxiety Disorders in midadolescence: A community sample. *American Journal of Psychiatry, 145,* 960–964.

Kaslow, N. J., & Thompson, M. P. (1998). Applying the criteria for empirically supported treatments to studies of psychosocial interventions for child and adolescent depression. *Journal of Clinical Child Psychology, 27,* 146–155.

Kassel, J. D., & Jackson, S. I. (2001). Twelve-step-based interventions for adolescents. In E. F. Wagner & H. B. Waldron (Eds.), *Innovations in adolescent substance abuse interventions* (pp. 329–342). Oxford: Elsevier Science.

Kavale, K. A., & Forness, S. R. (1996). Social skill deficits and learning disabilities: A meta-analysis. *Journal of Learning Disabilities, 29,* 226–237.

Kavale, K. A., Forness, S., & MacMillan, D. L. (1998). The politics of learning disabilities: A rejoinder. *Learning Disability Quarterly, 21,* 306–317.

Kazdin, A. E. (1996). Problem solving and parent management in treating aggressive and antisocial behavior. In E. D. Hibbs & P. S. Jensen (Eds.), *Psychosocial treatments for child and adolescent disorders* (pp. 377–408). Washington, DC: American Psychological Association.

Kazdin, A. E., Esveldt-Dawson, K., French, N. H., & Unis, A. S. (1987). Problem-solving skills training and parent management training in the treatment of antisocial behavior in children. *Journal of Consulting and Clinical Psychology, 55,* 76–85.

Kearney, C. A., Albano, A. M., Eisen, A. R., Allan, E. D., & Barlow, D. H. (1997). The phenomenology of Panic Disorder in youngsters: An empirical study of a clinical sample. *Journal of Anxiety Disorders, 11,* 49–62.

Kelley, M., Power, T. G., & Wimbush, D. D. (1992). Determinants of disciplinary practices in low-income Black mothers. *Child Development, 63,* 573–582.

Kendall, P. C. (1994). Treating Anxiety Disorders in children: Results of a randomized clinical trial. *Journal of Consulting and Clinical Psychology, 62,* 100–110.

Kendall, P. C. (2000). *Cognitive behavioral therapy for anxious children: Treatment manual* (2nd ed.). Aramore, PA: Workbook Publishing.

Kendall, P. C., Chansky, T. E., Kane, M. T., Kim, R. S., Kortlander, E., Ronan, K. R., Sessa, F. M., & Siqueland, L. (1992). *Anxiety disorders in youth: Cognitive behavioral interventions.* Needham Heights, MA: Allyn & Bacon.

Kendall, P. C., & Ronan, K. R. (1990). Assessment of children's anxieties, fears, and phobias: Cognitive-behavioral models and methods. In C. R. Reynolds & R. W. Kamphaus (Eds.), *Handbook of psychological and educational assessment of children* (Vol. 2, pp. 223–244). New York: Guilford Press.

Kendler, K. S., Gallagher, T. J., Abelson, J. M., & Kessler, R. C. (1996). Lifetime prevalence, demographic risk factors, and diagnostic validity of nonaffective psychosis as assessed in a U.S. community sample: The National Comorbidity Survey. *Archives of General Psychiatry, 53,* 1022–1031.

Kilpatrick, K. L., & Williams, L. M. (1997). Post-Traumatic Stress Disorder in child witness to domestic violence. *Journal of Orthopsychiatry, 67,* 639–644.

Kim, A.-H., Vaughn, S., Wanzek, J., & Wei, S. (2004). Graphic organizers and their effects on the reading comprehension of students with LD: A synthesis of research. *Journal of Learning Disabilities, 37,* 105–118.

Kim, W. J. (1995). A training guideline of cultural competence for child and adolescent psychiatric residencies. *Child Psychiatry and Human Development, 26,* 125–136.

King, N. J., Ollendick, T. H., Mattis, S. G., Yang, B., & Tonge, B. (1997). Nonclinical panic attacks in adolescents: Prevalence symptomatology and associated features, *Behaviour Change, 13,* 171–183.

Kinzl, J. (1992). Diagnosis and treatment of hypochondriacal syndromes. *Psychosomatics, 33,* 278–289.

Kinzl, J. F., Traweger, C., & Biebi, W. (1995). Family background and sexual abuse associated with somatization. *Psychotherapy and Psychosomatic Disorders, 64,* 82–87.

Klinger, L. G., & Dawson, G. (1996). Autistic Disorder. In E. J. Mash & R. A. Barkley (Eds.), *Child psychopathology* (pp. 311–313). New York: Guilford Press.

Knopik, V. (2001). Differential genetic etiology of reading-related difficulties as a function of IQ. *Dissertation Abstracts International: Section B: The Sciences & Engineering, 61,* 6729.

Koocher, G. P., & Keith-Spiegel, P. C. (1990). *Children, ethics, and the law: Professional issues and cases.* Lincoln: University of Nebraska Press.

Kotchick, B. A., & Forehand, R. (2002). Putting parenting in perspective: A discussion of the contextual factors that shape parenting practices. *Journal of Child and Family Studies, 11,* 255–270.

Kouzis, A. C., & Labouvie, E. W. (1992). Use intensity, functional elaboration, and contextual constraint as facets of adolescent alcohol and marijuana use. *Psychology of Addictive Behaviors, 6,* 188–195.

Kovacs, M., Akiskal, H. S., Gatsonis, C., & Parrone, P. L. (1994). Childhood Dysthymic Disorder: Clinical features and prospective naturalistic outcome. *Archives of General Psychiatry, 51,* 365–374.

Kovacs, M., & Devlin, B. (1998). Internalizing disorders in childhood. *Journal of Child Psychology and Psychiatry and Allied Disciplines, 39,* 47–63.

Kovacs, M., & Pollock, M. (1995). Bipolar Disorder and comorbid conduct disorder in childhood and adolescence. *Journal of the American Academy of Child and Adolescent Psychiatry, 34,* 715–723.

Kronenberger, W. G., & Meyer, R. G. (2001). *The child clinician's handbook, 2nd edition.* Needham Heights, MA: Allyn & Bacon.

Kunce, L., & Mesibov, G. B. (1998). Educational approaches to high-functioning autism and Asperger syndrome. In E. Schopler & G. B. Mesibov (Eds.), *Asperger Syndrome or high-functioning Autism? Current issues in autism* (pp. 227–261). New York: Plenum Press.

LaFromboise, T. D., & Graff Low, K. (2001). American Indian children and adolescents. In J. T. Gibbs & L. N. Huang (Eds.), *Children of color* (pp. 112–142). San Francisco: Jossey-Bass.

La Greca, A. M., Silverman, W. K., Vernberg, E. M., & Prinstein, M. (1996). Symptoms of posttraumatic stress in children after hurricane Andrew: A prospective study. *Journal of Consulting and Clinical Psychology, 64,* 712–723.

Larson, J., & Lochman, J. E. (2002). *Helping school children cope with anger: A cognitive-behavioral intervention.* New York: Guilford Press.

Last, C. G., Hersen, M., Kazdin, A. E., Finkelstein, R., & Strauss, C. C. (1987). Comparison of DSM-III separation anxiety and overanxious disorder: Demographic characteristics and patterns of comorbidity. *Journal of the American Academy of Child and Adolescent Psychiatry, 26,* 527–531.

Last, C. G., Hersen, M., Kazdin, A. E., Orvaschel, H., & Perrin, S. (1991). Anxiety Disorders in children and their families. *Archives of General Psychiatry, 48*(10), 928–934.

Last, C. G., Perrin, S., Hersen, M., & Kazdin, A. E. (1992). *DSM-III-R* anxiety disorders in children: Sociodemographic and clinical characteristics. *Journal of the American Academy of Child and Adolescent Psychiatry, 31,* 1070–1076.

Last, C. G., Perrin, S., Hersen, M., & Kazdin, A. E. (1996). A prospective study of child Anxiety Disorders. *Journal of the American Academy of Child and Adolescent Psychiatry, 35,* 1502–1510.

Lawford, B., Young, R. McD., Powell, J. A., Gibson, J. N., Feeney, G. F. X., Ritchie, T. L., Syndulko, K., & Noble, E. P. (1997). Association of the D2 dopamine receptor A1 allele with alcoholism: Medical severity of alcoholism and type of controls. *Biology and Psychiatry, 41,* 386–393.

Lazear, K., Doan, J., & Roggenbaum, S. (2003). *Youth suicide prevention school-based guide—Issue brief 9: Culturally and linguistically diverse populations.* Tampa, FL: Department of Child and Family Studies, Division of State and Local Support, Louis de la Parte Florida Mental Health Institute, University of South Florida. (FMHI Series Publication #218-9).

LeCroy, C. W. (1994). Social skills training. In C. W. LeCroy (Ed.), *Handbook of child and adolescent treatment manuals* (pp. 170–199). New York: Lexington.

Lehmkuhl, G., Blanz, B., Lehmkuhl, U., & Braun-Scharm, H. (1989). Conversion disorder (*DSM-III* 300.11): Symptomatology and course in childhood and adolescence. *European Archives of Psychiatry and Neurological Sciences, 238,* 155–160.

Leslie, A. (1988). Diagnosis and treatment of hysterical conversion reactions. *Archives of Disease in Childhood, 63,* 506–511.

Leutwyler, K. (1996). Paying attention: The controversy over ADHD and the drug Ritalin is obscuring a real look at the disorder and its underpinnings. *Scientific American, 272*(2), 12–13.

Levine, M. (1999). How can we differentiate between ADHD, Bipolar Disorder in children? *The Brown University Child and Adolescent Psychopharmacology Update, 8,* 4–5.

Lewinsohn, P. M., Clarke, G. N., Rhode, P., Hops, H., & Seeley, J. (1996). A course in coping: A cognitive-behavioral approach to the treatment of adolescent depression. In E. D. Hibbs & P. S. Jensen (Eds.), *Psychosocial treatments for child and adolescent disorders: Empirically based strategies for clinical practice* (pp. 109–135). Washington, DC: American Psychological Association.

Lewinsohn, P. M., Clarke, G. N., Seeley, J. R., & Rohde, P. (1994). Major depression in community adolescents: Age at onset, episode duration, and time of recurrence. *Journal of the American Academy of Child and Adolescent Psychiatry, 33,* 809–818.

Liddle, H. A., & Hogue, A. (2001). Multidimensional family therapy for adolescent substance abuse. In E. F. Wagner & H. B. Waldron (Eds.), *Innovations in adolescent substance abuse interventions* (pp. 229–261). Oxford: Elsevier Science.

Liebman, W. M. (1978). Recurrent abdominal pain in children: A retrospective survey of 119 patients. *Clinical Pediatrics, 17,* 149–153.

Litz, B. T. (1992). Emotional numbing in combat-related Post-Traumatic Stress Disorder: A critical review and reformulation. *Clinical Psychology Review, 12,* 417–432.

Lloyd, G. K., Fletcher, A., & Minchin, M. C. W. (1992). GABA agonists as potential anxiolytics. In C. D. Burows, S. M. Roth, & R. Noyes, Jr., (Eds.), *Handbook of anxiety* (Vol. 5, pp. 35–58). Oxford, England: Elsevier.

Lochman, J. E., Burch, P. R., Curry, J. F., & Lampron, L. B. (1984). Treatment and generalization effects of cognitive-behavioral and goal-setting interventions with aggressive boys. *Journal of Consulting and Clinical Psychology, 53,* 915–916.

Loeber, R., Green, S. M., Lahey, B. B., Christ, M. A., & Frick, P. J. (1992). Developmental sequences in the age of onset of disruptive child behaviors. *Journal of Child and Family Studies, 1,* 21–41.

Loeber, R., & Keenan, K. (1994). Interaction between Conduct Disorder and its comorbid conditions: Effects of age and gender. *Clinical Psychology Review, 14,* 497–523.

Loeber, R., & Stouthamer-Loeber, M. (1998). Development of juvenile aggression and violence: Some common misconceptions and controversies. *American Psychologist, 53,* 242–259.

Lonigan, C. J., Carey, M. P., & Finch, A. J., Jr. (1994). Anxiety and depression in children and adolescents: Negative affectivity and the utility of self reports. *Journal of Consulting and Clinical Psychology, 62,* 1000–1008.

Lonigan, C. J., Shannon, M. P., Saylor, C. M., Finch, A. J., & Sallee, F. R. (1994). Children exposed to disaster: II. Risk factors for the development of post-traumatic symptomatology. *Journal of the American Academy of Child and Adolescent Psychiatry, 33,* 94–105.

Lovaas, O. I. (1987). Behavioral treatment and normal educational and intellectual functioning of young autistic children. *Journal of Consulting and Clinical Psychology, 55,* 3–9.

Luby, J. L., Heffelfinger, A., Mrakotsky, C., Brown, K., Hessler, M., Wallis, J., & Spitznagel, E. (2003). The clinical picture of depression in preschool children. *Journal of the American Academy of Child and Adolescent Psychiatry, 42,* 340–348.

Lynch, E. W. (1998). Developing cross-cultural competence. In E. W. Lynch & M. J. Hanson (Eds.), *Developing cross-cultural competence* (2nd ed., pp. 47–90). Baltimore: Paul H. Brookes.

Lyon, G. R., & Shaywitz, S. E. (2003). Part I: Defining dyslexia, comorbidity, teachers' knowledge of language and reading. *Annals of Dyslexia, 53,* 1–14.

Lyons-Ruth, K., & Jacobvitz, D. (1999). Attachment disorganization: Unresolved loss, relational violence, and lapses in behavioral and attentional strategies. In J. Cassidy & P. R. Shaver (Eds.), *Handbook of attachment: Theory, research, and clinical applications* (pp. 520–554). New York: Guilford Press.

Macintosh, K. E., & Dissanayake, C. (2004). Annotation: The similarities and differences between Autistic Disorder and Asperger's disorder. A review of the empirical evidence. *Journal of Child Psychology and Psychiatry, 45*(3), 421–434.

MacMillan, D. L., & Forness, S. R. (1998). The role of IQ in special education placement decisions: Primary and determinative or peripheral and inconsequential. *Remedial and Special Education, 19,* 239–253.

Main, M., & Hesse, E. (1990). Parents' unresolved traumatic experiences are related to infant disorganized attachment status: Is frightened and/or frightening parental behavior the linking mechanism? In M. T. Greenberg, D. Cicchetti, & E. M. Cummings (Eds.), *Attachment in the preschool years: Theory, research, and intervention* (pp. 161–182). Chicago: University of Chicago Press.

Main, M., & Solomon, J. (1986). Discovery of a new, insecure-disorganized/disoriented attachment pattern. In T. B. Braxelton & M. W. Yogman (Eds.), *Affective development in infancy* (pp. 95–124). Norwood, NJ: Ablex.

Main, M., & Weston, D. (1981). The quality of the toddler's relationship to mother and to father: Related to conflict behavior and the readiness to establish new relationships. *Child Development, 52,* 932–940.

Mak, W., & Rosenblatt, A. (2002). Demographic influences on psychiatric diagnoses among youth served in California systems of care. *Journal of Child and Family Studies, 11,* 165–178.

Malmquist, C. P. (1986). Children who witness parental murder: Posttraumatic aspects. *Journal of the American Academy of Child and Adolescent Psychiatry, 25,* 320–325.

Malphurs, J. E., Field, T. M., Larraine, C., Pickens, J., Yando, R., & Bendell, D. (1996). Altering withdrawn and intrusive interaction behaviors of depressed mothers. *Infant Mental Health Journal, 17,* 152–160.

March, J., Amaya-Jackson, L., & Pynoos, R. S. (1994). Pediatric Posttraumatic Stress Disorder. In J. W. Weiner (Ed.), *Textbook of child and adolescent psychiatry* (pp. 507–527). Washington, DC: American Psychiatric Press.

Martini, D. R. (1995). Common Anxiety Disorders in children and adolescents. *Current Problems in Pediatrics, 25,* 271–280.

Mash, E. J., & Terdal, L. G. (1997). Assessment of child land family disturbance: A behavioral-systems approach. In E. J. Mash & L. G. Terdal (Eds.), *Assessment of childhood disorders, third edition* (pp. 3–70). New York: Guilford Press.

Matson, L. J., & Ollendick, H. T. (1988). *Enhancing children's social skills.* New York: Pergamon Press.

McAdoo, H. P. (1997). *Black families* (3rd ed.). Beverly Hills: Sage Publications.

McCabe, K., Yeh, M., Hough, R. L., Landsverk, J., Hurlburt, M., Culver, S., & Reynolds, B. (1999). Racial/ethnic representation across five public sectors of care for youth. *Journal of Emotional and Behavioral Disorders, 7,* 72–82.

McConaughy, S. H., & Achenbach, T. M. (1993). Comorbidity of externalizing and internalizing problems. *School Psychology Review, 22,* 421–436.

McDermott, B. M., & Palmer, L. J. (2002). Postdisaster emotional distress, depression, and event-related variables: Findings across child and adolescent developmental stages. *Australian and New Zealand Journal of Psychiatry, 36,* 754–761.

McDonald, W. L., and associates. (2004). *Child maltreatment 2002.* The report summarizes statistics submitted by states to the National Child Abuse and Neglect Data System (NCANDS), 166 pages. Retrieved October, 2004 from http://www.acf.dhhs.gov/programs/cb/publications/cm02/.

McFall, R. (1982). A review and reformulation of the concept of social skills. *Behavioral Assessment, 4,* 1–33.

McFarlane, A. (1987). Post-traumatic phenomena in a longitudinal study of children following a natural disaster. *Journal of the American Academy of Child and Adolescent Psychiatry, 26,* 764–769.

McLeer, S., Deblinger, E., Henry, D., & Orvaschel, H. (1992). Sexually abused children at high risk for Post-Traumatic Stress Disorder. *Journal of the American Academy of Child and Adolescent Psychiatry, 32,* 875–879.

McLellan, J. P., & Werry, J. S. (2003). Evidence-based treatments in child and adolescent psychiatry. *Journal of the American Academy of Child and Adolescent Psychiatry, 42,* 1388–1400.

McMahon, R. J., & Kotler, J. S. (2004). Treatment of conduct problems in children and adolescents. In P. M. Barrett & T. H. Ollendick (Eds.), *Handbook of interventions that work with children and adolescents* (pp. 395–425). Chichester, England: Wiley.

Meezan, W., & McCroskey, J. (1996). Improving family functioning through family preservation services: Results of the Los Angeles experiment. *Family Preservation Journal, 46,* 21–32.

Mellin, L. M., Irwin, C., & Scully, S. (1992). Prevalence of disordered eating in girls: A survey of middle class children. *Journal of the American Dietetic Association, 92,* 851–853.

MFT. (2003). *Monitoring the future.* Survey results for 2003. NIDA: www.nida.nih.gov

Michaelson, R. (1993). Flood volunteers build emotional levees. *APA Monitor, 24,* 30.

Miller, A. (1999). Appropriateness of psychostimulant prescription to children: Theoretical and empirical perspectives. *Canadian Journal of Psychiatry, 44*(10), 1017–1024.

Miller, J. N., & Ozonoff, S. (2000). The external validity of Asperger disorder: Lack of evidence from the domain of neuropsychology. *Journal of Abnormal Psychology, 109,* 227–238.

Miller, M. N., & Pumariega, B. (1999). Culture and eating disorders. *Psychiatric Times, XVI*(2). Retrieved October, 2004 from *http://www.psychiatrictimes.com/p990238.html.*

Mineka, S., Watson, D., & Clark, L. A. (1998). Comorbidity of anxiety and unipolar mood disorders. *Annual Review of Psychology, 49,* 377–412.

Minuchin, S. (1985). Families and individual development: Provocations from the field of family therapy. *Child Development, 56,* 289–302.

Minuchin, S., Rosman, B. L., & Baker, L. (1978). *Psychosomatic families: Anorexia Nervosa in context.* Cambridge, MA: Harvard University Press.

Mitchell, J. E., Pyle, R. L., & Miner, R. A. (1982). Gastric dilation as a complication of bulimia. *Psychosomatics, 23,* 96–97.

Moffit, E. E. (1990). Juvenile delinquency and Attention Deficit Disorder: Boys' developmental trajectories from age 3 to 15. *Child Development, 61,* 893–910.

Moffit, T. E., & Henry, B. (1989). Neurological assessment of executive functions in self-reported delinquents. *Development and Psychopathology, 1,* 105–118.

Molina, B. S., & Pelham, W. E. (2003). Childhood predictors of adolescent substance use in a longitudinal study of children with ADHD. *Journal of Abnormal Psychology, 112,* 497–507.

Monti, P. M., Abrams, D. B., Kadden, R. M., & Cooney, N. L. (1989). *Treating alcohol dependence: A coping skills guide.* New York: Guilford Press.

Morris, R. D., Stuebing, K. K., Fletcher, J. M., Shaywitz, S. E., Lyon, G. R., Shankweiler, D. P., Katz, L., Francis, D. J., & Shaywitz, B. A. (1998). Subtypes of reading disability: Variability around a phonological core. *Journal of Educational Psychology, 90,* 347–373.

MTA Cooperative Group. (1999). A 14-month randomized clinical trial of treatment strategies for Attention-Deficit/Hyperactivity Disorder. *Archives of General Psychiatry, 56,* 1073–1086.

Mundy, P. (1995). Joint attention and social-emotional approach behavior in children with autism. *Development and Psychopathology, 7,* 63–82.

Muris, P., Meesters, C., Merekelbach, H., Sermon, A., & Zwakhalen, S. (1998). Worry in normal children. *Journal of the American Academy of Child and Adolescent Psychiatry, 37,* 703–710.

Murphy, M. L., & Pichichero, M. E. (2002). Prospective identification and treatment of children with pediatric autoimmune neuropsychiatric disorder associated with Group A streptococcal infection (PANDAS). *Archives of Pediatric and Adolescent Medicine, 156,* 356–361.

Nachmias, M., Gunnar, M., Mangelsdorf, S., Parritz, R., & Buss, K. (1996). Behavioral inhibition and stress reactivity: The moderating role of attachment security. *Child Development, 67,* 508–522.

Nagata, D. K. (2001). The assessment and treatment of Japanese American children and adolescents. In J. T. Gibbs & L. N. Huang (Eds.), *Children of color* (pp. 68–111). San Francisco: Jossey-Bass.

National Institute of Drug Abuse (NIDA). (2003). Preventing drug use among children and adolescents: A research-based guide for parents, educators, and community leaders, 2nd edition. U.S. Department of Health and Human Services, National Institutes of Health, National Institute on Drug Abuse, Bethesda, MD: Author.

National Institute of Mental Health (NIMH). (2000). Depression in children and adolescents: A fact sheet for physicians. www.nimh.nih.gov.

National Institute of Mental Health (NIMH) Fact Sheet. (2000). Child and adolescent bipolar disorder: An update from the National Institute of Mental Health. www.nimh.nih.gov.

National Joint Committee on Learning Disabilities (NJCLD). (1987). Learning disabilities: Issues on definition. *Journal of Learning Disabilities, 20,* 107–108.

National Science Education Leadership Association (NSELA). (2003). Retrieved July 2003 from http://www.nsela.org/multicul.htm

Newcomb, M. D., & Felix-Ortiz, M. (1992). Multiple protective and risk factors for drug use and abuse: Cross-sectional and prospective findings. *Journal of Personality and Social Psychology, 63,* 280–296.

Nietzel, M. T., Bernstein, D. A., & Milich, R. (1994). *Introduction to clinical psychology, 4th edition.* Englewood Cliffs, NJ: Prentice Hall.

Norgate, R. (1998). Reducing self-injurious behavior in a child with severe learning difficulties: Enhancing predictability and structure. *Educational Psychology in Practice 14,* 176–182.

Offord, D. R., Boyle, M. H., & Szatmari, P. (1987). Ontario Child Health Study, II: Six-month prevalence of disorder and rates of service utilization. *Archives of General Psychiatry, 44,* 832–836.

Offord, D. R., Boyle, M. W., & Racine, Y. (1989). Ontario Child Health Study: Correlates of disorder. *Journal of the American Academy of Child and Adolescent Psychiatry, 28,* 855–860.

Ogbu, J. U. (1981). Origins of human competence: A cultural-ecological perspective. *Child Development, 52,* 413–429.

Olds, D., Henderson, C., Kitzman, H., Eckenrode, J., Cole, R., & Tatelbaum, R. (1998). The promise of home visitation: Results of two randomized trials. *Journal of Community Psychology, 26,* 5–21.

Ollendick, T. H. (1998). Panic Disorder in children and adolescents: New developments, new directions. *Journal of Clinical Child Psychology, 27,* 234–245.

Ollendick, T. H., & King, N. J. (1998). Empirically supported treatment for children with phobic and Anxiety Disorders: Current status. *Journal of Clinical Child Psychology, 27,* 156–167.

Ollendick, T. H., & King, N. J. (2004). Empirically supported treatments for children and adolescents: Advances toward evidence-based practice. In P. M. Barrett & T. H. Ollendick

(Eds.), *Handbook of Interventions that Work with Children and Adolescents* (pp. 3–26). West Sussex, U.K.: Wiley.

O'Shea, L. J., Sindelar, P. T., & O'Shea, D. J. (1985). The effects of repeated readings and attentional cues on reading fluency and comprehension. *Journal of Reading Behavior, 17,* 129–142.

Ostrov, E., Offer, D., & Howard, K. I. (1989). Gender differences in adolescent symptomatology: A normative study. *Journal of the American Academy of Child and Adolescent Psychiatry, 28,* 394–398.

Parker, J., & Asher, S. R. (1987). Peer relations and later personal adjustment: Are low-accepted children at risk? *Psychological Bulletin, 102,* 357–389.

Panerai, S., Ferrante, L., & Zingale, M. (2002). Benefits of the treatment and education of autistic and communication handicapped children (TEACCH) program as compared with a non-specific approach. *Journal of Intellectual Disability Research, 46,* 318–327.

Pate, J. E., Pumariega, A. J., Hester, C., & Gaarner, D. M. (1992). Cross-cultural patterns in eating disorders: A review. *Journal of the American Academy of Child and Adolescent Psychiatry, 31,* 802–808.

Patterson, G., Reid, J., Jones, R., & Conger, R. (1975). *A social learning approach to family intervention. Vol. 1: Families with aggressive children.* Eugene, OR: Castalia.

Patterson, G. R., & Capaldi, D. M. (1990). A mediational model for boys' depressed mood. In J. Rolf, A. S. Masten, D. Cicchetti, K. H. Nuechterlein, & S. Weintraub (Eds.), *Risk and protective factors in the development of psychopathology* (pp. 141–163). Cambridge: Cambridge University Press.

Patterson, G. R., Capaldi, D., & Bank, L. (1991). An early starter model for predicting delinquency. In D. Pepler & K. H. Rubin (Eds.), *The development and treatment of childhood aggression* (pp. 139–168). Hillsdale, NJ: Lawrence Erlbaum.

Patterson, G. R., DeBaryshe, B. D., & Ramsey, E. (1989). A developmental perspective on antisocial behavior. *American Psychologist, 44,* 329–335.

Patterson, G. R., & Gullion, M. E. (1968). *Living with children: New methods for parents and teachers.* Champaign, IL: Research Press.

Patterson, G. R., & Yoerger, K. (2002). A developmental model for early- and late-onset delinquency. In J. B. Reid, G. R. Patterson, & J. Snyder (Eds.), *Antisocial behavior in children and adolescents: A developmental analysis and model for intervention* (pp. 147–172). Washington, DC: American Psychological Association.

Pelham, E. E., & Milich, R. (1991). Individual differences in response to Ritalin in classwork and social behavior. In L. L. Grennhill & B. B. Osmon (Eds.), *Ritalin: Theory and patient management* (pp. 203–221). New York: Mary Ann Liebert.

Pelham, W. E., Jr., Wheeler, T., & Chronis, A. (1998). Empirically supported psychosocial treatments for Attention-Deficit/Hyperactivity Disorder. *Journal of Clinical Child Psychology, 27,* 190–205.

Perner, J., Frith, U., Leslie, A. M., & Leekam, S. R. (1989). Exploration of the autistic child's theory of mind: Knowledge, belief, and communication. *Child Development, 60,* 689–700.

Peterson, L., & Roberts, M. C. (1991). Treatment of children's problems. In C. E. Walker (Ed.), *Clinical psychology: Historical and research foundations.* New York: Plenum Press.

Pfefferbaum, B. (1997). Posttraumatic Stress Disorder in children: A review of the past 10 years. *Journal of the American Academy of Child and Adolescent Psychiatry, 36,* 1503–1511.

Phillips, K. A. (1996). Body Dysmorphic Disorder: Diagnosis and treatment of imagined ugliness. *Journal of Clinical Psychiatry, 57,* 61–64.

Piacentini, J., Bergman, R. I., Keller, M., & McCracken, J. (2003). Functional impairment in children and adolescents with Obsessive-Compulsive Disorder. *Journal of Child and Adolescent Psychopharmacology, 13,* 61–70.

Pickersgill, M. J., Valentine, J. D., Pincus, T., & Foustok, H. (1999). Girls' fearfulness as a product of mothers' fearfulness and fathers' authoritarianism. *Psychological Reports, 85,* 759–760.

Prior, M., Eisenmajer, R., Leekam, S., Wing, L., Gould, J., Ong, B., et al. (1998). Are there subgroups within the autistic spectrum? A cluster analysis of a group of children with autistic spectrum disorders. *Journal of Child Psychology and Psychiatry, 39,* 893–902.

Prior, M., & Werry, J. S. (1986). Autism, Schizophrenia, and allied disorders. In H. C. Quay & J. S. Werry (Eds.), *Psychopathological disorders of childhood* (3rd ed., pp. 156–210). New York: Wiley.

Puig-Antich, J., Geotz, D., & Davies, M. (1989). A controlled family history study of prepubertal Major Depressive Disorder. *Archives of General Psychiatry, 46,* 406–418.

Pynoos, R. S. (1990). Post-Traumatic Stress Disorder in children and adolescents. In B. Grafinkel, G. Carlson, & E. Weller (Eds.), *Psychiatric disorders in children and adolescents* (pp. 48–63). Philadelphia: W. B. Saunders Company.

Pynoos, R. S. (1994). Traumatic stress and developmental psychopathology in children and adolescents. In R. S. Pynoos (Ed.), *Posttraumatic Stress Disorder: A clinical review* (pp. 64–98). Lutherville, MD: The Sidran Press.

Pynoos, R. S., & Nader, K. (1993). Issues in the treatment of posttraumatic stress in children and adolescents. In J. P. Wilson & B. Raphael (Eds.), *International handbook of traumatic stress syndromes* (pp. 535–549). New York: Plenum Press.

Quay, H. C. (1986). Conduct disorders. In H. C. Quay & J. S. Werry (Eds.), *Psychopathological disorders of childhood* (3rd ed., pp. 1–34). New York: Wiley.

Rachmond, S. (1993). Obsessions, responsibility, and guilt. *Behavior Research and Therapy, 31,* 149–154.

Ramberg, C., Ehlers, S., Nyden, A., Johansson, M., & Gillberg, C. (1996). Language and pragmatic functions in school-age children on the autism spectrum. *European Journal of Disorders of Communication, 31,* 387–414.

Ramirez, O. (2001). Mexican American children and adolescents. In J. T. Gibbs & L. N. Huang (Eds.), *Children of color* (pp. 215–239). San Francisco: Jossey-Bass.

Rapee, R. M. (1997). Potential role of childrearing practices in the development of anxiety and depression. *Clinical Psychology Review, 17,* 47–67.

Rechsley, D. J. (2003). IDEA Reauthorization: Outcomes criteria and the bright future of school psychology. Presentation to the Florida Association of School Psychologists. Palm Harbor, Florida.

Reebye, P., Moretti, M. M., & Gulliver, L. (1995). Conduct Disorder and Substance Use Disorder: Comorbidity in a clinical sample of preadolescents and adolescents. *Canadian Journal of Psychiatry, 40,* 313–319.

Regan, J. J., & Regan, W. (1989). Somatoform Disorders. In C. G. Last & M. Hersen (Eds.), *Handbook of child psychiatric diagnoses* (pp. 343–355). New York: Wiley.

Renaud, J., Birmaher, B., Wassick, C. C., & Bridge, J. (1999). Use of selective serotonin reuptake inhibitors for the treatment of childhood Panic Disorder: A pilot study. *Journal of Child and Adolescent Psychopharmacology, 9,* 73–83.

Rey, J. M. (1993). Oppositional Defiant Disorder. *American Journal of Psychiatry, 150,* 1769–1777.

Richards, T., & Bates, C. (1997). Recognizing posttraumatic stress in children. *Journal of School Health, 67,* 441–443.

Ringwalt, C., et al. (2002). The prevalence of effective substance abuse prevention curricula in U.S. middle schools. *Prevention Science 2*(4), 257–265.

Robin, A. L., Bedway, M., Diegel, P. T., & Gilroy, M. (1996). Therapy for adolescent Anorexia Nervosa: Addressing cognitions, feelings, and the family's role. In E. D. Hibbs & P. S. Jensen (Eds.), *Psychosocial treatments for child and adolescent disorders: Empirically-based strategies for clinical practice.* Washington, DC: American Psychological Association.

Robins, L. N., & McEvoy, L. (1990). Conduct problems as predictors of substance abuse. In L. E. Robins & M. Rutter (Eds.), *Straight and devious pathways from childhood to adulthood* (pp. 182–204). Cambridge: Cambridge University Press.

Robinson, D. P., Greene, J. W., & Walker, L. S. (1988). Functional somatic complaints in adolescents: Relationship to negative life events, self concept, and family characteristics. *The Journal of Pediatrics, 113,* 588–593.

Rogers, H. R. (1986). *Poor women, poor families.* Armonk, NY: Sharpe.

Rogers, M. R., Ingraham, C. L., Bursztyn, A., Cajigas-Segredo, N., Esquivel, G., Hess, R. S., et al. (1999). Best practices in providing psychological services to racially, ethnically, culturally, and linguistically diverse individuals in the schools. *School Psychology International, 20,* 243–264.

Rogers, S. J. (1998). Empirically supported comprehensive treatments for young children with autism. *Journal of Clinical Child Psychology, 27,* 168–179.

Rogler, L. H. (1999). Methodological sources of cultural insensitivity in mental health research. *American Psychologist, 54*(6), 424–433.

Rosen, L. W., McKeag, D. B., Hough, D. O., & Curley, V. (1986). Pathogenic weight-control behavior in female athletes. *The Physician and Sports Medicine, 14*(1), 79–86.

Rosenheim, M. K., & Testa, M. F. (1992). *Early parenthood and coming of age in the 1990's.* New Brunswick, NJ: Rutgers University Press.

Rosenthal, R., & Jacobson, L. (1968). *Pygmalion in the classroom: Teacher expectation and pupils' "intellectual development."* New York: Rinehart and Winston.

Rourke, B. (1989). *Nonverbal learning disabilities: The syndrome and the model.* New York: Guilford Press.

Rubio-Stipec, M. W., & Murphy, J. (2002). Dimensional measures of psychopathology: The probability of being classified with a psychiatric disorder using empirically derived symptom scales. *Social Psychiatry and Psychiatric Epidemiology, 37,* 553–560.

Rutter, M. (1978). Diagnosis and definition. In M. Rutter & E. Schopler (Eds.), *Autism: A reappraisal of concepts and treatment.* New York: Plenum Press.

Ryan, N. D., Puig-Antich, J., Ambrosini, P., Rabinovich, H., Nelson, B., Iyengar, S., & Twomey, J. (1987). The clinical picture of major depression in children and adolescents. *Archives of General Psychiatry, 44,* 854–861.

Saavedra, L. M., & Silverman, W. K. (2002). Classification of Anxiety Disorders in children: What a difference two decades make. *International Review of Psychiatry, 14,* 87–101.

Sameroff, A. (1993). Models of development and developmental risk. In C. H. Zeanah, Jr. (Ed.), *Handbook of infant mental health* (pp. 3–13). New York: Guilford Press.

Sameroff, A. J., & Chandler, M. J. (1975). Reproductive risk and the continuum of caretaking casualty. In F. D. Horowitz, M. Hetherington, S. Scarr-Salapatek, & G. Siegel (Eds.), *Review of child development research* (Vol. 4, pp. 187–244). Chicago: University of Chicago Press.

Sattler, J. (2002). *Assessment of children: Behavioral and clinical applications, 4th edition.* LaMesa, CA: Author.

Scheeringa, M. S., & Zeanah, C. H. (1995). Symptom expression and trauma variables in children under 48 months of age. *Infant Mental Health Journal, 16,* 259–270.

Scheeringa, M. S., & Zeanah, C. H. (2001). A relational perspective on PTSD in early childhood. *Journal of Traumatic Stress, 14,* 799–815.

Schoenwald, S. K., Ward, D. M., Henggeler, S. W., & Rowland, M. D. (2000). Multisystemic therapy versus hospitalization for crisis stabilization of youth: Placement outcomes 4 months postreferral. *Mental Health Services Research, 2,* 3–12.

Schopler, R. (1985). Editorial: Convergence of learning disability, higher-level autism, and Asperger's syndrome. *Journal of Autism and Developmental Disorders, 15,* 359.

Schopler, R. (1994). A statewide program for the treatment and education of autistic and related communication handicapped children (TEACCH). *Psychology and Pervasive Developmental Disorders, 3,* 91–103.

Schor, E. (1986). Use of health care services by children and diagnoses received during presumably stressful life transitions. *Pediatrics, 77,* 834–841.

Scientific Panel rejects vaccines as cause of autism. *Infection Control Today. Posted May 19, 2004.* Retrieved October, 2004 from *http://www.infectioncontroltoday.com/hotnews/45h199856.html*

Seligman, M. E. P. (1975). *Helplessness.* San Francisco: W. H. Freeman.

Seligman, M., & Peterson, C. (1986). A learned helpless perspective on childhood depression: Theory and research. In M. Rutter, C. E. Izard, & P. B. Read (Eds.), *Depression in young people* (pp. 223–249). New York: Guilford Press.

Seltzer, W. (1985). Conversion Disorder in childhood and adolescence: A familial/cultural approach. Part I. *Family Systems Medicine, 3,* 261–280.

Semrud-Clikeman, M., Biederman, J., Sprich-Buckminster, S., Lehman, B. K., Faraone, S. V., & Norman, D. (1992). Comorbidity between ADDH and learning disability: A review and report in a clinically referred sample. *Journal of the American Academy of Child and Adolescent Psychiatry, 31,* 439–448.

Shaffer, D., & Craft, L. (1999). Methods of adolescent suicide prevention. *Journal of Clinical Psychiatry, 60,* 70–74.

Shaffer, D., Gould, M. S., Fisher, P., Trautment, P., Moreau, D., Kleinman, M., & Flory, M. (1996). Psychiatric diagnoses in child and adolescent suicide. *Archives of General Psychiatry, 53,* 339–348.

Shaywitz, S. (2003). *Overcoming dyslexia: A new and complete science-based program for reading problems at any level.* New York: Alfred A. Knopf.

Shedler, J., & Block, J. (1990). Adolescent drug use and psychological health. *American Psychologist, 45,* 612–630.

Sheeber, L., Hops, H., & Davis, B. (2001). Family processes in adolescent depression. *Clinical Child and Family Psychology Review, 4,* 19–35.

Siegel, M., & Barthel, R. P. (1986). Conversion Disorders on a child psychiatry consultation service. *Psychosomatics, 27,* 201–204.

Silverman, W. K., & Ginsburg, G. S. (1995). Specific phobias and generalized anxiety disorder. In J. S. March (Ed.), *Anxiety disorders in children and adolescents* (pp. 151–180). New York: Guilford Press.

Silverman, W. K., & Nelles, W. B. (2001). The influence of gender on children's ratings of fear in self and same-aged peers. *The Journal of Genetic Psychology, 148,* 17–21.

Silverman, W. K., & Saavedra, L. M. (2004). Assessment and diagnosis in evidence-based practice. In P. M. Barrett & T. H. Ollendick (Eds.), *Handbook of interventions that work with children and adolescents* (pp. 49–70). West Sussex, U.K.: Wiley.

Silverman, W. K., Saavedra, L. M., & Pina, A. A. (2001). Test-retest reliability of anxiety symptoms and diagnoses using the Anxiety Disorders Interview Schedule for *DSM-IV:* Child and Parent Versions (ADIS for *DSM-IV:*C/P). *Journal of the American Academy of Child and Adolescent Psychiatry, 40,* 937–944.

Slaff, B. (1989). History of child and adolescent psychiatry ideas and organizations in the United States: A twentieth-century review. In S. C. Feinstein et al. (Eds.), *Adolescent psychiatry: Developmental and clinical studies. Vol. 16* (pp. 31–52). Chicago: University of Chicago Press.

Smucker, M. R., Craighead, W. E., Craighead, L. W., & Green, B. J. (1986). Normative and reliability data for the Children's Depression Inventory. *Journal of Abnormal Child Psychology, 14,* 25–39.

Sonuga-Barke, E. J., Daley, D., Thompson, M., Laver-Bredbury, C., & Weeks, A. (2001). Parent-based therapies for preschool Attention-Deficit/Hyperactivity Disorder: A randomized, controlled trial with a community sample. *Journal of the American Academy of Child and Adolescent Psychiatry, 40,* 402–408.

Spaccarelli, S., Cotler, S., & Penman, D. (1992). Problem-solving skills training as a supplement to behavioral parent training. *Cognitive Therapy and Research, 27,* 171–186.

Spangler, G., & Grossman, K. (1999). Individual and psychological correlates of attachment disorganization in infancy. In J. Solomon & C. George (Eds.), *Attachment disorganization* (pp. 95–126). New York: Guilford.

Spence, S. (1997). Structure of anxiety symptoms in children: A confirmatory factor analytic study. *Journal of Abnormal Psychology, 106,* 280–297.

Spitz, A. (1946). Anaclitic depression. *Psychoanalytic Study of the Child, 2,* 313–342.

Sroufe, L. A. (1989). Pathways to adaptation and maladaptation: Psychopathology as developmental deviation. In D. Cicchetti (Ed.), *Rochester Symposia on Developmental Psychopathology* (Vol. 1, pp. 13–40). Hillsdale, NJ: Erlbaum.

Sroufe, L. A., & Rutter, M. (1984). The domain of developmental psychopathology. *Child Development, 55,* 17–29.

Stanger, C., & Lewis, M. (1993). Agreement among parents, teachers, and children on internalizing and externalizing behavior problems. *Journal of Clinical Child Psychology, 22,* 107–115.

Stanton, M. D., & Shadish, W. R. (1997). Outcome, attrition, and family/couples treatment for drug abuse: A review of the controlled, comparative studies. *Psychological Bulletin, 122,* 170–191.

Stanovich, K. E. (1986). Matthew effects in reading: Some consequences of individual differences in the acquisition of literacy. *Reading Research Quarterly, 21,* 360–407.

Stark, K. D., Swearer, S., Jurkowski, C., Sommer, D., & Bowen, B. (1996). Targeting the child and the family: A holistic approach to treating child and adolescent depressive disorders. In E. D. Hibbs & P. S. Jensen (Eds.), *Psychosocial treatments for child and adolescent disorders: Empirically based strategies for clinical practice* (pp. 207–238). Washington, DC: American Psychological Association.

Steiner, H. (2000). Evaluation and management of violent behavior in bipolar adolescents. In *Program and abstracts from the American Psychiatric Association, 153rd Annual Meeting, Abstract 19D.* Retrieved October, 2004 from http://www.medscape.com/viewarticle/420304.

Stevenson, H. W., Chen, C., & Lee, S. Y. (1993). Mathematics achievement of Chinese, Japanese, and American children: Ten years later. *Science, 259,* 53–58.

Stevenson, H. W., Chen, C., & Uttal, D. H. (1990). Beliefs and achievement: A study of black, white, and Hispanic children. *Child Development, 16,* 508–523.

Stone, W. L., & La Greca, A. M. (1990). The social status of children with learning disabilities: A reexamination. *Journal of Learning Disabilities, 23,* 32–37.

Strang, J. D., & Casey, J. E. (1994). The psychological impact of learning disabilities: A developmental neurological perspective. In L. F. Koziol & E. E. Scott (Eds.), *The neuropsychology of mental disorders: A practical guide* (pp. 171–186). Springfield, IL: Charles C. Thomas.

Strauss, C. C., Lease, C. A., Last, C. G., & Francis, G. (1988). Overanxious disorder: An examination of developmental differences. *Journal of Abnormal Child Psychology, 16,* 433–443.

Strober, M., Morrell, W., Lanpert, C., & Burroughs, J. (1990). Relapse following discontinuation of lithium maintenance therapy in adolescents with bipolar illness: A naturalistic study. *American Journal of Psychiatry, 147,* 457–461.

Strober, M., Freeman, R., Lampert, C., Diamond, J., & Kaye, W. (2000). Controlled family study of Anorexia Nervosa and Bulimia Nervosa: Evidence of shared liability and transmission of partial syndromes. *American Journal of Psychiatry, 157*(3), 393–401.

Swarr, A. E., & Richards, M. H. (1996). Longitudinal effects of adolescent girls' pubertal development, perceptions of pubertal timing, and parental relations on eating problems. *Developmental Psychology, 32,* 636–646.

Swedo, S. E., Rapoport, J. L., Leonard, H., Leanane, M., & Cheslow, D. (1989). Obsessive-

Compulsive Disorder in children and adolescents: Clinical phenomenology of 70 consecutive cases. *Archives of General Psychiatry, 46,* 335–341.

Szatmari, P., Boyle, M., & Offord, D. R. (1989). ADDH and Conduct Disorder: Degree of diagnostic overlap and differences among correlates. *Journal of the American Academy of Child and Adolescent Psychiatry, 28,* 865–872.

Tager-Flusberg, H., Calkings, S., Nolin, T., Baumberger, T., Anderson, M., & Chadwick-Dias, A. (1990). A longitudinal study of language acquisition in autistic and Down syndrome children. *Journal of Autism and Developmental Disorders, 20,* 1–20.

Taylor, A. (1986). Loneliness, goal orientation, and sociometric status: Mildly retarded children's adaptation to the mainstream classroom. Paper presented at the annual meeting of the American Educational Research Association, San Francisco.

Taylor, D. C., Szatmari, P., Boyle, M. H., & Offord, D. (1996). Somatization and the vocabulary of everyday bodily experiences and concerns: A community study of adolescents. *Journal of the American Academy of Child and Adolescent Psychiatry, 35,* 491–499.

Teplin, L. A., Abram, K. M., McClelland, G. M., Dulcan, M. K., & Mericle, A. A. (2002). Psychiatric disorders in youth in juvenile detention. *Archives of General Psychiatry, 59,* 1133–1143.

Terr, L. C. (1991). Childhood traumas: An outline and overview. *American Journal of Psychiatry, 148,* 10–20.

Thapar, A., Harold, G., & McGuffin, P. (1998). Life events and depressive symptoms in childhood: Shared genes or shared adversity? A research note. *Journal of Child Psychology and Psychiatry, 39,* 1153–1158.

Thomas, A., & Chess, S. (1977). *Temperament and development.* New York: Brunner/Mazel.

Thompson, J. (2004). *Supports Intensity Scale Manual.* Washington, DC: American Association on Mental Retardation.

Thompson, S. (1997). Nonverbal learning disorders revisited in 1997. *The Gram.* Retrieved October, 2004 from *http://www.ldaca.org/gram/thompsn1.html.*

Torgesen, J. K. (2000). Individual differences in response to early interventions in reading: The lingering problem of treatment resisters. *Learning Disabilities Research & Practice, 1,* 55–64.

Tremblay, R. E., Japel, C., Perusse, D., McDuff, P., Boivin, M., Zoccolillo, M., et al. (1999). The search for the age of "onset" of physical aggression: Rousseau and Bandura revisited. *Criminal Behaviour and Mental Health, 9,* 8–23.

Tueth, M. J., Murphy, T. K., & Evans, D. L. (1998). Special considerations: Use of lithium in children, adolescents, and elderly populations. *Journal of Clinical Psychiatry, 59,* 66–73.

U.S. Bureau of the Census. (1996). *Statistical abstract of the United States, 1996* (116th ed.). Washington, DC: U.S. Department of Commerce.

U.S. Department of Health and Human Services (USDHHS). (1999). *Mental health: A report of the surgeon general.* Rockville, MD: U.S. Department of Health and Human Services, Public Health Service, Office of the Surgeon General.

U.S. Department of Health and Human Services (USDHHS). (2001). *Mental health: Culture, race, and ethnicity. A supplement to* Mental Health: A Report of the Surgeon General. Rockville, MD: U.S. Department of Health and Human Services, Public Health Service, Office of the Surgeon General.

Valleni-Basile, L. A., Garrison, C. Z., Jackson, K. I., Waller, J. L., McKeown, R. E., Addy, C. L., et al. (1995). Family and psychosocial predictors of Obsessive-Compulsive Disorder in a community sample of young adolescents. *Journal of Child and Family Studies, 4,* 193–206.

Vaughn, S., Hogan, A., Kouzekanam, K., & Shapiro, S. (1990). Peer acceptance, self-perceptions, and social skills of learning disabled students prior to identification. *Journal of Educational Psychology, 82,* 101–106.

Velkamp, L. J., & Miller, T. W. (1994). *Clinical handbook of child abuse and neglect*. Madison, CT: International University Press.

Versi, M. (1995). Differential effects of cognitive behavior modification on seriously emotionally disturbed adolescents exhibiting internalizing and externalizing problems. *Journal of Child and Family Studies, 4,* 279–292.

Vik, P. W., Brown, S. A., & Myers, M. G. (1997). Adolescent substance abuse problems. In E. J. Mash & L. G. Terdal (Eds.), *Assessment of childhood disorders* (pp. 717–748). New York: Guilford Press.

Volkmar, F. R. (1987). Social development. In D. J. Cohen, A. M. Donnellan, & R. Paul (Eds.), *Handbook of autism and pervasive developmental disorder* (pp. 41–60). New York: Wiley.

Volkmar, F. R., & Mayes, L. C. (1990). Gaze behavior in autism. *Development and Psychopathology, 2,* 61–69.

Waldron, H. B. (1997). Adolescent substance abuse and family therapy outcome: A review of randomized trials. In T. H. Ollendick & R. J. Prinz (Eds.), *Advances in clinical child psychology* (vol. 19, pp. 199–234). New York: Plenum.

Waldron, H. B. (1998). Substance Abuse Disorders. In T. Ollendick (Ed.), *Comprehensive clinical psychology* (vol. 5, pp. 539–563). Oxford, U.K.: Elsevier Science.

Waldron, H. B., & Kern-Jones, S. (2004). Treatment of Substance Abuse Disorders in children and adolescents. In P. M. Barrett & T. H. Ollendick (Eds.), *Handbook of interventions that work with children and adolescents: Prevention and treatment* (pp. 329–342). Chichester, U.K.: Wiley.

Walker, L. S., Garber, J., & Greene, J. W. (1991). Psychosocial correlates of recurrent childhood pain: A comparison of pediatric patients with recurrent abdominal pain, organic illness, and psychiatric disorders. *Journal of Abnormal Child Psychology, 102,* 248–258.

Walker, S. (2002). Culturally competent protection of children's mental health. *Child Abuse Review, 2,* 380–393.

Walters, E. E., & Kendler, K. S. (1995). Anorexia Nervosa and anorexia-like syndromes in a population based female twin sample. *American Journal of Psychiatry, 152,* 64–71.

Warren, S. L., Huston, L., Egeland, B., & Sroufe, L. A. (1997). Child and adolescent Anxiety Disorders and early attachment. *Journal of the American Academy of Child and Adolescent Psychiatry, 36,* 637–644.

Webster-Stratton, C. (1984). Randomized trial of two parent-training programs for families with conduct-disordered children. *Journal of Consulting and Clinical Psychology, 52,* 666–678.

Weddle, K. D., & McKenry, P. C. (1995). Self-destructive behaviors among Black youth: Suicide and homicide. In R. L. Taylor (Ed.), *African American youth: Their social and economic status in the United States*. New York: Praeger.

Weems, C. F., Saltzman, K. M., Reiss, A. L., & Carrion, V. G. (2003). A prospective test of the association between hyperarousal and emotional numbing in youth with a history of traumatic stress. *Journal of Clinical Child and Adolescent Psychology, 32,* 166–171.

Weiss, M. D., Worling, D. E., & Wasdell, M. B. (2003). A chart review study of the Inattentive and Combined Types of ADHD. *Journal of Attention Disorders, 7*(1), 1–9.

Weissman, M. M., Wolk, S., Goldstein, R. B., et al. (1999). Depressed adolescents grow up. *Journal of the American Medical Association, 281,* 1701–1713.

Weisz, J. R., Weiss, B. B., Han, S. S., Granger, D. A., & Morton, E. (1995). Effects of psychotherapy with children and adolescents revisited: A meta-analysis of treatment outcome studies. *Psychological Bulletin, 117,* 450–468.

Wenar, C., & Kerig, P. (2000). *Developmental psychopathology, 4th edition*. Boston: McGraw Hill.

Wender, P. H., & Klein, D. F. (1981). *Mind, mood and medicine*. New York: Meridian.

Wielkiewicz, R. M. (1995). *Behavior management in the schools* (2nd ed.). Boston: Allyn & Bacon.

Willis, W. (1998). Families with African American roots. In E. W. Lynch & M. J. Hanson

(Eds.), *Developing cross-cultural competence* (2nd ed., pp. 165–208). Baltimore: Paul H. Brookes.

Wilmshurst, L. (2002). Treatment programs for youth with emotional and behavioral disorders: An outcomes study of two alternate approaches. *Mental Health Services Research, 4,* 85–96.

Windle, M., & Tubman, J. G. (1999). Children of alcoholics. In W. K. Silverman & T. H. Ollendick (Eds.), *Developmental issues in the clinical treatment of children* (pp. 393–414). Boston: Allyn & Bacon.

Wing, L. (1981). Asperger's syndrome: A clinical account. *Psychological Medicine, 11,* 115–129.

Winters, K. C., Latimer, W. W., & Stinchfield, R. (2001). Assessing adolescent substance use. In E. F. Wagner & H. B. Waldron (Eds.), *Innovations in adolescent substance abuse interventions* (pp. 1–29). Oxford: Elsevier Science.

Wilson, W. J., & Aponte, R. (1985). Urban poverty. *Annual Review of Sociology, 11,* 231–258.

Witelson, S. (1977). Developmental dyslexia: Two right hemispheres and none left. *Science, 195,* 309–311.

Wolpe, J. (1958). *Psychotherapy by reciprocal inhibition.* Stanford, CA: Stanford University Press.

Wolraich, M. L. (2000). Attention Deficit Hyperactivity Disorder: Current diagnosis and treatment. Paper presented at the American Academy of Pediatrics Annual Meeting. Retrieved October, 2004 from http://www.medscape.com/viewarticle/420198.

Wong, B. (1978). The effects of directive cues on the organization of memory and recall in good and poor readers. *Journal of Educational Research, 72,* 32–38.

Wong, M. G. (1995). Chinese Americans. In P. G. Min (Ed.), *Asian Americans: Contemporary trends and issues* (pp. 58–94). Beverly Hills: Sage Publications.

Wooley, S. C., & Wooley, O. W. (1985). Intense outpatient and residential treatment for bulimia. In D. M. Garner & P. E. Garfinkel (Eds.), *Handbook of psychotherapy for Anorexia Nervosa and bulimia* (pp. 391–430). New York: Guilford Press.

World Health Organization. (1993). The ICD-10 classification of mental and behavioral disorders: Clinical descriptions and diagnostic guidelines. Geneva: Author.

Yeh, C. J., & Huang, K. (2000). Interdependence in ethnic identity and self: Implications for theory and practice. *Journal of Counseling and Development, 78,* 420–429.

Yehuda, R., & McFarlane, A. C. (1995). Conflict between current knowledge about Posttraumatic Stress Disorder and the original conceptual basis. *American Journal of Psychiatry, 152,* 1705–1713.

Yule, W. (1998). Posttraumatic Stress Disorder in children and its treatment. In T. W. Miller (Ed.), *Children of trauma: Stressful life events and their effects on children and adolescents* (pp. 219–243). Madison, CT: International Universities Press.

Zeanah, C. H., Boris, N. W., & Larrieu, J. A. (1997). Infant development and developmental risk: A review of the past 10 years. *Journal of the American Academy of Child and Adolescent Psychiatry, 36,* 165–178.

Zoccolillo, M., & Cloniger, C. R. (1985). Parental breakdown associated with Somatization Disorder (hysteria). *British Journal of Psychiatry, 147,* 443–446.

Zohar, A. H., & Bruno, R. (1997). Normative and pathological obsessive-compulsive behavior and ideation in childhood: A question of timing. *Journal of Child Psychology and Psychiatry, 38,* 993–999.

Annotated Bibliography

Barrett, P. M., & Ollendick, T. H. (2004). *Handbook of interventions that work with children and adolescents: Prevention and treatment.* Chichester, U.K.: Wiley.

In Part I, the focus is on contemporary international views and trends in the area of evidence-based treatments. Part II provides information concerning specific evidence-based treatment programs for a variety of child and adolescent disorders, including, but not limited to, PTSD, depression, ADHD, and conduct problems. The final section discusses prevention initiatives as they relate to internalizing and externalizing disorders. 555 pages.

Cassidy, J., & Shaver, P. R. (Eds.). (1999). *Handbook of attachment: Theory, research, and clinical applications.* New York: Guilford Press.

The authors in this comprehensive handbook seek to integrate information on attachment with research and theories concerning the impact of the attachment process on developmental outcomes for children, adolescents, and adults. Chapters on attachment and psychopathology in childhood, attachment disorganization, and cross-cultural patterns of attachment are particularly relevant to studies of child psychopathology. 925 pages.

Comer, R. J. (2001). *Abnormal psychology, Fourth Edition.* New York: Worth.

Although the major focus of this text is adult psychopathology, its information on the ways various theoretical perspectives explain specific disorders can be readily applied to child psychopathology. Although the book discusses treatment, the major contribution of this book is in the integration of theory and research regarding the etiology of psychological disorders. Childhood disorders are discussed in one chapter; however, child and adolescent outcomes are mentioned throughout the text when applicable. 611 pages.

Gibbs, J. T., & Huang, L. H. (2001). *Children of color: Psychological interventions with culturally diverse youth.* San Francisco: Jossey Bass.

This multiauthored resource reveals information concerning relevant historical backgrounds and conceptual issues that result in increased understanding of families from diverse cultures. The book provides information on mental health issues faced by children from culturally diverse families and how the attitudes, beliefs, and values of distinct cultures may erect barriers to service delivery. Sections on how to improve the therapeutic alliance in culturally diverse families are of particular relevance to those working with children from diverse cultures. 410 pages.

Kronenberg, W. G., & Meyer, R. G. (2001). *The child clinician's handbook, 2nd edition.* Boston: Allyn & Bacon.

Kronenberg and Meyer provide a resource book for practicing clinicians that presents a prescribed focus and discusses information concerning the major disorders of childhood and adolescence in the following areas: clinical description (including characteristic features of children and adolescents), etiology, assessment, and treatment. The highlight of this book, in addition to assessment resources, is the description of disorders that goes beyond the DSM-IV and draws from empirical child-focused research. 557 pages.

Phares, V. (2003). *Understanding abnormal child psychology.* Hoboken, NJ: Wiley.

The text provides a unique focus that extends beyond psychology to include relevant information for students of social work and education. Although the book is research focused, the message is very applied and actually includes a chapter devoted to the application of material from the text to child-centered and family concerns. The book also includes more emphasis on the role of fathers in the parenting process, a topic that is often overlooked to a great extent in most texts on child psychopathology. 455 pages.

Sroufe, A., Cooper, R., & DeHart, G. (1999). *Child development: Its nature and course.* New York: McGraw-Hill.

Currently in its fourth edition, the book presents child development as it relates to research, theories, themes, and contexts. An entire chapter is devoted to the contexts of development and provides an ecological focus on how development is influenced by child and environmental characteristics. Each stage of development is introduced in opening vignettes that chronicle the lives of three diverse children. Empirical evidence is presented in a way that integrates research on child and environmental characteristics with everyday applications. Knowledge of child development is a necessary precursor to understanding child psychopathology. 672 pages.

Wenar, C., & Kerig, P. (2000). *Developmental psychopathology, 4th edition.* Boston: McGraw-Hill.

Wenar and Kerig explore the theme of maladaptive developmental outcomes by reviewing the literature concerning risk and protective factors that influence the trajectory of child development based on intrapersonal and interpersonal factors. The authors apply this framework to all the major disorders of childhood and adolescence in a comprehensive dialogue that focuses on the origins and course of emotional and behavioral disorders. The authors integrate information from diverse theoretical perspectives and empirically based findings that contribute to our understanding of the etiology, intervention, and treatment of child and adolescent disorders. 490 pages.

Wilmshurst, L. (2004). *Child and adolescent psychopathology: A casebook.* Thousand Oaks, CA: Sage Publications.

In Part I, readers are introduced to a Jeremy, a hyperactive, noncompliant 5-year-old raised by his mother and maternal grandmother. With Jeremy as a guide, readers are engaged in the development of a case formulation from various theoretical perspectives. In Part II, 14 extensive case studies (living files adapted from real life) illustrate the highly complex and comorbid nature of childhood disorders in a wide variety of high-incidence (ADHD, ODD) and more controversial areas (Asperger's, Reactive Attachment Disorder, Selective Mutism, Bipolar Disorder). Thought-provoking questions and current information on evidence-based treatments accompany each case. 308 pages.

Index